Lecture Notes in Computer Science   8195

Commenced Publication in 1973
Founding and Former Series Editors:
Gerhard Goos, Juris Hartmanis, and Jan van Leeuwen

Juliano Iyoda   Leonardo de Moura (Eds.)

Formal Methods: Foundations and Applications

16th Brazilian Symposium, SBMF 2013
Brasilia, Brazil, September 29 – October 4, 2013
Proceedings

 Springer

Volume Editors

Juliano Iyoda
UFPE, Centro de Informática
Recife, PE, Brazil
E-mail: jmi@cin.ufpe.br

Leonardo de Moura
Microsoft Research
Redmond, WA, USA
E-mail: leonardo@microsoft.com

ISSN 0302-9743 e-ISSN 1611-3349
ISBN 978-3-642-41070-3 e-ISBN 978-3-642-41071-0
DOI 10.1007/978-3-642-41071-0
Springer Heidelberg New York Dordrecht London

Library of Congress Control Number: 2013948105

CR Subject Classification (1998): D.2.4-5, D.2, F.3.1, F.4.1-2, D.3, K.6

LNCS Sublibrary: SL 2 – Programming and Software Engineering

Typesetting: Camera-ready by author, data conversion by Scientific Publishing Services, Chennai, India

Printed on acid-free paper

Springer is part of Springer Science+Business Media (www.springer.com)

Preface

This volume contains the papers presented at SBMF 2013: the 16th Brazilian Symposium on Formal Methods. The conference was held in Brasília, Brazil, colocated with CBSoft 2013, the 4th Brazilian Conference on Software: Theory and Practice.

The conference program included two invited talks, given by Christiano Braga (UFF, Brazil) and Kenneth McMillan (Microsoft Research, USA).

A total of 14 research papers were presented at the conference and are included in this volume; they were selected from 29 submissions. The submissions came from 10 countries: Australia, Brazil, Canada, Denmark, Israel, Germany, Norway, the UK, the USA, and Uruguay.

The deliberations of the Program Committee and the preparation of these proceedings were handled by EasyChair.

We are grateful to the Program Committee, and to the additional reviewers, for their hard work in evaluating submissions and suggesting improvements. In particular, special thanks go to Rohit Gheyi, co-chair of SBMF 2012, who was always available to help us and to share his experience and wisdom. SBMF 2013 was organized by the University of Brasília (UnB) under the auspices of the Brazilian Computer Society (SBC). We are very thankful to the organizers of this year's conference, Genaína Nunes Rodrigues (UnB) and Rodrigo Bonifacio de Almeida (UnB), who made everything possible for the conference to run smoothly.

The conference was sponsored by the following organizations, which we thank for their generous support:

- Brazilian National Institute of Science and Technology for Software Engineering (INES)
  - CAPES, the Brazilian Higher Education Funding Council
  - CNPq, the Brazilian Scientific and Technological Research Council
  - Google Inc.
  - Universidade de Brasília

July 2013

Juliano Iyoda
Leonardo de Moura

Organization

Program Committee

Aline Andrade	UFBA, Brazil
Wilkerson L. Andrade	UFCG, Brazil
David Aspinall	University of Edinburgh, UK
Luis Barbosa	Universidade do Minho, Portugal
Christiano Braga	UFF, Brazil
Michael Butler	University of Southampton, UK
Ana Cavalcanti	University of York, UK
Márcio Cornélio	UFPE, Brazil
Andrea Corradini	Università di Pisa, Italy
Marcelo d'Amorim	UFPE, Brazil
Jim Davies	University of Oxford, UK
Ana de Melo	USP, Brazil
Leonardo de Moura	Microsoft Research, USA
David Deharbe	UFRN, Brazil
Ewen Denney	SGT/NASA Ames, USA
Clare Dixon	University of Liverpool, UK
Jorge Figueiredo	UFCG, Brazil
Rohit Gheyi	UFCG, Brazil
John Harrison	Intel Corporation, USA
Rolf Hennicker	Ludwig-Maximilians-Universität München, Germany
Juliano Iyoda	UFPE, Brazil
Zhiming Liu	UNU-IIST, China
Gerald Luettgen	University of Bamberg, Germany
Patricia Machado	UFCG, Brazil
Narciso Marti-Oliet	Universidad Complutense de Madrid, Spain
Anamaria Martins Moreira	UFRN, Brazil
Tiago Massoni	UFCG, Brazil
Stephan Merz	Inria Lorraine, France
Alvaro Moreira	UFRGS, Brazil
Alexandre Mota	UFPE, Brazil
Arnaldo Moura	UNICAMP, Brazil
David Naumann	Stevens Institute of Technology, USA
Daltro Jose Nunes	UFRGS, Brazil

Jose Oliveira	Universidade do Minho, Portugal
Marcel Vinicius Medeiros Oliveira	UFRN, Brazil
Alexandre Petrenko	CRIM, Canada
Leila Ribeiro	UFRGS, Brazil
Augusto Sampaio	UFPE, Brazil
Leila Silva	UFS, Brazil
Adenilso Simao	ICMC/USP, Brazil
Heike Wehrheim	University of Paderborn, Germany
Jim Woodcock	University of York, UK

Local Organizers

Rodrigo Bonifacio de Almeida	UnB, Brazil
Genaína Nunes Rodrigues	UnB, Brazil

Program Chairs

Juliano Iyoda	UFPE, Brazil
Leonardo de Moura	Microsoft Research, USA

Steering Committee

Christiano Braga	UFF, Brazil
Jim Davies	University of Oxford, UK
Rohit Gheyi	UFCG, Brazil
Juliano Iyoda	UFPE, Brazil (Co-chair)
Carroll Morgan	University of New South Wales, UK
Leonardo de Moura	Microsoft Research, USA (Co-chair)
David Naumann	Stevens Institute of Technology, USA
Leila Silva	UFS, Brazil
Adenilso Simao	ICMC/USP, Brazil

Additional Reviewers

Edmunds, Andrew

Table of Contents

Meaningful Models
— A Research Agenda on Model-Driven Engineering —

Christiano Braga and Cássio Santos

Instituto de Computação
Active Documentation and Intelligent Design Laboratory
Universidade Federal Fluminense
{cbraga,cfernando}@ic.uff.br

Abstract. An important question in software engineering is whether a program (or system) is *correct with respect to its specification*. The model-driven engineering discipline (MDE) is an approach to software development that supports domain-engineering, is generative and language-driven. We believe that this set of characteristics enable MDE as a suitable approach for the rigorous development of correct software systems as it allows us to focus on models rather than code. In this paper, we illustrate how programming languages theory, through operational semantics, and logic in computer science, through Description Logics, may help us identify meta-properties and techniques to reason about MDE models.

1 Introduction

An important question in software engineering is whether a program (or system) is *correct with respect to its specification*. The boundaries of what can be automatically verified (decidability) and how efficiently it can be done (complexity) have been identified and are being challenged ever since. Informally, Göedel's first incompleteness theorem [15] states that a program can't list all that is true (theorems) about a (consistent axiomatic) system. Rice's theorem [18] states that expressive properties (i.e. non-trivial) are not verifiable (decidable) by a program. Cook's theorem [18] states that checking if there exits a valuation for a boolean expression (SAT) is unfeasible, unless $P = NP$.

These results are related to the *expressivity* (understood as decidability or complexity) of the language that a given system is described in and the properties that can be verified on these systems. Therefore, if we reduce the expressivity of the system description language, and also the properties to be checked, one may be able to *automatically* verify less expressive properties about abstractions (or models) of systems. A classical example is reasoning on database models [22].

The model-driven engineering discipline (MDE, e.g. [21]) appears to fit quite nicely within this approach. It supports domain engineering, is generative (which means that one only needs to convince oneself about correctness once, or, at least, only for a *class* of problems) and is *language-based*. This last characteristic is quite important as it allows for the definition of a *rigorous* foundation for

J. Iyoda and L. de Moura (Eds.): SBMF 2013, LNCS 8195, pp. 1–16, 2013.

MDE as there exists a solid theory for programming languages. Not only the theory of programming languages (PL), so to speak (that includes automata languages, formal languages, and formal semantics) may help us to build better (correct) software with MDE but also logic in computer science presents itself as an important foundation as it provides the machinery for *reasoning* about models.

In this paper, we illustrate how programming languages theory and logic in computer science may help us with meta-properties and techniques to reason about MDE models. In our discussion, we consider MDE models as *relational* models. They may represent domain models and also *transformations* among such models. Therefore, the techniques for the specification and reasoning about models nicely apply to model transformations as well.

This paper is organized as follows. Section 2 gives rigorous definitions for the model-driven engineering concepts that will be discussed in Sections 3 and 4. In Section 3 we understand model transformations as operational semantics specifications and study how meta-theoretical properties from PL theory can be adapted to the context of model transformations. Section 4 presents an ontological perspective and conjectures on model transformations as ontological alignment under contextualized ontologies. In Section 5 we discuss some related work on the specification and verification of model transformations. Section 6 concludes this paper with our final remarks.

2   Elements of Model-Driven Engineering

In this paper we will discuss three MDE concepts and two relations among them. The first concept is a *metamodel*, formalized in Definition 1, which is essentially a set of relations among classes. It may be understood as the description of the syntax of a modeling language. This is the understanding adopted in Section 3. With this understanding in mind, a well-formed object model, formalized by Definitions 2 and 3, is a syntactically correct program according to the syntax defined by its metamodel. Moreover, an object model in conformance with a given metamodel, formalized in Definition 4, is a well-formed model that has the properties defined in the given metamodel. From a programming languages perspective, checking for well-formedness may be understood as syntactical analysis with respect to the syntax defined by a given metamodel whereas conformance may be understood as type checking with respect to the properties defined by a given metamodel.

These elements may also be understood from a logical perspective, the one adopted in Section 4, where a metamodel together with the modeling language's properties may be understood as a theory in a suitable logic and an object model is a term. A well-formed object model with respect to a metamodel is a well-formed term with respect to the signature of logical theory associated with the given metamodel. Finally, an object model in conformance with a given metamodel and a set of properties is understood as semantic entailment between the term representing the object model and the logical theory representing the metamodel together with the modeling language's properties.

Definition 1 (Metamodel). *A metamodel $\mathcal{M}$ is a structure $\langle C, \mathcal{A} \rangle$ with C the set of classes of $\mathcal{M}$ comprised by a set of attribute declarations $Id \times (T \cup C)$ and a set of method declarations $Id \times (T \cup C)^* \times (T \cup C)$, and $\mathcal{A} \subseteq C^2 \times K^2$ the set of associations of $\mathcal{M}$ where K is the set of association's cardinalities given by intervals of the general form $[n_1..n_2]$, where $n_1, n_2 \in \mathbb{N}$ and $n_1 \leq n_2$.*

Definition 2 (Object model). *An object model m is a structure $\langle O, At, L \rangle$ where $O \subseteq Id \times Class$ is a set of objects with $o : C \in O$ an abbreviation for $\langle o, C \rangle \in O$ denoting that the object identified by o is an instance of class C; $At \subseteq Id \times Id \times Values$ is a set of object attributes with $a(o, v : T) \in A$ an abbreviation for $\langle a, o, (v, T) \rangle \in A$, a denotes an attribute of object o, and v a (typed) value attached to a, with $T \subseteq Value$; and $L \subseteq Id \times Id \times Id$ is a set of links relating objects in O with $l(o_1, o_2)$ an abbreviation for $\langle l, o_1, o_2 \rangle$.*

Definition 3 (Well-formed model). *Given an object model $m = \langle O, At, L \rangle$ and a metamodel $\mathcal{M} = \langle C, \mathcal{A} \rangle$, m is said* well-formed *with respect to $\mathcal{M}$, denoted by $m \in \mathcal{M}$, if and only if for every object $o : c \in O$ we have $c \in C$, each tuple formed by attributes in At indexed by o is an element of the product denoted by c, and for every link $l(o_1, o_2)$ in L, $o_1 : c_1 \in O$ and $o_2 : c_2 \in O$, with $c_1, c_2 \in C$, and there exists an $a \in \mathcal{A}$ such that $a = (c_1, c_2, k_1, k_2)$, with $k_1, k_2 \in K$.*

Definition 4 (Model conformance). *Given a model m and a metamodel $\mathcal{M}$, m is said* in conformance *with $\mathcal{M}$, denoted by $m \models \mathcal{M}$, if and only $m \models P_{\mathcal{M}}$, where $P_{\mathcal{M}}$ is the set of properties that must hold on every model $m \in \mathcal{M}$. When $P_{\mathcal{M}}$ is not empty, $\mathcal{M}$ is defined as a triple $\langle C, \mathcal{A}, P \rangle$.*

The last MDE concept considered in this paper is a model transformation. We understand a model transformation as a model that relates metamodels and we call such models *transformation contracts*. They are formalized in Definition 5. Example 1 illustrates the concept of a transformation contract through a model transformation from non-deterministic finite automata to deterministic finite automata, as defined in [18]. The symbol ⊶ denotes inheritance (or set inclusion from left to right). Standard notation for cardinality constraints is used when defining associations, as in $A \xrightarrow{1 \ R \ *} B$, where A and B are classes and R is an association with cardinality *one-to-many*.

Definition 5 (Transformation contract). *A transformation contract is a model $\mathcal{K}$ resulting from a model operation $\mathcal{S} \bowtie_{\mathcal{A}_{\mathcal{K}}} \mathcal{T}$ on two given metamodels $\mathcal{S}$ and $\mathcal{T}$ that* extends[1] *the metamodels $\mathcal{S}$ and $\mathcal{T}$ and: (i) disjointly unites[2] all the model elements of $\mathcal{S}$ and $\mathcal{T}$; (ii) declares associations $a \in \mathcal{A}_{\mathcal{K}}$ that relate classes in $\mathcal{S}$ with $\mathcal{T}$ and disjointly unites $\mathcal{A}_{\mathcal{K}}$ with $\mathcal{S}$ and $\mathcal{T}$; and (iii) declares properties $P_{\mathcal{K}}$ over $\mathcal{A}_{\mathcal{K}}$.*

---

[1] We use the word extends here in its algebraic sense that "junk" may be added but no "confusion", that is, new terms may be added but are not identified with old ones.

[2] The disjoint union avoids name clashing by *tagging* each model element name with the metamodel's name.

Example 1 (NFAtoDFA). Let $f \in \mathcal{T}.F, s_i \in \mathcal{S}.Q, t_i \in \mathcal{T}.Q, (t_i, t_j, a) \in \mathcal{T}.\delta,$

$$\mathcal{S} = \left\langle \begin{array}{c} \{\Sigma, Q, Q_0 \rightarrowtail Q, F \rightarrowtail Q, \delta\},\ Q \xrightarrow{1\ source\ *} \delta \xrightarrow{*\ target\ *} Q \\ {}^{*\ symbol\ 1}\Big| \\ \Sigma \end{array} \right\rangle$$

$$\mathcal{T} = \left\langle \begin{array}{c} \{\Sigma, Q, Q_0 \rightarrowtail Q, F \rightarrowtail Q, \delta\},\ Q \xrightarrow{1\ source\ *} \delta \xrightarrow{*\ target\ 1} Q \\ {}^{*\ symbol\ 1}\Big| \\ \Sigma \end{array} \right\rangle$$

$$\mathcal{A}_{\mathcal{K}} = \left\{ \begin{array}{c} \mathcal{S}.\Sigma \xrightarrow{1\ sigma\ 1} \mathcal{T}.\Sigma, \mathcal{S}.Q_0 \xrightarrow{1\ initial\ 1} \mathcal{T}.Q_0, \\ \\ \mathcal{S}.F \xrightarrow{*\ final\ *} \mathcal{T}.F, \mathcal{S}.\delta \xrightarrow{*\ delta\ 1} \mathcal{T}.\delta \end{array} \right\}$$

$$\mathcal{P}_{\mathcal{K}} = \{\ \mathcal{T}.Q \subseteq 2^{\mathcal{S}.Q},\ \forall f(f = \{s_1, s_2, \ldots, s_n\}, \exists s_i(s_i \in \mathcal{S}.F)), \\ \forall (t_i, t_j, a)(t_1 = \{s_1, s_2, \ldots, s_n\}, t_2 = \bigcup_{i=1}^{n} \mathcal{S}.\delta(s_i, a))\ \}$$

3   A Programming Languages Perspective

Operational semantics [19, 28] (OS) is a formalism for the description of the formal semantics of programming languages. An operational semantics specification $S = \langle \Sigma, R \rangle$ for a programming language L declares in Σ the grammar for L and R induces a finite state transition system [24] to programs in L. The rules in R capture either or both static and dynamic semantics of L.

Essentially, transformation contracts may be understood as operational semantics specifications by considering metamodels $\mathcal{S}$ and $\mathcal{T}$ as grammars, and associations in $\mathcal{A}_{\mathcal{K}}$ as rules with $\mathcal{P}_{\mathcal{K}}$ as premises. Formally,

$$[\![\langle \mathcal{S} \bowtie_{\mathcal{A}_{\mathcal{K}}} \mathcal{T}, \mathcal{P}_{\mathcal{K}} \rangle]\!] = \langle \mathcal{S} \uplus \mathcal{T}, \mathcal{P}_{\mathcal{K}} \Rightarrow \mathcal{A}_{\mathcal{K}} \rangle. \tag{1}$$

Operational semantics specifications may be implemented as rewriting logic theories [5, 23, 30] quite directly since they are almost in a one-to-one correspondence. (Some care must be taken to prevent the application of the congruence inference rule of rewriting logic.) As an indication of the soundness of Equation 1, we have implemented[3] the model transformation *NFAtoDFA* in Example 1 in the rewriting logic language Maude [12]. The implementation essentially represents the model transformation *NFAtoDFA* as a membership equational logic theory. Sorts, subsorting relations and operations represent classes and associations. Membership axioms and equations represent cardinality constraints. Finally, equations implement the properties in $\mathcal{P}_{\mathcal{K}}$ as a condition to the main equation that implements the model transformation. Listing 1.1 gives the declaration (Line 1) and equation (Lines 2–5) for operation **nfa2dfa**.[4] The signature

---

[3] It can be read at http://www.ic.uff.br/~cbraga/nfa2dfa.maude.

[4] Listing 1.1 is actually a simplification of the implementation in http://www.ic.uff.br/~cbraga/nfa2dfa.maude. There, we also implement deletion of useless states and transitions. Listing 1.1 suffices for the purposes of this paper.

of `nfa2dfa` relates terms from sort `Nfa` to terms from sort `Dfa`. A term in sort `Fa`, a super sort of both `Nfa` and `Dfa`, is a 5-tuple defined as usual in textbooks, that is, $\Sigma \times Q \times q_0 \times \delta \times F$. A membership axiom constraining the cardinality of the image of function δ properly types a term in `Fa` as a `Nfa` or `Dfa`. The conditions in Lines 3 to 5 represent the elements of set $\mathcal{P}_{\mathcal{K}}$ in Example 1, respectively.

```
1  op nfa2dfa : Nfa -> Dfa .
2  ceq nfa2dfa(<SS, QS, q0, DS, F>) = <SS, QS', q0, DS', F'>
3  if QS' := 2^ QS /\
4      F' := reachableFinalStates(DS') /\
5      DS' := deltaD((2^ QS), SS, DS)
```

Listing 1.1. Maude equation that implements transformation *NFAtoDFA*

We may now take advantage of meta-theoretical properties from operational semantics theory (e.g. [25]) to reason on transformation contracts.

3.1 Type Soundness Properties

In [31] the authors propose an approach to prove the soundness of Hindley/Milner-style polymorphic type systems based on the following properties,

Weak soundness : **if** $\triangleright e : \tau$ **then** $eval(e) \neq WRONG$,
Strong soundness : **if** $\triangleright e : \tau$ **then** $eval(e) \in V^\tau$

where the formula $\triangleright e : \tau$ denotes that expression e is well-typed; the function $eval : Programs \rightarrow Answers \cup \{WRONG\}$ is a partial function that defines the semantics of untyped programs, returns $WRONG$ when the given program causes a type error, and is undefined for programs that do not terminate; and V^τ denotes the set of values of type τ. Intuitively, the authors understand a static type system as a *filter* that selects well-typed programs from a universe of untyped programs. The *weak soundness* property essentially prevents type errors while *strong soundness* relates well-typed programs to proper answers.

As we mentioned before, the model transformation in Example 1 can be understood straightforwardly as an operational semantics specifications by the application of Equation 1. The weak soundness property may be written as follows for the *NFAtoDFA* model transformation

if $m \models NFA$ **then** $NFAtoDFA(m) \neq WRONG$.

To check that the *weak soundness* property holds in *NFAtoDFA* means to prove that given a source model in conformance with the *NFA* metamodel the model transformation will *never* produce a model that is not in conformance with the *DFA* metamodel. Note that, in this setting, *NFAtoDFA* is a *partial* function that could very well return *WRONG* for a source model not in conformance with the *NFA* metamodel. In Maude, this could be checked using the

ITP/OCL tool [13], an inductive theorem prover for membership equational logic. In Maude, the equality $t = WRONG$, where t is a term, would be denoted by checking that the type of t is not at the kind level, that is, t is properly sorted. In the context of *NFAtoDFA* model transformation we would have to make sure that any given term $NFAtoDFA(m)$, where $m : $ Nfa, would never be at the kind level of Fa, denoted [Fa].

The strong soundness property may be written as follows for the *NFAtoDFA* model transformation

$$\textbf{if } m \models \textbf{NFA then } \textit{NFAtoDFA}(m) \in \textit{DFA}.$$

To check that the *strong soundness* property holds in *NFAtoDFA* means to prove that given a source model in conformance with the *NFA* metamodel the model transformation will *always* produce a model that is in conformance with the *DFA* metamodel. In Maude, we would have to make sure that any given term $NFAtoDFA(m)$, where $m : $ Nfa, is always of type Dfa.

3.2   Bisimulation

Definition 6 recalls the concept of bisimulation from observation equivalence theory [24].

Definition 6 (Bisimulation). *Let $S = \langle \Gamma, L, \rightarrow \rangle$ be a transition system. A relation $R \subseteq \Gamma \times \Gamma$ is a simulation if for every pair of elements p, q in Γ with (p,q) in R, for all α in L such that for all p' in Γ, $p \xrightarrow{\alpha} p'$ implies that there exists a q' in Γ such that $q \xrightarrow{\alpha} q'$. R is said a strong bisimulation if its inverse R^{-1} is also a simulation. Moreover, a strong bisimulation relation, denoted $\sim$, is an equivalence relation, that is, $\sim$ is reflexive $(p \sim p)$, $\sim$ is symmetric $(p \sim q \Rightarrow q \sim p)$ and $\sim$ is transitive $(\exists r(p \sim q \wedge q \sim r \Rightarrow p \sim r))$.*

Let us move our attention back to Example 1. Relation *delta* in $\mathcal{A}_{\mathcal{K}}$ and the third property in $\mathcal{P}_{\mathcal{K}}$, which we recall here

$$\forall((t_1, t_2, a) \in \mathcal{T}.\delta, s_i \in \mathcal{S}.Q, t_i \in \mathcal{T}.Q)$$
$$(t_1 = \{s_1, s_2, \ldots, s_n\}, t_2 = \bigcup_{i=1}^n \mathcal{S}.\delta(s_i, a)),$$

induce a relation, say R, where $R \subseteq \mathcal{S}.Q \times \mathcal{T}.Q$.

Now, consider the *application* of *NFAtoDFA* to the automaton *NA3*, in Figure 1a, that recognizes the language $L = \{w \mid w \text{ has } aaa \text{ as sufix}\}$. The application *NFAtoDFA(NA3)* produces *DA3*, the DFA in Figure 1b. These automata are an example that the relation R induced by *NFAtoDFA* is not a strong bisimulation. R is actually a simulation. In *NFAtoDFA(NA3)*,

$$R = \{(p_0, q_0), (p_0, q_1), (p_0, q_2), (p_0, q_3), (p_1, q_1), (p_1, q_2), (p_1, q_3),$$
$$(p_2, q_2), (p_2, q_3), (p_3, q_3)\}$$

and $q_1 S^{-1} p_1$ is *not* a strong simulation since $q_1 \xrightarrow{b} q_0$ and $\nexists p(p_1 \xrightarrow{b} p \wedge q_0 S^{-1} p)$. Interestingly enough, $p_0 \sim q_0$.

(a) $NA3$ = NFA for L (b) $DA3$ = DFA for L

Programming languages theory and concurrency theory have contributed a lot to model-driven engineering (e.g. [20]). This Section is, of course, a shy example of it. But let us see now how logic in computer science and, in particular, how an ontological perspective can contribute to the model-driven engineering discipline.

4   An Ontological Perspective

This Section discusses a formalization of model-driven engineering concepts as ontologies in Description Logics [2]. In particular, we explore the semantics of transformation contracts as ontology alignments of contextualized ontologies [9]. Section 4.1 discusses how ontologies are represented as Description Logics theories. Section 4.2 formalizes model-driven engineering concepts in terms of Description Logics elements. In particular, we introduce the notion of *Extended TBox* to reason on the consistency of object models. Section 4.3 recalls from literature the concept of contextualized ontology and a set of algebraic operations on contextualized ontologies. Finally, Section 4.4 conjectures on transformation contracts as alignments of contextualized ontologies.

4.1   Ontologies as Theories in Description Logics

Description Logics is a family of logics defined to be efficiently decidable. Each fragment of the logic was carefully studied on its expressiveness and efficiency of reasoning. We will focus on $\mathcal{ALCQI}$, a particular Description Logic which is expressive enough for the purposes of this paper.

An ontology may be described as a *terminology box*, or TBox, in a Description Logic, which is comprised essentially by *concepts*, which denote sets; concept subsumption represented by $C \sqsubseteq C'$, denoting set inclusion, where C and C' are concepts ($C \equiv C'$ abbreviates $C \sqsubseteq C'$ and $C' \sqsubseteq C$); and *roles*, which are essentially binary relations.

The syntax of $\mathcal{ALCQI}$'s axioms is as follows:

$$C ::= A \mid \neg C \mid C_1 \sqcap C_2 \mid (\leq k\ R.C)$$
$$R ::= P \mid P^-$$

where C, C_1 and C_2 are concepts, A is an atomic concept, $k \in \mathbb{N}$, R is a role and P an atomic role with P^- its inverse.

Some abbreviations may help the definition of $\mathcal{ALCQI}$ TBoxes: (i) $\perp \equiv A \sqcap \neg A$, where A is an atomic concept; (ii) $\top \equiv \neg\perp$; (iii) $C_1 \sqcup C_2 \equiv \neg(\neg C_1 \sqcap \neg C_2)$; (iv) $C_1 \Rightarrow C_2 \equiv \neg C_1 \sqcup C_2$; (v) $\geq k\ R.C \equiv \neg(\leq (k-1)R.C)$; (vi) $(= 1C.R) \equiv (\geq 1C.R \sqcap \leq 1C.R)$; (vii) $\exists R.C \equiv (\geq 1\ R.C)$; and finally, $\forall R.C \equiv \neg\exists R.\neg C$.

The meaning of a TBox is defined in a standard way by means of an interpretation $\mathcal{I} = (\Delta^{\mathcal{I}}, \cdot^{\mathcal{I}})$, where $\Delta^{\mathcal{I}}$ is the domain of $\mathcal{I}$ and $\cdot^{\mathcal{I}}$ is the interpretation function that associates to a concept C, or relation R, a subset of the domain with the appropriate arity. The following rules specify the interpretation for $\mathcal{ALCQI}$ TBoxes.

$$\top^{\mathcal{T}} = \Delta^{\mathcal{I}}$$
$$P^{\mathcal{I}} \subseteq \top_2^{\mathcal{I}}$$
$$(P^-)^{\mathcal{I}} \subseteq \{(a, a') \in \Delta_2^{\mathcal{I}} \mid (a', a) \in P^{\mathcal{I}}\}$$
$$(\leq kR.C)^{\mathcal{I}} \subseteq \{a \in \Delta^{\mathcal{I}} \mid$$
$$\#\{a' \in \Delta^{\mathcal{I}} \mid (a, a') \in R^{\mathcal{I}} \wedge a' \in C^{\mathcal{I}}\} \leq k\}$$

$$\top_n^{\mathcal{T}} \subseteq (\Delta^{\mathcal{I}})^n$$
$$A^{\mathcal{I}} \subseteq \Delta^{\mathcal{I}}$$
$$(C_1 \sqcap C_2)^{\mathcal{I}} \subseteq C_1^{\mathcal{I}} \cap C_2^{\mathcal{I}}$$
$$\neg C^{\mathcal{I}} \subseteq \Delta^{\mathcal{I}} / C^{\mathcal{I}}$$

Given a TBox $\mathcal{T}$, an interpretation that satisfies all of $\mathcal{T}$'s assertions is called a *model* of $\mathcal{T}$. Similarly, $\mathcal{T}$ is said *consistent* if $\mathcal{T}$ has a model and inconsistent otherwise. A concept C is satisfiable in $\mathcal{T}$ if there exists an interpretation $\mathcal{I}$ of $\mathcal{T}$ such that $C^{\mathcal{I}}$ is not empty, that is, $C \not\sqsubseteq \perp$.

4.2   Models as DL Theories

We rely on the interpretation of class models defined in [3]. Definition 7 recalls it. (In this paper we do not consider OCL constraints as defined in [29]. We take them into account in [6].)

Definition 7 (TBox of a metamodel). *Given a metamodel $\mathcal{M}$, the TBox $\mathcal{T}$ associated with $\mathcal{M}$ is defined as follows:*

1. *For each* class *C in $\mathcal{M}$ there exists an atomic concept C in $\mathcal{T}$;*
2. *For each* generalization *between a class C and its child class C_1 in $\mathcal{M}$ there exists an inclusion assertion $C_1 \sqsubseteq C$ in $\mathcal{T}$. A class hierarchy is represented by the assertions $C_1 \sqsubseteq C, \ldots, C_n \sqsubseteq C$ in $\mathcal{T}$ when C_i inherits from C in $\mathcal{M}$. A disjointness constraint among classes $C_1, \ldots, C_n$ in D can be modeled as $C_i \sqsubseteq \sqcap_{j=i+1}^n \neg C_j$, with $1 \leq i \leq n-1$ in $\mathcal{T}$, while a covering constraint can be expressed as $C \sqsubseteq \bigsqcup_{i=1}^n C_i$ in $\mathcal{T}$;*
3. *Each* binary association *(or aggregation) A between a class C_1 and a class C_2, with multiplicities $m_l..m_u$ and $n_l..n_u$ on each end, respectively, in $\mathcal{M}$ is represented by the atomic role A, together with the inclusion assertion $\top \sqsubseteq \forall A.C_2 \sqcap \forall A^-.C_1$ in $\mathcal{T}$. The multiplicities are formalized by the assertions $C_1 \sqsubseteq (\geq n_l\ A.\top) \sqcap (\leq n_u\ A.\top)$ and $C_2 \sqsubseteq (\geq m_l A^-.\top) \sqcap (\leq m_u A^-.\top)$, where $\top$ denotes the largest concept (top) that includes all concepts and $\forall R.C$ is just syntactic sugar for $\leq 0\ R.\neg C$ in $\mathcal{T}$.*

An object model may be represented as a TBox by simply understanding each object as a class and each link as a role.

Definition 8 (TBox of an object model). *Given an object model* $\mathcal{O} = \langle O, A, L \rangle$, *the TBox of* $\mathcal{O}$, *denoted by* $\hat{\mathcal{O}}$, *is given by the application of the following mapping to* $\mathcal{O}$*: (i) for each object* $o \in O$ *there exists a concept* o *in* $\hat{\mathcal{O}}$, *and (ii) for each attribute* $a(o, v : T) \in A$ *there exists an axiom* $O \sqsubseteq a.T$ *in* $\hat{\mathcal{O}}$.

Now, we reduce conformance verification of a particular model m with respect to a metamodel $\mathcal{M}$ to the verification of the consistency of the DL theory resulting from the extension of the TBox that represents $\mathcal{M}$ with the TBox that represents m, as discussed in [6].

Definition 9 (Extended TBox). *Given a model* m *and a metamodel* $\mathcal{M}$, *such that* $m \in \mathcal{M}$ *and* $m \models \mathcal{M}$, *the TBox of* $\mathcal{M}$ *extended with respect to the TBox of* m, *or extended TBox for short, denoted by* $\hat{\mathcal{M}}_{\hat{m}}$, *is given by the union of* $\hat{\mathcal{M}}$, *given by Definition 7, with* $\hat{m}$, *given by Definition 8, together with: (i) axioms* $o \sqsubseteq C$, *for each concept* o *in* $\hat{m}$, *representing an object* o *in* m, *with* C *the concept representing* o's *class; (ii) disjointness axioms among objects of the same type* C *in* m *declared as* $o_i \sqsubseteq \prod_{j=i+1}^{n} \neg o_j$, *with* $1 \leq i \leq n-1$ *and* n *the cardinality of the set of objects of type* C *in* m, *(iii) completeness axioms among objects of the same type* C *in* m *declared as* $C \sqsubseteq \bigsqcup_{i=1}^{n} o_i$, *with* n *the cardinality of the set of objects of type* C *in* m, *(iv) let* L_A *be the set of links in* m *for association* A *in* $\mathcal{M}$, *then (a) for each link* $l(o_i, o_j) \in L_A$, *with* $A \subseteq C_1 \times C_2$, *axiom* $o_i \sqsubseteq= 1A.o_j$ *is in* $\hat{\mathcal{M}}_{\hat{m}}$, *and (b) for all* $l(o_i, o) \notin L_A$, *with* $o \in C_2$ *(and all* C_2's *child concepts), axiom* $o_i \sqsubseteq \neg \exists A.o$ *is in* $\hat{\mathcal{M}}_{\hat{m}}$.

Conjecture 1. $m \models \mathcal{M} \Leftrightarrow \bot \not\models \hat{\mathcal{M}}_{\hat{m}}$

4.3 The Algebra of Contextualized Ontologies

Informally, a contextualized ontology is a pair of ontologies where one ontology gives semantics (or context) to the other. Our intuition is that the ontology that represents a metamodel provides context to the ontology that describes a model. Conjecture 2 in Section 4.4 formalizes this intuition. Let us first recall the definition of contextualized ontologies and a few operations on them, as defined in [9].

Definition 10 (Contextualized ontology). *A* contextualized ontology *is a triple* (E, C, F) *where* E *and* C *are the entity and context ontologies, respectively, and* F *is the contextualization homomorphism* $F : E \rightarrow C$, *that is,* $F(f(e1, e2, \ldots, e_n)) = F(f)[F(e1), F(e2), \ldots F(e_n)]$, *where* e_i, $1 \leq i \leq n, n \in \mathbb{N}$ *are the parts of* E *related by* f. *Moreover, (i) any entity must have an identity link and thus the entity may be viewed as a context of itself; (ii) an entity is called the domain of a link, while a context is called codomain of a link; (iii) links can be composed in an associative way if the codomain of the first is the domain of the second.*

Definition 11 (Entity Integration). *Given two contextualized entities sharing the same context $e_1 : E_1 \to C$ and $e_2 : E_2 \to C$, the integration of E_1 and E_2 with respect to C is the contextualized entity $E \to C$, such that, (i) there exists $e'_1 : E \to E_1$ and $e'_2 : E \to E_2$ such that $e_1 \circ e'_1 = e_2 \circ e'_2$, and, (ii) for any other entity E'', with links $e''_1 : E'' \to E_1$ and $e''_2 : E'' \to E_2$, there exists a unique link $! : E'' \to E$ with $e'_1 \circ ! = e''_1$ and $e'_2 \circ ! = e''_2$.*

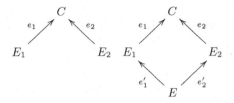

Fig. 1. Entity integration in contextualized ontologies

Definition 12 (Context Integration). *Given two contextualizations of the same entity $e_1 : E \to C_1$ and $e_2 : E \to C_2$, the context integration of C_1 and C_2 with respect to E is the contextualized entity $E \to C$, such that, (i) there exists $e'_1 : C_1 \to C$ and $e'_2 : C_2 \to C$ such that $e'_1 \circ e_1 = e'_2 \circ e_2$, and, (ii) for any other context C'', with maps $e''_1 : C_1 \to C''$ and $e''_2 : C_2 \to C''$ there exists a unique map $! : C \to C''$ with $! \circ e'_1 = e''_1$ and $! \circ e'_2 = e''_2$.*

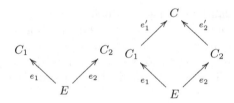

Fig. 2. Context integration in contextualized ontologies

Definition 13 (Relative Intersection). *Given two maps between contextualized entities $m_1 : CE_1 \to CE$ and $m_2 : CE_2 \to CE$, the relative intersection of CE_1 and CE_2 with respect to CE is the contextualized entity CE', with maps $m'_1 : CE' \to CE_1$ and $m'_2 : CE' \to CE_2$ such that, (i) $m_1 \circ m'_1 = m_2 \circ m'_2$, and, (ii) for any other contextualized entity CE'', with maps $m''_1 : CE'' \to CE_1$ and $m''_2 : CE'' \to CE_2$ there exists a unique map $! : CE'' \to CE'$ with $m'_1 \circ ! = m''_1$ and $m'_2 \circ ! = m''_2$.*

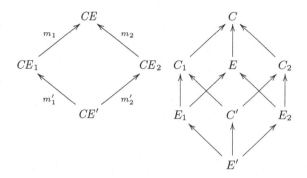

Fig. 3. Relative intersection in contextualized ontologies

4.4 Transformation Contracts and Ontological Alignment

As we mentioned in Section 4.3, our intuition is that the conformance relation may be understood as contextualization. We are now ready to formalize it as Conjecture 2. This conjecture appears to be sound based on the idea that conformance of a model with respect to a metamodel should preserve the metamodel's structure. That is precisely the idea of a homomorphism.

Conjecture 2 (Conformance is a contextualization homomorphism). Given a metamodel $\mathcal{M}$ and a model m, and their associated TBoxes $\hat{\mathcal{M}}$ and $\hat{m}$,

$$m \models \mathcal{M} \Leftrightarrow \hat{m} \to \hat{\mathcal{M}}.$$

Recall from Conjecture 1 that we believe that

$$m \models \mathcal{M} \Leftrightarrow \hat{\mathcal{M}}_{\hat{m}}.$$

Now, assuming Conjectures 1 and 2 correct, a consistent Extended TBox should be equivalent to a contextualized ontology. This is formalized in Conjecture 3.

Conjecture 3 (Extended TBox and contextualization). Given a metamodel $\mathcal{M}$ and a model m, and their associated TBoxes $\hat{\mathcal{M}}$ and $\hat{m}$,

$$\bot \not\models \hat{\mathcal{M}}_{\hat{m}} \Leftrightarrow \hat{m} \to \hat{\mathcal{M}}.$$

Our objective in this Section is to reach a semantics of transformation contracts in terms of relative intersection. (See Definition 13.) If the diagram in Figure 4 commutes then the properties of the transformation contract $\mathcal{K}$, taking R into account, are preserved in the application of the transformation contract $k(s)$.

The question now is to identify what is $\hat{R}$: it represents the ontology associated with the *dynamic semantics* of $\mathcal{K}$. For instance, R may specify a *simulation* relation, as recalled in Section 3.2, between the transition system induced by $\mathcal{S}$ and the transition system induced by $\mathcal{T}$.

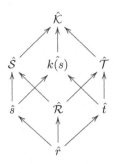

Fig. 4. Transformation contracts as relative intersection

Let us illustrate this discussion with a simple example borrowed from [24, pg. 19]. Figure 5 depicts two bisimilar transition systems. The bisimulation relation is represented in Figure 5 by dotted lines. Let us consider now that the transition system with states in $\{p_0, p_1, p_2\}$ represents the behavior of the source model of a model transformation and the transition system with states in $\{q_0, q_1, q_2\}$ represents the behavior of the model generated by the given model transformation. The relation r in Figure 4 would be represented by the dotted line in Figure 5, that is, $r = \{(p_0, q_0), (p_0, q_2), (p_1, q_1), (p_2, q_1)\}$.

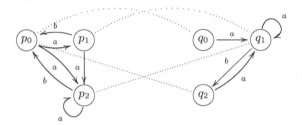

Fig. 5. Bisimilar transition systems

We can then use a Description Logics reasoner to verify some properties of r by reducing the verification of such properties to consistency checking of the associated DL theory. First, we need an encoding of transition systems in Description Logics by essentially representing states as concepts and labeled transitions as roles. For instance, the transition $p_0 \xrightarrow{a} p_1$ is specified by the axiom $p_0 \sqsubseteq \forall a.p_1$. (Note that due to open world semantics assumed by DL reasoners, one needs also to specify when two states are *not* related by a given labeled transition, such as $p_0 \xrightarrow{b} p_1$ in Figure 5.) The relation r is specified in a similar way with axioms that relate bisimilar states, such as $p_0 \sqsubseteq \forall r.q_1$. We also axiomatize the bisimulation property for every bisimilar pair of states. For instance, for the pair $(p_1, q_1) \in r$, since $p_1 \xrightarrow{a} p_2$ and $q_1 \xrightarrow{a} q_1$ then (p_2, q_1) should be in r. This is axiomatized in DL by the following concepts: $p_1 \sqsubseteq \forall a.p_2$, $q_1 \sqsubseteq \forall a.q_1$ and $p_1 \sqsubseteq r.q_1$. We also state that r should be reflexive, symmetric and transitive since, as recalled in Section 3.2, a bisimulation is an equivalence relation. The specification that r is the largest set that has the bisimulation property (see Definition 6) requires a fixpoint operator and therefore a DL that is more expressive then $\mathcal{ALCQI}$, such as $\mu\mathcal{ALCQI}$ [10].

Conjecture 4 formalizes that validity of the application of a model transformation could be understood as the relative intersection. Assuming Conjectures 3 and 4 correct, the validity of a particular model transformation application could be verified by checking the consistency of the associated Description Logics theory representing the relative intersection.

Conjecture 4 (Model transformation as relative intersection).

$$k(s) \models \mathcal{K} \Leftrightarrow \hat{r} \to \hat{\mathcal{R}} \text{ is the relative intersection of } \hat{s} \to \hat{\mathcal{S}} \text{ and } \hat{t} \to \hat{\mathcal{T}}$$
$$\text{with respect to } \widehat{k(s)} \to \hat{\mathcal{K}}.$$

5 Related Work

We organize the discussion of related work at the specification and verification levels. At the specification level, we adopt a *relational* approach towards the specification of a model transformation. It is similar in essence to [1, 4] but different from [11, 16]. In [11] the authors specify transformation contracts as OCL invariants from source and target model elements. We formalize our understanding of transformation contracts in Section 2 as opposed to the informal discussion in [1, 4, 16]. (The authors in [11, 16] also discuss the use of pre and postconditions but such predicates may also be represented as invariants.) The specification of a relation between the model elements of the metamodels related by a model transformation is essential to generalize from OCL invariants and understand that different *kinds* of properties may be specified *over such relation*. It is important to make *explicit* the relationship among the metamodels.

In [4] the idea of transformation model to specify model transformation is discussed. The authors describe the benefits of omitting details of the transformation process and concentrating in depicting the transformation as a model, in which models are instances of metamodels and transformations can be described in conformity to a metamodel. From this point it is possible to describe a transformation model in a formal way, thus it can be validated and verified. We share the idea of transformation models but in this work we make precise what we mean by transformation model (as the result of a disjoint union of two metamodels) and how it may be used to reason on model transformations, as opposed to [4].

OMG's Query View Transformations (QVT) [26] and Graph Grammars (GG, e.g. [17]) are other possible specifications for a model transformation that require specific theory and machinery to reason and implement model transformations. (In the case of GG, focus is on the verification of typical properties of term rewriting systems such as confluence and termination.) The transformation contracts approach proposed in this paper is not biased by any particular specification language and may be used with them as well. Note, however, that QVT is bound to OCL as the specification language for the properties of metamodels and there are properties, such as consistency, subject of this paper, best specified in other semantic frameworks. GG may not have QVT's restriction on the specification language for metamodel properties but a key aspect of our approach is that we apply to model transformation specification design the same specification languages and techniques one would to design a modeling language. No additional framework, such as QVT or GG, is necessary.

At the verification level, different kinds of properties may be reasoned upon besides OCL invariants. One such property is model consistency understood as satisfiability of a propositional formula representing a constrained model. In this paper, we check for the consistency of Description Logics theories associated with a given model. Note that, since we understand model transformations as models, their consistency may be checked as one would check the consistency of any given model, such as in [3].

In [7] the authors use an SMT-solver to check for the satisfiability of model transformations. The mapping is essentially built upon a first-order logic semantics for OCL in [14]. However, they are focused on a particular model transformation language. We believe that to be able to use the same modeling language to describe both the metamodels and model transformation is an important issue.

Some approaches to model verification consider the transformations of models into other languages and formalisms, in which the validation occurs by the use of solvers or theorem provers. In [8], Constraint Satisfaction Problem (CSP) is used to verify UML/OCL models using a translation method. After the translation, a constraint solver is used to verify if the constraint problem induced by the OCL specification is satisfiable. In [27] the authors propose the verification of model transformations specified in a language that extends QVT relations with CSP techniques. The use of CSP techniques is similar to our use of Description Logics however their approach is bound to QVT.

6   Final Remarks

In this paper we have discussed (in Section 3) how programming languages theory, through operational semantics, and logic in computer science (in Section 4), through Description Logics, may be used as a semantics and a logic framework, respectively, to specify and reason on model-driven engineering models. Both perspectives consider MDE models as relational models and build on the perception that model transformations are models as well, here called transformation contracts. Therefore, all the techniques for the specification and reasoning of MDE domain models apply to transformation contracts as well. In particular, in Section 4.4 we discuss what appears to be a novel semantics for transformation contracts which are understood as relative intersection on contextualized ontologies. We conjecture on the equivalence of reasoning on the application of the relative intersection operation and the so called Extended TBox of the given transformation contract.

Future work lies on further developing the research directions pointed out in this paper. In particular, we believe finite model theory [22] will allow us to define more expressive properties with the cost of incomplete models.

Acknowledgments. Christiano Braga would like to thank Leonardo Moura (a friend in need and indeed) and Juliano Iyoda, PC chairs of SBMF'13, for inviting him to give a keynote speech at SBMF'13, for the opportunity to write this paper, and also for their patience and encouragement while editing it. He also would like to thank Edward Hermann Haeusler (a mentor and friend), Isabel Cafezeiro and Alexandre Rademaker for the opportunities to discuss the ideas reported in this paper. This research was partially funded by FAPERJ.

References

1. Akehurst, D., Kent, S.: A relational approach to defining transformations in a metamodel. In: Jézéquel, J.-M., Hussmann, H., Cook, S. (eds.) UML 2002. LNCS, vol. 2460, pp. 243–258. Springer, Heidelberg (2002)
2. Baader, F., Diego Calvanese, D.M., Nardi, D., Patel-Schneider, P.: The Description Logic Handbook. Cambridge University Press (2003)
3. Berardi, D., Calvanese, D., Giacomo, G.D.: Reasoning on UML class diagrams. Artificial Intelligence 168, 70–118 (2005)
4. Bézivin, J., Büttner, F., Gogolla, M., Jouault, F., Kurtev, I., Lindow, A.: Model Transformations? Transformation Models! In: Wang, J., Whittle, J., Harel, D., Reggio, G. (eds.) MoDELS 2006. LNCS, vol. 4199, pp. 440–453. Springer, Heidelberg (2006)
5. Braga, C.: Rewriting logic as a semantic framework for modular structural operational semantics. PhD thesis, DI, PUC-Rio, Brasil (2001)
6. Braga, C., Santos, C., da Silva, V.T.: Consistency of model transformation contracts. Science of Computer Programming (with selected papers from SBMF 2011) (2011) (accepted for publication)
7. Büttner, F., Egea, M., Cabot, J.: On verifying ATL transformations using 'off-the-shelf' SMT solvers. In: France, R.B., Kazmeier, J., Breu, R., Atkinson, C. (eds.) MODELS 2012. LNCS, vol. 7590, pp. 432–448. Springer, Heidelberg (2012)
8. Cabot, J., Clarisó, R., Riera, D.: Verification of UML/OCL class diagrams using constraint programming. In: Proc. of IEEE Soft. Testing Verification and Validation Workshop, pp. 73–80 (2008)
9. Cafezeiro, I., Haeusler, E.H., Rademaker, A.: Ontology and context. In: Proc. of PERCOM 2008, pp. 417–422. IEEE Computer Society (2008)
10. Calvanese, D., Giacomo, G.D., Lenzerini, M.: Reasoning in expressive description logics with fixpoints based on automata on infinite trees. In: Proc. of IJCAI 1999, pp. 84–89 (1999)
11. Cariou, E., Marvie, R., Seinturier, L., Duchien, L.: OCL for the specification of model transformation contracts. In: Proc. of OCL and Model Driven Eng. Workshop, pp. 69–83 (2004)
12. Clavel, M., Durán, F., Eker, S., Lincoln, P., Martí-Oliet, N., Meseguer, J., Talcott, C.: All About Maude - A High-Performance Logical Framework. LNCS, vol. 4350. Springer, Heidelberg (2007)

13. Clavel, M., Egea, M.: ITP/OCL: A rewriting-based validation tool for UML+OCL static class diagrams. In: Johnson, M., Vene, V. (eds.) AMAST 2006. LNCS, vol. 4019, pp. 368–373. Springer, Heidelberg (2006)
14. Clavel, M., Egea, M., de Dios, M.A.G.: Checking unsatisfiability for OCL constraints. In: MODELS 2009. Elec. Comm. of the EASST, vol. 24, pp. 1–13 (2009)
15. Göedel, K.: On formally undecidable propositions of principia methematica and related systems. Dover (1992)
16. Van Gorp, P., Janssens, D.: Cavit: a consistency maintenance framework based on transformation contracts. In: Transformation Techniques in Soft. Eng., number 05161 in Dagstuhl Seminar Proc. (2006)
17. Hermann, F., Ehrig, H., Golas, U., Orejas, F.: Efficient analysis and execution of correct and complete model transformations based on triple graph grammars. In: Proc. of MDI 2010, pp. 22–31. ACM (2010)
18. Hopcroft, J.E., Motwani, R., Ullman, J.D.: Introduction to Automata Theory, Languages, and Computation, 2nd edn. Addison-Wesley (2000)
19. Kahn, G.: Natural semantics. In: Brandenburg, F.J., Wirsing, M., Vidal-Naquet, G. (eds.) STACS 1987. LNCS, vol. 247, pp. 22–39. Springer, Heidelberg (1987)
20. Kleppe, A.: Software Language Engineering. Addison-Wesley (2009)
21. Kleppe, A.G., Warmer, J., Bast, W.: MDA Explained. Addison-Wesley (2003)
22. Libkin, L.: Elements of Finite Model Theory, 1st edn. Springer (2010)
23. Meseguer, J., Roşu, G.: The rewriting logic semantics project. TCS 373(3), 213–237 (2007)
24. Milner, R.: Communicating and Mobile Systems: The π-calculus. Cambridge University Press (1999)
25. Mousavi, M.: Structuring Structural Operational Semantics. PhD thesis, Techsnische Universiteit Eindhoven (2005)
26. OMG. MOF QVT final adopted specification, OMG adopted specification ptc/05-11-01 (2005)
27. Petter, A., Behring, A., Mühlhäuser, M.: Solving constraints in model transformations. In: Paige, R.F. (ed.) ICMT 2009. LNCS, vol. 5563, pp. 132–147. Springer, Heidelberg (2009)
28. Plotkin, G.: A structural apporach to operational semantics. Journal of Logic and Algebraic Programming 60-61, 17–139 (2004)
29. Queralt, A., Artale, A., Calvanese, D., Teniente, E.: OCL-Lite: Finite reasoning on UML/OCL conceptual schemas. Data & Knowledge Eng. 73, 1–22 (2012)
30. Verdejo, A., Martí-Oliet, N.: Executable structural operational semantics in maude. The Journal of Logic and Algebraic Programming 67(1), 226–293 (2006)
31. Wright, A.K., Felleisen, M.: A syntactic approach to type soundness. Information and Computation 115, 38–94 (1994)

Deductive Generalization

Kenneth L. McMillan

Microsoft Research

Abstract. The empirical sciences are based on inductive inference, that is, the formation of theories by generalization from observations. In this process, scientists place a high value on the mathematical beauty or elegance of a theory. Apart from aesthetic concerns, mathematical simplicity has the virtue of constraining our speculations, preventing us from "over-fitting" the data, and thus increasing the chance that our theories will successfully account for new observations. This criterion is traditionally known as Occam's razor (after the medieval philosopher William of Ockham, a frequent user though not originator of the principle).

In mathematical proof we observe a similar phenomenon. That is, conjectures and lemmas are often formed by plausible generalizations from particular cases. Imagine, for example, proving a conjecture about an object in N dimensions. We might first try to prove the special case of two or three dimensions, and then generalize the argument to the N-dimensional case. We would prefer a proof of the two-dimensional case that is simple, on the grounds that it will be less prone to depend on particular aspects of this case, thus more likely to generalize.

The appearance of Occam's razor in logical proof should surprise us, since we require no heuristic justification of conclusions logically deduced from axioms. Nonetheless, such criteria can be highly valuable in the *search* for a proof, since they allow us to form conjectures that are plausibly valid and potentially useful, and thus to navigate the intractably large space of potential proofs.

We will illustrate these concepts by applying them to proofs about programs. To form generalizations, we use a methodology of *interpolation*: finding a hypothesis intermediate between a premise and a desired conclusion. We will set out heuristic criteria for generalizations in terms of evidence provided for both validity of the generalization and its utility in constructing a proof. These criteria can be used to discover inductive invariants that prove given properties of programs by considering only fragments of the program's behavior. We observe that evidence for generalizations comes at a computational cost, and that in practice it is important to strike a balance between cost and quality of generalizations.

Moreover, we observe a subtle but significant difference between the use of Occam's razor in deductive as opposed to inductive settings. That is, by considering the simplicity of the *proof* of a proposition in a particular case, we can make distinctions that cannot be made based on the simplicity of hypotheses alone.

J. Iyoda and L. de Moura (Eds.): SBMF 2013, LNCS 8195, p. 17, 2013.
© Springer-Verlag Berlin Heidelberg 2013

Unifying Theories of Logic and Specification

Victor Bandur and Jim Woodcock

The University of York, UK

Abstract. We propose a unifying treatment of multi-valued logic in the general context of specification, presented in the style of the Unifying Theories of Programming of Hoare and He. At a low level, UTP theories correspond to different types of three-valued logic. At higher levels they correspond to individual specifications. Designs are considered as their models, but members of other unifying theories of computation can serve as models just as well. Using this setup we have the opportunity to show correspondences between specification languages that use different logics.

1   Introduction

Previous work by Woodcock *et al.* [1] investigates the formal relationships between various logics that deal explicitly with undefinedness. The logics covered are Bochvar's strict logic [2], McCarthy's left-right logic [3] and Kleene's "lazy" logic as used in VDM's Logic of Partial Functions [4]. These are compared with classical and flavours of semi-classical logic. Semi-classical logics permit terms to be non-denoting, but are otherwise classical in character. Examples are the logic of Z [5], and LUTINS [6], the logic of the IMPS theorem prover. An information-theoretic theorem is there proven that orders these logics according to their resilience to undefinedness. In subsequent work [7] we make use of the features of Hoare and He's Unifying Theories of Programming (UTP) [8] to migrate the results of this work from a denotational semantics style to a fully algebraic one, enabling further expansion of the work to be carried out entirely using UTP. There we define an approach to encoding three-valued logics in classical logic in general and use the intrinsic theory structuring mechanism of UTP to construct theories of each logic.

With this logical basis in place, it is possible to start abstracting. Since every specification formalism is built on some underlying logic, it is natural to lift this investigation to the level of specification. Here we start exploring the formal connections existing between specification languages in general. We use a variant of our previous classical encoding to determine what correspondences are induced by the logic-level connections at the more abstract level of the specification languages built on these logics. We believe that the general view taken here will aid in the ongoing quest for a fully formal basis for theorem prover reuse.

1.1   Related Work

The structure of our approach is primarily inspired from the foundational work of Goguen and Burstall on *institutions* [9] and the work that followed from it

J. Iyoda and L. de Moura (Eds.): SBMF 2013, LNCS 8195, pp. 18–33, 2013.

[10–14]. Our intention, however, is not to continue in a categorical vein, but rather to explore the problem using the relational style of UTP. We believe that this move will address a comment made by Gavilanes-Franco and Lucio-Carrasco, that "the connections among different logics are sometimes presented in a cumbersome way" [15]. Indeed the treatment of how logics relate to each other is often application-specific and usually focused on a single pair of logics [16–21]. Usually no universal approach is taken. Our approach unifies the treatment of any type of logic and enables the investigation of relationships using the same mechanisms in all instances. These mechanisms are those intrinsic to UTP, like theory links and Galois connections. We believe that this approach regains a level of generality similar to that enjoyed by the categorical approach.

2   Classical Representation of Three-Valued Predicates

Since our primary aim is to give an account of the connections existing between various specification methods in use today, we restrict our investigations to three-valued logic only. The use of three truth values is most prominent in VDM [22], which employs the Logic of Partial Functions [4], and in the Overture tool for VDM [23], which employs a more operational flavour known as McCarthy's left-right logic [3]. Other three-valued logics help us understand how to better handle undefinedness in specification settings built over classical logic. Our starting point is Alan Rose's classical encoding of three-valued predicates.

Rose [24] proposes a representation of three-valued predicates taking on the values "true", "false" and "undefined", as a pair of classical predicates. A three-valued predicate P is there given a representation (P_l, P_r), where P_l represents the circumstances under which (the valuation of its free variables for which) P is true, and P_r represents the circumstances under which P is defined. Therefore, $P_l \wedge P_r$ captures the values for which P is both defined and true in the three-valued sense (the conjunction operator "$\wedge$" in this expression is classical conjunction). The free variables of P_l are those of P_r, which are in turn those of P itself, leading to the simple Venn diagram representation of P shown in Fig. 1. We adopt this representation for three-valued predicates, but depart immediately from it in two different ways. First, because we want to treat different logics in use today, we do not adopt the operators defined by Rose for these predicates. Our operators are introduced in Sect. 4.3. Second, our aim is to treat

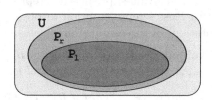

Fig. 1. Representation (P_l, P_r) of three-valued predicate P over its universe U

these different logics in their specification contexts, and to this end the free variables of our predicates are themselves allowed to range over predicates. Section 4 is dedicated to this topic.

3   Three-Valued Predicates in UTP

Starting with Rose's encoding, we must choose a way to represent these predicates as UTP alphabetized relations. What will primarily determine this encoding is the interpretation of the undefined truth value "⊥" in a specification context. This requires careful consideration, as different specification philosophies will attribute "⊥" different interpretations. In a multi-valued logic, the two possible interpretations are as missing information [25], and as too much, or contradictory, information (as considered by Belnap in a four-valued logic [26]). These two interpretations lead to differing views on what a specification statement says about those values which make it undefined. Here we take the position that undefined specification statements contain insufficient information. Therefore undefined specifications are *permissive* of those values that make them undefined. This naturally accommodates the refinement approach to specification, where such undefinedness can be refined away.

3.1   Three-Valued Predicate Representation

In the spirit of UTP designs, we want to give a syntactic *model* for three-valued predicates in terms of the individual components of Rose's predicate pair. Here we make the subscript notation used before formal. Therefore, for a three-valued predicate P, we use P_l for the left component (*i.e.*, the left projection) of Rose's pair, and P_r for the right component. The word "model" is used here to refer to this new syntactic representation. Later, where it will be made clear, the word is used in the model-theoretic sense.

Because in the most general sense P_l and P_r are not mandated to relate to each other, a device is required to bind them together in the desired way. In the theory of designs this binding is achieved through the introduction of the observation variable **ok**. For a design $P \vdash Q$, the variables **ok** and **ok'** are not definable in terms of each other, nor in terms of P and Q. They represent observable properties in the physical domain and are atomic and unanalyzable. Similarly, we introduce a variable **def** into the alphabet of each predicate pair (P_l, P_r), which reflects whether the three-valued predicate P represented is defined. Now we can combine **def** with Rose's representation to obtain our unifying model (*i.e.*, syntactic representation) of three-valued predicates.

Definition 1 (Three-valued predicate model). *A three-valued predicate P with alphabet $\alpha P \equiv \alpha(P_l, P_r)$ is represented in classical logic as,*

$$(P_l, P_r) \triangleq P_l \lhd \textbf{\textit{def}} \rhd \neg P_r \equiv (\textbf{\textit{def}} \wedge P) \vee (\neg \textbf{\textit{def}} \wedge \neg P_r) \ .$$
$$\alpha(P_l, P_r) \triangleq \{\textbf{\textit{def}}\} \cup \alpha P_l \ .$$

where $\alpha P_l = \alpha P_r$ and $\textbf{\textit{def}} \notin \alpha P_l$.

This conditional models the three-valued predicate P as follows. **def** reflects whether P is defined for some valuation of its free variables. P_r captures the space over which P is defined, whereas P_l captures the space over which P is true. **def** allows us to define how P_l and P_r capture properties of the predicate P that exist in the three-valued realm, which is itself represented in **def**.

Of course, there is nothing in place so far to prevent illegitimate combinations of **def**, P_l and P_r. The most important correspondence required of all predicates P represented thus is that between the definedness of P (as reflected in **def**) and the predicate P_r. This is suggested by the structure of the conditional itself. Whenever **def** is true, the conditional reduces to P_l, which is independent of P_r. But a guarantee is required that **def** and P_r agree at that point, otherwise nothing can be said about what P_l represents. This guarantee is provided by the following healthiness condition.

Definition 2 (Three-valued predicate healthiness). *Healthy predicate pairs exhibit agreement between **def** and* P_r.

$$\mathbf{H}(P_l, P_r) = \mathbf{\textit{def}} \Leftrightarrow P_r \ .$$

3.2   The Effect of Classical Operators

The development of our theory continues with the search for operators. Intuitively, the operators should be the logical operators which can combine alphabetized relations, which represent atomic predicates, into relations representing logical sentences in the usual way. Before trying to define the operators outright, it is natural to explore whether we can reuse any existing operators, so we first observe the effect of the classical logical operators, the logical operators of UTP itself, on our model of three-valued predicates.

We begin with the simplest case by considering the classical negation of a three-valued predicate (P_l, P_r). First we establish a straightforward lemma,

Lemma 1. *There exist two equivalent representations of predicate pairs* (P_l, P_r)*:*

$$P_l \lhd \mathbf{\textit{def}} \rhd \neg P_r \equiv (\mathbf{\textit{def}} \Rightarrow P_l) \wedge (\neg \mathbf{\textit{def}} \Rightarrow \neg P_r) \ .$$

Now the effect of classical negation on the predicate model can be observed:

$$
\begin{aligned}
\neg(P_l, P_r) &\equiv \neg(P_l \lhd \mathbf{\textit{def}} \rhd \neg P_r) && \textit{by Definition 1}\\
&\equiv \neg((\mathbf{\textit{def}} \wedge P_l) \vee (\neg \mathbf{\textit{def}} \wedge \neg P_r)) && \textit{definition of conditional}\\
&\equiv (\mathbf{\textit{def}} \Rightarrow \neg P_l) \wedge (\neg \mathbf{\textit{def}} \Rightarrow P_r) && \textit{distributivity of ``$\neg$''and}\\
& && \textit{definition of ``$\Rightarrow$''}\\
&\equiv (\neg P_l, \neg P_r) && \textit{by Lemma 1}
\end{aligned}
$$

The resulting pair represents a three-valued predicate which is true where the original was false, and which is defined where the original was undefined. Negating a three-valued predicate in this way does not in fact correspond to negation in any familiar three-valued logic because it makes defined predicates out of undefined ones and *vice versa*. In the logics we consider, negation is always contingent on predicates being defined in the first place. More importantly, the operators of the logics we consider are monotonic in the information order shown in Fig. 2, which classical negation in this case is not. We therefore abandon classical negation.

Fig. 2. Information ordering of the three logical values

Binary operators are more troublesome. According to Definition 1, all predicates share the observable *def*. Taking the classical conjunction, for instance, of two predicates (P_l, P_r) and (Q_l, Q_r) instantly reveals the need to discriminate between their respective *def*s. Consider the equivalence [8],

$$(P_l \triangleleft \textbf{\textit{def}} \triangleright \neg P_r) \wedge (Q_l \triangleleft \textbf{\textit{def}} \triangleright \neg Q_r)$$
$$\equiv (P_l \wedge Q_l) \triangleleft \textbf{\textit{def}} \triangleright (\neg P_r \wedge \neg Q_r) \qquad \textit{mutual distribution, Ex. 2.1.2}$$
$$\equiv (P_l \wedge Q_l, P_r \vee Q_r)$$

There are several problems with the resulting three-valued predicate. Since *def* is shared between P and Q, their classical conjunction yields the representation of a predicate that is defined when either P or Q is defined, but which is undefined when both are undefined. This reflects no three-valued conjunction we know, nor classical conjunction, and as it stands is too problematic to shed further light on the effect of classical operators on these representations.

We can try to tackle the problem of the shared *def* by using substitution to rename a predicate P's *def* so that it does not clash with the *def* of any other predicate. This can be done by referring to the predicate $P[\textbf{\textit{def}}_P / \textbf{\textit{def}}]$ instead. Taking the classical conjunction now, we obtain,

$$P[\textbf{\textit{def}}_P / \textbf{\textit{def}}] \wedge Q[\textbf{\textit{def}}_Q / \textbf{\textit{def}}] \equiv (P_l \triangleleft \textbf{\textit{def}}_P \triangleright \neg P_r) \wedge (Q_l \triangleleft \textbf{\textit{def}}_Q \triangleright \neg Q_r) \ .$$

Table 3 shows the consequence of this change. It is clear from the case, for instance, where P is defined and Q is not, that the result is similarly nonsensical. Since we know that $\textbf{\textit{def}}_Q$ and Q_r agree, the conjunction reduces to P_l. This again does not correspond directly to any logical operation in any of our three-valued logics. Applying the same renaming technique in the case of classical disjunction, we obtain the following identity, and result summary in Table 3.

$$P[\textbf{\textit{def}}_P / \textbf{\textit{def}}] \vee Q[\textbf{\textit{def}}_Q / \textbf{\textit{def}}] \equiv (P_l \triangleleft \textbf{\textit{def}}_P \triangleright \neg P_r) \vee (Q_l \triangleleft \textbf{\textit{def}}_Q \triangleright \neg Q_r) \ .$$

The trouble with this approach is that the definedness information of the entire conjunction (resp. disjunction) is lost, and to recover it we would have to do so

def_P	def_Q	Result
T	T	$P_l \wedge Q_l$
T	F	$P_l \wedge \neg Q_r$
F	T	$\neg P_r \wedge Q_l$
F	F	$\neg P_r \wedge \neg Q_r$

def_P	def_Q	Result
T	T	$P_l \vee Q_l$
T	F	$P_l \vee \neg Q_r$
F	T	$\neg P_r \vee Q_l$
F	F	$\neg P_r \vee \neg Q_r$

Fig. 3. Classical conjunction and disjunction of three-valued predicate models

by definition. We will return to the topic of classical conjunction and disjunction of three-valued predicate models in Sect. 4.5, where this classical behaviour is in fact reused, but to a different end. As for the immediate purpose of defining the theory's operators, this is done by first considering how the theory will be used.

4   Three-Valued Predicates as Specifications

This section continues to build on the three-valued predicate model by introducing the remaining components required for a complete lattice of three-valued predicates. The necessary partial order, theory operators, meet and join operators, and lattice top and bottom are defined.

4.1   Designs as Models of Specifications

We consider the case where a given relation's alphabet ranges over alphabetized relations in turn, *i.e.*, when a relation has second-order observation variables. As with first-order observation variables, we can assume that we have at our disposal the use of the substitution operator $[v_0/v]$ (implying knowledge of each relation's alphabet, which can be captured as a type on the variable [8]), logical operators, both those that are the operators of the source theory of the variable, as well as those of the classical logic employed in UTP, the construction of lists of alphabetized relations, and so on. Of course, all this must be consistent with the fact that the resulting characteristic predicate must be a classical predicate. Moreover, these predicates must be allowed to range in turn over alphabetized predicates in order to accommodate the expression of specification statements, as described below. Therefore, we consider the alphabet of a relation P to be composed of a first-order alphabet $\overset{F}{\alpha}P$, and a higher-order alphabet $\overset{H}{\alpha}P$:

Definition 3 (Alphabet partitioning). *The alphabet of any relation P is composed of a first-order alphabet $\overset{F}{\alpha}P$ and a higher-order alphabet $\overset{H}{\alpha}P$.*

$$\alpha P \triangleq \overset{F}{\alpha}P \cup \overset{H}{\alpha}P , \quad where \ \textbf{def} \in \overset{F}{\alpha}P .$$

This partitioning will help make the distinction between relations that represent three-valued predicates in general, and the subset that can be understood as specification statements in the usual sense of software specification.

In the UTP style, usually a specification is given as an input-output relation defining the behaviour of the entity that it names. This view can be generalized mathematically as follows. Consider an alphabetized relation $P = (in\alpha, out\alpha, p)$, where p is the characteristic predicate specifying the behaviour of the entity P. If we name this entity separately, say P°, then the specification describing the alphabetized relation P itself can be captured as,

$$\forall i, i' \bullet p(i, i') \Leftrightarrow P^\circ(i) = i' , \quad \text{where } \overset{\text{F}}{\alpha} = \{i, i'\} \text{ and } \overset{\text{H}}{\alpha} = \{P^\circ\} .$$

This second-order statement introduces the entity P° as a definition [27] that selects, from all possible entities, only those which satisfy the original input-output specification P: they are the only *models* that satisfy this formula (here we switch to the use of the word "model" in the model-theoretic sense of "interpretation"). In general, any alphabetized relation with only second-order alphabetical variables is a *specification* statement that introduces by definition the entities named by its second-order alphabet. This is in fact exactly the role of formal specification that is captured here. As expected, the stronger, more useful relationship of refinement of P° to P is also accommodated:

$$\forall i, i' \bullet P^\circ(i) = i' \Rightarrow p(i, i') .$$

This second definition of P° selects not only those entities which behave exactly in accordance with P, but also those that refine it.

Specifications can be more or less refined, naturally exhibiting the expected refinement order $P \sqsubseteq Q$. Real entities which make the refining specification Q true will make the refined specification P true as well. The healthiness condition selecting such a lattice of predicates from the complete space is exactly the predicate that expresses the *requirements* collected for one single specification. This is not meant to refer to a specific UTP predicate, but the logical statement, in any logic, of the requirements. Therefore, just as all specifications that are true to a set of (non-contradictory) requirements will satisfy all the requirements, so all the predicates in the resulting lattice will satisfy its healthiness condition, and represent all levels of refinement of one single specification.

If specifications are captured as unifying theories in the style described above, as second-order predicates ranging over entities which form their models, then the lowest-level description of these entities available to us in the UTP setting is the theory of designs. Designs (essentially abstract descriptions of *pieces of functionality*) naturally serve as models for specifications of large systems because they form a well-developed unifying theory in their own right. In fact, the various models of programming treated in UTP, namely designs, reactive designs, CSP processes, CCS processes *etc.* serve equally well as models of these specifications.

As a simple example, consider the specification of the "subp" function proposed by Jones [22], where $i, j : \mathbb{N}$.

$$\mathbf{pre} : i \le j \qquad \mathbf{post} : \text{subp}(i, j) = j - i .$$

Using the lifting approach described above, this specification can be captured as,

$$(S \Leftrightarrow \boldsymbol{res}' = j - i, i \le j) \equiv (S \Leftrightarrow \boldsymbol{res}' = j - i) \triangleleft \boldsymbol{def} \triangleright \neg(i \le j) .$$

where $\alpha S = \{i, j, \textbf{res}\}$, $\overset{\text{F}}{\alpha} = \alpha S$, $\overset{\text{H}}{\alpha} = \{S\}$ and $\textbf{res}$ is a *result* variable introduced so that the function subp may be represented as a relation. The alphabetical variable S ranges over all possible implementations for subp, designs for instance. One non-trivial implementation proposed by Jones has the recursive definition,

$$\text{subp}\,(i, j) \triangleq \text{if } i = j \text{ then } 0 \text{ else } \text{subp}\,(i+1, j) + 1 \ .$$

Adapted as a design with alphabet αS as described above, this becomes

$$S \triangleq true \vdash \exists r_0 \bullet ((\mu X \bullet \textbf{res}' = r_0 \lhd i = j \rhd X[i + 1/i, r_0 + 1/r_0]) \wedge r_0 = 0) \ .$$

Note that the precondition of the design intentionally matches that of Jones' recursive definition, and not that of the specification. Substitution into the specification relation now yields,

$$\exists r_0 \bullet ((\mu X \bullet \textbf{res}' = r_0 \lhd i = j \rhd X[i + 1/i, r_0 + 1/r_0]) \wedge r_0 = 0) \Leftrightarrow \textbf{res}' = j - i$$
$$\lhd \textbf{def} \rhd$$
$$\neg(i \leq j) \ .$$

First lifting the original three-valued specification into an alphabetized relation and then substituting into the resulting second-order variable a possible implementation of the defined entity subp, we arrive at an expression that verifies that, as expected, our candidate implementation indeed satisfies the original specification. This example is developed further using the defined three-valued logical operators in Sect. 4.3.

4.2 Partial Order for Three-Valued Predicates

We desire a partial order between pairs of relations that captures specification refinement in a particular logical setting. In the case of Kleene's three-valued logic (the logic used in VDM), if the refinement order is denoted $\sqsubseteq$ (is less refined than), then any two relations P and Q such that $P \sqsubseteq Q$ (Q refines P) must satisfy the following properties (we use the notation P^t for $P[true \,/\, \textbf{def}]$, and similarly for *false*):

Definition 4 (Properties of refinement).

1. Q *can refine two aspects of* P: *behaviours specified by* P *and situations where* P *is undefined:* $[Q^t \Rightarrow (P^t \vee P^f)]$.
2. Q *can not be undefined where* P *is defined:* $[Q^f \Rightarrow P^f]$.

It is clear that the standard reverse implication order usually employed in unifying theories can not be used as the refinement order, for one thing due to alphabet mismatch at $\textbf{def}$: our notion of refinement must discern between $\textbf{def}_{\text{P}}$ and $\textbf{def}_{\text{Q}}$, but the standard reverse implication is only defined for P and Q where $\alpha P = \alpha Q$.

It is therefore necessary to define a bespoke partial order that reflects a view of refinement in a three-valued logical specification setting as described above.

This order must be reflexive, antisymmetric and transitive. It must therefore be shown that these two sets of requirements are not at odds. That is, it must be shown that a partial order satisfying the two properties above can in fact be reflexive, antisymmetric and transitive.

Theorem 1 (Partial order). *The conditions of Definition 4 define a partial order on three-valued predicate models.*

The proof strategy is simple: for any two relations $P \sqsubseteq Q$, we assume the two properties of Definition 4 and prove reflexivity, antisymmetry and transitivity.

4.3   Theory Operators

Since characteristic predicates are built using the term expression language, our theory operators will then be the logical operators, allowing the construction of logical sentences from terms. For the sake of brevity, we only discuss the operators of Kleene's three-valued logic. Two other logics of interest are strict three-valued logic, as proposed by Bochvar [2], an approach to evaluating three-valued logical statements that is easily implementable, and McCarthy's left-right logic [3], a three-valued logic that retains more information than the strict variant, but is still tailored to easy implementation. McCarthy's logic is used in the Overture tool for VDM [23]. We justify the use of left-right logic in Overture elsewhere [7]. These logics are briefly explored in Sect. 5.

$\neg$			$\wedge$	**T**	**F**	**U**		$\vee$	**T**	**F**	**U**		$\forall x \bullet P$	Condition
T	F		**T**	T	F	U		**T**	T	T	T		**T**	P is true for all x.
F	T		**F**	F	F	F		**F**	T	F	U		**F**	P is false for at least one x.
U	U		**U**	U	F	U		**U**	T	U	U		**U**	Otherwise.

$\iota x \bullet P$	Condition
x	P is everywhere defined and there is exactly one x such that $P(x)$.
U	Otherwise.

Fig. 4. Kleene's three-valued logical operators

The definition of Kleene's logical operators is shown in Fig. 4.

Definition 5 (Kleene logic operators). *The operators of the unifying theory of three-valued Kleene logic are defined as follows.*

1. *Negation:* $\overset{K}{\neg} P \triangleq (\neg P_l, P_r)$.
2. *Conjunction:* $P \overset{K}{\wedge} Q \triangleq (P_l \wedge Q_l, (P_r \wedge Q_r) \vee (\neg P_l \wedge P_r) \vee (\neg Q_l \wedge Q_r))$.
3. *Disjunction:* $P \overset{K}{\vee} Q \triangleq (P_l \vee Q_l, (P_r \wedge Q_r) \vee (P_l \wedge P_r) \vee (Q_l \wedge Q_r))$.
4. *Universal Quantification:* $\overset{K}{\forall} x \bullet P \triangleq (\forall x \bullet P_l, [P_r] \vee \exists x \bullet \neg P_l \wedge P_r)$.
5. *Definite Description:* $\overset{K}{\iota} x \bullet P \triangleq (P_l, [P_r] \wedge \exists x \bullet P_l(x) \wedge \forall y \bullet P_l(y) \Rightarrow x = y)))$.

Note: *Under the assumption that predicates have finite alphabets, $\overset{\scriptscriptstyle K}{\forall}$, $\overset{\scriptscriptstyle K}{\iota}$ are actually finite families of operators, one for each combination of free variables in αP, represented by $\boldsymbol{x}$.*

Since $\overset{\scriptscriptstyle K}{\iota}$ is not a logical operator, it requires some explanation. In order to include it in our theory, it must operate on a predicate and yield a predicate in turn. It achieves this by changing its parameter P to behave in accordance with the behaviour of the definite description operator used in VDM. That is, it modifies an arbitrary P to only be defined and true for the unique x that satisfies it, if it exists.

Returning to the subp example, we can now explore the proof obligation required by VDM of the pre/postcondition specification given. The proof obligation, in LPF, is

$$\forall i, j : \mathbb{N} \bullet i \leq j \Rightarrow \operatorname{subp}(i, j) = j - i \ .$$

Since implication in LPF is defined in the usual way in terms of negation and disjunction, we shall focus instead on the statement,

$$\forall i, j : \mathbb{N} \bullet \neg(i \leq j) \vee \operatorname{subp}(i, j) = j - i \ .$$

The atoms of this formula are $i \leq j$ and $\operatorname{subp}(i, j) = j - i$. They are the two relations that will be combined using the operators of our theory to form the full relation representing the three-valued statement above. The atomic relations are $(i \leq j, true)$ and $(S \Leftrightarrow \boldsymbol{res'} = j - i, i \leq j)$, and the complete relation is,

$$\overset{\scriptscriptstyle K}{\forall} i, j \bullet \overset{\scriptscriptstyle K}{\neg} (i \leq j, true) \overset{\scriptscriptstyle K}{\vee} (S \Leftrightarrow \boldsymbol{res'} = j - i, i \leq j)$$
$$\equiv \forall i, j, \boldsymbol{res'} \bullet (\neg(i \leq j) \vee (S \Leftrightarrow \boldsymbol{res'} = j - i), true) \qquad \textit{by Definition 5}$$

This example illustrates how the atomic elements of logical sentences are chosen and represented as relations in our theory, and how the original sentences are then reconstructed using the theory's operators. Ignoring the characteristic predicate expression language at the level of the theory means that, if required, the characteristic predicates of the atomic relations can themselves use classical logical operators, ensuring that classical logic does not bleed into the sentences constructed inside the theory. And similarly, defining the theory's three-valued operators solely in terms of classical predicates ensures that undefinedness from the three-valued logic represented does not bleed back into the classical logic of UTP.

4.4   Strongest and Weakest Predicates

From Fig. 2 we know that the bottom element "$\perp$" of the information order on logical values is the undefined value. Happily this also corresponds to the most useless specification, the completely undefined specification, $\neg \boldsymbol{def}$. We therefore adopt $\neg \boldsymbol{def}$ as the bottom element.

The strongest element is a little less intuitive. It should be the specification that is not implementable. Such a specification is totally defined, but everywhere false. It would therefore admit no model. From Definition 1 we obtain,

$$\top \triangleq (false, true) \equiv \boldsymbol{def} \wedge \neg \boldsymbol{def} \equiv false \ .$$

At first sight this is not exactly the expression we desire, since it does not explicitly capture the fact that it represents a defined statement. But it is in fact neither defined, nor undefined, since neither $\boldsymbol{def}$ nor $\neg \boldsymbol{def}$ make it true. So on one hand it can be considered unimplementable from an even more fundamental point of view, which reveals that it can not even be established whether it is a defined statement in the first place; and on the other hand it is in fact technically strong enough to serve as our strongest specification and predicate.

4.5   Lattice Operators

In Sect. 3.2 we explored the effect of classical conjunction and disjunction on our model of three-valued predicates. Since these are the classical meet (greatest lower bound) and join (least upper bound) operators, we should investigate whether they can serve as same in our theory of three-valued predicates. First we establish the properties that the meet and join operators must possess in the context of specification.

Essentially we want the meet of two specifications to be only as prescriptive as the least prescriptive of the two. If undefinedness is present, then it dominates. First, it is reasonable to require that where the two specifications are defined, their meet is their disjunction, just as in the classical setting. That is, wherever $\neg P^f$ and $\neg Q^f$, then $(P \sqcap Q)^t = P^t \vee Q^t$ and $\neg (P \sqcap Q)^f$. Second, wherever both specifications are undefined, then their meet must also be undefined. That is, wherever P^f and Q^f, then $(P \sqcap Q)^f$. Third, wherever one of the two specifications is undefined, their meet must also be undefined. That is, wherever $\neg P^f$ and Q^f, or P^f and $\neg Q^f$, then $(P \sqcap Q)^f$. This condition is consistent with our view that undefined specifications do not constrain any behaviour. From Sect. 3.2 we observe that the classical disjunction of two three-valued predicate models satisfies all these conditions. Its behaviour is reproduced in the following definition:

Definition 6 (Meet). *The greatest lower bound of three-valued predicate models P and Q is defined as,*

$$P \sqcap Q \triangleq (P_l \vee Q_l, P_r \wedge Q_r) \equiv P \vee Q \ .$$

The greatest lower bound of a (possibly infinite) set S of three-valued predicate models is defined as,

$$\bigsqcap S \triangleq (\bigvee \{I_l | I \in S\}, \bigwedge \{I_r | I \in S\}) \ .$$

By a similar argument we have,

Definition 7 (Join). *The least upper bound of three-valued predicate models P and Q is defined as,*

$$P \sqcup Q \triangleq (P_l \wedge Q_l, P_r \vee Q_r) \equiv P \wedge Q \ .$$

The least upper bound of a (possibly infinite) set S of three-valued predicate models is defined as,

$$\bigsqcup S \triangleq (\bigwedge \{I_l | I \in S\}, \bigvee \{I_r | I \in S\}) \ .$$

To show that these definitions provide maximal (respectively minimal) bounds, we consider the case of the meet. The argument for join follows a similar line of reasoning. The statement to prove is the following second-order formula,

$$\forall P, Q \bullet ((P \sqcap Q \sqsubseteq P) \wedge (P \sqcap Q \sqsubseteq Q) \wedge (\forall S \bullet (S \sqsubseteq P \wedge S \sqsubseteq Q) \Rightarrow S \sqsubseteq P \sqcap Q)).$$

The first two conjuncts require that $P \sqcap Q$ is indeed a lower bound of P and of Q, and are clearly true. The third conjunct requires maximality.

According to condition 2 of Definition 4, two cases must be considered. First, we consider the case when P and Q are undefined. We know that S is also undefined and that $[P_r \Rightarrow S_r]$ and that $[Q_r \Rightarrow S_r]$, since $[P^f \Rightarrow S^f]$ and $[Q^f \Rightarrow S^f]$. Therefore it is the case that $[(P \sqcap Q)^f \Rightarrow S^f]$, since $[P_r \wedge Q_r \Rightarrow S_r]$. Second, we must consider the case when P is defined. If Q is also defined, then we have, for defined S, that $[P_l \vee Q_l \Rightarrow S_l]$ from $[P_l \Rightarrow S_l]$ and $[Q_l \Rightarrow S_l]$. The case for undefined S follows trivially. In the case of defined P and undefined Q, $P \sqcap Q$ is also undefined and from the hypothesis $S \sqsubseteq P \wedge S \sqsubseteq Q$ we have that S is undefined, yielding the conclusion directly.

It is interesting to see here why Kleene's operators do not serve well. Kleene's logical operators are very permissive of undefinedness in that they evaluate to a defined value using a minimal amount of information. The design of these definitions, to extract as much information as possible from arguments, is directly at odds with the notion of meet and join needed here, where undefinedness must prevail. The case of the disjunction of "F" and "U" in the disjunction table in Fig. 4 illustrates this contradiction clearly.

5   Connecting Theories

The various elements introduced in Sect. 4 define an unifying theory of Kleene logic, denoted K, with signature $\Sigma_K \triangleq (\overset{\kappa}{\neg}, \overset{\kappa}{\wedge}, \overset{\kappa}{\vee}, \overset{\kappa}{\forall}, \overset{\kappa}{\iota})$. Considering the top, bottom, meet and join operators defined in Sect. 4.5, it is easy to show that K is in fact a complete lattice of predicates, as desired. This section discusses briefly the unifying treatment of two other logics, and some connections between them. These theories possess the same lattice property. They are defined analogously to K and their operators mimic the operator definitions in Fig. 5. The details are here deferred [28].

5.1   Strict Logic and McCarthy Left-Right Logic

Bochvar's strict internal logic and McCarthy's left-right logic are two other variations on the theme of three truth values that regards undefinedness as useless information, but whose operators are defined with implementability in mind. They are reproduced in Figs. 5a and 5b. Similar to the definition of the operators of our theory of Kleene logic in Sect. 4.3, Definition 5, we define the operators of the corresponding theories of strict and left-right logics, bearing in mind the same observation on the families of operators $\overset{s}{\forall}, \overset{s}{\iota}, \overset{LR}{\forall}, \overset{LR}{\iota}$.

$\neg$		$\wedge$	T	F	U		$\vee$	T	F	U		$\forall x \bullet P$	Condition
T	F	**T**	T	F	U		**T**	T	T	U		**T**	P is true for all x.
F	T	**F**	F	F	U		**F**	T	F	U		**F**	P is false for at least one x.
U	U	**U**	U	U	U		**U**	U	U	U		**U**	P is undefined for any x.

$\iota x \bullet P$	Condition
x	P is everywhere defined and there is exactly one x such that $P(x)$.
U	Otherwise.

(a) Strict three-valued logical operators.

$\neg$		$\wedge$	T	F	U		$\vee$	T	F	U		$\forall x \bullet P$	Condition
T	F	**T**	T	F	U		**T**	T	T	T		**T**	P is true for all x.
F	T	**F**	F	F	F		**F**	T	F	U		**F**	P is false for at least one x.
U	U	**U**	U	U	U		**U**	U	U	U		**U**	P is undefined for any x.

$\iota x \bullet P$	Condition
x	P is everywhere defined and there is exactly one x such that $P(x)$.
U	Otherwise.

(b) Left-right three-valued logical operators.

Fig. 5. Strict and McCarthy left-right logical operators

Definition 8 (Strict and McCarthy left-right theory operators). *The operators of the unifying theories of strict and left-right three-valued logic are defined as follows.*

1. *Negation:* $\overset{s}{\neg} P = \overset{LR}{\neg} P \triangleq (\neg P_l, P_r)$.
2. *Conjunction:* $P \overset{s}{\wedge} Q \triangleq (P_l \wedge Q_l, P_r \wedge Q_r)$.
   $$P \overset{LR}{\wedge} Q \triangleq (P_l \wedge Q_l, (P_r \wedge Q_r) \vee (\neg P_l \wedge P_r)) .$$
3. *Disjunction:* $P \overset{s}{\vee} Q \triangleq (P_l \vee Q_l, P_r \wedge Q_r)$.
   $$P \overset{LR}{\vee} Q \triangleq (P_l \vee Q_l, (P_r \wedge Q_r) \vee (P_l \wedge P_r)) .$$
4. *Universal Quantification:* $\overset{s}{\forall} x \bullet P = \overset{LR}{\forall} x \bullet P \triangleq (\forall x \bullet P_l, [P_r])$.
5. *Definite Description:*
   $$\overset{s}{\iota} x \bullet P = \overset{LR}{\iota} x \bullet P \triangleq (P_l, [P_r] \wedge \exists x \bullet P_l(x) \wedge \forall y \bullet P_l(y) \Rightarrow x = y))) .$$

Then, $\Sigma_S \triangleq (\overset{s}{\neg}, \overset{s}{\wedge}, \overset{s}{\vee}, \overset{s}{\forall}, \overset{s}{\iota})$ and $\Sigma_{LR} \triangleq (\overset{LR}{\neg}, \overset{LR}{\wedge}, \overset{LR}{\vee}, \overset{LR}{\forall}, \overset{LR}{\iota})$ are the signatures of the resulting theories S and LR, respectively.

5.2   Relating Theories

There exist at least three different ways of relating the theories described so far. From the definedness ordering discovered by Woodcock *et al.* [1] between the three logics considered, we define the following relationships. Only S and LR are considered here, but the extension to K is straightforward. In what follows, let σ_{SLR} and σ_{LRS} be the signature morphisms that map the operators of S to those of LR and *vice versa*, respectively, expanded to the sentences of their respective theories. We also make use of the following theorem.

Theorem 2 (Equivalent behaviour). *There exists a function* $\tau : S \to LR$ *such that for all binary operators* $\overset{s}{\oplus}$ *of* S *and predicates* P *and* Q *in* S,

$$[P \overset{s}{\oplus} Q \equiv (\tau P)(\sigma_{SLR} \overset{s}{\oplus})(\tau Q)] .$$

The function τ can be defined by structural induction on members of S.

A *retract* [8] is a weakening, monotonic and idempotent endofunction on UTP theories. The following theorem confirms that LR is at least as resilient to undefinedness as S, and mirrors the corresponding part of the ordering theorem of Woodcock *et al.* A similar theorem exists for LR and K.

Theorem 3 (Retract). *The theory defined by the endofunction* $(\tau \circ \sigma_{LRS})$ *on* LR *is a retract.*

The intuition behind this result is illustrated by the application of σ_{LRS} alone to members of LR, but the subsequent application of τ is necessary to inject the resulting theory back into LR. τ achieves a simulation of the behaviour of S in LR and so weakening is shown. Monotonicity and idempotence are clear.

Since S, LR and K have signatures of the same size, we would expect that sentences can be transliterated between any two theories with no losses. The next theorem confirms that the logics are equally expressive *with respect to syntax*.

Theorem 4 (Isomorphism). S *and* LR *are isomorphic, since*

$$\sigma_{LRS} \circ \sigma_{SLR} = id_S \quad and \quad \sigma_{SLR} \circ \sigma_{LRS} = id_{LR} .$$

The result in Theorem 3 can be lifted to provide a more interesting class of connections between theories, as exemplified in the next theorem.

Theorem 5 (Galois connection). *The pair* (σ_{LRS}, τ) *forms a Galois connection between* S *and* LR.

Tighter Galois connections than this can be defined where the two adjoints can retain and reconstruct, respectively, varying amounts of information when moving from one theory to the other and back. This fact can be used to give a measure of the amount of information that a sentence can retain when translated between different logics.

6 Conclusions and Future Work

We have presented the foundations of work that aims to express and explore, in the unifying style of Hoare and He, the relationships between various flavours of logic, with an eye to understanding and automating the connection between various modern specification formalisms that employ these logics. This is not a new line of research, but it is the first attempt, as far as we have determined, that explores this problem in the UTP framework. In this installment we provide a classical model of three-valued predicates and explore the effect of the classical logical operators on this model, something that is rarely shown on the operators of new theories in the UTP literature. The model is used as the basis for UTP theories of three different three-valued logics, and a sampling of connections between them is shown. The interpretation of logical statements in these theories as specifications is explored, as well as one possible model theory. Future work includes exploration of alternative model theories using reactive designs and other process algebras, the meaning of connections in these contexts, treatment of types, direct application to Z, VDM and CML [29], and mechanization in Isabelle/HOL [30].

Acknowledgments. We are grateful to Simon Foster and to the anonymous reviewers for their helpful comments and recommendations. The results of this work have contributed to the semantics of CML, the modelling language developed in the EU FP7 project COMPASS (No. 287829).

References

1. Woodcock, J., Saaltink, M., Freitas, L.: Unifying theories of undefinedness. In: Summer School Marktoberdorf 2008: Engineering Methods and Tools for Software Safety and Security. NATO ASI Series F. IOS Press, Amsterdam (2009)
2. Bochvar, D.A., Bergmann, M.: On a three-valued logical calculus and its application to the analysis of the paradoxes of the classical extended functional calculus. History and Philosophy of Logic 2(1), 87–112 (1981)
3. McCarthy, J.: A basis for a mathematical theory of computation. In: Computer Programming and Formal Systems, pp. 33–70. North-Holland (1963)
4. Barringer, H., Cheng, J.H., Jones, C.B.: A logic covering undefinedness in program proofs. Acta Informatica 21 (1984)
5. Woodcock, J., Davies, J.: Using Z. Specification, Refinement, and Proof. Prentice-Hall (1996)
6. Farmer, W.M.: A partial functions version of Church's simple theory of types. Journal of Symbolic Logic, 1269–1291 (1990)
7. Woodcock, J., Bandur, V.: Unifying theories of undefinedness in UTP. In: Wolff, B., Gaudel, M.-C., Feliachi, A. (eds.) UTP 2012. LNCS, vol. 7681, pp. 1–22. Springer, Heidelberg (2013)
8. Hoare, C.A.R., He, J.: Unifying Theories of Programming. Prentice-Hall (1998)
9. Goguen, J.A., Burstall, R.M.: Institutions: Abstract model theory for specification and programming. Journal of the ACM 39(1), 95–146 (1992)

10. Goguen, J., Burstall, R.: A study in the foundations of programming methodology: Specifications, institutions, charters and parchments. In: Poigné, A., Pitt, D.H., Rydeheard, D.E., Abramsky, S. (eds.) Category Theory and Computer Programming. LNCS, vol. 240, pp. 313–333. Springer, Heidelberg (1986)

11. Meseguer, J.: General logics. In: Logic Colloquium 87, pp. 275–329. North Holland (1989)

12. Cerioli, M., Meseguer, J.: May I borrow your logic (transporting logical structures along maps). Theor. Comput. Sci. 173(2), 311–347 (1997)

13. Tarlecki, A.: Moving between logical systems. In: Haveraaen, M., Dahl, O.-J., Owe, O. (eds.) Abstract Data Types 1995 and COMPASS 1995. LNCS, vol. 1130, pp. 478–502. Springer, Heidelberg (1996)

14. Mayoh, B.: Galleries and institutions. Technical Report DAIMI PB-191, Aarhus University (1985)

15. Gavilanes-Franco, A., Lucio-Carrasco, F.: A First-Order Logic for Partial Functions. Theoretical Computer Science 74(1) (July 1990)

16. Hoogewijs, A.: Partial-predicate logic in computer science. Acta Informatica 24(4), 381–393 (1987)

17. Blikle, A.: Three-valued predicates for software specification and validation. In: Bloomfield, R.E., Jones, R.B., Marshall, L.S. (eds.) VDM 1988. LNCS, vol. 328, pp. 243–266. Springer, Heidelberg (1988)

18. Hoogewijs, A.: A partial-predicate calculus in a two-valued logic. Mathematical Logic Quarterly 29(4), 239–243 (1983)

19. Jones, M.: A typed logic of partial functions reconstructed classically. Acta Informatica 31 (1994)

20. Fitzgerald, J.S., Jones, C.B.: The connection between two ways of reasoning about partial functions. Information Processing Letters 107(3-4), 128–132 (2008)

21. Woodcock, J., Freitas, L.: Linking VDM and Z. In: ICECCS, pp. 143–152. IEEE Computer Society (2008)

22. Jones, C.B.: Systematic Software Development using VDM. Prentice Hall (1990)

23. Larsen, P.G., Battle, N., Ferreira, M., Fitzgerald, J., Lausdahl, K., Verhoef, M.: The Overture initiative – integrating tools for VDM. SIGSOFT Softw. Eng. Notes 35, 1–6 (2010)

24. Rose, A.: A lattice-theoretical characterisation of three-valued logic. Journal of the London Mathematical Society s1 - 25(4), 255–259 (1950)

25. Woodruff, P.W.: Logic and truth value gaps. In: Lambert, K. (ed.) Philosophical Problems in Logic: Some Recent Developments, pp. 121–142. D. Reidel Publishing Co., Dordrecht (1970)

26. Belnap, N.: A useful four-valued logic. In: Dunn, J.M., Epstein, G. (eds.) Modern Uses of Multiple-valued Logic, pp. 8–37. D. Reidel (1977)

27. Enderton, H.B.: A Mathematical Introduction to Logic. Academic Press, New York (1972)

28. Bandur, V.: Unifying Theories of Multi-Valued Logic and Specification. PhD thesis, The University of York (in preparation, 2013)

29. Woodcock, J., Cavalcanti, A., Fitzgerald, J., Larsen, P., Miyazawa, A., Perry, S.: Features of CML: A formal modelling language for systems of systems. In: 7th SoSE. IEEE Systems Journal, vol. 6. IEEE (July 2012)

30. Foster, S., Woodcock, J.: Unifying theories of programming in Isabelle. In: Liu, Z., Woodcock, J., Zhu, H. (eds.) Theories of Programming. LNCS, vol. 8050, pp. 109–155. Springer, Heidelberg (2013)

Institution-Based Semantics
for MOF and QVT-Relations

Daniel Calegari[1] and Nora Szasz[2]

[1] Facultad de Ingeniería, Universidad de la República, Uruguay
dcalegar@fing.edu.uy
[2] Facultad de Ingeniería, Universidad ORT, Uruguay
szasz@ort.edu.uy

Abstract. To cope with formal verification issues within the Model-Driven Engineering (MDE) paradigm, a separation of duties between software developers is usually proposed: MDE experts define models and transformations, while formal verification experts conduct the verification process. This is often aided by (semi)automatic translations form the MDE elements to their formal representation in the semantic domain used for verification. From a formal perspective, this requires semantic-preserving translations between the MDE elements and the semantic domain. The aim of this paper is to present formal semantics for the MOF and QVT-Relations languages which are standard languages for defining metamodels and model transformations, respectively. The semantics is based on the Theory of Institutions and reflect the conformance relation between models and metamodels, and the satisfaction of transformation rules between pairs of models. The theory assists in the definition of semantic-preserving translations between our institutions and other logics which will be used for verification.

Keywords: MOF, QVT-Relations, formal semantics, Theory of Institutions, verification.

1   Introduction

The Model-Driven Engineering paradigm (MDE, [1]) envisions a software development life-cycle driven by models representing different views of the system to be constructed. Its feasibility is based on the existence of a (semi)automatic construction process driven by model transformations, starting from abstract models of the system and transforming them until an executable model is generated. The Object Management Group (OMG) has conducted a standardization process of languages for MDE. They defined the MetaObject Facility (MOF, [2]) as the language for metamodeling as well as three transformation languages with different transformation approaches. The Query/View/Transformation Relations (QVT-Relations, [3]) is one of those languages and follows a relational approach which consists of defining transformation rules as mathematical relations between source and target elements. Since the quality of the whole development

J. Iyoda and L. de Moura (Eds.): SBMF 2013, LNCS 8195, pp. 34–50, 2013.

process strongly depends on the quality of the models and model transformations, verification is a must, and in some cases formal methods arise as a tool for strengthening verification results. To cope with this situation, a separation of duties between software developers is usually proposed. On the one side there are those experts in the MDE domain, and on the other, those in formal verification. This gives rise to different technological spaces [4], i.e. working contexts with a set of associated concepts, body of knowledge, tools, required skills, and possibilities. In general terms, MDE experts define models and transformations, while formal verification experts conduct the verification process, often aided by some (semi)automatic generation process which translates the MDE elements to their formal representation in the semantic domain used for verification purposes.

We are exploring a comprehensive formal environment enabling this scheme. This environment requires semantic-preserving translations between the MDE elements and the chosen semantic domain. Moreover, different logics (e.g. modal logic, predicate logic) can be used by verification experts. In this context, the biggest problem is perhaps the maintenance of multiple formal representations of the same MDE elements and the complexity of linking different semantic domains to perform a comprehensive verification using multiple semantic domains.

The aim of this paper is to present formal semantics for the MOF and the QVT-Relations languages in a flexible way to solve the problems described before. We base our proposal on the heterogeneous specification approach [5,6], which consists in having different mathematical formalism for expressing different parts of the overall problem and defining semantic-preserving mappings in order to allow "communication" between the formalisms. This approach uses as a basis the Theory of Institutions [7]. Using this theory we define institutions to represent the conformance relation between MOF models and metamodels and the satisfaction of QVT-Relations transformation rules between pairs of models. The theory also assists in the definition of semantic-preserving translations between our institutions and other logics which will be used for verification.

The remainder of the paper is structured as follows. In Section 2 we introduce the elements involved in the MDE technical space which will be part of this work and we introduce a running example. Then, in Section 3 we summarize the general schema we follow for defining formal semantics based on the Theory of Institutions. In Section 4 we formally define an institution for MOF, and in Section 5 we define the institution for QVT-Relations. Finally, in Section 6 we present some conclusions and guidelines for future work.

2 An Introduction to the MDE Technical Space

In MDE everything is a model, i.e. an abstraction of the system or its environment. Every model *conforms* to a metamodel, i.e. a model which introduces the syntax and semantics of certain kind of models. MOF is a standard language for metamodeling. A metamodel defines classes which can belong to a hierarchical structure and some of them must be defined as abstract (there are no instances of them). Any class has properties which can be attributes (named elements with an associated type which can be a primitive type or another class) and associations (relations between classes in which each class plays a role within the relation). Every property has a multiplicity which constraints the number of elements that can be related through the property. There are conditions (called invariants) that cannot be captured by the structural rules of these languages, in which case modeling languages are supplemented with another logical language, e.g. the Object Constraint Language (OCL, [8]).

Let us consider a simplified version of the well-known Class to Relational model transformation [3]. The metamodel on the left-hand side of Figure 1 defines UML class diagrams, where classifiers (classes and primitive types as string, boolean, integer, etc.) are contained in packages. Classes can contain one or more attributes and may be declared as persistent, whilst attributes have a type that is a primitive type. On the right-hand side of Figure 1 there is an example of a model composed by a persistent class of name ID within a package of name Package. The class has an attribute of name value and type String.

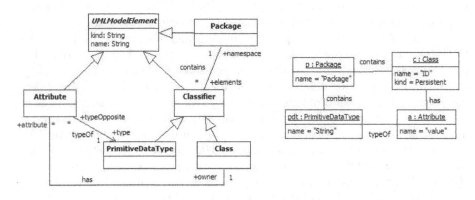

Fig. 1. Class metamodel and model of the example

A model transformation (or just transformation from now on) basically takes as input a model conforming to certain metamodel and produces as output another model conforming to another metamodel (possibly the same). QVT-Relations follows a relational approach which consists on defining transformation rules as mathematical relations between source and target elements. Although transformations can be defined between multiple metamodels at the same time, we will only consider a source and a target metamodel.

A transformation can be viewed as a set of interconnected relations which are of two kinds: top-level relations which must hold in any transformation execution, and non-top-level relations which are required to hold only when they are referred from another relation. We can view a relation as having the following abstract structure [3]:

```
[top] relation R {
    <R_var_set> <R_par_set>
    Domain {
        <domain_k_var_set> <domain_k_pat>
    } //k = 1,2
    [when <when_var_set> <when_cond>]
    [where <where_cond>]
}
```

Every relation has a set `<R_var_set>` of variables occurring in the relation, which are particularly used within the domains (`<domain_k_var_set>`) and in the when clause (`<when_var_set>`). Each relation defines a source and a target pattern `<domain_k_pat>` which is used to find matching sub-graphs in a model and can be viewed as a graph of typed pattern elements and pattern links, together with a predicate which must hold. Relations can also contain when (`<when_cond>`) and where (`<where_cond>`) clauses. A when clause specifies the conditions under which the relationship needs to hold, whilst the where clause specifies the condition that must be satisfied by all model elements participating in the relation. The when and where clauses, as well as the predicate of a pattern, may contain arbitrary boolean OCL expressions in addition to the relation invocation expressions. Finally, any relation can define a set of primitive domains which are data types used to parameterize the relation (`<R_par_set>`).

The standard checking semantics states that a rule holds if for each valid binding of variables of the when clause and variables of domains other than the target domain, that satisfy the when condition and source domain patterns and conditions, there must exist a valid binding of the remaining unbound variables of the target domain that satisfies the target domain pattern and where condition.

The Class to Relational transformation basically describes how persistent classes within a package are transformed into tables within a schema. Attributes of a class are transformed into columns of the corresponding table, and the primary key is defined by default. Below we show an excerpt of this transformation.

```
transformation umlToRdbms(uml:SimpleUML, rdbms:SimpleRDBMS) {
    top relation PackageToSchema {
        pn: String;
        domain uml p:Package {name=pn};
        domain rdbms s:Schema {name=pn};
    }
    top relation ClassToTable {
        cn, prefix: String;
        domain uml c:Class {namespace=p:Package {},kind='Persistent',name=cn};
        domain rdbms t:Table {schema=s:Schema {}, name=cn,
            column=cl:Column {name=cn+'_tid', type='NUMBER'},
            key=k:Key {name=cn+'_pk', column=cl}};
        when  { PackageToSchema(p,s); }
        where { prefix = ''; AttributeToColumn(c, t, prefix); }
    }
    relation AttributeToColumn { ... }
}
```

3   An Environment for Verification

We are exploring a comprehensive environment for the formal verification of different aspects of a model transformation using heterogeneous verification approaches [9]. The environment is based on representing models (from now on SW-models), metamodels, the conformance relation, transformations and verification properties in some consistent and interdependent way following the heterogeneous specification approach [5,6]. This approach is based on providing *Institutions* for the languages which are part of the environment. The concept of Institution [7] was originally introduced to formalize the notion of logical system, and many different logics as first-order, modal, rewriting, among others have been shown to be institutions. Informally, an institution consists of a collection of signatures (vocabularies for constructing sentences in a logical system), signature morphisms (allowing many different vocabularies at once), a collection of sentences and models (providing semantics) for a given signature, and a satisfaction relation of sentences by models, such that when signatures are changed (by a signature morphism), satisfaction of sentences by models changes consistently. The notion of an institution can be used to represent any specification language since it provides ways of representing the syntax and semantics of the language, as well as the relation between them by means of a satisfaction relation between them, as in [5]. In this work we provide an institution for QVT-Relations check-only unidirectional transformations. This kind of transformations only checks if a target model is the result of transforming the source SW-model according to the transformation rules. This institution needs a representation of SW-models and metamodels, therefore we first define an institution for MOF for expressing the conformance relation between them.

In order to use our institutions for verification purposes, there are two alternatives. The first one is to extend the institutions from a proof-theoretic point of view by defining a *logic*, i.e. equipping the institutions with an entailment system on sentences for conducting formal proofs. The second alternative is to formally translate our institutions into another logic. This can be done through *institution comorphisms* [10], which capture how a *weaker* institution can be represented in a *stronger* and *richer* one. The importance of comorphisms is such that it is possible (in some cases) to re-use (*borrow*) the entailment systems of an institution in order to prove properties.

We take the second alternative and define comorphisms from our institutions to a host logic and supplement this information with properties specified in the host logic. In particular, we are in the process of defining a comorphism to the Common Algebraic Specification Language (CASL, [11]), a general-purpose specification language. The institution underlying CASL is the sub-sorted partial first-order logic with equality and constraints on sets $SubPCFOL^{=}$, a combination of first-order logic and induction with subsorts and partial functions. The importance of CASL is that it is the main language within the Heterogeneous Tool Set (Hets, [6]), which is a tool meant to support heterogeneous multi-logic specifications. Hets allows defining institutions and comorphisms, and also provides proof management capabilities for monitoring the overall correctness of a heterogeneous specification whereas different parts of it are verified using (possibly different) proof systems. Hets already supports several interconnected logics (e.g. first-order and modal logics, among others). To the best of our knowledge, Hets does not support the MDE paradigm, i.e. it does not have specific languages for the specification of MDE elements. We plan to include our institutions as logics in Hets, in such a way that a developer can import a transformation (which is automatically translated into CASL through the comorphism), use the logics within Hets to specify additional verification properties which must be addressed, and perform the verification assisted by the tool.

3.1   Defining the Institutions

In Section 4 we define the institution for the MOF-based conformance relation, basing our proposal on the institution defined for UML class diagrams in [12,13]. Unlike [12], in our definition there are no derived relations (not used in transformations), the signature has an explicit representation of abstract classes and datatypes, and there are only 2-ary properties (associations and attributes). We also use an explicit syntactic representation of SW-models within the signature. In [13], instances (class objects and type values) are represented within the signature. However, there is no representation of links between these elements since they are used for other purposes. Moreover, unlike MOF, we do not consider aggregation, uniqueness and ordering properties within a property end, operations on classes, or packages. Properties and operations are not commonly used within transformations, whereas packages are just used for organizing metamodel elements. We follow the schema in Figure 2. From any metamodel we can derive a signature with a representation of types, properties, and SW-models, and a set of formulas stating invariants which must hold on every conforming SW-model. Up to now we have considered multiplicity constraints. However, it will be possible to add other kind of constraints through comorphisms as explained before. Any institution model (from now on just model) is a semantic representation of a potentially conforming SW-model. The model is composed by objects and relations between them, which must satisfy the multiplicity constraints. This allows us to define the satisfaction relation answering the question: does the SW-model conform to the metamodel?

In Section 5 we also define an institution for QVT-Relations check-only unidirectional transformations. For the definition of this institution we follow the schema shown in Figure 3. For the definition we do not consider black-box operations or rule and transformation overriding since they are advanced features not commonly used in practice. We neither consider keys definition since they are not used within the checking semantics. The institution takes the institutional representation of the source and target elements and supplements the formulas with a representation of the transformation rules. In this case, the satisfaction relation also answers the question: is the target SW-model the result of transforming the source SW-model according to the transformation rules?

As we mentioned before, the when and where clauses, as well as the predicate of a pattern, may contain arbitrary boolean OCL expressions. From a formal

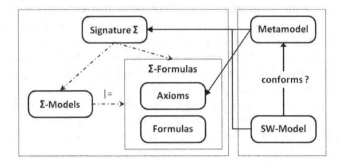

Fig. 2. The conformance relation as an institution

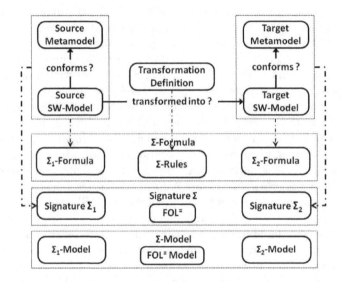

Fig. 3. A model transformation as an institution

perspective we would rather have an institution for OCL which would allow us to use the language not only for constraining the transformation rules, but also for expressing general constraints on metamodels. Unfortunately there is no institution for OCL, which is left for future work. However, in our work we consider an institution for first-order logic with equality ($FOL^=$) as defined in [14]. With this decision we are not losing expressive power (there are works [15] with the aim of expressing OCL into first-order logic).

3.2   Related Work

There are many works defining the semantics of MOF and the conformance relation in terms of a shallow embedding of the language by providing a syntactic translation into another one, e.g. into first-order logic [16] and rewriting logic [17]. We, on the contrary, do not want to depend on a general logic but to define a generic and minimal infrastructure allowing translations to other logics as needed. There are also some works with an algebraic/institutional approach, e.g. [18,19]. In these works the authors propose two alternatives: a generic algebraic representation of metamodels without an explicit representation of models, and concrete institutions for each metamodel. Unlike these works, we avoid the burden of defining a new institution for each metamodel, explicitly representing models to be used within proofs. In [12,13] the authors define institutions for simple and stereotyped UML Class Diagrams. As we said, we adapt those works for the purpose of defining the institution for the conformance relation. Finally, in [20] the authors define the semantics of class diagrams with OCL constraints by defining a translation into CASL. Although this is also a shallow embedding, as explained before, the translation (and the one proposed in [13]) could be useful for defining the comorphism from our institution to CASL.

With respect to QVT-Relations, there are also works defining the semantics of QVT-Relations in terms of a shallow embedding of the language, e.g. into rewriting logic [21] and coloured petri nets [22]. There are also embeddings into specific tools, as in the case of Alloy [23] and KIV [24], which provide model checking capabilities. As said before, we do not follow this approach. Moreover, in [18] transformations are represented as institution comorphisms, which is somehow restrictive since it assumes a semantic relation between metamodels. Finally, in [25] the authors present a formal semantics for the QVT-Relations check-only scenario based on algebraic specification and category theory. The definition of the institution is much more complex than ours and the work does not envision a scenario in which the elements of the transformation are translated to other logics for verification.

4   An Institution for MOF

In this section we present the formal definition of an institution $\mathcal{I}^C$ for the MOF-based conformance relation. As said before, this definition is based on the institutions for UML class diagrams defined in [12,13], but adapted for representing the conformance relation. Along the definition we will illustrate the concepts introduced with the example presented in Section 2.

A class hierarchy is a partial order $\boldsymbol{C} = (C, \leq_C)$ where C is a set of class names, and $\leq_C \subseteq C \times C$ is the subclass (inheritance) relation. By $\boldsymbol{T(C)}$ we denote the *type extension* of $\boldsymbol{C}$ by primitive types and type constructors. $\boldsymbol{T(C)}$ is likewise a class hierarchy $(T(C), \leq_{T(C)})$ with $C \subseteq T(C)$ and $\leq_C \subseteq \leq_{T(C)}$. As in [13], in order to provide generic access to primitive types, like Boolean, and String, we treat these as built-ins with a standard meaning (they must be defined within $T(C)$). All other classes are assumed to be inhabited, i.e., to contain at least one object. However, unlike [13] in which it is assumed the existence of an object *null*, we impose that if $c \in C|_{abstract}$ then there exists another $c' \in T(C)$ downwards in the hierarchy having at least one object.

As we mentioned before, from a metamodel we can derive a signature $\Sigma = (\boldsymbol{T}, \boldsymbol{P}, \boldsymbol{M})$ declaring:

- A type extension of a finite class hierarchy $\boldsymbol{T} = (T(C), \leq_{T(C)}, C|_{abstract})$ extended with a subset $C|_{abstract} \subseteq C$ denoting abstract classes.
- A properties declaration (attributes and associations) $\boldsymbol{P} = (R, P)$ where R is a finite set of role names and P is a finite set $(p_w)_{w \in (R \times T(C)) \times (R \times T(C))}$ of property names indexed over pairs of a role name and a class (or type) name, such that for any class or type name $c \in C$, the role names of the properties in which any $c' \leq_{T(C)} c$ is involved are all different. If $p_w \in P$ with $w = ((r_1, c_1)(r_2, c_2))$, we write $p(r_1 : c_1, r_2 : c_2) \in P$.
- A SW-model declaration (instances and links) $\boldsymbol{M} = (I, L)$ where I is a finite set of instances of the form $o : c$ with $c \in T(C)$; and L is a finite set of links between instances of the form $p_w(x, y)$ with $p_w \in P$, $w = ((r_1, c)(r_2, d))$, $x : c$, $y : d \in I$.

From a metamodel it is also possible to derive a set of formulas (multiplicity constraints) constraining the set of SW-models conforming to it. Given a signature as defined before, any Σ-formula is defined by:

$$\Phi ::= \#\Pi = n \mid n \leq \#\Pi \mid \#\Pi \leq n$$
$$\Pi ::= R \bullet P$$

where $n \in \mathbb{N}$. The #-expressions return the number of links in a property when some roles are fixed. We use $\bullet$ as the select/partition operator in Π representing the selection of the elements in the opposite side of role R in property P.

Let $\Sigma_i = (\boldsymbol{T}_i, \boldsymbol{P}_i, \boldsymbol{M}_i)$ $(i = 1, 2)$ with $\boldsymbol{T}_i = (T(C_i), \leq_{T(C_i)}, C_i|_{abstract})$, $\boldsymbol{P}_i = (R_i, P_i)$, and $\boldsymbol{M}_i = (I_i, L_i)$. A signature morphism $\sigma : \Sigma_1 \to \Sigma_2$ is a tuple of maps $\langle \sigma_T, \sigma_R, \sigma_P, \sigma_I \rangle$ between class names, role names, property names, and instances. Signature morphisms extend to formulas over Σ_1 as follows. Given a Σ_1-formula φ, $\sigma(\varphi)$ is the canonical application of the signature morphism to every role and property in the formula such that $\sigma(r \bullet p) = \sigma_R(r) \bullet \sigma_P(p)$.

Given a class hierarchy $\boldsymbol{C} = (C, \leq_C)$, a $\boldsymbol{C}$-object domain $\boldsymbol{O}$ is a family $(O_c)_{c \in C}$ of sets of object identifiers verifying $O_{c_1} \subseteq O_{c_2}$ if $c_1 \leq_C c_2$. Given moreover a type extension $\boldsymbol{T}$, the *value extension* of a $\boldsymbol{C}$-object domain $\boldsymbol{O} = (O_c)_{c \in C}$ by primitive values and value constructions, which is denoted by $V_{\boldsymbol{C}}^{\boldsymbol{T}}(\boldsymbol{O})$, is a $\boldsymbol{T}(C)$-object domain $(V_c)_{c \in T(C)}$ such that $V_c = O_c$ for all $c \in C$. We consider disjoint sets of objects within the same hierarchical level.

We adapt the definition of a Σ-interpretation in order to 'reduce' the interpretation to those elements and relations in $\boldsymbol{M}$, i.e. there is an isomorphism between these elements and those in the interpretation. A Σ-interpretation $\mathcal{I}$ consists of a tuple $(V_{\boldsymbol{C}}^{\boldsymbol{T}}(\boldsymbol{O}), \boldsymbol{A}, K^{\mathcal{I}})$ where

- $V_{\boldsymbol{C}}^{\boldsymbol{T}}(\boldsymbol{O}) = (V_c)_{c \in T(C)}$ is a $\boldsymbol{T}(C)$-object domain
- $\boldsymbol{A}$ contains a relation $p^{\mathcal{I}} \subseteq V_{c_1} \times V_{c_2}$ for each relation name $p(r_1 : c_1, r_2 : c_2) \in P$ with $c_1, c_2 \in T(C)$
- $K^{\mathcal{I}}$ maps each $o : c \in I$ to an element of V_c
- $c_2 \in C|_{abstract}$ implies $O_{c_2} = \bigcup_{c_1 \leq_C c_2} O_{c_1}$

- $K^{\mathcal{I}}(o_1 : c) \neq K^{\mathcal{I}}(o_2 : d)$ iff $o_1 : c \neq o_2 : d$
- $V_c = \bigcup_c K^{\mathcal{I}}(o : c)$ with $o : c \in I$, for all $c \in T(C)$
- $p^{\mathcal{I}} = \{(K^{\mathcal{I}}(x : c), K^{\mathcal{I}}(y : d)) \mid p_w(x, y) \in L, x : c, \ y : d \ \in I\}$

Given a Σ-interpretation $\mathcal{I} = (\boldsymbol{V_C^T(O)}, \boldsymbol{A}, K^{\mathcal{I}})$, the interpretation evaluates relations as follows: if $p(r_1 : c_1, r_2 : c_2)$ then $(r_i \bullet p)^{\mathcal{I}} = \{\{t \in p^{\mathcal{I}} \mid \pi_i(t) = o\} \mid o \in V_{c_i}\}$ ($i = 1, 2$). The evaluation $(r_i \bullet p)^{\mathcal{I}}$ gives a set of sets of pairs of semantic elements connected through property p, grouped by the semantic elements having role r_i. Note that this set can be empty if the element with role r_i is not connected with any one.

Given a signature Σ, a formula φ, and a Σ-interpretation $\mathcal{I}$, the interpretation satisfies φ, written $\mathcal{I} \models_{\Sigma} \varphi$, if one of the following conditions holds:

- φ is $\#(r \bullet p) = n$ and $|S| = n$ for all $S \in (r \bullet p)^{\mathcal{I}}$
- φ is $n \leq \#(r \bullet p)$ and $n \leq |S|$ for all $S \in (r \bullet p)^{\mathcal{I}}$
- φ is $\#(r \bullet p) \leq n$ and $|S| \leq n$ for all $S \in (r \bullet p)^{\mathcal{I}}$

This means that the number of elements related through a property p with any element with role r in such property, satisfies the multiplicity constraints. This definition can be trivially defined for a set of formulas Φ.

Finally, the satisfaction condition holds for given signatures Σ_i ($i = 1, 2$), a signature morphism $\sigma : \Sigma_1 \to \Sigma_2$, a Σ_2-interpretation $\mathcal{I}$, and a Σ_1-formula ψ: $\mathcal{I}|_\sigma, \models_{\Sigma_1} \psi$ iff $\mathcal{I} \models_{\Sigma_2} \sigma(\psi)$. This can be trivially extended to a set of formulas.

Given that the satisfaction condition holds we can state that $\mathcal{I}^C$ consisting of signatures, morphisms, formulas, interpretations, reducts, and the satisfaction relation, defines an institution. For space reasons we omit here several definition (e.g. signature morphisms, reducts) and proofs, which can be completely found in [26].

4.1   Running Example

From the class metamodel and the SW-model in Figure 1 we derive the signature $(\boldsymbol{T}, \boldsymbol{P}, \boldsymbol{M})$ with $\boldsymbol{T} = (T(C), \leq_{T(C)}, C|_{abstract})$, $\boldsymbol{P} = (R, P)$, and $\boldsymbol{M} = (I, L)$ such that:

$$
\begin{aligned}
T(C) \quad &= \{\text{UMLModelElement}, \text{Package}, ..., \text{String}\} \\
\leq_{T(C)} \quad &= \{\text{Package} \leq_{T(C)} \text{UMLModelElement}, ...\} \\
C|_{abstract} &= \{\text{UMLModelElement}\} \\
R \quad &= \{\text{namespace}, \text{elements}, \text{type}, \text{typeOpposite}, ...\} \\
P \quad &= \{\text{contains}(\text{namespace} : \text{Package}, \text{elements} : \text{Classifier}), \\
&\quad\ \ \text{name}(\text{UMLModelElement} : \text{UMLModelElement}, \text{name} : \text{String}), \\
&\quad\ \ \text{typeOf}(\text{typeOpposite} : \text{Attribute}, \text{type} : \text{PrimitiveDataType}), ...\} \\
I \quad &= \{\text{p} : \text{Package}, \text{c} : \text{Class}, \text{a} : \text{Attribute}, ..., \text{String} : \text{String}\} \\
L \quad &= \{\text{contains}(\text{p}, \text{c}), \text{contains}(\text{p}, \text{pdt}), \text{has}(\text{c}, \text{a}), \text{type}(\text{a}, \text{pdt}), \\
&\quad\ \ \text{name}(\text{p}, \text{Package}), \text{kind}(\text{c}, \text{Persistent}), \text{name}(\text{pdt}, \text{String}), ...\}
\end{aligned}
$$

The set of formulas φ is defined by:

$$\varphi = \{\#(\text{UMLModelElement} \bullet \text{name}) = 1, \#(\text{UMLModelElement} \bullet \text{kind}) = 1,$$
$$\#(\text{elements} \bullet \text{contains}) = 1, \#(\text{attribute} \bullet \text{has}) = 1, ...\}$$

An interpretation $\mathcal{I}$ can be defined as follows, in which each element has a correspondence with one in the signature:

– A $\boldsymbol{T(C)}$-object domain consisting of
$$
\begin{aligned}
V_{\text{Class}} &= \{c1\} \\
V_{\text{PrimitiveDataType}} &= \{pdt1\} \\
V_{\text{Package}} &= \{p1\} \\
V_{\text{Attribute}} &= \{a1\} \\
V_{\text{String}} &= \{Pac, Str, Per, nul, ID, val\}
\end{aligned}
$$

– A set $\boldsymbol{A}$ consisting of relations
$$
\begin{aligned}
\text{contains}^{\mathcal{I}} &= \{(p1,c1),(p1,pdt1)\} \\
\text{name}^{\mathcal{I}} &= \{(p1,Pac),(c1,ID),(c2,nul),(a1,val)\} \\
\text{kind}^{\mathcal{I}} &= \{(p1,nul),(c1,Per),(a1,nul),(pdt1,nul)\} \\
\text{type}^{\mathcal{I}} &= \{(a1,pdt1)\}
\end{aligned}
$$
...

The property contains(namespace : Package, elements : Classifier) represents that a package contains classifiers. The interpretation $\mathcal{I}$ has the following interpretation of this property: $\text{contains}^{\mathcal{I}} = \{(p1,c1),(p1,c2)(p1,pdt1),(p1,pdt2)\}$, such that there is only one package object $p1$, and it contains two classes ($c1$ and $c2$) and two primitive datatype objects ($pdt1$ and $pdt2$). This interpretation evaluates $(\text{namespace} \bullet \text{contains})^{\mathcal{I}}$ as the set $\{(p1,c1),(p1,c2),(p1,pdt1),(p1,pdt2)\}$ since there is only one object with role namespace which is the package object $p1$, and those elements in the opposite side of the property are those in $\text{contains}^{\mathcal{I}}$.

Now, we check that $\mathcal{I}, \beta \models_{\Sigma} \varphi$ for every formula φ defined before. For example it holds in the following cases.

– $\#(\text{UMLModelElement} \bullet \text{name}) = 1$ and $|S| = 1$
 for all $S \in (\text{UMLModelElement} \bullet \text{name})^{\mathcal{I}} =$
 $\{\{(p1,Pac)\}, \{(c1,ID)\}, \{(a1,val)\}, \{(pdt1,Str)\}\}$

– $\#(\text{elements} \bullet \text{contains}) = 1$ and $|S| = 1$
 for all $S \in (\text{elements} \bullet \text{contains})^{\mathcal{I}} = \{\{(p1,c1)\}, \{(p1,pdt1)\}\}$

5   An Institution for QVT-Relations

We finally introduce an institution $\mathcal{I}^{\text{QVT}}$ for QVT-Relations check-only unidirectional transformations, and then we continue illustrating the concepts introduced with the example presented in Section 2.

A signature in $\mathcal{I}^{\text{QVT}}$ is a triple $\langle \Sigma_1^C, \Sigma_2^C, \Sigma^{\text{FOL}} \rangle$ with $\mathcal{I}^C$-signatures Σ_i^C ($i = 1, 2$) representing the source and target metamodels and models of the transformation, and a $FOL^=$ signature Σ^{FOL} such that there are sorts for every type ($\bigcup_i T(C_i) \subseteq S$) and there is a predicate for each property declaration ($\bigcup_i P_i \subseteq \Pi$). We assume that there are no name clashes (types, roles and properties) between source and target metamodels. In fact, if a transformation has the same source and target metamodels, we can use a prefix to identify elements on each side. A signature morphism is defined as a triple of morphisms of the corresponding institutions.

A Σ-formula is of the form $\langle \varphi_1^C, \varphi_2^C, \varphi^{\text{rules}} \rangle$ such that φ_i^C is a Σ_i^C-formula and φ^{rules} is a formula representing the transformation specification. i.e. a tuple $\langle \text{Rules}, \text{top} \rangle$ such that Rules is the set of transformation rules, and top $\subseteq$ Rules the set of top rules of the transformation.

A rule Rule $\in$ Rules is a tuple $\langle \text{VarSet}, \text{Pattern}_i \ (i = 1, 2), \text{when}, \text{where} \rangle$ such that VarSet $\subseteq X^s$ with $s \in S$ is the set of variables of the rule, $\text{Pattern}_i \ (i = 1, 2)$ are the source and target patterns, and when/where are the **when**/**where** clauses of the rule, respectively. We will denote by k_VarSet (k $= 1, 2$) the variables used in pattern k that do neither occur in the other domain nor in the **when** clause.

A pattern $\text{Pattern}_i \ (i = 1, 2)$ is a tuple $\langle E_i, A_i, Pr_i \rangle$ such that $E_i \subseteq (X^c)_{c \in C_i}$ is a set of class-indexed variables, A_i is a set of elements representing associations of the form $rel(p, x, y)$ with $p \in P_i$ and $x, y \in E_i$, and Pr_i is a $FOL^=$-formula.

A **when** clause is a pair $\langle \text{when}_c, \text{when}_r \rangle$ such that when_c is a $FOL^=$-formula with variables in VarSet, and when_r is a set of pairs of transformation rules and set of variables which are the parameters used for the invocation of each rule. We will denote by WhenVarSet the set of variables ocurring in the **when** clause. Finally, a **where** clause is a pair $\langle \text{where}_c, \text{where}_r \rangle$ such that where_c is a $FOL^=$-formula with variables in VarSet, and where_r is a set of pairs of transformation rules and set of variables (parameters). Only variables used in a **where** clause (as **prefix** in the example) are contained in 2_VarSet.

A Σ-model is a triple $\langle \mathcal{M}_1^C, \mathcal{M}_2^C, \mathcal{M}^{\text{FOL}} \rangle$ of $\text{Sign}_i^C \ (i = 1, 2)$ models, and a Sign^{FOL} first-order structure, such that the interpretation of elements in Sign_i^C must be the same in $\mathcal{M}_i^C$ and $\mathcal{M}^{\text{FOL}}$. This means that $|D|_t = V_t. \forall t \in \bigcup_i T(C_i)$, and $p_D = p^{\mathcal{I}}. \forall p \in \bigcup_i P_i$. In the case of $t \in T(C) \backslash C$ (primitive types) we have that $V_t \subseteq |D|_t$ since $\mathcal{M}^{\text{FOL}}$ can have more elements than those in the source and target institutions: type constants (e.g. the empty string) and elements created using type constructors (e.g. new strings using type constructor $++$).

Given variables $X^s = (X^s)_{s \in S}$, the binding of a variable $x^c \in X^c$, denoted by $|x^c|$, is the set of possible interpretations of such a variable which corresponds to the carrier set of the corresponding sort, i.e. $|x^c| = |D|_c$. Moreover, the binding of a set of variables $(x_1, ..., x_n)$, denoted by $|(x_1, ..., x_n)|$, is defined as $\{(y_1, ..., y_n) \mid y_i \in |x_i| \ (i = 1..n)\}$. We can also view $|(x_1, ..., x_n)|$ as a set of variable assignments. We denote by $\mu[x_1, ..., x_n]$ the function with an assignment for variables $x_1, ..., x_n$. We also denote by $\mu_1 \cup \mu_2$ an assignment unifying the former ones, assuming that if there is variable clash, the assignment takes for those variables the values in μ_2.

A **when** clause $\langle \text{when}_c, \text{when}_r \rangle$ is satisfied with respect to a first-order structure $\mathcal{M}^{\text{FOL}}$ and a variable assignment μ, denoted by $\mathcal{M}^{\text{FOL}}, \mu \models \langle \text{when}_c, \text{when}_r \rangle$ if

$\mathcal{M}^{\mathrm{FOL}}, \mu \models_{\mathrm{FOL}}$ when$_c$ $\wedge$ $(\forall(r, v) \in$ when$_r$. $\mathcal{M}^{\mathrm{FOL}}, \mu[v] \models r)$ Here, $\models_{\mathrm{FOL}}$ is the satisfaction relation in $FOL^=$, and $\models$ is the satisfaction of the parametric transformation rule r using the variable assignment $\mu[v]$ as a parameter. The satisfaction of a `where` clause is defined in the same way.

A pattern Pattern $= \langle E, A, Pr \rangle$ is satisfied with respect to a first-order structure $\mathcal{M}^{\mathrm{FOL}}$ and a variable assignment μ (which must include a valuation for the elements in E), denoted by $\mathcal{M}^{\mathrm{FOL}}, \mu \models$ Pattern if there is a matching subgraph $\forall \, rel(p, x, y) \in A. \, (p_D(\mu(x), \mu(y)) \in \mathcal{M}^{\mathrm{FOL}})$, and the predicate holds in $FOL^=$ ($\mathcal{M}^{\mathrm{FOL}}, \mu \models_{\mathrm{FOL}} Pr$).

A rule Rule $= \langle \mathrm{VarSet}, \mathrm{Pattern}_i \ (i = 1, 2), \mathrm{when}, \mathrm{where} \rangle$ is satisfied with respect to a first-order structure $\mathcal{M}^{\mathrm{FOL}}$ and a variable assignment μ, denoted by $\mathcal{M}^{\mathrm{FOL}}, \mu \models$ Rule if one of the following properties hold.

1. If WhenVarSet $= \emptyset$

$$\forall \, \mu^1[x_1, ..., x_n] \in |\mathrm{VarSet} \backslash 2\_\mathrm{VarSet}|,$$
$$(\, \mathcal{M}^{\mathrm{FOL}}, (\mu^1[x_1, ..., x_n] \cup \mu) \models \mathrm{Pattern}_1 \rightarrow$$
$$\exists \, \mu^2[y_1, ..., y_m] \in |2\_\mathrm{VarSet}|,$$
$$(\, \mathcal{M}^{\mathrm{FOL}}, (\mu^1 \cup \mu^2 \cup \mu) \models \mathrm{Pattern}_2 \wedge$$
$$\mathcal{M}^{\mathrm{FOL}}, (\mu^1 \cup \mu^2 \cup \mu) \models \mathrm{where}))$$

2. If WhenVarSet $\neq \emptyset$

$$\forall \, \mu^w[z_1, ..., z_o] \in |\mathrm{WhenVarSet}|,$$
$$(\, \mathcal{M}^{\mathrm{FOL}}, (\mu^w[z_1, ..., z_o] \cup \mu) \models \mathrm{when} \rightarrow$$
$$\forall \, \mu^1[x_1, ..., x_n] \in |\mathrm{VarSet} \backslash (\mathrm{WhenVarSet} \cup 2\_\mathrm{VarSet})|,$$
$$(\, \mathcal{M}^{\mathrm{FOL}}, (\mu^1 \cup \mu^w \cup \mu) \models \mathrm{Pattern}_1 \rightarrow$$
$$\exists \, \mu^2[y_1, ..., y_m] \in |2\_\mathrm{VarSet}|,$$
$$(\, \mathcal{M}^{\mathrm{FOL}}, (\mu^1 \cup \mu^2 \cup \mu^w \cup \mu) \models \mathrm{Pattern}_2 \wedge$$
$$\mathcal{M}^{\mathrm{FOL}}, (\mu^1 \cup \mu^2 \cup \mu^w \cup \mu) \models \mathrm{where})))$$

The satisfaction relation is defined in such a way that a model $\mathcal{M}$ satisfies φ, written $\mathcal{M} \models_{\Sigma} \varphi$, if $\mathcal{M}_i^C \models_{\Sigma_i^C}^C \varphi_i^C$ ($i = 1, 2$) and $\mathcal{M} \models_{\Sigma} \varphi^{\mathrm{rules}}$. In other words, a model satisfies a formula if the SW-models conform to the corresponding metamodels, and they fulfill the top transformation rules. The satisfaction relation $\mathcal{M} \models_{\Sigma} \varphi^{\mathrm{rules}}$ is defined to hold if for all Rule$_i \in$ top. $\mathcal{M}^{\mathrm{FOL}}, \emptyset \models$ Rule$_i$. We take $\emptyset$ as the empty variable assignment, since for rules it will be used only in the case of non top and explicit called rules.

Finally, given signatures Σ_i, a signature morphism $\sigma : \Sigma_1 \rightarrow \Sigma_2$, a Σ_2-model $\mathcal{M}$, a set of variables X_2, and a Σ_1-formula ψ with variables in $X_2|_\sigma$, the following satisfaction condition holds (see [26]): $\mathcal{M}|_\sigma \models_{\Sigma_1} \psi$ iff $\mathcal{M} \models_{\Sigma_2} \sigma(\psi)$. Thus, we can state that $\mathcal{I}^{\mathrm{QVT}}$ consisting of the definitions given before, defines an institution. Complete definitions and proofs can be found in [26].

5.1   Running Example

The signature $\Sigma = \langle \Sigma_1^C, \Sigma_2^C, \Sigma^{FOL} \rangle$ contains the signature Σ_1^C of the source metamodel, which is the one presented in Section 4.1, the signature Σ_2^C of the target metamodel, which is not shown here but can be derived in the same way, and a $FOL^=$ signature Σ^{FOL} with at least one sort for each type name in $\bigcup_i T(C_i)$ and a predicate for each property in $\bigcup_i P_i$.

A transformation between two SW-models is represented as a formula φ of the form $\langle \varphi_1^C, \varphi_2^C, \varphi^{rules} \rangle$ such that, for example, φ_1^C is the formula introduced in Section 4.1, which represents the multiplicity constraints of the metamodel in Figure 1, φ_2^C is another formula representing the target SW-model (not shown here), and $\varphi^{rules} = \langle \text{Rules}, \text{top} \rangle$ is the formula representing the transformation specification which has three relations named $\texttt{PackageToSchema} \in \text{top}$, $\texttt{ClassToTable} \in \text{top}$ and $\texttt{AttributeToColumn}$.

As an example, the relation $\texttt{PackageToSchema}$ is defined as follows:
$\texttt{PackageToSchema} = \langle \text{VarSet}, \text{Pattern}_i \; (i = 1, 2), \text{when}, \text{where} \rangle$ such that

- VarSet $= \{\text{pn}, \text{p}, \text{s}\}$ with $\text{pn} \in X^{String}$, $\text{p} \in X^{Package}$, and $\text{s} \in X^{Schema}$.
- Pattern$_1 = \langle E_1, A_1, Pr_1 \rangle$ with $E_1 = \{\text{p}\}$, $A_1 = \emptyset$, and $Pr_1 = \texttt{name(p,pn)}$ (name is also a property in the source metamodel)
- Pattern$_2 = \langle E_2, A_2, Pr_2 \rangle$ with $E_2 = \{\text{s}\}$, $A_2 = \emptyset$, and $Pr_2 = \texttt{name(s,pn)}$.
- when $= \langle \emptyset, \emptyset \rangle$ and where $= \langle \emptyset, \emptyset \rangle$.

A model $\mathcal{M} = \langle \mathcal{M}_1^C, \mathcal{M}_2^C, \mathcal{M}^{FOL} \rangle$ can be composed by $\mathcal{M}_1^C = (\mathcal{I}, \beta)$ as defined in Section 4.1, $\mathcal{M}_2^C = (\mathcal{I}', \beta')$ is a target model not shown in this paper, and $\mathcal{M}^{FOL}$ is a first-order structure. Binding of variables depends on the type of elements. If the variable is of a class, we have that the set of possible values coincides with the set of elements within the MOF institutions, e.g. $|\text{p}| = V_{Package} = \{p1\}$. However, if the variable is of a primitive type, we have than $V_t \subseteq |D|_t$ since transformation rules can use other elements besides those in the MOF institutions, for example those strings created using the type constructor $++$, e.g. $|\text{pn}| = \{Pac, Str, ID, ..., pk, tid, ..., ID + +tid, ID + +numb, ...\}$

We have that $\mathcal{M} \models_\Sigma \varphi$, if $\mathcal{M}_i^C \models_{\Sigma_i^C} \varphi_i^C$ $(i = 1, 2)$ and $\mathcal{M} \models_\Sigma \varphi^{rules}$. We already showed that $\mathcal{M}_1^C \models_{\Sigma_1^C} \varphi_1^C$, and we prove in the same way that $\mathcal{M}_2^C \models_{\Sigma_2^C} \varphi_2^C$ for a valid SW-model. Thus, we need to prove that $\mathcal{M} \models_\Sigma \varphi^{rules}$, and this holds if $\mathcal{M}^{FOL}, \emptyset \models \texttt{ClassToTable}$, and $\mathcal{M}^{FOL}, \emptyset \models \texttt{PackageToSchema}$.

As an example, we prove that $\mathcal{M}^{FOL}, \emptyset \models \texttt{PackageToSchema}$ considering a valid target SW-model with only one schema (semantically represented as $s1$) having the same name as the package (semantically represented as Pac). We know that $|\text{pn}| = V_{String} = \{Pac, Str, Per, nul, ID, val, ...\}$, and $|\text{p}| = V_{Package} = \{p1\}$, so $|\{\text{pn}, \text{p}\}|$ is $\{(Pac, p1), (Str, p1), (ID, p1), (nul, p1), (Per, p1), (val, p1), ...\}$.

We also have that $|\text{s}| = V_{Schema} = \{s1\}$. Thus, the rule holds if

$$\forall \; \mu^1[\text{pn}, \text{p}] \in \{(Pac, p1), (Str, p1), (ID, p1), (Per, p1), (val, p1), (nul, p1), ...\},$$
$$(\; \mathcal{M}^{FOL}, \mu^1 \models \text{Pattern}_1 \rightarrow \exists \; \mu^2[\text{s}] \in \{s1\},$$
$$(\; \mathcal{M}^{FOL}, (\mu^1 \cup \mu^2) \models \text{Pattern}_2 \; \wedge \; \mathcal{M}^{FOL}, (\mu^1 \cup \mu^2) \models \text{where}))$$

For every $\mu^1[\text{pn}, \text{p}]$ different from $(Pac, p1)$ we have that Pattern$_1$ does not hold, since it depends on the predicate name(p,pn). Thus, in these cases the implication holds. Now, in the case of $(Pac, p1)$, we have that Pattern$_1$ holds, and that the only possible value for s is $s1$. In this case, we also have that $\mathcal{M}^{\text{FOL}}, (\mu^1 \cup \mu^2) \models$ Pattern$_2$ since the predicate name(s,pn) holds. Moreover, since the **where** clause is empty, $\mathcal{M}^{\text{FOL}}, (\mu^1 \cup \mu^2) \models$ where trivially holds. Finally, we conclude that $\mathcal{M}^{\text{FOL}} \models$ PackageToSchema indeed.

6   Conclusions and Future Work

In this paper we have defined institutions to represent the conformance relation between MOF models and metamodels, and the satisfaction of QVT-Relations check-only unidirectional transformations between pairs of models. These definitions neither depend on a shallow embedding of the languages by providing a syntactic translation into other logics, nor on the definition of specific institutions for each metamodel or model transformation. On the contrary, we defined a generic and minimal infrastructure within a theory which allows the definition of semantic-preserving translations from the MDE elements to potentially any logic defined as an institution, with the advantage that there is no need to maintain multiple formal representations of the same MDE elements.

Unlike MOF, we do not consider some constructions (e.g. aggregation, operations on classes) since they are elements not commonly used within transformations. We neither consider black-box operations or rule and transformation overriding within transformations since they are advanced features not commonly used in practice, nor keys definition since they are used for object creation not within the checking semantics. However, an inclusion of these elements within our institutions will strengthen the formal environment for MDE.

Our institutions contribute to the definition of a comprehensive formal environment for the verification of model transformations. We plan to define comorphisms from our institutions to a host logic and supplement this information with properties specified in the host logic. In particular, we have an initial formal definition of comorphism to CASL, the main language within Hets, and we are developing a first functional prototype of the running example using such definition as a way to test the main concepts. The native inclusion of MOF and QVT within Hets (by implementing the necessary Haskell code), as well as of the comorphisms, is within our medium-term goals.

Although we are for now focusing on MOF and QVT-Relations, we envision to extend the environment to support other transformation approaches.

References

1. Kent, S.: Model driven engineering. In: Butler, M., Petre, L., Sere, K. (eds.) IFM 2002. LNCS, vol. 2335, pp. 286–298. Springer, Heidelberg (2002)
2. Object Management Group: Meta Object Facility (MOF) 2.0 Core Specification. Specification Version 2.0 (2003)

3. Object Management Group: Meta Object Facility (MOF) 2.0 Query/View/Transformation. Final Adopted Specification Version 1.1 (2009)
4. Kurtev, I., Bezivin, J., Aksit, M.: Technological spaces: An initial appraisal. In: Intl. Symposium on Distributed Objects and Applications (2002)
5. Cengarle, M.V., Knapp, A., Tarlecki, A., Wirsing, M.: A heterogeneous approach to UML semantics. In: Degano, P., De Nicola, R., Meseguer, J. (eds.) Concurrency, Graphs and Models. LNCS, vol. 5065, pp. 383–402. Springer, Heidelberg (2008)
6. Mossakowski, T.: Heterogeneous specification and the heterogeneous tool set. Tech. Rep., Universitaet Bremen, Habilitation thesis (2005)
7. Goguen, J.A., Burstall, R.M.: Institutions: Abstract Model Theory for Specification and Programming. J. ACM 39(1), 95–146 (1992)
8. Object Management Group: Object Constraint Language. Formal Specification Version 2.2 (2010)
9. Calegari, D., Szasz, N.: Bridging techological spaces for the verification of model transformations. In: Conf. Iberoamericana de Software Engineering, Uruguay (2013)
10. Goguen, J.A., Rosu, G.: Institution morphisms. Formal Aspects of Computing 13, 274–307 (2002)
11. Mossakowski, T., Haxthausen, A.E., Sannella, D., Tarlecki, A.: Casl - the common algebraic specification language: Semantics and proof theory. Computers and Artificial Intelligence 22, 285–321 (2003)
12. Cengarle, M.V., Knapp, A.: An institution for UML 2.0 static structures. Tech. Rep. TUM-I0807, Institut für Informatik, Technische Universität München (2008)
13. James, P., Knapp, A., Mossakowski, T., Roggenbach, M.: Designing domain specific languages – A craftsman's approach for the railway domain using CASL. In: Martí-Oliet, N., Palomino, M. (eds.) WADT 2012. LNCS, vol. 7841, pp. 178–194. Springer, Heidelberg (2013)
14. Sannella, D., Tarlecki, A.: Foundations of Algebraic Specification and Formal Software Development. Springer (2012)
15. Beckert, B., Keller, U., Schmitt, P.: Translating the Object Constraint Language into first-order predicate logic. In: VERIFY Workshop, Denmark (2002)
16. Shan, L., Zhu, H.: Semantics of metamodels in UML. In: 3rd IEEE Symposium on Theoretical Aspects of Software Engineering, pp. 55–62. IEEE Computer Society (2009)
17. Rivera, J., Durán, F., Vallecillo, A.: Formal specification and analysis of domain specific models using Maude. Simulation 85(11-12), 778–792 (2009)
18. Boronat, A., Knapp, A., Meseguer, J., Wirsing, M.: What is a multi-modeling language? In: Corradini, A., Montanari, U. (eds.) WADT 2008. LNCS, vol. 5486, pp. 71–87. Springer, Heidelberg (2009)
19. Orejas, F., Wirsing, M.: On the specification and verification of model transformations. In: Palsberg, J. (ed.) Semantics and Algebraic Specification. LNCS, vol. 5700, pp. 140–161. Springer, Heidelberg (2009)
20. Bidoit, M., Hennicker, R., Tort, F., Wirsing, M.: Correct realizations of interface constraints with OCL. In: France, R.B. (ed.) UML 1999. LNCS, vol. 1723, pp. 399–415. Springer, Heidelberg (1999)
21. Boronat, A., Heckel, R., Meseguer, J.: Rewriting Logic Semantics and Verification of Model Transformations. In: Chechik, M., Wirsing, M. (eds.) FASE 2009. LNCS, vol. 5503, pp. 18–33. Springer, Heidelberg (2009)

22. de Lara, J., Guerra, E.: Formal Support for QVT-Relations with Coloured Petri Nets. In: Schürr, A., Selic, B. (eds.) MODELS 2009. LNCS, vol. 5795, pp. 256–270. Springer, Heidelberg (2009)
23. Anastasakis, K., Bordbar, B., Küster, J.M.: Analysis of model transformations via Alloy. In: 4th MoDeVVa Workshop, pp. 47–56 (2007)
24. Stenzel, K., Moebius, N., Reif, W.: Formal verification of QVT transformations for code generation. In: Whittle, J., Clark, T., Kühne, T. (eds.) MODELS 2011. LNCS, vol. 6981, pp. 533–547. Springer, Heidelberg (2011)
25. Guerra, E., de Lara, J.: An algebraic semantics for QVT-relations check-only transformations. Fundamenta Informaticae 114, 73–101 (2012)
26. Calegari, D., Szasz, N.: Institution-based semantics for MOF and QVT-Relations (extended version). Tech. Rep. 13-06, InCo-PEDECIBA (2013) ISSN 0797-6410, http://www.fing.edu.uy/inco/pedeciba/bibliote/reptec/TR1306.pdf

Derivation and Verification of Parallel Components for the Needs of an HPC Cloud

Thiago Braga Marcilon and Francisco Heron de Carvalho Junior

Mestrado e Doutorado em Ciência da Computação,
Universidade Federal do Ceará, Brazil
{thiagomarcilon,heron}@lia.ufc.br

Abstract. Cloud computing platforms are considered a promising approach for provision of High Performance Computing services. HPC Storm is an ongoing research project that is proposing a component-oriented view of HPC resources in a cloud, towards the development and provision of large-scale parallel computing systems. In this context, a system of contracts have been proposed for representing functional and non-functional properties of components. This paper is interested in evaluating the use of the Circus specification language for specifying the functional and behavioral subset of computational component contracts. For that, a process is proposed for their development and some case studies with real programs in the HPC domain are used to validate it in practice.

1 Introduction

The provisioning of High Performance Computing (HPC) services under the cloud computing perspective [2] is an important challenge [21]. We envisage HPC cloud services as interfaces where large-scale workflows are configured for orchestrating a set of computationally intensive tasks deployed in high-end parallel computing platforms, aiming at solving challenging problem by using abstractions of the application domain. Thus, through these services, the computational resources that will perform the workflows should be transparent to the users. In other words, the users should not be aware of the physical location and architecture of the parallel computing platforms used for performing the workflow in the prescribed timeline. However, the current cloud computing initiatives in HPC are restricted to either IaaS (Infrastructure-as-a-Service), for provisioning of access to virtual parallel computing platforms, or SaaS (Software-as-a-Service), for provisioning of application services in a specific domain of interest.

We are developing HPC Storm, a general-purpose platform for provisioning of HPC services, where parallel components represent building-block abstractions for developing, deploying and executing parallel computing systems (hardware and software). HPC Storm blurs the distinction between the IaaS, SaaS and PaaS (Platform-as-a-Service) perspectives, according to the kind of user.

In HPC Storm, a workflow is an orchestration of a set of components of different kinds, some of which represent computations that must be deployed in parallel computing platforms, each one represented by a *contract* that defines

J. Iyoda and L. de Moura (Eds.): SBMF 2013, LNCS 8195, pp. 51–66, 2013.
© Springer-Verlag Berlin Heidelberg 2013

the requirements that must be satisfied by a set of compliant components and the parallel computing platforms to which their performance are tuned.

The goals of this paper are twofold. Firstly, it introduces the use of formal methods for defining a development process for building components in HPC Storm, where they may be certified with respect to the computation specified by their contracts. For that, we use Circus [22], a specification language that has expressiveness for describing behavioral and computational properties of components, as well as providing a refinement calculus for deriving component implementations from contracts. We rely on an extension of Circus for specification of parallel components developed in a previous work [7]. Secondly, the proposed process is evaluated regarding the feasibility of refining contracts and translating them to source code, using kernels of NPB (NAS Parallel Benchmarks) [3]. The selected kernels have "pencil-and-paper" descriptions, from which we can derive contracts, and realistic tuned implementations developed by HPC programmers, which may be used for evaluating the performance of the produced code.

In HPC, the use of formal methods for code generation is poorly disseminated, despite the high cost of errors in long running programs [10]. The codes in HPC programs are often hand-tuned for the characteristics of the target execution platform. On the contrary, refinement and translation approaches favor the generation of portable and generic code, using high level abstractions of programming languages for simplifying code generation by reducing the semantic gap. For this reason, one of the main concerns in our research, but not yet approached in this paper, is developing techniques for deriving high performance code, which is optimal for running on the target parallel computing platforms.

This paper comprises four more sections. Section 2 overviews HPC Storm. Section 3 motivates and describes the proposed process of formal derivation of certified components for the requirements of HPC Storm. Section 4 presents the case studies for evaluating the feasibility of refining and translating contracts, written in an extension of Circus, to source code. Finally, Section 5 present our conclusions about the contributions of this paper and a discussion about the next steps of our research about certification of components in HPC Storm.

2   HPC Storm: The Cloud of (Parallel) Components

HPC Storm is an on-going project for implementing a cloud computing platform that serves a collection of components of different kinds to its clients. They are aimed at representing the hardware and software building blocks of parallel computing systems, that implement HPC applications.

The abstraction of clouds may provide a transparent view of HPC resources from the perspective of a set of stakeholders. They are: **users**, the final clients, which access applications of the domain of their expertise; **providers**, which offer applications to their target users, built from a set of components; **developers**, which write optimized components for a class of parallel computing platforms; and **maintainers**, which offer a set of virtual parallel computing platforms, represented by components of kind *platform*, to the applications.

HPC Storm has its basis in our previous work on the *Hash component model* [5], the *Hash Programming Environment* (HPE) [8] and the *Hash Type System* (HTS), introduced in the next sections with important concepts for understanding the architecture of HPC Storm and the contributions presented in this paper.

2.1   The **Hash** Component Model, HPE and HTS

The Hash component model [5] brings to CBHPC (Component-Based High Performance Computing) a general abstraction to represent parallel components, i.e. components that are able to exploit the potential performance of distributed-memory parallel computing platforms. They are so-called *#-components*.

A #-component is formed by a set of *units*, represented by processes running at distinct processing nodes of a parallel computing platform. Thus, units may be viewed as distributed agents that cooperate in addressing the concern of the #-component. For that, a unit of a #-component *c* is specified by the orchestration of units from a set of *inner components*, i. e. #-components from which *c* depends to address its own concern. This is so-called overlapping (hierarchical) composition [6], since it is described by an *overlapping function* that maps the units of the inner components of *c* to the units of *c*. The *slices* of a unit *u* of *c* are the units of the inner components of *c* mapped to *u* by the overlapping function. A *configuration* is a description of the units, inner components and overlapping function of a #-component, using an architecture description language (ADL). For that purpose, we have developed HCL (Hash Configuration Language).

Besides units and overlapping composition, a component platform that complies with the Hash component model supports *component kinds*. Component kinds group #-components that comply with the same component model, making it possible to represent domain-specific building block abstractions.

HPE (*Hash Programming Environment*) [8] is a general-purpose CBHPC platform that complies with the Hash component model, targeted at cluster computing platforms. It supports eight component kinds: *computations*, *data structures*, *synchronizers*, *topologies*, *platforms*, *environments*, *applications*, and *features*. It implements a choreography of services of three types: the **Front-End**, from which a programmer build configurations and implementations of #-components and control their life cycle; the **Core**, for cataloging #-components in a distributed library; and the **Back-End**, for managing a parallel computing platform where #-components are deployed and executed. The interfaces of the **Core** and the **Back-End** are *Web Services*. In turn, the **Front-End** is an Eclipse plugin that provides a visual editor for building configurations. The **Back-End** has been implemented on top of the Mono virtual execution engine [1].

HTS is the type system of HPE for dynamic discovery and binding of #-components, through a service provided by the **Core** to the **Back-End**. An *abstract component* represents a set of #-components that address the same concern for different assumptions about the application and the target parallel computing platforms. Such assumptions are described through *context parameters*, each one associated to a *bound* subtype restriction, defined by an *instantiation type*. In turn, an instantiation type is recursively defined by the application of instantiation types as arguments to each context parameter of an abstract component by respecting its bound restrictions. In HPE, the inner components of a #-component and #-components itself are typed by instantiation types. In execution, a resolution procedure will traverse the subtypes of the instantiation type of an inner component in a certain order, trying to find a #-component whose instantiation type matches it, which will supply the inner component.

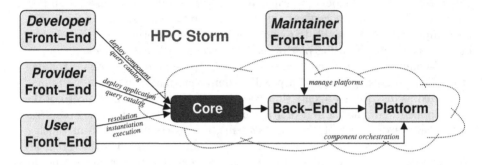

Fig. 1. HPC Storm Architecture

2.2 The Architecture of HPC Storm

The Figure 1 depicts the main architectural elements of HPC Storm, clearly inspired by HPE. The infrastructure is represented by the **Core** and the **Back-End**. The **Core** provides the main abstraction layer, providing access and management for the catalog of *contracts* provided by HPC Storm.

Contracts is a key abstraction of HPC Storm, generalizing abstract components of HPE by including number valued context parameters and the functional specification of its set of compliant components. They make it possible the selection of the most tuned components of contextual contracts that specifies the components of an application, according to their sets of context arguments.

From the *User* **Front-End**, a user may configure an application to be performed in HPC Storm, by using the domain-specific language supported by the application. A computation of the application is mapped to a workflow specification, described using the underlying workflow language of HPC Storm, which specifies the orchestration of a set of components represented by contextual contracts. Some of these components represent concrete computations that will be deployed to a parallel computing platform. By submitting the workflow to the **Core**, the application receives a set of candidates for each component, sorted according to a classification strategy supported by HPC Storm, generalizing the resolution algorithm of HTS. Then, the application selects a candidate and instantiate it through the **Core**, which communicates with the maintainer that provides the component through its **Back-End** service. A platform is instantiated by the **Back-End** in some parallel computing platform offered by the maintainer, where the component is instantiated. Finally, a reference to the component is returned to the application, which may use it to communicate directly with the component in the workflow execution.

From the **_Provider_ Front-End**, providers develop applications using the *application framework*. In turn, developers write components and contracts from the **_Developer_ Front-End**. They ask the **Core** for querying the catalog for finding and registering contracts, as well as deploying new components.

3   A System of Formal Contracts for Parallel Components

The users of HPC Storm may demand for guarantees from providers of prevention against unexpected errors and performance bottlenecks in long-running workflow executions. In turn, providers may demand for similar guarantees from developers, regarding the behavior and performance of the available components from which their applications are built.

In this context, it is relevant to provide means for helping providers and developers in certifying the applications and components they provide in HPC Storm. For that, we propose a development process that aims at offering guarantees that components implement the computation specified in their contracts. Using this process, providers and developers may check whether components satisfy properties they consider relevant.

Fig. 2. Component Certification by Derivation and Verification Steps

3.1   Overview of the Formal Derivation Process

The certification process of components in HPC Storm, depicted in Figure 2, comprises two main activities: *derivation* and *verification*. Derivation consists in producing a component implementation tuned for a given *context* from a *contract*, i. e. a specification that formally describes the computation performed by the component. For that, derivation is divided in two steps: the *refinement* of the contract towards a so-called *concrete specification* and its *translation* onto the source code of the component. In turn, the verification consists in checking whether the concrete specification of an arbitrary component in the HPC Storm complies with a given contract, even if it has been not derived from it.

The contract abstraction introduced in this paper generalizes abstract components of HTS, by including a way of specifying the computations that must be performed by components. Thus, contracts also support contexts, representing the assumptions about the architecture and requirements of the target parallel computing platforms and applications, respectively, that will guide the derivation process towards production of tuned component implementations.

The *refinement step* takes the contract and successively applies a set of refinement laws that turn the source specification onto a more concrete target specification that preserves the properties of the source one. After that, the resulting concrete specification may be translated to a programming language. The case study carried out in this paper uses C♯ and MPI.NET, but different sets of translation rules may exist for distinct programming languages.

With contract contexts, the translation process may take into account the architecture of the target parallel computing platform and application requirements, besides the target programming language, for promoting a better use of the available computational resources and improving the performance of individual components. For instance, one should deal with specific HPC requirements, such as the pervasive use of multidimensional arrays, the support to complex and floating point numbers, the ordering of loops for improving locality when accessing memory hierarchies, and so on. However, requirements that depend on the architecture of the target parallel computing platform are not usually supported by formal specification languages that support refinement.

The certification process involves providers and developers of HPC Storm. In turn, the HPC Storm infrastructure is responsible in verifying whether components of applications comply with their contracts, giving preference to components that assure that they respect the contract from which they were derived. In simple terms, certified components are that ones developed using the proposed process. For that, in the environment of components, it is necessary to bundle the component and the concrete specification from which it has been derived, in such way that this bundle is unforgeable and HPC Storm may verify whether or not a component complies with a contract. We are planning to apply proof-carrying code techniques [14] for accomplishing this.

3.2   The Chosen Specification Language: Circus

The formal specification language suitable for the proposed process must be able to specify both functional and behavioral aspects of parallel components. Furthermore, it must support a validated refinement calculus by means of practical experiences on code generation from specifications [15,16,4].

Circus is a formal specification language designed around a refinement calculus for concurrent programs. It combines the Z specification language, widely used in academia and industry, with the CSP (*Communicating Sequential Processes*) process algebra, which has been designed around the notion of refinement. Circus also incorporates the guarded command language of Dijsktra [9]. A specification in Circus is basically a combination of Z paragraphs [20,12], guarded commands of Dijkstra [9] and CSP combinators [11]. Indeed, it is possible to write specifications, designs and even programs using Circus.

The Z specification language and the guarded command language may be used to specify the computations that must be performed by a component, while CSP is able to describe its behavioral aspects. Also, the refinement and code generation support of Circus have been validated by other works [19,15,17,4]. These are the reasons for choosing Circus for the specification of certifiable components in HPC Storm, fitting the requirements of the proposed process.

3.3 Circus/HCL

Circus/HCL will be adopted for the specification of component contracts in HPC Storm. It is an extension of Circus for specifying components in HPE [7]. HCL stands for *Hash Configuration Language*, an architecture description language (ADL) for describing configurations of components in HPE. Furthermore, additional syntactic sugar and abstractions have been introduced to Circus/HCL, aiming at fitting the HPC requirements of highly tuned code generation. HCL is used by Circus/HCL as a glue for plugging together Circus specifications of #-components. A Circus/HCL specification may be directly translated to Circus. Indeed, all refinement rules that are valid for Circus are valid for Circus/HCL.

A grammar for Circus/HCL, and its translation to Circus, is presented in [7].

computation VECVECPRODUCT $\langle N \rangle$ (u, v, i)
$\quad\quad\quad [accelerator\_type = A : \text{ACCELERATORTYPE},$
$\quad\quad\quad number\_of\_cores = M : \text{INTEGER}]$ **where**

inner data u: VECTOR$\langle N \rangle$ $[accelerator\_type = A, number\_of\_cores = M]$
inner data v: VECTOR$\langle N \rangle$ $[accelerator\_type = A, number\_of\_cores = M]$
inner computation sum: REDUCE$\langle N \rangle$ $[accelerator\_type = A, number\_of\_cores = M,$
$\quad\quad\quad\quad\quad\quad\quad\quad\quad\quad\quad\quad\quad\quad\quad\quad reduce\_operator = \text{SUM}]$
inner data i: REALSCALAR$\langle N \rangle$

unit $dot\_product \,\widehat{=}\, \left|\middle|\middle|\right. i : \{0..N-1\} \bullet$
begin
$\quad\quad$ **slice** $u.vector[i], v.vector[i], sum.reduce[i], i.value[i]$
$\quad\quad$ **state** $State \,\widehat{=}\, [u::*, v::*, sum::*, i::* \mid u::dim = v::dim]$
$\quad\quad computeLocal \,\widehat{=}\, [\Delta State \mid sum::k' = \sum_{j=0}^{v::dim-1} v::v[j] \times u::v[j]]$
$\quad\quad updValue \,\widehat{=}\, [\Delta State \mid i::k' = sum::k]$
$\quad\quad$ **action** $perform \,\widehat{=}\, computeLocal;\, \textbf{do } sum;\, updValue$
$\quad\quad \bullet\, perform$
end

Fig. 3. Contract VECVECPRODUCT for a Vector-Vector Product $i = u \times v$

The Figure 3 shows the contract VECVECPRODUCT, in Circus/HCL, formed by a parallel unit identified by *dot_product*, representing processes that perform a dot product between vectors u and v whose result is stored in scalar i.

In a Circus/HCL component specification, the *units* are denoted by a set of Circus processes. Besides a set of slices, which are described as in HCL, a unit may declare a *state*, a set of *actions*, a set of *conditions*, and a *protocol*. The protocol is defined by the main action of the specification.

The unit state may inherit the state of the unit slices, by means of ⟨*slice*⟩ ::*,
where ⟨*slice*⟩ is the name of a slice. Also, using ⟨*slice*⟩ :: ⟨*item*⟩, it may refer to a
variable (⟨*item*⟩) of the slice's state.

Actions and conditions may be public or private and may be referred in other
actions and in the protocol. However, only public actions and conditions may be
referred in the actions and in the protocol of the enclosing unit where the unit
is a slice. Therefore, actions are defined by the combination of its own actions
and public actions from its slices, using CSP action combinators. The use of slice
actions must satisfy the restriction imposed by the protocol of their respective
slices. For instance, if an action of a unit slice is not referred in its protocol, then
this action can be used freely in the actions and in the protocol of the unit.

Units, in Circus/HCL, communicate through channels, defined as primitive
components of kind *communicator* that encapsulate message passing primitives.
For that, such components contain a unit called *receive*, for receiving messages,
and a unit called *send*, for sending messages.

The abstraction of parallel units is represented as processes replicated by the
interleaving CSP operator (|||), since units run independently of each other.

VECVECPRODUCT declares four inner components, which define the slices of
dot_product: *u*, *v*, *sum* and *i*. Also, there is a public action, identified by *perform*,
and two private actions, identified by *updValue* and *computeLocal*, referred in
perform. There is no channel, since the units do not need to communicate for
performing a parallel dot product. The protocol is simply defined by the *perform*
action. The vectors *u* and *v* are updated in the *computeLocal* action. The local
values are added by the protocol of the unit *reduce* of the inner component *sum*,
and stored in its variable *k*. Finally, the action *updValue* store this value in the
variable *k* in the state of the unit *value* of inner component *i*.

The reader may have noticed the context parameters **accelerator_type** and
number_of_cores in VECVECPRODUCT. They state that components that
may be derived from it may be optimized according to the kind of accelerator
coupled to the processing units (e.g. GPU, FPGA or MIC), if one exists, and
the number of cores per processor in a processing unit.

In the derivation process, implementations of components will be produced
from Circus/HCL contracts through the application of refinement steps followed
by translation to the target programming language.

3.4 Overview of Refinement Laws and Translation Rules

Circus offers a large set of proven refinement laws [19,16]. For the sake of simplicity, since it is not possible to present a comprehensive resume of all these laws
in this section, we only refer to the set of six refinement laws that have been
applied in the case studies of Section 4, which are:

- *Basic Conversion*, which transforms a schema in the Z notation into an
  instruction in the guarded command language;
- *Sequential composition*, which divides a complex specification instruction in
  two, more simple, specification instructions;

- *Assignment Introduction*, which transforms a specification instruction into an assignment;
- *Alternative/Guard - Exchange*, which transforms a guard in CSP into a guard in the guarded command language and vice-versa;
- *Alternative Introduction*, which transforms a specification instruction into an alternative structure;
- *Strengthen Postcondition*, which transforms a specification instruction into another specification instruction with a more strong postcondition.

Using these laws, one may build concrete specifications from contracts, targeting component implementations free of loops, function calls, and recursion, approaching the usual programming practices of HPC programming.

The translation rules from concrete specifications to C#/MPI.NET programs do not yet take contexts into consideration for applying different translation rules according to assumptions about the architecture of the target parallel computing platforms and the requirements of the application. The translation involves data structures, expressions and HCL declarations, which come from the guarded command language and CSP. So, they may be translated into programming language constructions by using appropriate techniques for circumventing the existing semantic gaps. One may consult [13], at http://www.lia.ufc.br/~heron/storm/certification, for the set translation rules used in Section 4.

3.5   Automating Tools for the Certification Process

In HPC Storm, realistic component contracts written in Circus/HCL may be quite large and complex, making it difficult and error-prone the task of specifying, refining and translating them to high performance code, even for expert developers. Thus, automating tools are necessary to help programmers in these tasks, implementing existing techniques for dealing with their complexity, such as refinement tactics [18]. They must guide developers in choosing the appropriate translation rules, being aware about the relevant characteristics of both the architecture of the target parallel computing platform and the target programming language.

Before approaching the problem of designing appropriate tools for the needs of HPC Storm, we decided to define an initial fixed set of refinement laws and translation rules for generating typical HPC code, aiming at evaluating the proposed process. For that, it is essential to work with practical HPC code whose granularity makes them natural candidates to be encapsulated in a component of HPC Storm. The existence of some specification of the code, formal or informal, written before implementation, would be also important, making it possible to derive the Circus/HCL specification from them, to apply refinement laws and translation rules for producing the code, and, finally, to compare the performance of the generate code with the original code. In the next section, we will present a case study that takes these premises into consideration.

4   Case Studies and Discussion

For the purpose of evaluating the feasibility of the proposed process, we have selected two kernels from the NAS Parallel Benchmarks (NPB) [3].

The NPB is a benchmarking package developed by the NASA Advanced Supercomputing division (NAS) for the performance evaluation of parallel computers[1]. It has been implemented in various programming languages such as C, Java and Fortran, using both the message-passing model, through MPI, and the shared memory model, through OpenMP and Java Threads.

NPB is now in version 3.3, consisting of 12 programs, among kernels and simulated applications, and five standard workload levels for each program. The two benchmarks selected for this paper are: **IS** (*Integer Sort*), for parallel sorting of a set of integers using the bucketsort algorithm; and **CG** (*Conjugate Gradient*), which uses the inverse power iteration method to find the lowest eigenvalue of a sparse positive-definite symmetric matrix.

NPB has been adopted because it provides typical hand-tuned codes from scientific computing applications, developed by experts in the field. IS and CG were chosen due to their simplicity and availability of official "pencil-and-paper" specifications. Furthermore, they have the typical granularity of components in the HPC Storm. Thus, we can derive specifications and code from the same official specification from which the optimized codes of IS and CG were derived, making it possible to compare the resulting code, regarding readability and performance.

The methodology of this case study starts from the "pencil-and-paper" specifications of IS and CG, used for obtaining concrete implementations of components encapsulating them using the derivation process outlined in Section 3.1. For that, three stages will be applied: (1) specification of the computationally significant components of the two applications using Circus/HCL, building *contracts* that preserve the original properties of the applications; (2) *refinement* of the contracts towards concrete specifications of components; (3) *translation* of concrete specifications onto components, written in C♯.

Unfortunately, it is not possible to describe all the details about the application of the derivation process to IS and CG in this paper. For details, we recommend the Marcilon's Master Dissertation [13] and the web page at http://www.lia.ufc.br/~heron/storm/certification, where all the contracts, refined specifications and derived source codes may be consulted. The case studies results are outlined in the following sections, with our conclusions about them.

4.1   Integer Sort

The IS kernel consists of sorting integer keys in parallel, using the *bucketsort* algorithm. The key values do not exceed a predetermined value *Bmax*. The value of *Bmax* depends on the workload level. In practice, it is widely used in HPC applications, since it is a fundamental operation.

---

[1] http://www.nas.nasa.gov/publications/npb.html

For IS, we have developed a contract named INTEGERSORT, written in Circus/HCL. It specifies a parallel version of the bucketsort algorithm, where each process represents a "bucket" where the keys in a given interval will be put. It has a parallel unit named *sorter*, whose state includes the following variables:

- **ord**, keeping the number of elements in the i-th bucket;
- **rank**, keeping the rank of the first key in the i-th bucket, if $ord[i]$ is nonzero;
- **b_0** and **b_1**, storing the value of the first and last values whose ranks are to be computed by the bucket.

The paragraph *rank* of unit *sorter* specifies the procedure for ranking the keys. First, each unit redistributes the keys outside the $[b_0, b_1]$ interval and receives keys of this interval from other units. In the meantime, they compute the vector *ord*. After this step, all units have your keys. Then, the rank of each key is computed based on *ord*. The communication are performed trough the channel c. It does not need to be connected to the component environment, since it serves for communication between the units, being encapsulated into the component.

In what follows, for illustrating the derivation process, we present a fragment of *rank* where the array *rank* is computed:

$$\vdots$$

$$\textbf{if } i = 0 \rightarrow rank : [\forall j : b_0..b_1 \bullet rank[j] = (\textstyle\sum_{l=b_0}^{j-1} ord[l]) + 1];$$
$$c.i.(i+1)!(rank[b_1] + ord[b_1]) \rightarrow SKIP$$
$$[\!] (i > 0) \wedge (i < N - 1) \rightarrow c.(i-1).i?aux \rightarrow$$
$$rank : [\forall j : b_0..b_1 \bullet rank[j] = (\textstyle\sum_{l=b_0}^{j-1} ord[l]) + aux];$$
$$c.i.(i+1)!(rank[b_1] + ord[b_1]) \rightarrow SKIP$$
$$[\!] i = N - 1 \rightarrow c.(i-1).i?aux \rightarrow rank : [\forall j : b_0..b_1 \bullet rank[j] = (\textstyle\sum_{l=b_0}^{j-1} ord[l]) + aux]$$
$$\textbf{fi}$$

$$\vdots$$

For refining INTEGERSORT, it is necessary to refine all the specification instructions and Z schemas of the unit *sorter*. In the above fragment of *rank*, we have the following specification instructions to be refined:

- $rank : [\forall j : b_0..b_1 \bullet rank[j]' = \left(\sum_{l=b_0}^{j-1} ord[l] \right) + aux]$
- $rank : [\forall j : b_0..b_1 \bullet rank[j]' = \left(\sum_{l=b_0}^{j-1} ord[l] \right) + 1]$

In order to refine the above specification instructions, we apply the *Sequential composition* and *Assignment Introduction* laws twice. The resulting concrete specification of the above contract fragment is presented below:

$$\vdots$$

$$\textbf{if } i = 0 \rightarrow rank[b_0] := 1; \; \overset{\circ}{\underset{9}{}} m : b_0 + 1..b_1 \bullet rank[m] := rank[m - 1] + ord[m - 1];$$
$$c.i.(i+1)!(rank[b_1] + ord[b_1]) \rightarrow SKIP$$
$$[\!] (i > 0) \wedge (i < N - 1) \rightarrow c.(i-1).i?aux \rightarrow rank[b_0] := aux;$$
$$\overset{\circ}{\underset{9}{}} m : b_0 + 1..b_1 \bullet rank[m] := rank[m - 1] + ord[m - 1];$$
$$c.i.(i+1)!(rank[b_1] + ord[b_1]) \rightarrow SKIP$$
$$[\!] i = N - 1 \rightarrow c.(i-1).i?aux \rightarrow rank[b_0] := aux;$$
$$\overset{\circ}{\underset{9}{}} m : b_0 + 1..b_1 \bullet rank[m] := rank[m - 1] + ord[m - 1]$$

$$\vdots$$

Finally, the translation of concrete specification to source code, using the translation rules specified in [13], is presented below:

```
:
if (getRank()==0) {
    rank[b_0] = 1;
    for(m=b_0+1; m<=b_1; m++)
        rank[m] = rank[m−1] + ord[m−1];
    c.Send(rank[b_1]+ord[b_1], getRank()+1, 0);
}
else if ((getRank() > 0) && (getRank() < getSize() −1)) {
    aux = c.Receive<ulong>(getRank()−1,0);
    rank[b_0] = aux;
    for(m=b_0+1; m<=b_1; m++)
        rank[m] = rank[m−1] + ord[m−1];
    c.Send(rank[b_1]+ord[b_1], getRank()+1, 0);
}
else if (getRank() == getSize()−1) {
    aux = c.Receive<ulong>(getRank()−1,0);
    rank[b_0] = aux;
    for(m=b_0+1; m<=b_1; m++)
        rank[m] = rank[m−1] + ord[m−1];
}
else{
    Environment.Exit(1);
}
:
```

The verification may be applied by the dynamic resolution algorithm for checking whether a given component satisfies a given contract, i. e. if it is a valid implementation of the contract, even if it was not derived from the contract. It starts by transforming the Circus/HCL concrete specifications and the contracts in pure Circus specification. Then, the formula $[\exists\ C.State;\ C.State' \bullet C.Act] \Rightarrow [\exists A.State;\ A.State' \bullet A.Act]$ is checked, where $C.Act$ and $A.Act$ are the translated concrete specification and the contract, repectively.

4.2 Conjugate Gradient

The CG kernel estimates the lowest eigenvalue of a sparse, symmetric and positive-definite matrix using the inverse power iteration method. It uses the method of *conjugate gradient* to solve the system of linear equations needed to find the smallest eigenvalue of a given matrix. The size of the array, the number of iterations and other constants are defined according to the workload level.

The method of *conjugate gradient* is an iterative numeric method used to solve systems of linear equations where the matrix that represents them are sparse, symmetric and positive-definite.

The contract CONJUGATEGRADIENT specifies the CG kernel, depending on other contracts. They are: ALLGATHER, MATVECPRODUCT and REDUCE. ALLGATHER and REDUCE specify well known collective communication operations, whereas MATVECPRODUCT specifies the product between a matrix and a vector. In addition to the variables inherited from the states of ALLGATHER, MATVECPRODUCT and REDUCE, it includes the following variables:

- **A**, **z** and **x**, the operands of the system of equations $A \times z = x$, to be solved, which are assumed to be initialized outside the component;
- **dim**, the dimension of the matrix **A**, also assumed to be initialized before the execution of the component;
- **$lines$**, the number of lines of matrix A and vectors x e z, in each unit;
- array **r**, whose i-th element is the residue ($r = x - A \times z$) in iteration i;

The contract CONJUGATEGRADIENT describes the conjugate gradient method where each unit contains a number of rows, represented by the value $lines$, of the matrix A and vector x. The paragraph $init$ is responsible for describing the initialization of the component state. Its specification code is shown below for illustrating the derivation process:

$$
\begin{aligned}
init \ \widehat{=}\ &lines : \big[\, (i = N - 1 \wedge lines' = dim - (N - 1) \times \lfloor \tfrac{dim}{N} \rfloor) \vee (i \neq N - 1 \wedge lines' = \lfloor \tfrac{dim}{N} \rfloor) \,\big]; \\
&z : [\forall j : 0..lines - 1 \bullet z[j]' = 0]; \ \ r : [\forall j : 0..lines - 1 \bullet r[j]' = x[j]]; \\
&mv::A : [\forall j : 0..lines - 1 \bullet \forall k : 0..dim - 1 \bullet mv::A[j, k]' = A[j, k]]; \\
&mv::dim : [mv::dim' = dim]; \\
&a::dim : [a::dim' = dim]
\end{aligned}
$$

In order to refine the contracts ALLGATHER, MATVECPRODUCT, REDUCE and CONJUGATEGRADIENT, the six laws described in Section 3.4 are enough. The concrete specification of the $init$ paragraph is presented below:

$$
\begin{aligned}
init \ \widehat{=}\ &\textbf{if}\, i = N - 1 \rightarrow lines := dim - (N - 1) \times \lfloor dim/N \rfloor \\
&[\![\, i \neq N - 1 \rightarrow lines := \lfloor dim/N \rfloor \\
&\textbf{fi}; \\
&\overset{\circ}{\underset{9}{}} m : 0..lines - 1 \bullet z[m] := 0; \ \ \overset{\circ}{\underset{9}{}} m : 0..lines - 1 \bullet r[m] := x[m]; \\
&\overset{\circ}{\underset{9}{}} m : 0..lines - 1 \bullet \overset{\circ}{\underset{9}{}} l : 0..dim - 1 \bullet mv::A[m, l] := A[m, l]; \\
&mv::dim := dim; \ \ a::dim := dim
\end{aligned}
$$

After application of the translation rules, the above concrete specification results in the following code:

```
void init ()
{
    if (getRank () == getSize ()−1) {
        lines = dim − (getSize ()−1) * System.Math.Floor ((( double )dim )/ getSize ());
    }
    else if (getRank () != getSize ()−1) {
        lines = Math.floor ((( double )dim )/ getSize ());
    }
    else { Environment.Exit (1); }
    for (int m = 0; m <= lines −1; m++) z [m] = 0;
    for (int m = 0; m <= lines −1; m++) r [m] = x [m];
    for (int m = 0; m <= lines −1; m++)
        for (int l = 0; m <= dim −1; m++) mv.A[m, l] = A[m, l];
    mv.Dim = dim;
    a.Dim = dim;
}
```

The verification occurs in the same way as in the contract INTEGERSORT. However, the verification process must be applied recursively for each one of its constituent contracts (ALLGATHER, MATVECPRODUCT and REDUCE).

4.3 Discussion

As expected, both the specification of contracts of IS and CG and manual derivation of their C♯ source codes from the contracts have been shown to be time consuming and error prone tasks, requiring high mathematical skills from the developer, as well as familiarity with proof techniques. Thus, the case study highly enforces the need of designing and implementing appropriate tools for guiding the derivation process towards component certification in HPC Storm.

The case study has also shown that it is possible to guide the derivation process towards tuned code according the characteristics of the target execution platform by choosing the appropriate sequence of refinement laws and translation rules. Indeed, we have defined translation rules according to our knowledge about generation of scientific efficient code in C♯, making use of rectangular multidimensional arrays and ordering loops for improving cache performance. For that, the existing codes of IS and CG, in C and Fortran, respectively, were useful as a baseline to guide definition and application of translation rules.

Also, we have confirmed that it is useful, and often necessary, to augment the underlying specification language, i. e. Circus, with some abstractions, such as multidimensional arrays. For the needs of the case study, the type $Array_k(T)$ was introduced to Circus/HCL, where T represents a Z primitive type, as a syntactic sugar for functions over naturals: $Array_k(T) == \mathbb{N}^k \nrightarrow T$. Also, the indexing operator is defined as: $\_[\_,\_,\ldots,\_] == Array(T) \times \mathbb{N}^k \to T$. This syntactic sugar may also be used for array update.

5   Conclusions and Lines for Further Works

The use of formal methods for derivation and verification of software parts in HPC applications that make use of parallel computing platforms is still incipient. This is mainly due to the tight coupling between the usual HPC programming techniques and the hardware characteristics, for tuning software performance, as well as the use of portable scientific computing libraries whose reliability comes from their reputation obtained from many years of successful use. However, HPC Storm has shown to us that formal methods may be very useful for the requirement of component certification in component-oriented parallel computing systems, in the context of general-purpose cloud computing platforms aimed at provisioning high-level HPC services.

The contributions of this paper were twofold. First, it introduced a certification process for ensuring that components in HPC Storm performs the computations specified in their contracts, based on well-known software derivation and verification techniques. Secondly, it presented case studies for evaluating the use of this process for derivation and verification of typical code of HPC programs, aiming at collecting evidences about our main research hypotheses and analysing the appropriateness of existing formal derivation and verification techniques for the requirements of HPC Storm. The contracts, concrete specifications and sources codes of IS and CG, outlined in Section 4, may be consulted at http://www.lia.ufc.br/~heron/storm/certification.

Our study has enforced the need for designing and implementing tools for guiding the process of component certification for applying the process proposed in this paper, provisioned as a subset of the HPC Storm's cloud services, targeting developers and providers. This conclusion may appear rather obvious, but HPC Storm introduces additional complexity in the problem. For instance, it introduces the requirement to derive tuned component implementations, taking into consideration assumptions about both the requirements of the enclosing application and the architecture of the target parallel computing platform.

For addressing this problem, we plan to study how to take *contexts*, a concept of the contract system of HPC Storm, into consideration in the derivation process, for systematically guiding the choice of refinement laws and translation rules. In practice, this may be viewed as the systematization of the use of contexts for deriving tuned component implementations, which is now performed informally by the component developer, which codes a #-component by knowing the context assumptions that are specified in context arguments applied to the context parameters of the contract. As far as we know, this is an innovative part of our research with component certification.

As pointed ou in the end of Section 3.1, we are also interested in studying proof-carrying code techniques for component certification.

Finally, our experience with the case studies has also shown that it may be necessary to extend the underlying specification language (Circus) with new abstractions, aimed at derivation of typical HPC programming constructs. Identifying them is a complex part of our further works, since it is necessary a wide knowledge about HPC programming uses cases and techniques.

References

1. The Mono Project (2006), http://www.mono-project.com
2. Antonopoulos, N., Gillam, L.: Cloud Computing: Principles, Systems and Applications. Computer Commmunications and Networks. Springer (2011)
3. Bailey, D.H., et al.: The NAS Parallel Benchmarks. International Journal of Supercomputing Applications 5(3), 63–73 (1991)
4. Barrocas, S.L.M., Oliveira, M.V.M.: JCircus 2.0: an extension of an automatic translator from Circus to Java. In: Communicating Process Architectures 2012, vol. 34, pp. 15–36. Open Channel Publishing (August 2012)
5. Carvalho Junior, F.H., Lins, R.D.: Separation of Concerns for Improving Practice of Parallel Programming. INFORMATION, An International Journal 8(5), 621–638 (2005)
6. Carvalho Junior, F.H., Lins, R.D.: An Institutional Theory for #-Components. Electronic Notes in Theoretical Computer Science 195, 113–132 (2008)
7. Carvalho Junior, F.H., Lins, R.D.: Composition Specification of Parallel Components Using Circus. Electronic Notes in Theoretical Computer Science 260, 47–72 (2010)

8. de Carvalho Junior, F.H., Rezende, C.A.: A Case Study on Expressiveness and Performance of Component-Oriented Parallel Programming. Journal of Parallel and Distributed Computing 73(5), 557–569 (2013)
9. Dijkstra, E.W.: Guarded Commands, Nondeterminacy and Formal Derivation of Programs. Commun. ACM 18, 453–457 (1975)
10. Gopalakrishnan, G.L., Kirby, R.M.: Top Ten Ways to Make Formal Methods for HPC Practical. In: Proceedings of the FSE/SDP Workshop on Future of Software Engineering Research, FoSER 2010, pp. 137–142. ACM, New York (2010)
11. Hoare, C.A.R.: Communicating Sequential Processes. Communications of the ACM 21(8), 666–677 (1978)
12. Jacky, J.: The Way of Z: Practical Programming with Formal Methods. Cambridge University Press, New York (1996)
13. Marcilon, T.B.: Contratos Formais para Derivação e Verificação de Componentes Paralelos. Master's thesis, Departamento de Computação, Universidade Federal do Ceará (2012)
14. Necula, G.C., Lee, P.: Safe, Untrusted Agents Using Proof-Carrying Code. In: Vigna, G. (ed.) Mobile Agents and Security. LNCS, vol. 1419, pp. 61–91. Springer, Heidelberg (1998)
15. Oliveira, M., Cavalcanti, A.: From Circus to JCSP. In: Davies, J., Schulte, W., Barnett, M. (eds.) ICFEM 2004. LNCS, vol. 3308, pp. 320–340. Springer, Heidelberg (2004)
16. Oliveira, M.V.M., Gurgel, A.C., Castro, C.G.: CRefine: Support for the Circus Refinement Calculus. In: Proceedings of the IEEE International Conference on Software Engineering and Formal Methods (SEFM 2008), pp. 281–290 (2008)
17. Oliveira, M.V.M., Gurgel, A.C., Castro, C.G.: CRefine: Support for the Circus Refinement Calculus. In: Proceedings of the 2008 Sixth IEEE International Conference on Software Engineering and Formal Methods, pp. 281–290. IEEE Computer Society, Washington, DC (2008)
18. Oliveira, M.V.M., Zeyda, F., Cavalcanti, A.L.C.: A Tactic Language for Refinement of State-rich Concurrent Specifications. Science of Computer Programming 76(9), 792–833 (2011); Special issue based on the 2008 Refinement Workshop, Turku (May 27, 2008)
19. Sampaio, A., Woodcock, J., Cavalcanti, A.: Refinement in circus. In: Eriksson, L.-H., Lindsay, P.A. (eds.) FME 2002. LNCS, vol. 2391, pp. 451–470. Springer, Heidelberg (2002)
20. Stephen, B., John, N.: Z Base Standard, Verson 1.0. Technical Report 107, Oxford University (1992)
21. Vecchiola, C., Pandey, S., Buyya, R.: High-Performance Cloud Computing: A View of Scientific Applications. In: 10th International Symposium on Pervasive Systems, Algorithms, and Networks (ISPAN 2009), pp. 4–16. IEEE (2009)
22. Woodcock, J., Cavalcanti, A.: The semantics of circus. In: Bert, D., Bowen, J.P., Henson, M.C., Robinson, K. (eds.) ZB 2002. LNCS, vol. 2272, pp. 184–203. Springer, Heidelberg (2002)

An Executable Semantics for a Multimedia Authoring Language

Joel dos Santos[1,2], Christiano Braga[2], and Débora C. Muchaluat-Saade[1,2]

[1] MídiaCom Lab
[2] Instituto de Computação, Universidade Federal Fluminense, Brazil
{joel,debora}@midiacom.uff.br,
cbraga@ic.uff.br

Abstract. The Nested Context Language is a multimedia authoring language which is part of the standard for digital television in Brazil and in Latin America and the ITU standard for IPTV services. The need for proper support for the development of NCL applications is growing with the increasing demand for digital TV applications. Rigorous means to assure that multimedia presentations in NCL will behave as expected is an example. Since NCL applications may be understood as finite transition systems, standard model-based verification techniques directly apply. This paper discusses a formalization of NCL semantics and its realization in a verification tool.

1   Introduction

Nested Context Language (NCL) [1] is a declarative multimedia document authoring language, that is, it allows for the specification of user interaction with multimedia content and a temporal order for their presentation. NCL is part of the standard for digital television in Brazil and in Latin America. It is also part of the ITU standard for IPTV services [16]. As the use of NCL for the authoring of multimedia interactive applications grows, it is also expected a growth in interest for authoring tools to help NCL developers to create interactive applications. An NCL document with many components, and possibly organized within a complex structure, may present specification problems and/or fall victim of potentially undesired behaviors in its presentation. Syntactical problems arise when the document does not follow the authoring language grammar and multimedia players may not even be able to open a given document. Undesired behaviors during the presentation of a document arise when the computation induced by the document declaration produces an unexpected presentation.

In [9] we have identified a set of desirable properties for NCL documents that appear to be desirable by the multimedia document authoring community (e.g. [8, 18, 19]). They are classified as structural and behavioral properties. Structural properties, part of NCL's static semantics, rule the authoring language syntax rules by means of invariants. Behavioral properties, part of NCL's dynamic semantics, are those used for representing desired behaviors in a document's presentation.

As part of our project [10] that aims at developing formal support for NCL document reasoning using model-driven development techniques, we define a rewriting logic

J. Iyoda and L. de Moura (Eds.): SBMF 2013, LNCS 8195, pp. 67–82, 2013.

theory for the specification of NCL's semantics. Invariants representing the structural properties and temporal logic formulas representing the behavioral properties are verified in the Maude system [7] by equational reduction and model checking, respectively, thus guaranteeing that a given NCL document has the desired properties.

The remainder of this paper is structured as follows. Section 2 presents related work considering the verification of multimedia documents. Section 3 discusses the properties that are currently supported by our approach. Section 4 describes the rewriting logic semantics of NCL. Section 5 discusses the implementation of the verification of NCL documents. Section 6 concludes this paper highlighting its contributions and pointing to future work.

2   Related Work

The literature is rich on the discussion about the verification of multimedia documents. In general, it describes *either* the behavioral or structural verification. Therefore, this section presents related work separating contributions on the structural verification from those focusing on the behavioral verification.

2.1   Structural Verification

Honorato and Barbosa in [13] present the NCL-Inspector tool. This tool, based on other tools for code quality critique, supports the author in terms of code quality. With this tool, besides the possibility of verifying the NCL code searching for coding problems, it is possible to suggest modifications regarding best programming practices. The code verification, or inspection, is done following a set of rules, forming a rule repository. Each rule presents an NCL code pattern and an action realized when that pattern is found. For the inspection of an NCL document, NCL-Inspector parses the document. After that step, the tool creates an abstract syntax tree that represents the NCL document being inspected. Then it walks through the tree searching for violations of the existent rules. The violations found are presented to the user so he can correct the application code.

Neto et al. in [18] discuss an approach for the incremental structural verification of NCL documents. It defines a metalanguage for representing NCL elements with a set of primitives. The primitives define rules that must be satisfied by language elements. The structural verification is done by verifying if each element satisfies the rules defined in its related primitives. For the incremental verification, only the elements recently modified and the ones related to them are verified. An additional structure is used for identifying the elements that have to be verified.

Troncy et al. in [21] present VAMP, an approach to structurally verify MPEG-7 descriptions [14], created with different annotation tools. VAMP intends to allow the interoperability of annotation tools by reducing the variability in the use of MPEG-7 descriptions. Besides, it is also used for verifying descriptions according to constrains defined by the standard and the MPEG-7 profile [15] used. Although both MPEG-7 and MPEG-7 profiles define an XML Schema, it is not sufficient for the consistency checking of MPEG-7 descriptions. In [21] authors present a set of so called violations in descriptions that yield perfectly valid documents with respect to the MPEG-7 XML Schema. Therefore, to verify those descriptions structurally, VAMP uses an ontology (OWL-DL [22]) for representing the concepts described in the profile and logical rules (Horn clauses [2]) to represent the constrains in the use of description elements.

A common approach for the structural verification of XML documents (common representation for multimedia documents) is using XML Schema [23] based validators. Such approach verifies if Schema restrictions are satisfied by the XML-based language. Restrictions are defined over element types and not over element instances. Therefore, it can not be used, for example, to verify if two distinct element instances refer to a common element instance. This kind of verification is important for our work and others like [18].

2.2 Behavioral Verification

Santos et al. in [19] discuss an approach for the behavior verification of the presentation of multimedia documents by translating them into RT-LOTOS, a real-time process algebra framework. The modularity and hierarchy of RT-LOTOS allow the combination of processes specifying the document presentation with other processes modeling the available platform. The verification itself consists on the interpretation of the minimum reachability graph built from the formal specification to prove if the event corresponding to the document presentation end can be reached from the document's initial state. Each node in the graph represents a reachable state and each edge, the occurrence of an event or temporal progression. The tool presented in [19] can verify NCM (Nested Context Model) [20] and SMIL (Synchronized Multimedia Integration Language) [25] documents.

Oliveira et al. in [8] introduce the Hypermedia Model Based on Statecharts (HMBS). An HMBS multimedia application is described by a statechart that represents its structural hierarchy, regarding nodes and links, and its *human-consumable* components. Those components are expressed as information units, called pages and anchors. A statechart state is mapped into pages and transactions and events represent a set of possible link activations. For the presentation behavior verification, the statechart reachability tree for a specific configuration is used for verifying if some page is unreachable. In a similar manner, it is possible to determine if a certain group of pages is presented simultaneously searching state configurations containing the states associated to those pages. The reachability graph also allows the detection of configurations from which no other page may be reached or that present cyclical paths.

Felix in [12] presents an approach for the verification of temporal properties of multimedia documents through the application of model checking techniques. The work presents a notation used for the description of NCL relevant characteristics, as its temporal characteristics. Such a description is transformed into a timed automata net that indicates the document temporal behavior. The transformation creates a state machine for each document media and a synchronizer machine for each document link. A synchronizer machine is used for tying together the occurrence of events in the media node state machines. The work also presents a tool where the author can define temporal-logic formulas for verification of temporal properties. The temporal verification is done with a model-checker.

Bertino et al. in [3] propose an authoring model based on constraints. A multimedia application in that model consists of several sub-presentations, each one representing a topic composed of multimedia objects semantically related. All relations, temporal, layout and structural, are specified in a single step. So, the author defines a set of high-level constraints that will be used by the system to automatically group the objects into topics. The application generation process is responsible for three main tasks: consistency checking, presentation structure generation and topics generation.

The presentation consistency is checked by applying compatibility rules to each pair of constraints, detecting inconsistencies. Before checking, several inference rules are applied to the initial declaration to determine constraints that, even not defined explicitly, are consequences of the constraints defined. If an inconsistency arises, the system applies relaxation techniques, reducing the constraint set until the presentation becomes consistent or, when it is not possible, the author must review the declaration. The presentation structure generation process creates a structure that reflects the given application declaration. The structure is represented by a direct graph where each vertex represents a topic and the edges, connections among them. This process always returns a consistent graph, otherwise, the author should review the declaration. After this step, the system relates media objects to topics. According to the constraints, it creates connections among topics and checks the consistency before returning the final generated graph. If any failure occurs, the author is warned about the inconsistencies found.

Elias et al. in [11] present an algorithm for dynamic checking spatio-temporal relations. In the paper, dynamic means that the checking is done during presentation declaration. Temporal inconsistencies occur when a set of constrains can not be satisfied at the same time. Incompleteness of a constraint set occurs when there is a discontinuity in the presentation, that is, there is a media object set that is not reached during presentation. In case an inconsistency occurs in a constraint set, one of the constraints must be removed in order to obtain a consistent set. That removal is done by relating a priority value to each constraint. In case two inconsistent constraints present the same priority, relaxation techniques are applied to determine the constraint to be removed.

The paper presents two operators *TEMPORAL* and *SPATIAL*, to model temporal and spatial relations, respectively. The consistency checking is done by finding the minimum spanning tree T for the graph defined by media objects (vertices) and relationships among them (edges). In order to maintain the presentation consistency and the acyclic nature of T, a relationship that creates cycles must be removed. The choice is done by taking into account the priority of each relationship. For the completeness checking, all vertices must be found in the set that contains the first media object. If this search returns the vertex set of T, then all presentation media objects are reached directly or indirectly from the initial object. Otherwise, the algorithm presents an error message so the author can define restrictions that make the constraint set complete. With the use of the *SPATIAL* operator, it is possible to determine if A overlaps B and vice versa. The spatial consistency is checked the same way as the temporal one.

Bossi and Gaggi in [4,5] propose an authoring system that includes a semantic vefirication module for multimedia document temporal behavior evaluation. This is obtained by defining a formal semantics for the SMIL language [25]. The proposed semantics is defined through a set of inference rules inspired by Hoare logic. The main characteristic of Hoare logic is that it describes how a command, or code part, changes the computation state. So, the SMIL structure may be enriched with assertions expressing temporal properties that may be used during the authoring phase. Another application resulting from the defined formal semantics is the concept of equivalence, which guarantees that two sets of SMIL tags may be replaced, without changing the application behavior. The verification is done during the authoring phase, whenever the author wants or when he saves the application. This is done to diminish the occurrence of error messages during the application creation. The assertions defined by the semantics proposed in the paper specify the system temporal state before and after the execution of a SMIL tag or set of tags. For the system correctness verification, the tool applies axioms, also defined by the proposed semantics, in order to verify if a tag, or set of tags, correctly changes the system temporal state. Otherwise, it presents to the author the problem found so it can be corrected.

Júnior et al. in [17] use a model-driven approach for the presentation behavior verification of NCL documents. The verification is achieved by transforming an NCL document into a Petri Net. This transformation is done in two steps. In the first step, the document is represented in a language called FIACRE as a set of components (representing nodes) and processes (representing the behavior of a component). The second step transforms the FIACRE representation into a Petri Net. The verification uses a model-checking tool and temporal logic formulas representing the properties to be verified. The automation of the transformation process is left as a future work.

2.3 Related Work Comparison

Sections 2.1 and 2.2 presented works focusing on the verification of multimedia documents. The study of the literature cited in these sections helped us on the design of the approach presented in this paper. The main influences are: (i) choosing a formal approach, since it brings correctness, verified with tool support, of the approach by using precise descriptions of the multimedia language used for document authoring; (ii) the definition of the set of common properties for NCL documents presented in Section 3.

In this section, our approach and related work from Sections 2.1 and 2.2 are compared. A conceptual comparison is presented here, since most of the tools are not currently available for practical tests.

Each work focuses on either the structural *or* the behavioral verification of multimedia documents. It is important to guarantee that a multimedia document has been structurally verified before verifying its behavior, since a failure of the former may turn the latter impossible to be performed. However, it was not possible to identify if the works presented in Section 2.2 perform some form of structural verification prior to the document behavioral verification. We, on the other hand, propose a tool that addresses both the structural and behavioral verification of multimedia documents.

In [17, 18] the authors claim to be capable of verifying a multimedia document in an incremental way. Such kind of verification is not supported in this work, where the complete document is verified.

3   Verification Properties

In [9, Chapter 2] we studied different approaches to the verification of multimedia documents. We identify the properties in [8, 18, 19] as the most relevant ones and the set of properties discussed below is based on them. The properties in [18] are similar (and gave origin) to the structural properties here presented. On the other hand, the resource property was discussed in [19] and the reachability property in [8]. Besides, termination properties were found in both works.

Our set of properties are classified here as structural or behavioral properties. Structural properties are the ones used for representing the authoring language syntax rules defined by its grammar and structural invariants induced by its static semantics. Each structural property gives origin to a set of equations representing invariants in the rewriting logic theory, one for each element of the authoring language where the given property is applicable.

The **syntactic** property specifies that the lexical and syntactic structure of a document should be well-formed and in accordance to the authoring language's grammar. For example, the XML tags [24] used must be correctly closed and in the language *namespace*. The **hierarchical** property specifies that every document element must only contain valid child elements and in the correct cardinality. The **attribute** property specifies that every document element must only contain valid attributes and the required ones must be defined. It also specifies that every element identifier must be unique and attributes with related values must follow the constraints defined by the authoring language (as an example, suppose attributes "type" and "subtype").

The **reference** property specifies constraints on references between elements (such as a media or a composition of medias). The **compositionality** property specifies that elements inside a composition can not refer to the ones outside. The **composition nesting** property specifies that compositions can not create loops. The **reuse** property specifies that elements being reused can not create loops.

Behavioral properties are used for representing desired document presentation behaviors. Each behavioral property gives rise to a temporal logic formula [6].

The **reachability** property specifies that every document element has to be reached during a document's execution. The **anchor termination** property specifies that a document's element presentation must end. The **document termination** property specifies that the execution of the document as a whole must end, up to an upper bound duration. The document execution ends if every anchor inside the document end and there is no execution loops inside the document (for example an anchor restarting its presentation every time it ends). The **resource** property specifies that two distinct anchors (that is, references to media elements or to parts of it) should not use the same resource simultaneously, avoiding their superposition.

4   NCL Semantics

4.1   Rewriting Logic

A *rewriting logic theory* is a tuple $\mathcal{R} = (\Sigma, E, R)$, with:

- (Σ, E) an equational theory with function symbols Σ and equations E; and
- R a set of *labeled rewrite rules* of the general form

$$r : t \rightarrow t'$$

with r a label and t, t' Σ-terms which may contain variables in a countable set X of variables which we assume fixed in what follows; that is, t and t' are elements of the term algebra $T_\Sigma(X)$. In particular, their corresponding sets of variables, $vars(t)$, $vars(t')$ are both contained in X.

Given $\mathcal{R} = (\Sigma, E, R)$, the sentences that $\mathcal{R}$ proves are rewrites of the form, $t \rightarrow t'$, with $t, t' \in T_\Sigma(X)$, which are following *rules of deduction*:

- **Reflexivity**. For each $t \in T_\Sigma(X)$,

$$\overline{t \rightarrow t}$$

- **Equality**.

$$\frac{u \rightarrow v \qquad E \vdash u = u' \qquad E \vdash v = v'}{u' \rightarrow v'}$$

- **Congruence**. For each $f : k_1 \ldots k_n \rightarrow k$ in Σ, and $t_i, t_i' \in T_\Sigma(X)$, $1 \leq i \leq n$,

$$\frac{t_1 \rightarrow t_1' \qquad \cdots \qquad t_n \rightarrow t_n'}{f(t_1, \ldots, t_n) \rightarrow f(t_1', \ldots, t_n')}$$

- **Replacement**. For each rule $r : t \rightarrow t'$ in R, with, say, $vars(t) \cup vars(t') = \{x_1, \ldots, x_n\}$, and for each substitution $\theta : \{x_1, \ldots, x_n\} \rightarrow T_\Sigma(X)$, with $\theta(x_l) = p_l$, $1 \leq l \leq n$, then

$$\frac{p_1 \rightarrow p_1' \qquad \cdots \qquad p_n \rightarrow p_n'}{\theta(t) \rightarrow \theta'(t')}$$

where for $1 \leq i \leq n$, $\theta'(x_i) = p_i'$.
- **Transitivity**.

$$\frac{t_1 \rightarrow t_2 \qquad t_2 \rightarrow t_3}{t_1 \rightarrow t_3}$$

4.2 NCL Syntax

NCL is a XML-based [23] language, which uses XML elements to represent the entities defined by the *Nested Context Model* (NCM) [20].

An NCL document is divided in two parts, its *head* and its *body*. The document head is where layout information is defined (e.g. regions of the screen in pixels and presentation descriptors such as sound volume). The document body is where the document content (i.e. its *nodes*) and behavior (i.e. its *links*) are defined. NCL defines two types of nodes: content nodes and composite nodes. A content node represents a media object inside the document, while a composite node represents a grouping of other nodes (content and/or composite). A content node in NCL is called *media*. A composite node, in NCL, can be either a *context* or a *switch*. A switch node is a special kind of node used to define alternative content to be presented, therefore only one of its inner nodes are presented at a time. Links define a relationship among nodes inside the same context.

NCL provides the possibility of defining interfaces for each node. A node interface is used to allow links be defined over parts of nodes. The interface for an NCL media is an *anchor*. NCL contexts define *ports* which maps an interface to the interface of an inner node.

Figure 2 illustrates the structure of a simple NCL document pictorially and Figure 4 exemplifies NCL's syntax.

4.3 NCL Static Semantics

NCL static semantics is given by the equational theory $N_S = \langle \Sigma, E \rangle$ where (i) Σ denotes the signature of N_S declaring NCL elements, such as regions, contexts, medias, anchors, together with their attributes, types and parent element, and (ii) E denotes a set of equations representing the invariants that any given NCL document must fulfill. An NCL document is interpreted as a term t such that $N_S \vdash inv(t)$, where inv is an equation representing the conjunction of all NCL invariants in N_S. An NCL document is said well-typed when $N_S \vdash inv(t) = true$ and ill-typed otherwise.

The invariants specify the hierarchical property, attribute property, reference property, compositionally property, composition nesting property and reuse property, informally discussed in Section 3. These properties apply to different elements in NCL. For instance, we have defined invariants representing the reference property for port, bind, and mapping NCL elements. Equation 1 specifies the invariant for a bind element. A bind element references a node and an interface. The invariant verifies if the interface is a child element of the node in a given bind element,

$$eq\ inv\_refer\_bind(ei) = (getElement(getAttributeComponent(ei)) \neq empty) \Rightarrow$$
$$(getElement(getAttributeInterface(ei))in \qquad (1)$$
$$getChildrenReuse(getAttributeComponent(ei))).$$

where ei is an identifier for the bind element inside a term t representing an NCL document. The complete set of invariants defined for the NCL language is available in [9].

4.4 NCL Dynamic Semantics

NCL dynamic semantics is given by the rewriting logic theory $N_D = \langle \Sigma, E, R \rangle$ where Σ denotes the signature of N_D declaring the state of a document, which is comprised by the states of the anchors that compose the given document. Anchors are the smallest information units of an NCL document.

From one hand, the signature Σ in N_D is simpler than Σ in N_S since presentation attributes are disregarded as they are not important for the specification of the dynamic semantics of an NCL document. Moreover, N_D does not define *composite* nodes nor *content* nodes which are essentially groups of anchors.

On the other hand, state attributes are necessary to specify the state of an anchor. Therefore, Σ in N_D includes part of Σ in N_S and extends it with state information.

Every anchor is associated to its presentation, selection or attribution events, where each event is in one of the following states: *occurring*, *sleeping* and *paused*. Each multimedia event follows the NCM (NCL's reference model) state machine shown in Figure 1.

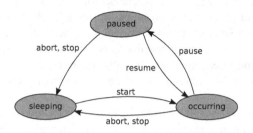

Fig. 1. Multimedia event state machine

The state of anchors may be changed by links. A link has conditions and actions. Conditions must be satisfied in order to activate the link and actions are executed as the link is active, modifying the document's state. A link condition is triggered by multimedia event transitions related to its source anchors and may define tests over anchor states or values. A link action defines a multimedia event transition that will be induced over a multimedia event state related to its target anchor. A link action may also define a delay in time before it is applied.

The state of the presentation of a multimedia document, specified in Definition 1 and denoted by $\rho \vdash d$ with $\rho \in Env$ and $d \in DocState$, is represented in N_D by the environment resulting from a document's declaration and the document' state. The document environment ρ is comprised by the definition of the document anchors, links and its initial actions that should be applied as a document's presentation begins. The document state d is given by the state of every anchor inside the document and, possibly, pending actions to be applied on delayed anchors.

Definition 1 (NCL document).

$$DocState = AnchorSet \times PendingLinkActionSet,$$
$$Env = (LinkId \mapsto_{fin} LinkSet) \times (DocAnchors \mapsto_{fin} AnchorSet) \times$$
$$(InitActions \mapsto_{fin} PendingLinkActionSet).$$

Sets E and R in N_D specify the document's behavior. The presentation of a document is formalized by Rule 2 that specifies the relation *docPresentation* defined in R in N_D.

$$\frac{elapse(d_1) = d_2 \qquad d_2 \rightarrow_{natural} \langle as_3, ps_3, es \rangle \qquad \langle as_3, ps_3, es \rangle \rightarrow_{applyLinks} \langle as_4, ps_4, es' \rangle}{d_1 = \langle as_1, ps_1 \rangle \rightarrow_{docPresentation} \langle as_4, ps_4 \rangle} \quad (2)$$

A document state (d_i) is given by the state of its anchors (as_i) and delayed link actions (ps_i). Every anchor and delayed action has a countdown clock, representing its presentation duration and its remaining delay, respectively. Function *elapse*, defined in

E in N_D, uses the value of these clocks (in d_1) to calculate the maximum leap that can be performed, i.e. the smallest clock value among the active anchors and delayed actions. After calculating the leap value, function *elapse* decrements this value from the anchor and action clocks (resulting in d_2).

Relation *natural*, defined in R in N_D, checks for event occurrences on anchors (in d_2). It can be the end of an anchor presentation (once its clock reaches zero) or the selection of an anchor. Since every anchor being presented can be selected by the user of the multimedia document, concurrent document states will be created, representing the permutation of the selected anchors. Finally, relation *natural* applies the actions whose delay has ended thus changing the state of document anchors (resulting in d_3 and ps_3)

Event occurrences (es), resulting from the evaluation of *natural*, may trigger links in a document. Relation *applyLinks*, defined in R in N_D, evaluates the document links that are enabled by these event occurrences. A link is considered enabled when its conditions match the document state. The application of a link consists of changing the state of anchor presentation, selection or assignment events (resulting in as_4, ps_4 and es'). All enabled links are applied to all possible orders, so different document states can be reached after a link application.

Definition 2 specifies the transition system induced by theory N_D.

Definition 2 (The transition system of an NCL document). *Given an NCL document d, the declarations resulting from N induce a transition system $\mathcal{S}_N(d)$ as follows,*

$$\mathcal{S}_N(d) = (\Gamma, \rightarrow_{docPresentation}), where$$
$$\Gamma = \rho \vdash d, \rho \in Env, d \in DocState.$$

4.5   The Behavioral Semantics of an NCL Document

In order to obtain a transition system for a given NCL document we defined a transformation $\tau : \Sigma_{N_S} \rightarrow \Sigma_N$, where N is a rewriting logic theory that that extends N_D with additional signature specifying the initial state of the given document together with sorts and operations that represent the link relations among the many anchors that a document has. The transformation τ discards elements which are not relevant for document behavior. The transformation "flattens" the document structure by: (i) replacing nodes from the document structure by the set of anchors within the document's nodes, and (ii) adjusting links to relate anchors and not nodes.

Node Flattening. For each content node the flattening process gathers the anchors defined for it. For every content node there is an anchor representing the node itself, called lambda anchor. The flattening node process produces, for a given content node, the lambda anchor together with all anchors declared for the content node.

For each composite element (context, switch and the body of an NCL document) the transformation computes which anchors are related to the given composite by hierarchical composition. Formally speaking, we compute the transitive closure of the hierarchical composition relation for each composite. This relation is used later on by the link adjustment phase so that links relate only anchors and not composite elements. For example, in Figure 2, context C_1 is related to anchors representing nodes N_1 and N_2.

A composite may have several ports. Therefore, we need to identify, in the transitive closure of the hierarchical composition relation of a given composite, which anchors are associated with the ports of the given composite. This information is important in the link adjustment phase so that only such anchors are started when the composite is started by a link.

Theorem 1. *Document structure is preserved by node flattening.*

Proof. (Sketch.) Anchors are the smallest elements of NCL documents. They are preserved by the flattening process. NCL element composition is a hierarchical relation. The flattening composite process computes the transitive closure of the hierarchical composition relation. Therefore, all content information is preserved by this transformation modulo hierarchical structure, which is not relevant for behavioral semantics. This step computes the necessary information for preservation of all actions over nodes which are preserved by link adjustment.   □

Link Adjustment. Once the anchors of each node (composite or otherwise) have been calculated, we only need to adjust the links such that the anchors of a given node are referenced in a link instead of the node itself. Moreover, all the actions that apply to a node are preserved in link adjustment taking in consideration eventual delays among the presentation of the anchors.

Theorem 2. *Document behavior is preserved by link adjustment.*

Proof. (Sketch.) Link adjustment replaces content nodes and composite nodes by their associated anchors on each link. This step also makes sure that actions are properly applied to anchors. For a content node, the start action must preserve the order of anchor presentation. If an anchor has a delay in its presentation, with respect to the lambda anchor, such a delay must be included in the link action. (See Section 4.4.) For a composite node, the application of the start action is preserved by link adjustment because only the anchors identified as associated with the ports of the composite are enacted. For the remaining actions, all the anchors in the transitive closure of the composite node are enacted.   □

Example. Figure 2 presents an NCL document in pictorial form. The document defines two nodes N_1 and N_2, both inside composition C_1, and port P_1 that maps to node N_1. That means that node N_1 will be executed as the document (composition C_1) begins. The document also defines link L_1 that will start the presentation of node N_2 when node N_1 is selected by the user.

Figure 3 presents the representation of the document in Figure 2 as a term in N_D, that is, after the application of transformation $\tau : \Sigma_{N_S} \to \Sigma_{N_D}$. Notice that nodes N_1 and N_2 are represented by their lambda anchors (a_{N_1} and a_{N_2}). Link L_1 is represented as a relation, which takes the state of the NCL document from a state where anchor

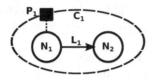

Fig. 2. NCL document example

$$doc = (A_{doc}, L_{doc}, I)$$
$$A_{doc} = \{a_{N_1}, a_{N_2}\}$$
$$L_{doc} = \{((a_{N_1}, selection, start) \rightarrow (a_{N_2}, presentation, start))\}$$
$$I_{doc} = \{(a_{N_1}, presentation, start)\}$$

Fig. 3. N_D document example

a_{N_1} is selected to a state where anchor a_{N_2} is being presented. The port mapping is represented by an initial action that starts anchor a_{N_1} as the document execution begins.

5   NCL Analyzer

We have implemented a verification tool for NCL documents as a Java library called aNaa (API for NCL Authoring and Analysis). Further details about the API architecture and its implementation are available in [9]. With the aNaa API we have been able to process all NCL documents in the NCL Club[1], which do not use any external language to implement node behavior. NCL Club is a repository for NCL applications built by the NCL community. The results given by aNaa are encouraging based on the problems we have found (if it was the case) for each document. Each problem found was confirmed by a manual inspection of the application. Besides a web interface built on top of aNaa library is available online[2] for a massive test of aNaa with respect to real user acceptance.

The verification is performed by aNaa in three steps as follows. From a given NCL document d, aNaa creates its representation as a rewriting theory $d \in \Sigma_{N_S}$ and applies the equations $e_i \in E_{N_S}$ representing the NCL invariants to d, as described in Section 4.3. If an invariant does not hold in d, aNaa presents a message to the author indicating that e_i has failed. If all invariants hold in d then aNaa applies the transformation $\tau : \Sigma_{N_S} \rightarrow \Sigma_N$ to d, as described in Section 4.5, creating a term in N where temporal formulas representing the behavioral properties in Section 3 are verified using model checking.

The semantics described in Section 4 has been implemented in the Maude [7] system. The implementation is quite direct since Maude is an implementation of rewriting logic. The rewriting system in Maude is bissimilar to the transition system in Definition 2 essentially because all state information is preserved by the transformation to Maude

---

[1] http://club.ncl.org.br
[2] http://www.midiacom.uff.br/~joel/anaa4web

and every transition in the transition system induced by N gives rise to a rewrite in the transition system induced by the generated Maude code.[3]

We now present a very simple document, where structural properties (reference, compositionality and reuse) and behavioral properties (reachability, anchor and document termination) do not hold. Figure 4 presents the NCL code for that document.

```
1  <ncl id='scenario' xmlns='http ://www. ncl . org . br /NCL3 . 0/ EDTVProfile '>
2      <head>
3          <regionBase>
4              <region id='reg '/>
5          </regionBase>
6          <descriptorBase>
7              <descriptor id='desc' region='reg '/>
8          </descriptorBase>
9      </head>
10     <body>
11         <port id='p_body' component='fig' interface='p_inner '/>
12         <media id='video' src='video.mp4' descriptor='desc '/>
13         <context id='inner' refer='inner '>
14             <port id='p_inner' component='fig '/>
15             <media id='fig' src='fig1 .png' descriptor='desc '/>
16         </context>
17     </body>
18  </ncl>
```

Fig. 4. Example document

Structural Analysis. The reference property does not hold because port *p_body* makes reference to node *fig* and interface *p_inner*, which is not a child of node *fig*. The compositionality property does not hold because port *p_body* makes reference to node *fig*, which is not in the same composition as *p_body*. The reuse property does not hold because context *inner* reuses itself through its attribute *refer*. Each problem is identified by aNaa with the invariants shown in Figure 5, instances of the reference, compositionality and composition nesting properties, where $ei \in ElementId$.

To correct the identified problems, the author should change attribute *component* of port *p_body* to *inner*. The port remains mapping to node *fig* but now respects the compositionality property since context *inner* is one of its siblings. It also respects the reference property since attribute *interface* now makes reference to an interface of the node referred in attribute *component*. Finally, the author should remove attribute *refer* from context *inner* so it does not reuse itself anymore.

Behavioral Analysis. The reachability property does not hold because media *video* is never presented during document execution. Also, both the anchor and document termination properties do not hold because media *fig*, which started its presentation at document initialization, never ends its presentation. The document environment ρ in N_D (see Section 4.4) resulting from the document in Figure 4 is presented in Figure 6.

Each problem is identified by the Maude model checker with the linear temporal logic (LTL) formulas described in Figure 7. Syntax F and G denote their homonymous

---

[3] As a more technical note, all rewritings occur at the top level term, that is, the congruence rule of the rewriting logic calculus is controlled. (See Section 4.1.)

```
1 | — Reference  property  instance  invariant
2 | (getElement(getAttributeComponent(ei)) =/= empty) implies
3 | (getElement(getAttributeInterface(ei)) in getChildrenReuse(getAttributeComponent(
  |     ei)))
4 |
5 | — Compositionality  property  instance  invariant
6 | (getParent(ei) =/= empty) implies
7 | (getElement(getAttributeComponent(ei)) in getChildren(getParent(ei)))
8 |
9 | — Reuse  property  instance  invariant
10| not(getElement(ei) in refer(getElement(ei)))
```

Fig. 5. Invariants for the example document

```
1 | mod NCLDOC is
2 |     eq DocAnchors = CONTENT(video | sleeping, 0, 0, −, 100, −)
3 |         CONTENT(fig | sleeping, 0, 0, −, INF, −).
4 |
5 |     eq InitActions = ACTION(fig, pre, start) .
6 |
7 |     eq DocLinks = none .
8 | endm
```

Fig. 6. Document environment resulting from the example document

```
1 | — Reachability  property  instance  formula
2 |     F pre−occurring(video)
3 |
4 | — Anchor  termination  property  instance  formula
5 |     GF pre−occurring(fig1) implies GF pre−sleeping(fig)
6 |
7 | — Document  termination  property  instance  formula
8 |     GF doc−end
```

Fig. 7. LTL properties for the example document

modal operators, *pre-occurring*, *pre-sleeping* and *doc-end* are predicates specified over the document state that hold when the given anchors (*video* or *fig*) reach their homonymous state, where the prefix *pre* denotes a state in the presentation state machine of an anchor. The verification of the termination property is bound to a maximum document duration which is a parameter of the Maude specification.

To correct the reachability problem, the author should either create another port mapping to media *video* or create a link to start the presentation of media *video* as the presentation of media *fig* starts. To solve the remaining problems, the author should either create a link to stop the presentation of media *fig* as the presentation of media *video* stops or define an explicit duration for media *fig* in its descriptor.

6 Final Remarks

Multimedia document verification is an important task with the growing market of digital TV. The Nested Context Language is an important authoring language in digital TV application development in Brazil and worldwide. Since NCL documents maybe understood as finite transition systems standard model-based techniques apply to their verification. In this paper we discuss NCL's formal semantics and its implementation in a verification tool development in the Maude system. We have been able to process all NCL documents in the NCL Club[4], a repository for NCL applications built by the NCL community, that do not use any external language to implement node behavior. The results are encouraging based on the problems we have found and the efficiency of the prototype.

Future work points to two important directions: first, based on preliminary studies, we believe that the formal semantics we propose in Section 4 may be able to represent other multimedia authoring languages such as SMIL [25] and HTML 5 [26]. Second, we plan to support for the verification of user defined properties.

References

1. ABNT. Digital Terrestrial Television — Data Coding and Transmission Specification for Digital Broadcasting — Part 2: Ginga-NCL for Fixed and Mobile Receivers — XML Application Language for Application Coding. ABNT 15606-2:2011 (2011)
2. Baral, C., Gelfond, M.: Logic programming and knowledge representation. The Journal of Logic Programming 19, 73–148 (1994)
3. Bertino, E., Ferrari, E., Perego, A., Santi, D.: A Constraint-Based Approach for the Authoring of Multi-Topic Multimedia Presentations. In: ICME, pp. 578–581 (2005)
4. Bossi, A., Gaggi, O.: Enriching SMIL with assertions for temporal validation. In: ACM Multimedia, pp. 107–116 (2007)
5. Bossi, A., Gaggi, O.: Analysis and verification of SMIL documents. Multimedia Systems 17(6), 487–506 (2011)
6. Clarke, E.M., Grumberg, O., Peled, D.A.: Model Checking. The MIT Press (2000)
7. Clavel, M., Durán, F., Eker, S., Lincoln, P., Martí-Oliet, N., Meseguer, J., Talcott, C.: All About Maude - A High-Performance Logical Framework. LNCS, vol. 4350. Springer, Heidelberg (2007)
8. de Oliveira, M., Turine, M., Masiero, P.: A statechart-based model for hypermedia applications. In: ACM TOIS, pp. 28–52 (2001)
9. dos Santos, J.A.F.: Multimedia and hypermedia document validation and verification using a model-driven approach. Master's thesis, UFF (2012)
10. dos Santos, J.A.F., Braga, C., Muchaluat-Saade, D.C.: A Model-driven Approach for the Analysis of Multimedia Documents. In: Eisenecker, U.W., Bucholdt, C. (eds.) Proceedings of the Doctoral Symposium of the 5th International Conference on Software Language Engineering 2012. CEUR Workshop Proceedings, vol. 935, pp. 37–44. ceur-ws.org (September 2012) ISSN 1613-0073, http://ceur-ws.org/Vol-935/p_07.pdf
11. Elias, S., Easwarakumar, K., Chbeir, R.: Dynamic consistency checking for temporal and spatial relations in multimedia presentations. In: ACM SAC, pp. 1380–1384 (2006)

---

[4] http://club.ncl.org.br

12. Felix, M.F.: Formal Analysis of Software Models Oriented by Architectural Abstractions. PhD thesis, PUC-Rio (2004) (in Portuguese)
13. Honorato, G.S.C., Barbosa, S.D.J.: NCL-Inspector: Towards Improving NCL Code. In: ACM SAC, pp. 1946–1947 (2010)
14. ISO/IEC 15938. Multimedia content description interface (2001)
15. ISO/IEC 15938-9. Multimedia content description interface - Part 9: profiles and levels (2005)
16. ITU H.761. Nested Context Language (NCL) and Ginga-NCL for IPTV services (2009), http://www.itu.int/rec/T-REC-H.761-200904-S
17. Júnior, D.P., Farines, J., Koliver, C.: An Approach to Verify Live NCL Applications. In: WebMedia, pp. 223–232 (2012)
18. Neto, J.R.C., Santos, R.C.M., Neto, C.S.S., Teixeira, M.M.: Método de Validação Estrutural e Contextual de Documentos NCL. In: WebMedia, pp. 1–8 (2011) (in Portuguese)
19. Santos, C., Soares, L., de Souza, G., Courtiat, J.: Design methodology and formal validation of hypermedia documents. In: ACM Multimedia, pp. 39–48 (1998)
20. Soares, L.F.G., Rodrigues, R.F., Muchaluat-Saade, D.C.: Modeling, authoring and formatting hypermedia documents in the HyperProp system. Multimedia Systems, 118–134 (2000)
21. Troncy, R., Bailer, W., Höffernig, M., Hausenblas, M.: VAMP: a service for validating MPEG-7 descriptions w.r.t. to formal profile definitions. Multimedia Tools and Applications 46(2), 307–329 (2010)
22. W3C Recommendation. OWL Web ontology language: reference (2004)
23. W3C Recommendation. XML Schema Part 0: Primer, 2nd edn. (2004)
24. W3C Recommendation. Extensible Markup Language (XML) 1.0, 5th edn. (2008)
25. W3C Recommendation. Synchronized Multimedia Integration Language - SMIL 3.0 Specification (2008)
26. W3C Recommendation. HTML5: A vocabulary and associated APIs for HTML and XHTML (2011)

On the Use of SPIN for Studying the Behavior of Nested Petri Nets*

Mirtha Lina Fernández Venero and Flávio Soares Corrêa da Silva

Department of Computer Science, University of São Paulo, Brazil, 05508-090

Abstract. Nested Petri nets have been applied for modelling interaction protocols, mobility, adaptive systems and interorganizational workflows. However, few results have been reported on the use of automated tools for analyzing the behavior of these nets. In this paper we present a translation from a subclass of recursive nested Petri nets into PROMELA and explain how some properties of these nets can be studied using SPIN model checker.

Keywords: nested Petri nets, model checking, SPIN.

1 Introduction

Petri nets (PNs) are one of the most widely used formalisms for analyzing concurrent and distributed systems. The key to their success is the combination of few and simple primitives, a convenient graphical representation and several tools for simulation and verification. Therefore, they have been extended in several ways in order to increase the modelling power. One of the ideas applied to complex models was the use of nesting and recursion. For instance, recursive nets and nets within nets have been used to specify interaction protocols and mobility in the context of distributed multi-agent systems [25,19,13,12].

The nested Petri nets (NPNs) form a representative class of this kind of nets. In a NPN, the tokens may be PNs which fire their transitions autonomously or in synchrony with other net tokens [16]. This provides a high degree of modularity and flexibility for the dynamic creation, transportation and removal of concurrent processes. Therefore, its application has been extended to areas such as the coordination of inter-organizational workflows [21] and adaptive systems [18]. NPNs are more powerful than classical PNs and some properties (e.g. reachability and boundedness) are undecidable [15]. However, for important subclasses, such as the multi-level nets and the recursive nested nets with autonomous elements, termination and the inevitability problem can be decided [16]. In spite of this fact, to best of our knowledge, there is no automated tool for analyzing the behavior of NPNs.

---

* This work has been supported by the São Paulo Research Foundation (FAPESP) under the grant 2010/52505-0.

J. Iyoda and L. de Moura (Eds.): SBMF 2013, LNCS 8195, pp. 83–98, 2013.

In this paper we propose the use of SPIN for this purpose. SPIN [10] is one of most successful tools for simulation and verification of concurrent and distributed software systems. Given a finite-state model of the system behavior, SPIN verifies it against temporal properties by an exhaustive inspection of all possible system states. If some property is violated, a counterexample is provided. SPIN uses a C-like language to specify models called PROMELA (Process Meta Language). Unlike other model checkers, SPIN allows recursive processes; besides, its buffered channels are suitable for implementing the synchronizations in a NPN. The model checking approach suffers from the state-space explosion problem, but clever algorithms have been developed in SPIN to deal with it.

The subclass of NPNs that we address in this paper is introduced in Section 2 and its translation into PROMELA is presented in Section 3. Section 4 explains how termination, boundedness and some reachability properties can be studied using SPIN. Section 5 illustrates the feasibility of our translation with an example of a NPN modelling an interoganizational workflow. Section 6 discusses the related work and draws some concluding remarks and future work.

2   Nested Petri Nets

A Petri net [20] is a 4-tuple $N = (P, T, A, W)$ where P and T are non-empty, finite and disjoint sets of places and transitions resp; $A \subseteq (P \times T) \cup (T \times P)$ is a set of arcs and W is a function defined from A to multisets of uncolored tokens (black dots). A *marking* of a N is a function attaching a multiset of tokens to each place. Transitions represent events (called *firings*) which may change the marking of the net according to W. The tokens in a PN have no structure or information. In colored Petri nets (CPNs) [11], each place has a type; thus, it may host tokens with different data values, i.e. colors. The arcs are labelled by multiset expressions containing variables. Therefore, firing of a transition is conditioned to the binding of the variables in the input arcs.

Nested Petri nets [17] are CPNs in which tokens can also be Petri nets and thus they may fire their own internal transitions. More precisely, a NPN is a tuple $(SN, EN_1, \ldots, EN_n)$ of CPNs, one of them called *system net* (SN) and the rest *element nets*. Each EN_i is considered as a type whose set of values consists of marked net tokens. The firing of a transition t is performed according to the classical PN rules. But in addition, a net token may synchronize the firing with other net tokens at the same place (*horizontal synchronization step*) or with the parent net (*vertical synchronization step*). The synchronization is defined by means of labels that are attached to transitions.

In this paper, we deal with the subclass of *NPNs with autonomous elements*, i.e. those where the vertical steps remove the net tokens involved. Therefore, the next definition is a simplified version of the one provided in [17]. As usual in CPNs, we have a set of basic types Σ and a set of basic constants Σ_c belonging to these types. The element nets represent both types and constants. The places are divided into two kinds, places with basic type or net type. For simplicity, we have avoided the use of arities for places; hence the horizontal synchronization is restricted to two net tokens[1]. We slightly adapt the definition for sharing some basic places of SN with the element nets. This way, the system net can control the firing of some transitions in the net tokens. Nevertheless, no shared place can be an input of a labelled transition. We assume that arc expressions are multisets over constants, basic-typed variables and the integer 1. The latter is used to denote a single token, regardless its value. We denote as $Var(m)$ the set of variables occurring in the multiset m.

Definition 1. *Let* $N = (\Sigma, P_s, L, (EN_0, EN_1, \ldots, EN_n))$ *be a NPN s.t.* Σ *is a finite set of basic types,* P_s *is a finite set of shared places and* L *is the disjoint union of the sets of labels* L_h *and* L_v. *The set* L_v *is s.t.*

- *for each* $l \in L_v$, *there is a complementary label* $\bar{l} \in L_v$ *s.t.* $\bar{\bar{l}} = l$ *and*
- *for all* $l_1, l_2 \in L$, $l_1 \neq l_2$ *implies* $\bar{l}_1 \neq \bar{l}_2$.

For all $i = 0 \ldots n$, $EN_i = (P_i, V_i, C_i, I_i, T_i, \Lambda_i, A_i, W_i)$ *is a colored Petri net, called net component, where*

- EN_0 *is called the* system net, *denoted as* SN,
- P_i *is a finite set of places s.t.* $P_s \subset P_i$ *if* $i = 0$ *and* $P_i \cap P_s = \emptyset$ *if* $i > 0$,
- V_i *is a set of variables,*
- $C_i : P_i \cup V_i \to \Sigma \cup \mathcal{P}(\{EN_1, \ldots, EN_n\})$ *is a type function s.t. for all* $x \in V_i$ *either* $C_i(x) \subseteq \Sigma$ *or* $C_i(x) = \{EN_1, \ldots, EN_n\}$. *Furthermore, for all* $p \in P_s$, $C_0(p) \in \Sigma$,
- I_i *is the initial function defined from* P_i *into multisets over* Σ_c *s.t. for all* $p \in P_i$, $I_i(p) \subseteq C_i(p)$,
- T_i *is a finite set of transitions s.t.* $P_i \cap T_i = \emptyset$,
- Λ_i *is a partial function from* T_i *to* L,
- $A_i \subseteq ((P_s \cup P_i) \times T_i) \cup (T_i \times (P_s \cup P_i))$ *is a set of arcs s.t. for all* $(p,t) \in A_i$, *if* $\Lambda_i(t)$ *is defined then* $p \in P_i$,
- W_i *is an arc expression function defined from* A_i *to multisets over* $V_i \cup \Sigma_c \cup \{EN_1, \ldots, EN_n\}$ *s.t.*
  - *(a) the type of each element in the multiset of an input (output) arc must be included in the type of the corresponding input (output) place,*
  - *(b) there are no net constants in input arc expressions,*
  - *(c) every variable has at most one occurrence in each input arc expression,*
  - *(d) given two different input arcs* (p_1, t_1) *and* (p_2, t_2), $Var(W_i(p_1, t_1)) \cap Var(W_i(p_2, t_2)) = \emptyset$;
  - *(e) for each variable* $x \in Var(W_i(t, q))$, $C_i(x) \subseteq \Sigma$ *and there should be one input arc of* t *s.t.* $x \in Var(W_i(p, t))$.

Example 1. Figure 1 depicts a NPN with two net components SN and F. Places are drawn as ellipses and transitions as bars. We omit the arc labels $\{1\}$ as well as the braces for multisets of a single element. The element net F, adapted from [17], simulates the recursive calls for computing the factorial function. Here F shares

---

[1] Our translation can be extended to allow horizontal steps between several net tokens.

two places from SN: $p1$ which initially may store $a \geq 0$ black tokens and $p5$ which is initially empty. The places $p3$ and $p7$ are net-typed while the rest are uncolored. The net SN simulates the computation of the factorial of an integer $0 \leq b \leq a$.

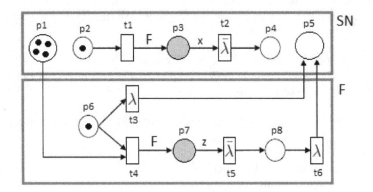

Fig. 1. Example of NPN for simulating the factorial computation calls

Markings. A *marking of an element net* EN_i over N, $1 \leq i \leq n$, is inductively defined as follows.

- A function M, mapping each place $p \in P_i$ to a finite multiset over Σ is a marking of EN_i over N. The pair (EN_i, M) is called a marked element net or a net token of EN_i.
- Let $\bar{\Sigma}$ be a set of marked element nets. Then, a function mapping each place $p \in P_i$ to a finite multiset over $\bar{\Sigma} \cup \Sigma$, is also marking of EN_i over N.

A *marking* of EN_0 over N is a function mapping each place $p \in P_0$ to a finite multiset over $\bar{\Sigma} \cup \Sigma$. Any marking must agree with the type definition of the places. Hence, for all $p \in P_i$, if $C_i(p) \in \Sigma$, then $M(p)$ is a multiset over $C_i(p)$; otherwise $M(p)$ is a multiset of net tokens of $C_i(p)$. To avoid confusion, it can be assumed that places, transitions, variables and arcs of two net tokens of the same element net are different. Notice that, no net token of SN is allowed and places belonging to P_s are shared by all net tokens.

A *marking of a NPN* N is a marking of SN. The initial marking of any net component is obtained from the initial function (I_i) which, by definition, has no net token. The constant EN_i represents the marked net (EN_i, I_i). The initial marking of N, obtained from I_0, is denoted as M_0.

Occurrence and Replacement. A net token $nt' = (EN_i, M')$ occurs in M if there is a place p s.t. either $nt' \in M(p)$ or there exists $(EN_j, M'') \in M(p)$ and nt' occurs in M''. The occurrence of two net tokens at the same place in a marking is defined analogously. The replacement of nt' in M by a net token $nt'_1 = (EN_i, M'_1)$ (denoted as $M[nt' \to nt'_1]$) is defined as the marking M_1 s.t. $M_1(p) = M(p) - \{nt'\} \cup \{nt'_1\}$ if $nt' \in M(p)$; $M_1(p) = M(p) - \{(EN_j, M'')\} \cup \{(EN_j, M''[nt' \to nt'_1])\}$ if nt' occurs in M''; and $M_1(p') = M(p')$ otherwise.

Bindings. Let t be a transition in a net token or the system net of N. Let $EN = (P, C, I, T, \Lambda, A, W, V)$ be the CPN s.t. $t \in T$. We write $Var(t)$ for the set of all variables occurring in input arcs of t. Hereafter, we assume that $W(p,t)$ (resp. $W(t,p)$) is the empty set if $(p,t) \notin A$ (resp. $(t,p) \notin A$). A *binding* for t is a function b assigning to each variable $x \in Var(t)$ a value from $\bar{\Sigma} \cup \Sigma$ (of the corresponding type). It may be applied to multisets in a straightforward way. The set $\{b(x) \mid x \in Var(t) \wedge C(x) \notin \Sigma\}$ are the net tokens involved in t w.r.t. b.

Firings. Let M be marking of a NPN N. A transition $t \in T_0$ is *enabled* in M w.r.t. a binding b, if for all $a = (p,t) \in A_0$, $b(W_0(a)) \subseteq M(p)$. In this case, t may fire. After the firing, a new marking M_n is obtained s.t. for any place $p \in P_0$, $M_n(p) = M(p) - b(W_0(p,t)) \cup b(W_0(t,p))$.

Let (EN_i, M') be a net token occurring in M at some place p'. A transition t of (EN_i, M') is *enabled* in M w.r.t. a binding b, if for all $a = (p,t) \in A_i$, $b(W_i(a)) \subseteq M'(p)$. If t fires, a new marking M'' is obtained from M' s.t. for any place $p \in P_i$, $M''(p) = M'(p) - b(W_i(p,t)) \cup b(W_i(t,p))$. Furthermore, a new marking M_n is obtained from M s.t. for any place $p \in P_s$, $M_n(p) = M(p) \cup b(W_i(t,p))$; for any place $p \notin P_s \cup \{p'\}$, $M_n(p) = M(p)$; and $M_n(p') = M[(EN_i, M') \rightarrow (EN_i, M'')](p')$.

Steps. An *autonomous step* is the firing of an unlabelled transition in SN or in a net token of N. This step is denoted as $M[t\rangle M_n$ where M_n is the resulting marking. A *horizontal* step is the firing of transitions t_1 and t_2 in two different net tokens nt_1 and nt_2 s.t. nt_1 and nt_2 occurs in M at the same place and $\Lambda(t_1) = \Lambda(t_2) \in L_h$. This step is denoted as $M[t_1 \, t_2\rangle M_n$. A *vertical step* is the firing of a transition t in some net net token that occurs in M s.t. $l = \Lambda(t) \in L_v$, and the firing of a transition labelled as $\bar{l}$ in all net tokens involved in the binding of t. This step is also denoted as $M[t\rangle M_n$ but the notation may also include the transitions fired in the child net tokens. A marking M is called *reachable* if there is a sequence of zero or more steps $M_0[\rangle M_1[\rangle \ldots [\rangle M_k$ s.t. $M_k = M$. This is denoted as $M_0[*\rangle M$. It is called *dead* if no step can be done from it.

We point out that, since labelled transitions do not share input places, the order for firing the transitions involved in a synchronizing step is irrelevant. Besides, by condition (e) on W_i, autonomous and vertical steps consume the net tokens involved. Hence, all the steps of a net token occur at the same place.

Example 2. The firing sequence below corresponds to the NPN in Figure 1. We write a marking as a sequence of pairs $p : M(p)$ enclosed by the symbols $\prec$ and $\succ$. Uncolored places are marked with non-negative integers instead of multisets of black dots. We use superscripts for the places and transitions in net tokens.

$$\prec p_1 : 4, p_2 : 1, p_3 : \emptyset, p_4 : 0, p_5 : 0 \succ \; [\mathbf{t_1}\rangle$$
$$\prec p_1 : 4, p_2 : 0, p_3 : (F^1, \prec p_6^1 : 1, p_7^1 : \emptyset, p_8^1 : 0 \succ), p_4 : 0, p_5 : 0 \succ \; [\mathbf{t_4^1}\rangle$$
$$\prec p_1 : 3, p_2 : 0, p_3 : (F^1, \prec p_6^1 : 0, p_7^1 : (F^2, \prec p_6^2 : 1, p_7^2 : \emptyset, p_8^2 : 0 \succ), p_8^1 : 0 \succ),$$
$$p_4 : 0, p_5 : 0 \succ \; [\mathbf{t_3^2 \, t_5^1}\rangle$$
$$\prec p_1 : 3, p_2 : 0, p_3 : (F^1, \prec p_6^1 : 0, p_7^1 : \emptyset, p_8^1 : 1 \succ), p_4 : 0, p_5 : 1 \succ \; [\mathbf{t_6^1 \, t_2}\rangle$$
$$\prec p_1 : 3, p_2 : 0, p_3 : \emptyset, p_4 : 1, p_5 : 2 \succ$$

The two first steps of this sequence create two nested net tokens (say nt_1 and nt_2) at p_3 and p_7^1 resp. After that, the inner net token performs a vertical step with its parent, firing the transitions t_3^2 and t_5^1 resp. This step adds a black dot at p_5 and p_8^1 and consumes nt_2. Another vertical step occurs between nt_1 and SN involving the transitions t_6^1 and t_2 resp. As before a black dot is added at p_5 and also at p_4; besides nt_1 is consumed. Then, no further step can be done in the net. An alternative sequence is obtained if in the second step above, we choose the transition t_3^1 instead of t_4^1. In this case, the sequence is the next:

$$<p_1 : 4, p_2 : 1, p_3 : \emptyset, p_4 : 0, p_5 : 0 > \ [\mathbf{t_1})$$
$$<p_1 : 4, p_2 : 0, p_3 : (F, <p_6^1 : 1, p_7^1 : \emptyset, p_8^1 : 0>), p_4 : 0, p_5 : 0 > \ [\mathbf{t_3^1 \ t_2})$$
$$<p_1 : 4, p_2 : 0, p_3 : \emptyset, p_4 : 1, p_5 : 1>$$

In general, when the net reaches a dead marking M we have $M(p_4) = 1$, $M(p_5) = b + 1$ for some $0 \leq b \leq a$ (i.e. the number of net tokens - factorial calls), $M(p_1) = a - b$, $M(p_2) = 0$ and $M(p_3) = \emptyset$.

3   Translating Nested Petri Nets into PROMELA

In this section we explain how to translate the NPNs defined in the previous section into PROMELA. We will assume the reader is familiar with the basics of PROMELA and SPIN semantics of executability.

The Translation. We represent each element net using a `proctype` definition; thus each net token is a process. We assume $L \subseteq [1, 254]$ and we denote the label of a transition t for vertical synchronization as `Lv(t)` and its complementary label as `-Lv(t)`. For unlabelled transitions, we define `Lv(t)=0` and `-Lv(t)=255`. We also assume that each transition has an identity number, denoted as `id(t)`.

Uncolored places are represented as non-negative integer variables. A colored basic place may be translated into an array or a buffered channel or it can be unfolded into several uncolored ones. We will use the last option; hence hereafter we deal with nets where all the basic-typed places are uncolored. A net place will be translated as channel, intended for exchanging messages between the parent net process and the processes corresponding to net tokens at the place. Each message consists of four fields. The first holds the instantiation number (`_pid`) of the net token process sending or receiving the message. The second and the third fields are the label and the identity number of the transition which is enabled, resp. The last bit field defines the type of the message: 0 for a synchronization request and 1 for the response. The messages should be inserted in the channel in a non-deterministic way to simulate a multiset. Nevertheless, for the sake of readability, we will use the standard SPIN statement for sending messages.

Shared places must be declared as global variables while non-shared ones are local to the process definition of the net component. We assume that the initial marking is defined as part of the variable declaration. The system net is represented in the `init` process. Its behavior is simulated via a do-loop where each option corresponds to the firing of a transition [10]. The general structure of the translation is shown in Figure 2.

```
typedef NetPlace { chan d =          init(){
  [Msg] of {byte,byte,byte,bit} }       /* Non-Shared Places    */
                                         /* Initial  Marking     */
/* Shared Places */                      /* Auxiliary variables */
byte sp1, sp2,...;                       byte nt, it;
                                         do :: atomic{        /*(a)*/
/* Auxiliary Definitions */                    enableTest_t ->
inline sP(p, n)                                 sP(_pid, 3);
  { set_priority(p,n) }                         consumeActions_t;
                                                produceActions_t;
/* Element Nets */                              sP(_pid, 1) }
                                         :: ...
                                         od }
```

Fig. 2. General structure of PROMELA specification for a NPN

Firings. Each transition t in SN is translated as shown in Figure 2(a). The expression enableTest is the conjunction of an enabling condition for each input arc (p, t). This condition, denoted as enableTest$_p$, depends on the label $W(p, t)$. Similarly, consumeActions is the sequence of instructions for removing the tokens on each input label $W(p, t)$. Finally, produceActions is the sequence of instructions for adding the tokens in $W(t, p)$ to each output place p. We use priorities to simulate the steps involving net tokens.

We assume the arcs from/to an uncolored place p are labelled by natural numbers. Hence, if $W(p, t) = n$ then enableTest$_p$ is the expression p >= n and consumeActions$_p$ is the instruction p = p - n. If $W(t, p) = n$, produceActions$_p$ is defined as p = p + n. For a net place np, the labels of the incidents arcs are multisets. By condition (b) in Definition 1, no net constant appears in any input arc label $W(np, t)$, just variables. On the contrary, the label of an output arc $W(t, np)$ includes just net constants. To keep enableTest$_{np}$ simple, we assume that the label of any input arc $W(np, t)$ is a single variable[2]. We impose no condition on $W(t, np)$; hence, the instructions in produceActions$_{np}$ create a net token for each constant in $W(t, np)$. The next table shows the PROMELA expression and instructions for dealing with net-typed arc labels.

enable(x)	consumeAction(x)	produceAction(ENi)

np.d ?? [_,-Lv(t),_,0]	np.d ?? nt,-Lv(t),it,0;
	 consNetTok(np.d);
	 np.d ! nt,Lv(t),it,1;
	 sP(nt, 3)
		nt = run ENi(np.d);
		 np.d ! nt,255,0,0

As the last cell shows, a child net token nt is produced by creating a process instance for the corresponding element net. In addition, an initial message is sent to the the channel attached to the place np. This message represents the net token and allows the removal of nt without vertical synchronization, e.g. by

---

[2] We explain how to get rid of this restriction in Section 6.

unlabelled transitions. A transition t s.t. $W(np, t)$ is a variable may consume nt if the channel contains a request message, previously written by nt, with the complementary label of t. When t is enabled and fires, consumeActions$_{np}$ removes from the channel the remaining request messages of nt (consNetTok). Then, a response message is sent that will force the termination of the process nt. By changing the priority of nt we ensure that once t completes the firing, the child net processes will be executed in order to finish the synchronization.

Element Nets. We use a proctype definition with two nested do-loops, as shown in Figure 3. The inner loop includes options for the autonomous steps and the requests for synchronization. This loop is broken when a response message is received, using an unless instruction. Therefore, each option is enclosed in a deterministic region.

Autonomous Steps. Unlabelled transitions that do not produce net tokens are translated as in Figure 2 (a). However, a process instance cannot be created inside a d_step. Hence, the firing of the autonomous steps producing net tokens is split into two parts. The first takes place inside the inner loop and has the form: enableTest -> sP(_pid, 3); consumeActions; pc!_pid,0,idt,1. The inner cycle terminates after sending the request message with the identity of the transition. The second part of the step is performed as an if option, as shown in Figure 3(a).

```
proctype elNetName(chan pc){          /* horizontal steps    (b)*/
  /* Non-Shared Places    */            :: it == idt ->
  /* Initial  Marking     */               consumeActions;
  /* Auxiliary Variables */                produceActions
  byte nt, it;                         /* vertical steps       (c)*/
  do:: {                                 :: it == idt ->
    do :: d_step{/* aut-step */}           consumeActions;
       ...                                 produceActions;
       :: d_step{/* sync-req */}           break
       ...                              /* net removed          (d)*/
    od }                                  :: it == 0 -> break
  unless atomic{                         fi;
  pc ?? eval(_pid),_,it,1;               sP(_pid, 1) }
  /* autonomous steps                  od;
     creating net tokens    (a)*/      d_step{     /* stop child nets */
  if :: it == idt ->                     consNetsAtPlace(np1); ... }
        produceActions                 sP(_pid, 1) }
```

Fig. 3. PROMELA specification for an element net

Vertical Steps. We divide the transitions labelled for vertical synchronization into *net-typed* and *basic-typed*. The former transitions have at least an input net place and consume the net tokens involved. For these transitions, the translation for autonomous steps effectively applies. A basic-typed labelled transition has all the input places of basic types; hence its firing entails the removal of the net. Due to this, the firing is split into two steps. The first is

performed once the transition is enabled and it simply sends a request message to the parent. The corresponding option in the inner loop has the form:
`enableTest && ! pc??[eval(_pid),Lv(t),_,0] -> pc!_pid,Lv(t),id(t),0.`

The second step is executed as soon as the process receives the parent response message, as shown in Figure 3(c). When the firing is completed, the outer loop is broken and the child nets that may be still active at some place are removed without synchronization. The `d_step` at the end deals with this situation by means of the macro `consNetsAtPlace`. The last `if`-option (Figure 3(d)) applies here and also when the net is consumed by an unlabelled transition.

Conflicts Involving Labelled Transitions. A labelled transition t may be disabled by the firing of another transition t' in the same net token (e.g. t_3 and t_4 in Example 1). In this case, if a synchronizing request message from t was already written in the parent channel, then it should be removed. This may be done after the `consumeActions` for t', using the next PROMELA macro.

```
inline dT(idt){ if:: ! enableTest(idt) && pc??[eval(_pid),_,idt,0] ->
                   pc??eval(_pid),_,idt,0
          :: else fi }
```

Horizontal Steps. The translation of a horizontal transition is also divided into two steps. But, in this case, the request part consists of two options. If there is no request message with this label in the parent channel, then the message is sent. Otherwise a test for horizontal synchronization is done. If the test is valid, the response messages are written on the channel. The PROMELA instructions are the next. Here the label of t is denoted as `Lh(t)`.

```
enableTest_t && ! pc??[_,Lh(t),_,0]  -> pc!_pid,Lh(t),id(t),0    /* fT */
enableTest_t && ! pc??[eval(_pid),Lh(t),_,0] &&                  /* cT */
                   pc??[_,Lh(t),_,0]  ->
          sP(_pid, 3); pc??nt,Lh(t),it,0;
          pc!_pid,Lh(t),id(t),1; pc!nt,Lh(t),it,1; sP(nt, 3);
```

The firing is executed outside the inner cycle, as shown in Figure 3(b). We remark that, when these transitions consume net tokens, the label used for `enable` and `consume` is the one for vertical synchronization (`Lv(t)=0` as for unlabelled transitions). Therefore, the translation of the firing is the same.

In order to demonstrate the correctness of the above translation schema first note that all entities of a NPN are properly transformed into PROMELA constructions. The marking of the net is encoded in the values of global and local variables. Each step in the net corresponds to the execution of a sequence of atomic or deterministic regions with priority 3 in the PROMELA program. The execution path corresponding to a sequence of NPN steps may include additional deterministic regions between the net steps, due to the synchronization requests. But these regions do not affect the underlying marking. Besides, they are executed once, before the synchronization, unless they are disabled by another firing. Since the firings in a synchronizing step are interleaved, several execution paths in the model may correspond to the same firing sequence in the NPN.

4   Investigating Behavioral Properties with SPIN

The NPNs with autonomous elements is a subclass of recursive nested nets for which termination is decidable [17]. This was proved by constructing a finite coverability tree where each node represents a reachable marking. The method classifies the nodes as *internal, final, covering* and *iterative*. Internal nodes have at least one reachable marking as direct descendant while the remaining nodes are leaves of the tree. Covering nodes represent infinite cycles in the net and are detected by means of a quasi-ordering compatible with the relation [⟩. Iterative nodes have a nested net token leading to an infinite recursive firing sequence. Final nodes represent dead markings; thus the net is terminating if all the leaves are final. As far as we know, no tool has been implemented this method yet.

The translation proposed in previous section can be used for studying the behavior of NPNs. The simulation facilities provided by SPIN may help in the validation of specific firing sequences. Besides, some properties can be verified, in particular termination. Those states of the PROMELA model where every active process is blocked at the inner loop correspond to the final nodes of the coverability tree. These states should be marked as valid **end** states for SPIN. This way, the default verification will report an error if there exists an invalid end-state. Since SPIN deals with finite-state models, iterative nodes and covering nodes increasing the marking will lead to invalid states. But such states may also be due to a long terminating sequence exceeding SPIN limits (number and bound of channels, processes, etc). SPIN guided simulation or advanced options (e.g. -DVECTORSZ, -DBITSTATE, -DCOLLAPSE) will provide insights of the real situation. When the search is completed without errors, the verifier may report some unreachable states. One of these states should be the end of **init** since *SN* cannot be consumed. Other unreachable states may be due to transitions which are never fired or net tokens which are never consumed.

If the net has cycles, a further analysis should be done in order to conclude termination. This is because some covering nodes may lead to cycles in the space state of the model that are not detected by the default verification. Instead a search for acceptance cycles should be performed. To this end, we should add **accept** labels in front of the inner loop of the **proctype** definition of each element net and the also the loop of **init**. If the new search is completed and no acceptance cycle is found by SPIN then the NPN is terminating.

It is important to remark that priorities are key to approximate the synchronizing steps. This feature was recently introduced in PROMELA (SPIN Version 6.2.0 - May 2012) and some errors have been reported on the current implementation (version 6.2.5 - May 2013). Besides, it requires compilation without the partial order reduction (-DNOREDUCE). Therefore, in order to take advantage of the full verification power of SPIN, priorities may be disabled in the translation, just by defining **sP(p, n)** as **skip**. This entails that a number of steps may be interleaved between the firings involved in a synchronization. However, this does not affect the verification since labelled transitions do not share input places. Hence, if a PROMELA model without priorities satisfies a property, the same holds for the NPN. Nevertheless, in our experiments the verification with priorities exhibited a better performance than without using this feature.

Example 3. The translation for the element net F in Figure 1 is shown below. Since the NPN has no cycle, termination can be proved by a default verification of the PROMELA model[3]. SPIN took $0.001s$ for this analysis, running in a notebook Intel Core I3, 2.4GHz, 4Gb RAM. For $p1 = 34$, the time was $0.211s$ but for $p1 = 35$ the verification could not be completed. The same happens if, as in [17], we remove the places p1 and p5, leading to an infinite recursive firing sequence. In both cases the same error trail is obtained. However, for the terminating version, increasing the size of state vector (-DVECTORSZ=2048) was enough for completing the verification for $p1 = 70$ in $3.46s$.

```
proctype netF(chan pc){                       p8++; sP(_pid, 1); }
byte p6=1,p8,nt,it; NetPlace p7;         :: d_step{ p8 > 0 &&
do:: {                                         !pc ?? [eval(_pid),10,6,0]->
 do:: d_step{ p6 >0 &&                         pc ?? eval(_pid),10,6,0] }
     !pc ?? [eval(_pid),10,3,0]->      od }
     pc ! eval(_pid),10,3,0] }         unless atomic{
  :: d_step{ p6 > 0 && p1 > 0 ->       pc ?? eval(_pid),_, it,1 ->
     sP(_pid, 3);                      if:: it == 4 ->
     p1--; p6--; dT(3);                   nt = run netF(p7.d);
     pc ! _pid,0,4,1 }                    p7.d ! nt, 255,0,0 ;
  :: d_step{                           :: it == 3 ->
     p7.d ?? [_,10,_,0] ->                p6--; p5++; break
     sP(_pid, 3);                      :: it == 6 ->
     p7.d ?? nt,10,it,0;                  p8--; p5++; break
     consNetTok(p7.d, nt);             :: it == 0 -> break
     p7.d ! nt,11,it,1;                fi; sP(_pid, 1) }
     sP(nt, 3);                        od; sP(_pid, 1) }
```

Other properties can be verified for a terminating NPN. For example, bounded-ness can also be studied with the default verification by means of bounds for the channels and assertions on the variables for places. Some reachability conditions, in particular those that are restricted to places in SN, can also be investigated using LTL properties or never claims. To this end, the non-shared places of SN should be declared as global instead local variables. Conditions involving net tokens should be encoded in a **never**-claim, in order to gain access to the value of local places through remote references. But this is only possible if the total number of net tokens is known in advance. Never-claims may also help to analyze some properties of non-terminating nets. However, SPIN provides support just for process-level weak fairness; thus strong fairness should be embedded inside the claim.

Example 4. The last statement in Example 1 can be proved with SPIN. To this end, we declared all places of SN as global variables. Besides, we included two

---

[3] See http://www.ime.usp.br/~mirtha/factEx.pml. We assume $\lambda = 10$ and $\bar{\lambda} = 11$.

additional variables: a for saving the initial marking of p1 and f for counting the number of net tokens created. The statement can be specified using the LTL property `<>[](p4==1 && p2==0 && len(p3.d)==0 && p1==a-f+1 && p5==f)`. The analysis took $0.02s$.

The main disadvantage of SPIN is that the number of active processes and channels is limited to 255. Hence, large nets must be analyzed by means of smaller abstract models. To reduce the state space, it is important to avoid large bounds for the channels and use data types such as `unsigned` and `bit` instead of `byte`.

5   Application to Inter-organizational Workflow Nets

In the next we illustrate the use of our translation by means of an example of a NPN for an inter-organizational workflow. A workflow can be modelled using a PN in which transitions represent either tasks or routing patterns while places represent casual dependencies. Such a net, called Workflow Net (WF-net) [26], has a place i with no incoming arc (*source node*) and another place o with no outgoing arc (*sink node*). Furthermore, every other place or transition is on a path from i to o. The initial and final markings have a single token at i and o resp. An inter-organizational WF-net (IOWF-net) is the combination of several WF-nets with asynchronous and synchronous communication relations between tasks [26]. An asynchronous relation (AC) between $T1$ and $T2$ implies that $T2$ must be executed after $T1$ is completed. To this end an additional place is used. A synchronous relation (SC) between $T1$ and $T2$ implies that they are executed at the same time. These transitions are merged into a single one.

IOWF-nets can be modelled as NPNs [21]. In this approach, each local WF-net is an element net having a sink transition from o labelled for vertical synchronization. The communication relations are represented using an independent element net AC and labels for horizontal synchronization. The system net has also source and sink places and a place for storing the WF-net tokens and a single AC net token. Since the local WF-nets only expose the labels, this approach provides more flexibility, modularity, autonomy and privacy.

Figure 4 shows a NPN modelling an IOWF-net. It consists of two WF-nets $LWF1$ and $LWF2$ with labels $L_h = \{l_1, l_2, l_3, l_4, l_5, l_6, l_7, l_8\}$ and $L_v = \{\lambda, \bar{\lambda}\}$. Transitions in different WF-nets with the same horizontal label belong to SC. The asynchronous communication relation is modelled as the element net AC. From the initial marking of SN, a net token of each type is created. Then, several autonomous and horizontal steps are performed. When a WF-net reaches its final marking, a vertical synchronization with SN occurs. Once both WF-net tokens are consumed, the last transition fires, the AC net token is also consumed and SN reaches its final marking. Figure 4 also includes the PROMELA translation[4] for $LWF1$ and SN. We have used the label number as the identity for horizontal transitions.

---

[4] See `http://www.ime.usp.br/~mirtha/ioWFEx.pml`.

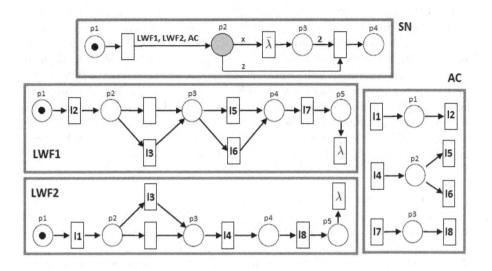

```
proctype netLWF1(chan pc){              init{
bit p1=1,p2,p3,p4,p5;                   bit p1=1; unsigned p3:2;
unsigned nt:3; unsigned it:4;           unsigned nt:3; NetPlace p2;
do :: {                                 do :: atomic{ p1 > 0 ->
 do :: fT(p1,2) :: cT(p1,nt,2)              sP(_pid,3); p1--;
    :: fT(p2,3) :: cT(p2,nt,3)              nt = run netLWF1(p2.d);
    :: d_step{p2 > 0 ->                     p2.d ! nt, 255,0;
       sP(_pid, 3); p2--; dT(3);            nt = run netLWF2(p2.d);
       p3++; sP(_pid,1) }                   p2.d ! nt, 255,0;
    :: fT(p3,5) :: cT(p3,nt,5)              nt = run netAC(p2.d);
    :: fT(p3,6) :: cT(p3,nt,6)              p2.d ! nt, 255,0;
    :: fT(p4,7) :: cT(p4,nt,7)              sP(_pid,1) }
    :: fT(p5,10)                     :: atomic{
 od }                                       p2.d ?? [_,10,0] ->
unless atomic{                              sP(_pid,3);
pc ?? eval(_pid),it,1 ->                    p2.d ?? nt,10,0;
if :: it==2 -> p1--; p2++                   consNetTok(p2.d, nt);
   :: it==3 -> p2--; p3++                   p2.d ! nt,11,1; sP(nt,3);
   :: it==5 -> p3--; dT(6); p4++            p3++; sP(_pid,1) }
   :: it==6 -> p3--; dT(5); p4++     :: atomic{ p3 >= 2 &&
   :: it==7 -> p4--; p5++                   p2.d ?? [_,255,0] ->
   :: it==11-> break                        sP(_pid,3); p3 = p3-2;
   :: it==0 -> break                        p2.d ?? nt,255,0;
 fi; sP(_pid, 1) }                          consNetTok(p2.d, nt);
od; sP(_pid, 1) }                           p2.d ! nt,0,1; sP(nt,3);
                                            p4++; sP(_pid,1) }
bit p4;                                 od }
```

Fig. 4. NPN for an IOWF-net and part of its PROMELA translation

The behavior of a workflow is correct if its WF-net is *sound* [26]. Three conditions are required to satisfy this property: (1) from the initial marking, it is always possible to reach the final marking; (2) the final marking should be the only marking reachable with a token at o; and (3) every task must be performed for at least one execution of the workflow. In [27], it was shown how SPIN can be used for proving soundness of acyclic WF-nets. In particular, the first property can be verified using the LTL formula <>(o>0). An IOWF-net is sound if the local WF-nets are sound and the condition (1) is valid for the NPN [21]. The WF-nets $LWF1$ and $LWF2$ are sound. The soundness of the NPN in Figure 4 was verified using the PROMELA model in $1.8s$.

6   Conclusions

Several variations of PNs and PN-like formalisms, (e.g. workflows, business processes, UML diagrams) have been translated into DVE [14], LTSA [22], NuSMV [6] and SPIN [9,7,23,27,24,2]. DVE, LTSA and NuSMV cannot be used in this context because they have no support for recursion. Among the PROMELA translations, the one presented in [2] is the closest to the NPN framework. Nevertheless, it is restricted to two-level nested nets without horizontal synchronization or net tokens removal. In [7], two-level object nets are encoded into Prolog and verified using the XTL model checker. Although the method is intended for arbitrary nesting, the encoding for the synchronization in the multi-level case is not provided. Rewriting logic has been used to express the semantics of recursive algebraic nets [1]. But these nets do not include horizontal steps. Translating NPNs into PROMELA is simpler and more amenable for simulation that using rewriting rules or logic programming. Regarding verification, SPIN outperforms Maude model checker in execution time and memory requirements [5]. According to [8], SPIN is faster than XTL model checker and can handle a larger number of properties and instances.

As far as we know, this is the first translation integrating multi-level and recursive nested nets as well as horizontal and vertical synchronization steps. Our translation applies to a subclass of NPNs where the vertical steps remove the net tokens involved. We have shown that SPIN may be an effective tool for verifying behavioral properties of these nets such as termination, boundedness and LTL properties. We illustrated the use of the translation in a practical application: the verification of the soundness for an interorganizational workflow. For simplicity and space limitations, we imposed some additional restrictions on the nets. In particular, we did not consider basic colored places, variables and expressions on output arcs; but these features are easily included. The input arcs from net-typed places are labelled by a single variable. But we can get rid of this restriction by means of an additional channel for each net place, to keep track of the number of request messages for each label. This extension will also allow horizontal synchronization steps involving more than two nets. The inclusion of transportation steps can be achieved by sending channels via channels. When a net token is moved, the parent net should send to the child process the channel corresponding to the new place (e.g. via a global channel). All pending requests from the child should also be moved to the new channel.

The ideas presented in this paper constitute a first step towards the verification of recursive interaction protocols in a coordination middleware called JamSession [3]. This middleware is composed by protocols that execute specific services and manage distributed agents and resources by means of predicates. The agents are hosted at locations and can be moved between them. The protocols combine movements and predicates using logical connectives and can be nested and recursive. The movements play a relevant role in JamSession coordination model. However, they may lead to synchronization errors that may be difficult to trace. Therefore, in JamSession, it is a crucial issue to provide means for verifying that the execution of the interactions meets the desired properties.

In [4] it was shown that when the JamSession protocols are not recursive, they can be translated into hierarchical CPNs. The recursive protocols can be modelled using a NPN where each protocol definition generates an acyclic element net . We had run some preliminary experiments using the PROMELA translation and also a direct translation from JamSession to PROMELA. The running times are similar for both versions but the direct approach slightly reduces the size of the state space. However, the NPN approach allows to understand the error traces more easily. Besides, the properties to be verified can be formulated in a simpler and uniform way. As future work, we plan the construction of an environment for the analysis of these nets, based on the ideas behind the translation and SPIN model checking techniques.

References

1. Barkaoui, K., Hicheur, A.: Towards analysis of flexible and collaborative workflow using recursive eCATNets. In: ter Hofstede, A.H.M., Benatallah, B., Paik, H.-Y. (eds.) BPM Workshops 2007. LNCS, vol. 4928, pp. 232–244. Springer, Heidelberg (2008)
2. Chang, L., He, X.: A model transformation approach for verifying multi-agent systems using SPIN. In: Proc. ACM Symposium on Applied Computing, pp. 37–42 (2011)
3. Corrêa da Silva, F.S.: Knowledge-based interaction protocols for intelligent interactive environments. Knowledge and Information Systems 30, 1–24 (2012)
4. Corrêa da Silva, F.S., Venero, M.L.F., David, D.M., Saleemb, M., Chung, P.W.H.: Interaction protocols for cross-organisational workflows. Knowledge-Based Systems 37, 121–136 (2013)
5. Eker, S., Meseguer, J., Sridharanarayanan, A.: The Maude LTL Model Checker. In: Proc. WRLA. ENTCS, vol. 71, pp. 162–187 (2002)
6. Eshuis, R.: Symbolic model checking of UML activity diagrams. ACM Trans. Softw. Eng. Methodol. 15(1), 1–38 (2006)
7. Farwer, B., Leuschel, M.: Model checking object petri nets in Prolog. In: Proc. 6th ACM SIGPLAN Int. Conf. on Principles and Practice of Declarative Programming, pp. 20–31 (2004)
8. Frappier, M., Fraikin, B., Chossart, R., Chane-Yack-Fa, R., Ouenzar, M.: Comparison of model checking tools for information systems. In: Proc. 12th Int. Conf. on Formal Engineering Methods and Software Engineering, pp. 581–596 (2010)

9. Gannod, G.C., Gupta, S.: An automated tool for analyzing Petri Nets using SPIN. In: Proc. 16th IEEE Int. Conf. on Automated Software Engineering, pp. 404–407. IEEE Computer Society (2001)

10. Holzmann, G.J.: The SPIN Model Checker: Primer and Reference Manual. Addison-Wesley (2003)

11. Jensen, K.: Coloured Petri Nets. Basic Concepts, Analysis Methods and Practical Use. Springer (1992)

12. Kissoum, Y., Sahnoun, Z.: A recursive colored petri nets semantics for AUML as base of test case generation. In: Proc. IEEE/ACS Int. Conf. on Computer Systems and Applications, pp. 785–792 (2008)

13. Köhler, M., Moldt, D., Rölke, H.: Modelling mobility and mobile agents using nets within nets. In: van der Aalst, W.M.P., Best, E. (eds.) ICATPN 2003. LNCS, vol. 2679, pp. 121–139. Springer, Heidelberg (2003)

14. Leyla, N., Mashiyat, A.S., Wang, H., MacCaull, W.: Towards workflow verification. In: Proc. Conference of the Center for Advanced Studies on Collaborative Research, pp. 253–267 (2010)

15. Lomazova, I.A., Schnoebelen, P.: Some decidability results for nested petri nets. In: Bjorner, D., Broy, M., Zamulin, A.V. (eds.) PSI 1999. LNCS, vol. 1755, pp. 208–220. Springer, Heidelberg (2000)

16. Lomazova, I.A.: Nested petri nets: Multilevel and recursive systems. Fundamenta Informaticae 47, 283–293 (2001)

17. Lomazova, I.A.: Recursive nested petri nets: Analysis of semantic properties and expessibility. Programming and Computer Software 27(4), 183–193 (2001)

18. Lomazova, I.A.: Nested petri nets for adaptive process modeling. In: Avron, A., Dershowitz, N., Rabinovich, A. (eds.) Pillars of Computer Science. LNCS, vol. 4800, pp. 460–474. Springer, Heidelberg (2008)

19. Mazouzi, H., Seghrouchni, A.F., Haddad, S.: Open protocol design for complex interactions in multi-agent systems. In: Proc 1st Int. Joint Conf. on Autonomous Agents and Multiagent Systems, AAMAS 2002, pp. 517–526 (2002)

20. Murata, T.: Petri nets: Properties, analysis and applications. Proc. of the IEEE 77(4), 541–580 (1989)

21. Prisecaru, O., Jucan, T.: Interorganizational workflow nets: a petri net based approach for modelling and analyzing interorganizational workflows. In: Proc 4th Int. Workshop on Enterprise and Organizational Modeling and Simulation, pp. 64–78 (2008)

22. Regis, G., Ricci, N., Aguirre, N.M., Maibaum, T.: Specifying and verifying declarative fluent temporal logic properties of workflows. In: Gheyi, R., Naumann, D. (eds.) SBMF 2012. LNCS, vol. 7498, pp. 147–162. Springer, Heidelberg (2012)

23. Ribeiro, O.R., Fernandes, J.M.: Translating Synchronous Petri Nets into PROMELA for verifying behavioural properties. In: Int. Symposium on Industrial Embedded Systems, pp. 266–273 (2007)

24. Sbai, Z., Missaoui, A., Barkaoui, K., Ben Ayed, R.: On the verification of business processes by model checking techniques. In: Proc. 2nd Int. Conf. on Software Technology and Engineering, vol. 1 (2010)

25. Seghrouchni, A.F., Haddad, S.: A recursive model for distributed planning. In: Proc. Int. Conf. on Multi-Agent Systems, pp. 307–314 (1996)

26. van der Aalst, W.M.P.: Interorganizational workflows: an approach based on message sequence charts and petri nets. Systems Analysis–Modelling–Simulation 34(3) (1999)

27. Yamaguchi, S., Yamaguchi, M., Tanaka, M.: A soundness verification tool based on the SPIN model checker for acyclic workflow nets. In: Proc. 23rd Int. Conf. on Circuits/Systems, Computers and Communications, pp. 285–288 (2008)

Specifying a Linked Data Structure in JML for Formal Verification and Runtime Checking

Christoph Gladisch[1] and Shmuel Tyszberowicz[2]

[1] Institute for Theoretical Informatics, Karlsruhe Institute of Technology (KIT)
[2] School of Computer Science, The Academic College Tel Aviv-Yaffo

Abstract. We show how to write a concise and elegant specification of a linearly linked data structure that is applicable for both verification and runtime checking. A specification of linked lists is given as an example. The concept of a list is captured by an observer method which is a functional version of a reachability predicate. The specification is written in the Java Modeling Language (JML) and does not require extensions of that language. This paper addresses a mixed audience of users and developers in the fields of formal verification, runtime checking, and specification language design. We provide an in-depth description of the proposed specification and analyze its implications both for verification and for runtime checking. Based on this analysis we have developed verification techniques that fully automate the verification process, using the KeY tool, and that are also described here.

1 Introduction

Linked data structures have been specified and verified in many works. Yet, the specifications we found in the literature either are complex and therefore difficult to understand by engineers or use logics and formulas which cannot be employed by runtime checkers[1] for popular languages such as Java. JML [11] is a specification language that has been designed for verification and runtime checking, but the language is used differently depending on which of the two approaches is used. This often results in specifications that are incompatible for the other approach. L. du Bousquet et al. [7] show that specifications used for verification or for runtime checking, even if written in JML, often cannot be exchanged for the other purpose. The combination of both approaches is, however, important due to their complementary strengths (see, e.g., [7,18]).

We have developed JML specifications for a selection of methods that operate on linked lists (`get`, `size`, `acyclic`, `remove`, `insert`). They are compatible with deductive program verification on the actual source code level as well as with runtime checking tools. For the verification we have used KeY [3] and for runtime checking the testing tool JET [5]. Both tools use JML as the specification language. The goal of the paper, however, is not only to provide ready-to-use

---

[1] We use the term *runtime checker* as a synonym for *testing tool*. The term is motivated by the runtime assertion checker (RAC) that is provided with JML [11].

J. Iyoda and L. de Moura (Eds.): SBMF 2013, LNCS 8195, pp. 99–114, 2013.
© Springer-Verlag Berlin Heidelberg 2013

specifications, but to explain the design decisions with respect to verification and runtime checking. Our goal is to explain to engineers that use runtime checkers how to write specifications that are compatible with formal verification tools and vice-versa.

To achieve readable and executable specifications we have decided to use queries, also known as inspector or observer methods, instead of list abstractions using ghost fields. Since no ghost state has to be managed, (a) the implementation can be executed as it is, without the need to extend it with code that updates the ghost state in parallel to the normal execution, and (b) the user does not have to think about and to specify two kinds of states. However, regarding verification, reasoning with queries is not easy and has been even proposed as a verification challenge [12]. During this research we created experiments with over 5.000 LOC as steps towards a clear and automatically provable specification. A great amount of work was to extend the proving techniques of the KeY tool, as briefly described in Section 6. Specification readability and clear semantics of the specification elements are crucial for ensuring correctness. We have developed specifications that are readable and understandable also by software engineers that are not experts in deductive verification.

Reachability is crucial for reasoning about linked data structures [14]. To illustrate our approach, we specify the query method Node get(Node o, int n) (Figure 2) which provides access to the n'th node of the list starting at node o, following the field next. It can be seen as a functional version of a reachability predicate but additionally it identifies the position of list nodes. Quantification over the integer n (second parameter) results in quantification over all elements of the list o (first parameter). This enables to express properties that involve transitive closure of the list, that a requirement holds for all elements of the list or in a specific range, and that an element exists (is reachable) which fulfills a certain property. Transitive closure and reachability cannot be expressed in first-order logic, but they can be expressed in first-order logic with integers [4].

JML provides the reachability predicate \reach, which returns the set of objects reachable from a particular reference. Dealing with this predicate requires reasoning about sets, something that we tried to avoid in order to reduce complexity. Not all tools that use JML as a specification language fully support this predicate, e.g. KeY and JET. Also, sometimes different semantics of the predicate are needed [1]. In contrast, the semantics of get is given by its specification or implementation, providing an easy way of *exporting* the semantics to various tools. Using a self-defined method instead of a built-in function or predicate is also more flexible for the user.

Structure of the Paper. Section 2 describes related work. A short introduction to JML is given in Section 3. In Section 4 the query get is described which is the basis for our specifications. Section 5 describes the specification of modifier methods, i.e., methods that change the program state, as well as additional queries. Section 6 describes verification techniques we have developed, experience with runtime checking, and additional insights. Section 7 concludes the paper and describes future work.

2   Related Work

Specification Using Queries and/or Model Fields. linked list specifications mostly either (a) describe the effect of mutator methods in terms of query methods, or (b) use an abstraction of the concrete data structure implementation.

The usage of inspector methods within specifications to abstract away from the concrete implementation is promoted by [8]. An explicit heap encoding limits the information on which those methods depend. In [6], a formalization of pure methods is presented that allows reasoning about method calls in JML specifications. Pure methods are encoded by uninterpreted function symbols and axioms. The encoding can be applied to JML's model fields, specification-only fields that encode abstractions of the concrete state of a data structure.

A full JML specification for `java.util.LinkedList` can be found in [2]. It has complex dependencies due to its hierarchy of containers but it hides implementation details. Our focus is different, it is on proving and testing the actual implementation of a linked data structure. Ideas from both specifications can be combined. Some technical differences are: they use model fields, we do not; they use no recursive specification of the `get` method and it is not connected with a "next" pointer; their specification of `remove` uses disjunctions (DNF versus CNF) which is incompatible with our verification technique (item 3 in Section 6).

Dafny is used to specify and verify a linked list in [13]. The class node uses two ghost fields: the sequence of data values stored in a node and its successors, and a set consisting of the node and its successors. In contrast to our approach, the specifications do not use any reachability predicate.

Specification Using FOL. Analysis of programs that manipulate linked lists by using first-order axiomatizations of reachability information has been extensively studied (e.g., [16,10]). The verification in [10] provides a first-order approximation of a reachability predicate. Two predicates characterize reachability of heap cells. These predicates allow reasoning uniformly about both acyclic and cyclic lists. While theoretically incomplete, the authors of [10] believe that the approach is complete enough for most realistic programs.

In [14], the authors explore how to harness existing theorem provers for first-order logic to prove reachability properties of programs that manipulate dynamically allocated data structures. The paper also provides a set of axioms for characterizing the reachability predicate, which works only for acyclic lists.

Two abstractions, a predicate abstraction and a canonical abstraction, of a (cyclic) singly-linked list are studied in [15]. The state of a program is represented using a 3-valued FOL structure. The intuition is that a heap containing only singly-linked lists is characterized by the connectivity relations between a set of nodes and the length of list segments.

Specification Using HOL or Separation Logic. Zee et al. [20] verify full functional correctness of linked data structure implementations. The correctness properties include intractable constructs such as quantifiers and transitive closure. The specification is written in higher-order logic (including set comprehension, λ-expressions, transitive closure, cardinality of finite sets, etc.), and for verification

—— JAVA + JML ————————————————————————————

```
1    public class Node {
2    //@ public model static JMLDataGroup footprint;
3    public /*@ nullable */ Node next;  //@ in footprint;
4    ... }
```

————————————————————————————— JAVA + JML ——

Fig. 1. The class Node, representing list elements

the Jahob system was used. For some verifications (e.g., a sized list), additional provers such as SPASS, MONA, and BAPA have been used by Jahob.

Separation logic, a generalization of Hoare logic, is powerful for handling the framing problem which occurs with reasoning about heaps. In [9], linked lists with views are investigated which is not immediately expressible in frameworks such as JML. Separation logic is usually used for verification but it has also been utilized for runtime checking [17]. An approach that combines separation logic and dynamic frames is described in [19].

3   JML

Java Modeling Language (JML) is a behavioral interface specification language used to specify the behavior of Java modules. Following is a short description of JML clauses used in the paper. Full details can be found in [11].

The pre-state of a method call is the state of the program after passing parameters and before running the method's code. The post-state is the state of the program just before the method normally returns or throws an exception.

The **public normal_behavior** clause is used to specify behavior of method calls that return normally. The **requires** clause specifies the method's precondition, evaluated at the pre-state of the method call. The **ensures** clause specifies properties that are guaranteed to hold at the end of the method call, in case that the method returns normally. Two keywords that are used in **ensures** are \old and \result. The first refers to the value of fields at the pre-state, and the second is the value returned by the method when normally terminating. The expression (\forall int i;ϕ;ψ) denotes the formula $\forall i : int.(\phi \rightarrow \psi)$.

The clauses **assignable** and **accessible** declare the frame properties of a method. The former defines which (memory) locations can be updated during method execution and the latter states the locations that the method may read from. A set of locations can be declared using a model field of class JMLDataGroup. For instance, the model field **footprint** in Lines 2-3 of Figure 1 denotes the location set of the field **next** for all receiver objects of class Node. The empty set is denoted as \nothing.

The **measured_by** clause is used when the specification is recursive. It enables to describe a termination argument, ensuring that the specification is well-defined. It defines an integer-valued expression that must always be at least zero and it has to decrease strictly for each (recursive) call.

—— JAVA + JML ——————————————————————————————

```
1    /*@ public normal_behavior
2      requires   n>=0;
3      assignable \nothing;
4      accessible Node.footprint;
5      ensures (o==null || n==0) ==> \result == o;
6      ensures              n>0   ==> \result == (get(o,n-1)!=null?
7                                                get(o,n-1).next : null);
8      measured_by n;
9    @*/
10   public static /*@nullable pure*/ Node get(/*@nullable*/Node o, int n){
11       int i=0; Node oldo = o;    //oldo is a temporary variable
12       /*@ loop_invariant 0<=i && i<=n && o == get(oldo,i);
13             assignable \nothing;  //syntactically not supported by JET
14             decreases n-i; @*/
15       while(i<n && o!=null) {
16           o=o.next;
17           i++;
18       }
19       return o;
20   }
```

—————————————————————————————————————— JAVA + JML ——

Fig. 2. Specification and implementation of the query method get

Member fields, formal parameters, and method return types are by default considered to be non_null. In order to enable them to have a null value, they explicitly have to be annotated with the modifier nullable.

4   The Observer Method Get

In order to express properties of a list, we use the method Node get(Node o, int n) (Figure 2) which provides access to the n'th node of the list starting at node o, following the field next. It can be seen as a functional variant of a reachability predicate, allowing quantification over list elements. The chosen signature is a functional version of a *get*-method where the usually implicit this pointer is made explicitly as the first argument. The rational was to allow the first element to be the null pointer during our experiments. However, different signatures can be used, e.g. get(int n), where o is a field or the this pointer.

4.1   Specification of the Get Query

Figure 2 presents a recursive specification of the method get. Line 5 defines the base-case, where either the element at position 0 is accessed or the list is empty, i.e. null. Lines 6-7 define the step-case for n>0, with a case distinction that checks whether the element at position n-1 is null. If it is not null, then get(o,n) is defined as get(o,n-1).next; otherwise, it is also null.

For modular reasoning, the framing properties of `get` must be defined in addition to the functional specification. Framing properties are important to help verification and do not have to be used for runtime checking, as the latter does not abstract the code. The `assignable` clause expresses what locations might have been modified by a method (cf. Section 3). More interesting, however, is the inverse, i.e., the locations that have not been modified. For every field f not mentioned in the `assignable` clause, the implicit postcondition `f==\old(f)` can be assumed. This information is important for verification to relate pre- and post-state. The method `get` is (strictly) pure, thus it does not modify the heap's state and can be used in specifications.

The result of `get` depends not only on the values of the parameters o and n, but also on the `next` field values of the `Node` objects of the list starting at node o. Hence, whenever an assignment to `next` has been made, the value of the method may have been changed. The difficulty in specification and verification when using observer methods is in tracking the return values of the observer methods according to the changes in states they depend on. The `accessible` clause, also called dependency clause, describes which memory locations the method depends on. The dependency clause in Line 4 of Figure 2 is an over-approximation. The state of all locations that are not mentioned in the dependency clause can be ignored when evaluating the method, which considerably simplifies verification.

4.2   Implementation of the Get Query

The specification of `get` can be used both for specifying and for verifying properties of a list. The first method that we have verified using `get` is the implementation of `get` itself. A recursive code is the most trivial to implement and to verify. However, we demonstrate the more interesting iterative implementation, since a loop invariant, which uses the recursively defined query `get`, has to be provided or computed. As can be seen in Figure 2, the loop invariant is very concise—which is one of our goals. The code annotations, however, bear some problems that will be described next, together with the solutions that we have successfully applied.

Required Lemma. The specification of `get` (Figure 2) implicitly implies that if i is the last element's index, then for all n, with $i < n$, `get` returns `null`. This is needed for the verification, to prove the postcondition for the case that the loop in Lines 15-18 terminates due to the condition o==null, and i<n evaluates to true. If a verification system is not able to derive this knowledge automatically, it must be provided by the user—for instance as a lemma. One possibility to do this in JML is to declare a pure void method, say `lem_getTransNull`, which contains the lemma in its postcondition (see Figure 3). A runtime checker, however, will not be able to execute the postcondition as it uses unbounded quantification. In such cases it may just ignore the postcondition. Since the lemma is needed only as a hint for the verification tool, this lack of compatibility with runtime checking is not a problem. To use it for verification, `lem_getTransNull` can be inserted into the code in Figure 2 after Line 18. An implementation that ensures i==n at loop exit does not need the lemma.

```
       JAVA + JML
1  /*@ public normal_behavior
2    assignable \nothing;
3    ensures (\forall int j; 0<=j && get(o,j)==null;
4                  (\forall int k; j<k; get(o,k)==null)); @*/
5  public static void lem_getTransNull(/*@nullable */ Node node){};
                                                        JAVA + JML
```

Fig. 3. Encoding of a null transitivity lemma of the query method **get**

```
       JAVA + JML
1    ... measured_by n; */
2  public /*@nullable pure*/ Node getImpl(/*@nullable*/Node o, int n){
3    int i=0;  Node oldo = o;
4    /*@ loop_invariant 0<=i && i<=n && o == get(oldo,i);  ...
                                                        JAVA + JML
```

Fig. 4. Implementation of the query method **get**

Well-definedness Issues: The measured_by Clause. The specification of the **get** query (Figure 2) contains the **measured_by n;** clause. This clause requires that each time the method is called a) the value of the argument **n** is decreased and b) $n \geq 0$. These conditions ensure the method's termination and hence its well-definedness. However, the loop invariant in Figure 2 is problematic, as it permits **i==n**. When the subformula **o==get(oldo,i)** is evaluated and **i==n**, the call **get(oldo,n)** is encountered which violates condition a) of the **measured_by** clause. This can be a problem also for runtime checking, and not only for verification: the checker may not terminate when checking the loop invariant. To enforce the first condition, the following two solutions can be applied:

Solution 1. Distinction between the Program and the Specification Function. This solution explicitly distinguishes between the **get** query, which will be used for specification only, and the method used for implementation, say **getImpl** (Figure 4). Both queries **get** and **getImpl** co-exist. The expression **n** following the **measured_by** clause of **get** is independent of that employed in **getImpl**. In order to use **get** also by a runtime checker, the implementation must be provided.

Solution 2. Expanding the Definition of get in the Loop Invariant. Since the second argument of **get** is decreased in each recursion step, manual expansion of the specification of **o==get(oldo,i)** ensures the satisfaction of the required conditions of the **measured_by** clause. However, the specification is larger and less readable.

5   Specification of Modifier Methods

Modifier methods, also called mutators, are non-pure ones, i.e., they can modify fields of objects. We will show two of them: **remove** and **insert**. Figure 5 shows an implementation of the `remove` method. A trivial specification of the method is shown in Figure 6, where Line 5 of the specification describes the effect of the assignment in Line 3 of the implementation. The specification formalizes how the `next` field is changed by the method when the precondition is satisfied. The specification is strong and correct, but it is not suitable for our approach as it does not specify how the result of `get` has changed.

The problem is that, in contrast to runtime checking, in verification a query that uses recursion or a loop cannot be simply executed as this execution would not terminate for arbitrary inputs. Instead, the value of the query has to be deduced. This is not just the *framing problem* but the question of *how exactly* values have changed. The addressed problem is typical for specifications with queries used in modular verification. Handling this problem has been proposed as a verification challenge [12] and is addressed in different works (see Section 2). It can be explained using an example, summarized by the following three lines:

assume	value of `get(o,i)` is known
assign	`u.next:=b`
assert	$\phi(\texttt{get(o,i)})$

Assume that the value of `get(o,i)` is known, e.g. from a precondition. Then a reference value `b` is assigned to the field `next` of an object `u` of class `Node`. Such an assignment may occur in a modifier method, for instance `remove`. Since the field `next` has been modified and the query is heap-dependent, the return value of the query may have changed after the assignment. The problem is in determining the value of the `get(o,i)` query after the state change in order to check whether it fulfills some condition ϕ, e.g. the postcondition. In contrast to runtime checking, in modular verification the query is not executed but rather only the information from its specification is used[2]. However, whereas the value of the field `next` in Figure 6 is specified, the evaluation of the `get` query is not.

—— JAVA ——

```
1    public static void remove(Node o, int i){
2        Node n=get(o,i-1);
3        n.next=n.next.next;
4    }
```

—— JAVA ——

Fig. 5. Implementation of the modifier method `remove`

A similar problem occurs also with the other queries: `size` and `acyclic`. When verifying a program which invokes the query `remove` two times in a row, e.g. `remove(o,i);remove(o,k);`, the postcondition of the first invocation of `remove` must imply the precondition of the second invocation:

---

[2] Also in verification the implementation of the query can be used instead of the specification, but since the state space is infinite, or arbitrarily large, it cannot be flattened to a finite set of executions.

——— JML ——

```
1    public normal_behavior
2    requires   0<i && i<size(o) && acyclic(o);
3    assignable Node.footprint; //for KeY: get(o,i-1).next;
4    accessible Node.footprint;
5    ensures    \old(get(o,i-1)).next==\old(get(o,i+1));
```

——— JML ———

Fig. 6. A precise specification of the method **remove**

——— JML ——

```
1    /*@ public normal_behavior
2    requires 0<i && i<size(o) && acyclic(o);
3    assignable Node.footprint; //for KeY: get(o,i-1).next;
4    accessible Node.footprint;
5    ensures  (\forall int j;0<=j && j<i; get(o,j)==\old(get(o,j)));
6    ensures  (\forall int k;i<k && k<=\old(size(o));
7                                get(o,k)==\old(get(o,k+1)));
8    ensures  size(o) == \old(size(o))-1 && acyclic(o);          @*/
```

——— JML ———

Fig. 7. Specification of the method **remove** using the query **get**

$$\overbrace{\ldots \backslash \mathrm{old}(\mathrm{get}(o,i-1)).\mathrm{next} = \backslash \mathrm{old}(\mathrm{get}(o,i+1))}^{\text{postcondition of } \mathtt{remove(o,i)}} \to \overbrace{0 < k \wedge k < \mathrm{size}(o) \wedge \mathrm{acyclic}(o)}^{\text{precondition of } \mathtt{remove(o,k)}}$$

where '...' stands for additional assumptions, e.g. $0 < k < i < \mathrm{size}(o)$, to ensure validity of the formula. In order to prove this formula, knowledge is needed of how the new information about the field **next** changes the evaluation of **size** and **acyclic**. This knowledge can be provided either in the form of a lemma, or, following our approach, in the postcondition of the modifier method.

5.1 Specification of the Method Remove Using Queries

A specification of the **remove** method that uses the **get** query is provided in Figure 7. Since the specification describes the return value of **get** after calling **remove**, one can regard it also as a specification of the query with respect to the execution of **remove**. The specification contains three postconditions. The first

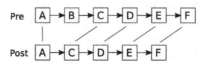

Fig. 8. Correspondence of list nodes before and after removing element B

—— JAVA + JML ——————————————————————————————————

```
1   /*@ public normal_behavior
2     requires 0<i && i<=size(o) && acyclic(o);
3     requires e.next==null && (\forall int i;0<=i && i<=size(o);get(o,i)!= e);
4     assignable Node.footprint;
5     accessible Node.footprint;
6     ensures (\forall int j;0<=j && j<i;get(o,j)==\old(get(o,j)));
7     ensures get(o,i) == e;
8     ensures (\forall int k; i<k && k<=\old(size(o))+2;get(o,k)==\old(get(o,k-1)));
9     ensures size(o) == \old(size(o))+1 && acyclic(o); @*/
10    public static void insert(/*@nullable */ Node o, int i, Node e){
11      Node tmp = get(o,i-1);
12      lem_getTransNull(o); //this is a lemma, see Figure 3
13      e.next = tmp.next;
14      tmp.next = e;
15    }
```

——— JAVA + JML ——

Fig. 9. Specification and implementation of **insert** using queries

—— JAVA + JML ——————————————————————————————————

```
1   /*@ public normal_behavior
2     requires (\exists int i; ((o==null && i==0) ||
3              (i>0 && get(o,i-1)!=null && get(o,i)==null)) );
4     assignable \nothing;
5     accessible Node.footprint;
6     ensures ((o==null && \result==0) ||
7       (\result>0 && get(o,\result-1)!=null && get(o,\result)==null));   @*/
8   public static int /*@ pure */ size(/*@nullable */ Node o){...};
```

——— JAVA + JML ——

Fig. 10. Specification of the query method **size**

(Line 5) describes the new value of the query with respect to its old one (i.e., before executing the method) for the list interval that has not been changed. The second postcondition (Lines 6 and 7) describes the interval after the removed element; here the list has been shifted as depicted in Figure 8. These two postconditions solve the problem of proving the following assertion:

assume	value of get(o,i) is known
invoke	remove(o,j)
assert	$\phi(\text{get(o,i)})$

If the formula $\phi(\text{get(o,i)})$ is true, it can be proved using the specification given in Figure 7 instead of the one in Figure 6. The reason is that full information about **get** is available after invoking **remove**.

The third postcondition (Figure 7, Line 8) specifies the return values of **size** and **acyclic** in the post state of **remove**. Hence, when calling **remove** twice in a row, sufficient knowledge is provided to the theorem prover to prove that the postcondition of the first invocation implies the precondition of the second one.

The specification of **insert** (Figure 9) follows similar principles to those of **remove**. Programs constructed with these methods can therefore be verified using the methods' contracts.

5.2   List Size and Acyclicity

The `size` query, which returns the list's length, is used in Lines 2, 6, and 8 of Figure 7. Note that the length of the list is arbitrary and not fixed, i.e., the correctness proof is valid for every length. The specification is also correct without the upper bound `\old(size(o))` of the quantification (Line 6), as `get(o,i)==null` when `i>size(o)`. Omitting the upper bound even simplifies the verification since less queries are used, the formula is smaller, less case distinctions have to be made, and quantifier instantiation—a well-known problem in theorem proving—is simpler. However, we have included the quantification bound as it is important for runtime checking tools. Such tools check the quantified formula explicitly for all elements of the quantification domain, e.g., by using a for-loop, thus they usually cannot handle unbounded quantifiers.

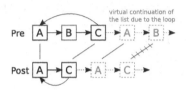
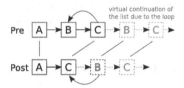

Fig. 11. Removing element B within a cycle of a cyclic list

Fig. 12. Removing element B at the beginning of the cycle of a cyclic list

One way to refer to the list's size is by storing it in a field of the class `Node`. The value of this field can be defined using a class invariant and has to be explicitly updated by the methods that modify the list. This approach simplifies verification since in our approach the return value of `size` has to be deduced from the list structure every time it is used. Nevertheless, we decided to use a query in order to follow rigorously one approach.

Figure 10 shows the specification of `size` that we have used for verification. It uses neither recursion nor quantifiers. Since the query is used inside other specifications, keeping it small and simple is very important for reducing proof complexity. When using other variants to specify `size`, e.g. a recursive specification, automatic proof attempts of `remove` were more complicated or even failed. For cyclic and infinite lists the precondition of `size` is *false* and its return value is undefined. Acyclicity of the list must be ensured from the context where the query is used as it is the case for the specifications of `remove` and `insert`.

Acyclicity is required for using the modifier methods (e.g., Figure 7, Line 2). It can be implicity expressed as `\exists int i;i==size(o)`. However, using an explicit specification of acyclicity is much more efficient and practical. Figure 13 shows the specification of the query `acyclic`. A cycle exists if there are two distinct integers i and j such that `get(o,i)==get(o,j)` and `get(o,i)!=null`.

The methods `remove` and `insert` can be generalized for cyclic lists. However, then the specification and verification become more complicated. The problem occurs when removing an element within the cycle, as shown in Figure 11. When traversing the list in the pre- and poststate of `remove`, the size of the interval on which the list is shifted is increased each cycle. A solution is to redefine `size`

—— Java + JML ——————————————————————————

```
1   /*@ public normal_behavior
2     assignable \nothing;
3     accessible Node.footprint;
4     ensures \result == (\forall int i;0<=i && i<=size(o);
5                          (\forall int j;i<j && j<=size(o);
6                          (get(o,i)!=null==>get(o,i)!=get(o,j)))); @*/
7   public static boolean /*@ pure */ acyclic(/*@nullable*/ Node o){...};
```

—————————————————————————————— Java + JML ——

Fig. 13. Specification of the query method `acyclic`

such that it will return the length of the list before the cycle repeats. To handle cyclic lists, also the implementation of `remove` (Figure 5) has to be changed. The reason is that if the element that is removed is the first in the cycle, then two pointers, rather than one, must be changed. Otherwise, the shape of the list may change without actually removing the element (Figure 12).

5.3   The Order of Postconditions Reflects Semantic Dependencies

The postconditions are connected via a conjunction. Nevertheless, the order of the postconditions is structured in a specific way to assist a verification tool in finding a proof. To prove one of the postconditions, but the first, in the specification of `remove` and `insert`, the preceding postcondition must be assumed as a premise. For instance, a proof of the postcondition in Lines 6-7 of Figure 7 requires the postcondition in Line 5 as an assumption. The reason is that to prove that the list has been shifted by one element after the removed element (Lines 6-7), the assumption is needed that it was not shifted on the interval before the removed element (Line 5); see also Figure 8. The postcondition in Line 8 adds another layer to the specification, which semantically depends on the postconditions in Line 5-7. It formalizes properties of `size` and `acyclic` in the poststate of `remove`. These queries are defined in terms of `get`, i.e., when replacing the queries by their postconditions, a formula is obtained that uses `get` as the only query. Hence, to prove the postcondition in Line 8, those in Lines 5-7 must be used as premises, as full information about `get` in the poststate of `remove` is needed. A similar argumentation explains also the sequential dependency of the postconditions of `insert` in Figure 9. This is a new technique, hence existing tools need to be extended, as we did in KeY, to utilize the postcondition order.

6   Verification, Runtime Checking, and Discussion

Verification. To verify the code presented in the listings we have used an extended version of KeY, a tool that enables automatic and interactive verification. Some techniques used by it are: symbolic execution of Java programs, handling of pointer aliasing, first-order theorem proving with quantifier handling via E-matching, and reasoning with integer arithmetics. It also allows applying an induction rule interactively by supplying an induction hypothesis. Such features, or equivalent ones, are needed for the verification of the code.

To achieve fully automatic verification of the presented code we have investigated the verification conditions that arose and developed techniques that increase KeY's power by several orders of magnitude for programs with recursive specifications and queries. I.e., each improvement eliminated a big set of user interactions of a certain category that were needed. A detailed description of these techniques cannot be given in this paper due to lack of space. We briefly point out three techniques that we have developed as a result of this research:

(1) *A set of strategies for replacing occurrences of queries in verification conditions by their definitions, i.e. by their pre- and postconditions.* Originally, KeY performed such replacements randomly, but for handling recursive queries such as `get` well-designed strategies are needed. Since the query `get` is specified recursively, the effect of the query expansion is that the second argument of the query is subtracted by one. Performing such a replacement is required in order to prove equality between terms. For instance, in order to prove $\Phi \rightarrow get(o, i) = get(o, i + 1)$, where Φ contains some assumptions that are not shown here, it may be necessary to apply query expansion to the term $get(o, i+1)$, i.e., to get a term with $get(o, (i+1) - 1)$ that will match the term $get(o, i)$. Originally KeY has chosen randomly which queries to expand but this approach did not lead to successful proofs. We have developed several query expansion heuristics which improved verification also of other kinds of programs than those described in this paper. The following three query expansion heuristics are required: expansion of queries after execution of the loop body; breadth-first query expansion (all queries expanded once, then twice, etc.); and detection and suppression of infinite loops in the proof caused by unfolding of recursive queries.

(2) *Automatic application of integer induction on postconditions that use quantifiers* (Figures 7 and 9). Induction is essential to prove these postconditions. A characteristic of the quantified formulas in the specifications is that they put two terms with the query `get` which are evaluated in two different states, i.e. pre- and poststate, into relation, e.g.:

$$\texttt{get(o,j)==\textbackslash old(get(o,j)).} \tag{1}$$

The only useful reasoning step that can be applied to this equation is unfolding these queries which, leads among other formulas to the equation

$$\texttt{get(o,j-1)==\textbackslash old(get(o,j-1)).} \tag{2}$$

Hence, if we assume (2), then the original Equation (1) can be proved. However, repeating such unfolding does not terminate, because j stands for an arbitrary number. Only for a concrete value, e.g. where $j = 0$, the Equation (1) can be proved using unfolding. Looking closely at these steps one can see that this is induction. We have extended KeY to perform automatically integer induction on the postconditions with quantified formulas. Fortunately, it is sufficient to use the quantified formulas as induction hypotheses that occur in the postconditions to prove them, hence no additional complicated techniques are needed to generate induction hypotheses.

(3) *Reuse already proved formulas as lemmas for further proofs.* The postconditions are proved sequentially and used as premises or lemmas for proving

following postconditions. This extension was necessary due to the semantic dependencies between the postconditions (see Section 5.3). This approach mimics the proving style of the theorem prover Isabelle. Hence, from a broad perspective this idea is not new but we have not seen this style of specification in JML or being applied for the specification of lists in the related work.

With these improvements the verification proof of `remove` involves approximately 100.000 rule applications and the proof of `insert` is in the range of 150.000 rule applications. In comparison, using KeY to verify code of similar size (not related to lists) that does not use recursion and that does not require induction can be typically proved using approximately 1.000 rule applications.

Runtime Checking. For testing the code and the specifications using a runtime checker we have used the automatic random testing tool JET [5]. No changes to the code have been required. However, to create more meaningful tests we have encapsulated the test code with a test driver. The goal was not to check if the code and specification are correct—they already have been formally verified—but rather to check if the specification is compatible with a runtime checker. KeY and JET do not use the same JML dialect, thus we have been required to change the way frame conditions are written (see remark in Section 4.1). Since our approach does not use sophisticated frame conditions but rather only safe approximations, the transformation of specifications between both dialects is safe and trivial. The most important change we have used for an intermediate specification was to introduce upper bounds of quantification in the specification, using the query `size`. Adding the `size` query and the upper bound to the quantifications made the verification more difficult, thus more improvements in KeY were required.

Discussion. We have compared our approach to alternative ones. One alternative is to use arrays or sequences as abstract data types for lists. Such an abstraction stores a copy of the list and provides direct access to its elements via an index, e.g. `a[i]`, similar to `get(o,i)`. The fundamental difference is that an array (sequence) has its own (ghost-) state that exists in parallel to the state of the actual list, whereas the method `get` *derives* a value from the state of the list. Specification and verification of list operations using arrays (sequences) abstraction differ from approaches employing query methods. A coupling invariant that relates the content of the array (sequence) with the state of the list is needed. When the list is modified, the array (sequence) must also be changed explicitly using JML's `set` keyword. For runtime checking this means that the original code must be extended with ghost code. We found that these additional annotations and ghost state simplify verification, since induction is not needed. However, this overhead can make specifications larger and harder to understand, issues which we tried to avoid by using the suggested approach. The approach we followed can also be generalized for handling data types other than lists.

To ensure that the specifications of the methods also work for verification in practice when reasoning with method contracts, we have verified some simple programs that use these methods. Specifying and automatically verifying disjointness of two lists after calling the modifier methods was no problem. We yet have not investigated programs with shared lists, where the nodes u and o are distinct and there exist integers i and j such that $\mathtt{get}(u, i) = \mathtt{get}(o, j)$. To verify such programs, additional lemmas are needed. We have verified some of them, such as $\forall o, u : Node. \, \forall i : int.u = \mathtt{get}(o, i) \rightarrow \mathtt{get}(u, j) = \mathtt{get}(o, i + j)$.

We have experimented also with specifications for trees. Quantification over the nodes of a tree is complicated due to the branching nature of a tree. One possibility is using quantification over arrays which describe paths in the tree. However, runtime checking tools have problems with such quantification and also reasoning is difficult. Several possibilities exist for precisely indexing nodes in a tree using integers. Quantification over integers works for runtime checking but the arithmetics is very complicated for verification. A more suitable specification approach for verification is using a "contains" query for specifying containment of nodes and subtrees. This approach is, however, problematic for runtime checking due to quantification over nodes. Whether it is possible to write specifications for trees that are compatible with verification and runtime checking is thus an open question.

7   Conclusion and Future Work

The paper describes how a specification of a linked data structure can be written that is compatible with runtime checking and verification—a goal that existing specifications often do not satisfy [7]. As an example, we presented a specification of linked list operations using JML that is readable, that is based on first-order logic with integers, and that is, to the best of our knowledge, unique considering all its characteristics. Along that presentation we elaborated problems that arise, related to verification and runtime checking, and our solutions. We developed the ideas and techniques based on several hundred experiments consisting of verification tasks that were conducted during this research.

Using queries for specification makes verification difficult, and has been proposed as a challenge in verification [12]. However, such specifications are easily readable, can be executed by runtime checkers, and can be used as abstractions in verification. Using the self-defined query $\mathtt{get}$ rather than a special construct, i.e. JML's reachability predicate, enables flexibility, as users can define their own queries. The semantics of such a query is given by its implementation and specification, thus it can be understood by other tools.

We have investigated what verification techniques are needed for automatic verification. Additional techniques we have developed are: strategies for replacing (recursive) queries by their definition in formulas; automatic application of integer induction on the postconditions that contain quantifiers; and reuse of already proven postconditions as premises for proving succeeding postconditions.

Future plans are handling of shared lists and extension of the approach to other linked data structures. One idea is deducing of framing conditions for queries.

Acknowledgment. We would like to thank Thorsten Bormer and Mattias Ulbrich for valuable discussions. We also thank the referees for their helpful comments and suggestions.

References

1. Albert, E., Bubel, R., Genaim, S., Hähnle, R., Román-Díez, G.: Verified resource guarantees for heap manipulating programs. In: de Lara, J., Zisman, A. (eds.) FASE 2012. LNCS, vol. 7212, pp. 130–145. Springer, Heidelberg (2012)
2. Becker, K., Leavens, G.T.: Class LinkedList, http://www.eecs.ucf.edu/~leavens/JML-release/ javadocs/java/util/LinkedList.html#removeint
3. Beckert, B., Hähnle, R., Schmitt, P.H. (eds.): Verification of Object-Oriented Software. LNCS (LNAI), vol. 4334. Springer, Heidelberg (2007)
4. Beckert, B., Trentelman, K.: Second-order principles in specification languages for object-oriented programs. In: Sutcliffe, G., Voronkov, A. (eds.) LPAR 2005. LNCS (LNAI), vol. 3835, pp. 154–168. Springer, Heidelberg (2005)
5. Cheon, Y.: A quick tutorial on JET. Technical Report UTEP-CS-07-40, Department Technical Reports (CS), University of Texas at El Paso (June 2007)
6. Darvas, A., Müller, P.: Reasoning about method calls in interface specifications. Journal of Object Technology 5(5), 59–85 (2006)
7. du Bousquet, L., Ledru, Y., Maury, O., Oriat, C., Lanet, J.-L.: Reusing a JML specification dedicated to verification for testing, and vice-versa: Case studies. Journal of Automated Reasoning 45, 415–435 (2010), 10.1007/s10817-009-9132-y
8. Jacobs, B., Piessens, F.: Inspector methods for state abstraction. Journal of Object Technology 6(5), 55–75 (2007)
9. Jensen, J.B., Birkedal, L., Sestoft, P.: Modular verification of linked lists with views via separation logic. Journal of Object Technology 10(2), 1–20 (2011)
10. Lahiri, S.K., Qadeer, S.: Verifying properties of well-founded linked lists. In: Proceedings of POPL, pp. 115–126. ACM (2006)
11. Leavens, G.T., Baker, A.L., Ruby, C.: Preliminary design of JML: a behavioral interface specification language for Java. SEN 31(3), 1–38 (2006)
12. Leavens, G.T., Leino, R., Müller, P.: Specification and verification challenges for sequential object-oriented programs. Formal Asp. Comput. 19(2), 159–189 (2007)
13. Leino, K.R.M.: Specification and verification of object-oriented software. In: Engineering Methods and Tools for Software Safety and Security. NATO Science for Peace and Security, vol. 22, pp. 231–266. IOS Press (2009)
14. Lev-Ami, T., Immerman, N., Reps, T.W., Sagiv, M., Srivastava, S., Yorsh, G.: Simulating reachability using first-order logic with applications to verification of linked data structures. Logical Methods in Computer Science 5(2) (2009)
15. Manevich, R., Yahav, E., Ramalingam, G., Sagiv, M.: Predicate abstraction and canonical abstraction for singly-linked lists. In: Cousot, R. (ed.) VMCAI 2005. LNCS, vol. 3385, pp. 181–198. Springer, Heidelberg (2005)
16. Nelson, G.: Verifying reachability invariants of linked structures. In: Proceedings of POPL, pp. 38–47. ACM (1983)
17. Nguyen, H.H., Kuncak, V., Chin, W.-N.: Runtime checking for separation logic. In: Logozzo, F., Peled, D.A., Zuck, L.D. (eds.) VMCAI 2008. LNCS, vol. 4905, pp. 203–217. Springer, Heidelberg (2008)
18. Rajamani, S.K.: Verification, testing and statistics. In: Bensalem, S., Peled, D.A. (eds.) RV 2009. LNCS, vol. 5779, p. 25. Springer, Heidelberg (2009)
19. Smans, J., Jacobs, B., Piessens, F.: Implicit dynamic frames: Combining dynamic frames and separation logic. In: Drossopoulou, S. (ed.) ECOOP 2009. LNCS, vol. 5653, pp. 148–172. Springer, Heidelberg (2009)
20. Zee, K., Kuncak, V., Rinard, M.: Full functional verification of linked data structures. In: Proceedings of PLDI, pp. 349–361 (2008)

Toward the Revision of CTL Models through Kripke Modal Transition Systems

Paulo T. Guerra[1], Aline Andrade[2], and Renata Wassermann[1]

[1] University of São Paulo
{paulotgo,renata}@ime.usp.br
[2] Federal University of Bahia
aline@ufba.br

Abstract. In this paper we consider the problem of automatic repair of models in the context of system partial specification. This problem is a challenge involving theoretical and practical issues and the theory of belief revision is an alternative to give theoretical support to its solution. A Kripke structure is widely used to model systems, but it does not express partial information explicitly and a set of these structures might be required to represent several possibilities of behavior. A more general structure is the Kripke Modal Transition System (KMTS) which can specify systems with partial information and can be interpreted as a set of Kripke models. In this paper, we propose a framework for the repair of KMTS based on belief revision combined with model checking as an approach to revise sets of Kripke structures. We demonstrate the advantages of our approach, even with the existing restrictions in representing general sets of CTL models over the KMTS formalism.

1 Introduction

In the preliminary phases of system development it can be necessary to deal with incomplete information because generally not all requirements are already known. To specify an undetermined system it is desirable that models can represent partial information, such as possible behaviors. When a model does not explicitly express partial information, an alternative is to take several models as possible candidates for the system behavior. In both cases the models should be able to be formally verified and when a desired property is not satisfied the models must be repaired, ideally automatically.

We consider in this work the technique of model checking [1] for the verification of systems, particularly model checking over Kripke structures as CTL (Computation Tree Logic) models. A CTL model checker solves the decision problem: given a Kripke structure K, an initial state s_0 and a CTL formula φ, does K satisfy ϕ from s_0? ($K, s_0 \models \phi$?). When the property is not satisfied, the model checker shows a counter-example that can guide the repair of the model.

A CTL model does not express partial information explicitly. A set of these structures might be required to represent several possibilities of behavior. A more general Kripke structure is the Kripke Modal Transition System (KMTS) which is adequate for the specification of systems with partial information [2] and can

J. Iyoda and L. de Moura (Eds.): SBMF 2013, LNCS 8195, pp. 115–130, 2013.
© Springer-Verlag Berlin Heidelberg 2013

be expanded in a set of CTL models. KMTS is interpreted over a 3-valued logic and can represent behavior that must or may occur. Model checking over KMTS [2], besides *true* and *false* values, can return *indefinite* meaning both values may be consistent.

The automatic repair of models is not straightforward and presents several challenges. The theory of belief revision [3] can be applied to this problem by considering models as beliefs [4,5]. In [4], a revision operation is defined to repair a set of CTL models when they are inconsistent with a desired property.

In this paper, we define the revision of a set of CTL models through the revision of a KMTS model when the KMTS model checking returns *false* or *indefinite*. We compare it with the revision of a set of CTL models as proposed in [5] and show the correspondence between these two approaches. Although there are some restrictions in representing a general set of Kripke models, we argue that the compact representation of KMTSs has advantages during the revision process. We show how revision can be implemented, using model checking through 3-valued model checking game as proposed in [6].

To the best of our knowledge this is the first work on revision of a set of CTL models through KMTS. In [7] the authors propose an algorithm to repair KMTS models based on primitive changes defined in [8]. Unlike our proposal this work is not based on belief revision and it does not make reference to any other theory of change and its context is abstract model checking, where a KMTS model represents an abstraction of a concrete Kripke structure as proposed by [6].

This paper is organized as follows. In Section 2, we briefly introduce CTL and the model revision approach. In Section 3 we introduce KMTS and how it is expanded into Kripke structures. In Section 4 we define revision of KMTS, its operations, the minimality criterion and proofs of its correctness. We describe how to implement KMTS revision in Section 5 based on a model checking game. Finally in Sections 6 and 7 we discuss this approach and conclude the paper.

2   Preliminaries

2.1   Computation Tree Logic

The computation tree logic (CTL) [9,10] is a temporal logic where the future is represented by a time-branching structure. CTL is suitable for example to describe properties over computer program and its different execution paths. The CTL syntax is given by the following Backus-Naur form:

$$\phi ::= \top \mid \bot \mid p \mid (\neg \phi) \mid (\phi \vee \phi) \mid (\phi \wedge \phi) \mid (\phi \rightarrow \phi) \mid EX\phi \mid$$
$$AX\phi \mid EF\phi \mid AF\phi \mid EG\phi \mid AG\phi \mid E[\phi U \phi] \mid A[\phi U \phi]$$

where its temporal operators comprise: path quantifiers (E, "there is a path", or A, "for all paths"); and state operators (X, "neXt state", U, "Until", G, "Globally in states" or F, "some Future state").

The semantics for CTL is defined over a labelled transition system called Kripke structure. These structures are described by Definition 1.

Definition 1. *A Kripke structure is a tuple $M = (AP, S, S_0, R, L)$ where AP is a set of atomic propositions; S is a finite set of states, $S_0 \subseteq S$ is the set of initial states, $R \subseteq S \times S$ is transition relation over S, and $L : S \to 2^{AP}$ is a labelling function of truth assignment over states.*[1]

For convenience, we frequently refer to Kripke structures as CTL models.

2.2 CTL Model Revision

Guerra and Wassermann [4,5] propose a model repair framework using principles of belief revision theory [3]. Belief revision deals with how to rationally adapt dynamic beliefs set in order to incorporate new information, even if it is inconsistent with what is believed. This rationality principle usually involve a minimal change assumption, that is also intended to the model repair: the solution should preserve as much information as possible from the original model.

The authors define a model revision operator $\circ_c$ based on a set of basic model change operations, as proposed by [8]. These change operations represent all primitive structural changes over a CTL model:

PU1: Adding one pair to the relation R
PU2: Removing one pair from the relation R
PU3: Changing the labelling function on one state
PU4: Adding one state to S
PU5: Removing one isolated state of S

Let M and M' be two CTL models, we denote by $Diff_{PU_i}(M, M')$ the structural difference between M and M' produced by applications of PU_i, for example, $Diff_{PU_1}(M, M')$ denotes the transitions added to M in order to achieve M'.

A model change is said to be *admissible* if it produces a model M' from M such that M' satisfies the desired property and there is no model M'' obtained from M such that $Diff_{PU_i}(M, M'') \subseteq Diff_{PU_i}(M, M')$, $i = 1, ..., 5$ and $Diff_{PU_i}(M, M'') \subset Diff_{PU_i}(M, M')$, for some $i = 1, ..., 5$. Guerra and Wassermann define a minimality criterion over admissible changes in order to select minimal changes according to belief revision principles, therefore defining the following revision operator:

$$Mod(\psi \circ_c \phi) = Min_{Mod(\psi)}(Mod(\phi)),$$

where ψ, ϕ are CTL formulas that represent the initial beliefs and the new information, respectively, $Mod(\alpha)$ all CTL models of a formula α and $Min_{\mathcal{B}}(\mathcal{A})$ the set of all minimal models of $\mathcal{A}$ according to any admissible modification on any model of $\mathcal{B}$. The authors show that $\circ_c$ satisfies the rationality postulates for belief revision as presented in [11].

Guerra and Wasserman [4] also proposed an algorithm for CTL model revision. The algorithm receives as input a CTL formula ϕ and a set of CTL models

---

[1] Usually the transition relation is defined as total. Although it makes simple the definition of many temporal logic semantics, this requirement is not needed.

that do not satisfy ϕ, then by repairing each model individually and filtering these repaired models according to their belief revision ordering criterion, the algorithm returns as result a set of revised models representing possible corrections to the original models relative to the formula ϕ.

3   Kripke Model Transition System as Sets of CTL Models

KMTS are expressive models to represent undetermined or sub-specified systems. They have two types of transitions, transitions that *must* occur and transitions that *may* occur, which represent necessary and possible behavior, respectively.

Specification over KMTS are written in the $\mu - calculus$ and in this work we use this language in its negation normal form.

Definition 2. *($\mu - calculus$). Let AP be a set of atomic propositions and V a set of propositional variables. The set of literals over AP is defined as $Lit = AP \cup \{\neg p \mid p \in AP\}$. The $\mu - calculus$ in its negation normal form over AP is defined by $\varphi ::= l \mid Z \mid \varphi \wedge \varphi \mid \varphi \vee \varphi \mid AX\varphi \mid EX\varphi \mid \mu Z.\varphi \mid \upsilon Z.\varphi$ where $l \in Lit$ and $Z \in V$. AX means for all successors and EX means there exists a successor. μ denote the least fixpoint and υ denote the greatest fixpoint. A formula φ is closed if all its variables Z are bounded by a fixpoint operator μ or υ.*

CTL formulas can be specified in $\mu - calculus$ by the following translation: $EF\phi \equiv \mu Z.\phi \vee EXZ; AF\phi \equiv \mu Z.\phi \vee AXZ; EG\phi \equiv \upsilon Z.\phi \wedge EXZ; AG\phi \equiv \upsilon Z.\phi \wedge AXZ; E[\phi U\phi] \equiv \mu Z.\phi \vee (\phi \wedge EXZ);$ and $A[\phi U\phi] \equiv \mu Z.\phi \vee (\phi \wedge AXZ)$.

Definition 3. *A Kripke modal transition system (KMTS) is a tuple $M = \langle AP, S, S_0, R^+, R^-, L \rangle$, where S is a set of finite sates, $S_0 \subseteq S$ is the set of initail states, $R^+ \subseteq S \times S$ and $R^- \subseteq S \times S$ are transition relations such that $R^+ \subseteq R^-$, and $L : S \to 2^{Lit}$ is a label function, such that for all state s and $p \in AP$, at most one between p and $\neg p$ occur. The transitions R^+ e R^- correspond to the transitions must and may respectively.*

The semantics defined below is presented in [6]. A complete semantics of $\mu - calculus$ is presented in [12].

Definition 4. *The semantics of three values $\|\varphi\|_3^M$ of a closed formula φ with respect to a KMTS M is a map from S to $\{T, F, \perp\}$. The interesting cases are defined below.*

$$\| l \|_3^M (s) = T \ if \ l \in L(s), F \ if \ \neg l \in L(s), \perp \ otherwise.$$

$$\|AX\varphi\|_3^M (s) = \begin{cases} T, & if \ \forall t \in S, if \ R^-(s,t) \ then \ \|\varphi\|_3^M (t) = T \\ F, & if \ \exists t \in S \ such \ that \ R^+(s,t) \ and \ \|\varphi\|_3^M (t) = F \\ \perp, & otherwise. \end{cases}$$

And dually for $EX\varphi$ exchanging F and T.

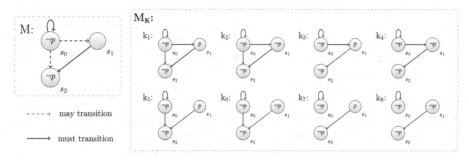

Fig. 1. (a) Example of a KMTS M   (b) Expansion M_K of M

3.1   Expanding KMTS into CTL Models

In this section we formally define a KMTS expansion into a set of Kripke structures showing its capacity to compactly represent CTL models and some limitations of this representation.

Definition 5. *Let $M = \langle AP, S, S_0, R^+, R^-, L \rangle$ be a KMTS, the KMTS expansion of M, denoted by M_K, is the set of all Kripke models $K' = \langle AP', S', S'_0, R', L' \rangle$ such that $AP' = AP$, $S' = S$, $S'_0 = S_0$, $R^+ \subseteq R' \subseteq R^-$ and $L(s) \subseteq L'(s)$, for all $s \in S$.*

The KMTS expansion may lead to an exponential set of Kripke models, as stated in Proposition 1. On the other hand, it shows the capacity of this formalism to compactly represent a huge set of CTL models in one single structure. It is important to note that KMTS may not be expressive enough to represent all possible sets of CTL models, as shown in Proposition 2.

Proposition 1. *Let $M = \langle AP, S, S_0, R^+, R^-, L \rangle$ be a KMTS with $m = |R^- \setminus R^+|$ genuine (strictly) may transitions and $n = |\{s \in S \mid p \in AP \text{ and } p, \neg p \notin L(s)\}|$ state indeterminations. M can be expanded into 2^{m+n} Kripke structures.*

Proof. It follows straight from the number of possible combinations of each KMTS indetermination that can be realized or not in the Kripke structures.

Proposition 2. *Let $K = \{k_1, ..., k_n\}$ any set of kripke structures $k_i = \langle AP, S, S_0, R_i, L_i \rangle$. Not necessarily exists a KMTS $M = \langle AP, S, S_0, R^+, R^-, L \rangle$ that can be expanded into K.*

Proof. Take for example $K = \{k_3, k_5\}$ of Figure 1(b). No KMTS $M = \langle \{p\}, \{s_0, s_1, s_2\}, \{s_0\}, \{(s_0, s_0), (s_1, s_2)\}, R_-, L \rangle$ can be expanded in this set. This is because the KMTS formalism does not provide any way of expressing interdependency between indeterminations. In this example, we could not express in M that the transitions (s_0, s_1) and (s_0, s_2) should not occur at the same time.

To represent any set of Kripke structures we have two alternatives: (1) to associate a selection function to a KMTS that selects the desired Kripke models among its expanded models; (2) to consider a set of KMTS models that represent the set of Kripke models. In the second alternative, in the worse case, each KMTS will be a Kripke model.

Proposition 3. *Let M be a KMTS and $K = \{k_1, ..., k_n\}$ the Kripke structures expanded from M. Consider s_0 the initial state of M. For all closed formula φ of $\mu - calculus$, if the semantic value of $\|\varphi\|_3^M (s_0)$ is equal to*

1. $\perp$, then $\exists k_i, k_j \in K, i \neq j$ such that $(\|\varphi\|^{k_i} (s_0) = T$ and $\|\varphi\|^{k_j} (s_0) = F$

2. T, then $\forall k_i \in K, \|\varphi\|^{k_i} (s_0) = T$

3. F, then $\forall k_i \in K, \|\varphi\|^{k_i} (s_0) = F$

Proof. It follows straight from the semantics of KMTS and the expansion of it.

4   Revision of KMTS Models

In this section we define the KMTS model revision operation, through the specification of minimal change criterion over KMTS models and showing its correspondence to the minimal changes over sets of KMTS expanded Kripke models. This minimality criterion is similar to that proposed by [5], but now considering a different set of primitive operations which represent possibilities of changes in KMTS models, as shown below.

> P1: Removing one pair from the relation R^-
> P2: Removing one pair from the relation R^+
> P3: Transforming one pair (s_i, s_j) of R^- to (s_i, s_j) of R^+
> P4: Changing a defined literal on one state label
> P5: Assigning a literal to a a state label if it is undefined in it

For the definitions below we consider some notation. X_{Pn} denotes a set of changes relative to operation $P_n, 1 \leq n \leq 5$. Each change in X_{Pn} is represented as (s_i, s_j) or (s_i, l), where l is a literal, depending on whether the change is relative to transitions or to state labels, respectively. A change X is represented as $X = (X_{P1}, ..., X_{P5})$, where X_{Pn} can be an empty set if no change of type P_n occurs. We say that $X = (X_{P1}, ..., X_{P5}) \subset Y = (Y_{P1}, ..., Y_{P5})$ if for each $X_{Pn} \subseteq Y_{Pn}$ and at least one $X_{Pi} \subset Y_{Pi}$. The application of X to a model A results in another model denoted by $A(X)$. We refer to $M, s_0 \models \varphi$ is *True, False* or $\perp$ to indicate the result of model checking φ in M from s_0.

Our definition of minimal change over KMTS is based on the operations P2 and P4, the operations P1, P3 and P5 are disregarded. This makes sense because among the Kripke models expanded of the KMTS there are models without the transitions of P1, which already have the transitions of case P3, and those where the state label already has the literal of P5 assigned. In this sense, these modifications should not be considered for all models. We then define minimal changes considering a reduced change $X/$ of a change X as defined below.

Definition 6. *Let $X = (X_{P1}, ..., X_{P5})$, the reduced change $X/$ of X is defined as $X/ = (X_{P2}, X_{P4})$.*

A reduced change $X/ = (X_{P2}, X_{P4})$ over a KMTS M induces changes in $K \in M_K$: all $(s_i, s_j) \in X_{P2}$ induces a change (s_i, s_j) of type $PU2$ in K and all $(s_i, l) \in X_{P4}$ induces a change (s_i, l) of type $PU3$ in K. So, we also refer X_{P2} and X_{P4} as changes over K meaning its corresponding induced changes.

Definition 7. *Given two changes $X1 = (X1_{P1}, ..., X1_{P5})$ and $X2 = (X2_{P1}, ..., X2_{P5})$, $X1 \leq X2$ iff for all n, $X1/_{Pn} \subseteq X2/_{Pn}$. $X1 < X2$ iff $X1 \leq X2$ and there is at least one n, such that $X1/_{Pn} \subset X2/_{Pn}$. If there is no $X2$ such that $X2 < X1$, $X1$ is said to be minimal.*

Propositions 4, 5 and 6 show that the defined minimality criterion for KMTS correspond to the minimality criterion (presented in section 2.2) for the set of Kripke models expanded of the KMTS, i.e. the revision of a set of Kripke models can be achieved by the revision of a KMTS that represents them. The next proposition specifies that any change in a Kripke model, that belongs to M_K, can be achieved through a change in M.

Proposition 4. *Let M be a KMTS, M_K its corresponding expansion, $K1$ a model in M_K and $Y = (Y_{P2}, Y_{P4})$ a change in $K1$. Then there is a change X in M such that $M(X)_K$ contains the model $K1(Y)$.*

Proof. Construct $X = (X_{P1}, X_{P2}, X_{P3}, X_{P4}, X_{P5})$: X_{P1} contains all (s_i, s_j) may transitions such that (s_i, s_j) are not transitions of $K1$; X_{P2} contains (s_i, s_j) $\in Y_{P2}$ if (s_i, s_j) is a must transition in M, otherwise (s_i, s_j) is included in X_{P1}; X_{P3} contains all (s_i, s_j) may transitions which correspond to (s_i, s_j) transitions of $K1$; X_{P4} contains $(s_i, l) \in Y_{P4}$ if l or $\neg l \in label(s_i)$ in M, otherwise include it in X_{P5}. Take a model $K2$ from M_K which differs from $K1$ in two ways: 1) for all $(s_i, l) \in X_{P5}, l \in label(s_i)$ in $K2$; 2) $K2$ does not have the transitions (s_i, s_j) of Y_{P2} if they are may transitions in M ($K2$ exists because the expansion of M generates all Kripke models resulting from all the possibilities of transforming indetermination in M in determinations in Kripke models, in the best case $K2 = K1$ and $X/ = Y$). Therefore $M(X)_K$ contains the model $K2(X/)$ which is equal to $K1(Y)$.

Proposition 5. *Let M be a KMTS and $X = (X_{P1}, X_{P2}, X_{P3}, X_{P4}, X_{P5})$ be a minimal change in M. Then $X/ = (X_{P2}, X_{P4})$ is a minimal change in M_K.*

Proof. Suppose $X/$ is not minimal in M_K, so there is a change $Y = (Y_{P2}, Y_{P4})$ in M_K such that $Y < X/$. The transitions of Y_{P2} are not may transitions in M and all literals of the states in Y_{P4} are defined literals in the respective states in M. By the proposition 4 there is a change Z in M constructed from Y such that $Z/ = Y$. So, $Z/ < X/$ which implies that $Z < X$, a contradiction.

Proposition 6. *Let M be a KMTS such that $M, s_0 \models \varphi$ is False, $X = (X_{P1}, X_{P2}, X_{P3}, X_{P4}, X_{P5})$ a minimal change in M such that $M(X), s_0 \models \varphi$ is True. So, there is a model K in M_K such that $K(X/), s_0 \models \varphi$ is True.*

Proof. Take a model K of M_K such that K does not have the transitions of X_{P1}, has the transitions of X_{P3} if $X_{P3} \neq \emptyset$ and for all (s_i, l) in X_{P5}, $l \in$ labels of s_i of K. For all K_i of $M(X)_K$, $K_i, s_0 \models \varphi$ is True because $M(X), s_0 \models \varphi$ is True (see proposition 3). The model $K(X/)$ is one of the K_i models.

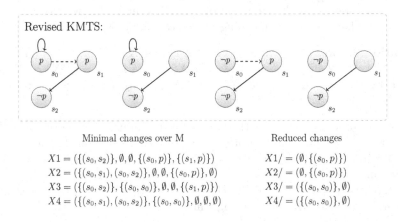

Revised KMTS:

Minimal changes over M	Reduced changes

$X1 = (\{(s_0, s_2)\}, \emptyset, \emptyset, \{(s_0, p)\}, \{(s_1, p)\})$ $X1/ = (\emptyset, \{(s_0, p)\})$
$X2 = (\{(s_0, s_1), (s_0, s_2)\}, \emptyset, \emptyset, \{(s_0, p)\}, \emptyset)$ $X2/ = (\emptyset, \{(s_0, p)\})$
$X3 = (\{(s_0, s_2)\}, \{(s_0, s_0)\}, \emptyset, \emptyset, \{(s_1, p)\})$ $X3/ = (\{(s_0, s_0)\}, \emptyset)$
$X4 = (\{(s_0, s_1), (s_0, s_2)\}, \{(s_0, s_0)\}, \emptyset, \emptyset, \emptyset)$ $X4/ = (\{(s_0, s_0)\}, \emptyset)$

Fig. 2. Revision by AXp of the KMTS M (Fig. 1(a))

Figures 2 and 3 show an example of the relation between minimal changes of a KMTS M and minimal changes of the set M_K. They present the minimal possible changes (with the operations P_1 to P_5 above) in M to satisfy the property AXp from s_0 and their respective reduced changes which correspond to the minimal changes of M_K. Consider the change $X = (\emptyset, \emptyset, \emptyset, \{(s_0, p), (s_2, p)\}, \{(s_1, p)\})$, it is not minimal because $X1 < X$. To exemplify the Proposition 4 consider the model K_4 (Fig. 1(b)) and the change $Y = (\emptyset, \{(s_0, p), (s_1, p)\})$, the model $K_4(Y) = K_3(X_2/)$. As an example of Proposition 6, consider the model K_3 (Fig. 1(b)) and the change X_1 of M (Fig. 2), $M(X_1), s_0 \models AXp$ is True and $K_3(X_1/), s_0 \models AXp$ is True.

In the case that the KMTS model checking returns $\bot$, the KMTS revision selects among its expanded Kripke models those that are consistent with the

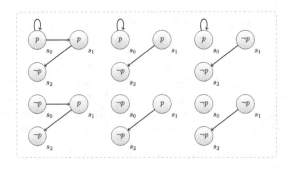

Fig. 3. Revision by AXp of the expansion M_K (Fig 1(b))

verified property. This result is aligned to the result produced by the operator $\circ_c$. When the KMTS model checking returns *false*, changes effectively modify the KMTS model. As stated before in this paper we consider only changes in state labels and removal of transitions. Although these changes seem relatively restrictive, the results presented in this paper are still relevant to domains where the KMTS completely defines the consistent information, and thus no other information such as new states can be added. Our approach is also a step forward in the definition of a general KMTS revision operator with all kinds of changes, which we intend to define afterwards.

5 Implementing Revision of KMTS Models

The revision of a KMTS model M might occur when $M, s_0 \models \varphi$ is $\bot$ or F. In case $\bot$ the revision consists of refining the KMTS to be expanded into only Kripke structures where the required property is satisfied. In case F, the KMTS should be repaired resulting in KMTSs where model checking results in T causing changes in the expanded Kripke structures.

In this section we present the 3-valued model checking game proposed by Grumberg in [12] and our proposal of an abstract algorithm over this game to refine a KMTS model.

5.1 The 3-valued Model Checking Game

In the $\mu - calculus$ 3-valued model checking game proposed in [12], Grumberg introduces the concept of non-losing strategy to identify the causes of $\bot$ in model checking besides the known concept of winning strategy. These games are defined between two players, $\exists$ and $\forall$, where the player $\exists$ tries to verify the formula and the $\forall$ tries to refute the formula.

The game for model checking a formula φ consists of a graph of configurations of type $s \vdash \psi$ where s is a state of the model and ψ is a subformula of φ. These configurations are determined from the decomposition of the formula φ in its subformulas according to the rules presented in Figure 4, considering the states and transitions of the KMTS model.

In Figure 5 we show an example of a graph of configurations of a 3-valued model checking game. A configuration is classified as a $\exists$ configuration when ψ is of the form of the antecedent of an $\exists$ rule and is represented as an ellipse in the game graph and is classified as a $\forall$ configuration if ψ is of the form of the antecedent of an $\forall$ rule and is represented as a rectangle in the game graph. Dotted edges correspond to KMTS genuine may transitions $(R_- \setminus R_+)$ and normal edges correspond to both KMTS must transitions and other moves generated from the rules that do not involve transitions of the model.

The players move from their configurations according to a strategy. A strategy of a player σ is a function between its configurations and all the configurations of the game graph. A winning strategy of player σ is such that it makes σ win a game independent of the strategy used by the other player. When neither players win the game, both of them have a non-losing strategy and the game results $\bot$. For example, in Figure 5 the bold edges are part of non-losing strategies of the $\forall$ player.

Rules of player $\exists$:

$$\dfrac{s \vdash \psi_0 \vee \psi_1}{s \vdash \psi_i} : i \in \{0,1\} \qquad \dfrac{s \vdash EX\psi}{t \vdash \psi} : R^+(s,t) \text{ or } R^-(s,t)$$

$$\dfrac{s \vdash \eta Z.\psi}{s \vdash Z} : \eta \in \{\mu, \upsilon\} \qquad \dfrac{s \vdash Z}{s \vdash \psi} : \text{if } f_p(Z) = \eta Z.\psi, \eta \in \{\mu, \upsilon\}, \text{ and } f_p(Z) \text{ is the unique subformula identified by } Z$$

Rules of player $\forall$:

$$\dfrac{s \vdash \psi_0 \wedge \psi_1}{s \vdash \psi_i} : i \in \{0,1\} \qquad \dfrac{s \vdash AX\psi}{t \vdash \psi} : R^+(s,t) \text{ or } R^-(s,t)$$

Fig. 4. Rules of the model checking game

A play can be finite or infinite and it is defined as a sequence of configurations $C_0, C_1, \ldots$ such that there is an edge from C_i to C_{i+1}. Each configuration of the graph is colored depending on the result of all plays starting from this configuration: with T if the player $\exists$ wins, with F if the player $\forall$ wins, or $\bot$ if both players do not win (or do not lose). A necessary condition for a player to win a play is to obey the restriction that all of his/her movements in the configurations of the play are through normal edges, meaning that the player does not move between configurations that corresponds to genuine may transitions of the model. Moreover, there are other conditions to determine the winner of a play as presented below.

Conditions for the player $\exists$ win a play $C_0, C_1, \ldots$:
1. To exist a $n \in N$ such that $C_n = t \vdash l$ and the state t of the model is labelled with l or
2. To exist a $n \in N$ such that $C_n = t \vdash AX\psi$ and there does not exist $t' \in S$ such that (t, t') is a transition in the model or
3. the outermost variable that occurs infinitely often is of type υ

Conditions for the player $\forall$ win a play $C_0, C_1, \ldots$:
1. To exist a $n \in N$ such that $C_n = t \vdash l$ and the state t of the model is labelled with $\neg l$ or
2. to exist a $n \in N$ such that $C_n = t \vdash EX\psi$ and does not exits $t' \in S$ such that (t, t') is a transition in the model or
3. the outermost variable that occurs infinitely often is of type μ

If neither player wins a play, the result of it is $\bot$, meaning that both players have a non-losing strategy for that play. A player wins a game if he/she wins all the plays in the game from the initial configuration $(s_0 \vdash \varphi)$.

To calculate the result of the game, one can color each configuration of the graph bottom up with T, F or $\bot$ depending on whether $\exists$ has a winning strategy, or $\forall$ has a winning strategy, or both players have a non-losing strategy, respectively, in all plays starting from that configuration. Initially the deadend configurations are colored (a deadend configuration is one that does not reach another configuration), then the coloring proceeds to other configurations taking other plays until all the configurations are colored as explained in next section. The result of the game will be the color of the root node of the graph (configuration $s_0 \vdash \varphi$). Figure 5 presents a game graph with the colored configurations (represented by the symbols enclosed in parenthesis inside the node of the configuration) and with edges that belong to the non-losing strategies of player $\forall$, represented as bold edges.

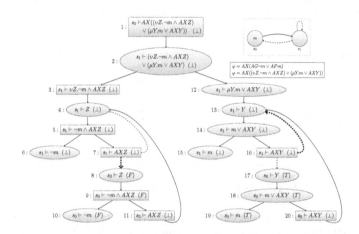

Fig. 5. Example of failure witnesses of non-losing strategy of player $\forall$

5.2   Implementing KMTS Repair

In this section we develop an algorithm to refine the KMTS (case $M, s_0 \models \varphi$ is $\bot$) based on the repair of the 3-valued model checking game. The algorithm considers non-losing strategies (that are not winning strategies) for both players $\forall$ and $\exists$ defined in [12] to determine the witnesses of the failure. Our algorithm consists of reducing the KMTS to represent only the Kripke structures that satisfy the property φ by eliminating genuine may transitions, or transforming genuine may transitions into must transitions, or changing the labels of undefined states. At the end of this section we present a quick overview of an algorithm to implement the repair when $M, s_0 \models \varphi$ is *False*.

From now on we will refer to the configurations of the game as nodes. Let ψ be a subformula of φ. We define a witness of a failure in case $M, s_0 \models \psi$ is $\bot$ one of the following transitions, which belongs to non-losing strategies of $\forall$ or $\exists$, found bottom up in the game graph: (1) a genuine may edge, coming from a node of type AX colored $\bot$, to a child node colored F or $\bot$, (2) a genuine may edge, coming from a node of type EX colored $\bot$, to a child node colored T or $\bot$, (3) a must edge, coming from a node of type EX colored $\bot$, to a child node colored $\bot$, (4) an edge coming from a node of type $s_i \vdash l \wedge \psi$ to a node $s_i \vdash l$

colored with $\perp$, (5) an edge from a node of type $s_i \vdash l \vee \psi$ where its child node $s_i \vdash l$ is colored with $\perp$ and the other child is colored $\perp$ or F. In Figure 5 the bold edges are examples of failure witnesses.

In order to obtain all the Kripke models that satisfy the property, all failure witnesses might be considered, resulting in different KMTSs. It is not necessary to consider all possible combinations of changes in order to generate all possible Kripke models because the KMTS expresses possibilities by the may transitions. For example if a node $s_0 \vdash EXp$ colored $\perp$ has two may children nodes $s_1 \vdash p, s_2 \vdash p$ both colored T, it is enough to change only one may edge at a time (to be a must edge), because the resultant KMTSs expresses the Kripke models with both transitions as must.

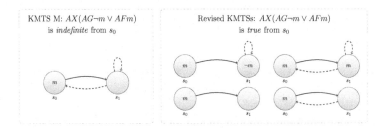

Fig. 6. Example of KMTS refinement

The algorithm Revision-game controls the refinements of the model M from the sequence of failure witnesses (Fwitness) identified by procedure Check-model, which determines them from a the 3-valued model checker game. One failure of Fwitness at a time is processed by Refine-game until no more failures exists in Fwitness. For the game of Figure 5, Fwitness will be initialized with the sequence of failure witnesses $((7,8),(16,13),(14,15))$, where a pair (m,n) represents the edge from the node m to the node n of the game. Other failure witnesses are considered by Refine-game to complement the change $X = (\{(s_1, s_0)\}, \emptyset, \emptyset, \emptyset, \emptyset)$ such as $(5,6)$ and $(16,13)$. The algorithm returns 4 KMTSs (see Figure 6) that satisfy φ with the changes: (1) $X = (\{(s_1, s_0)\}, \emptyset, \emptyset, \emptyset, \{(s_1, \neg m)\})$, (2) $X = (\{(s_1, s_0),(s_1,s_1)\}, \emptyset, \emptyset, \emptyset, \emptyset)$, (3) $X = (\{(s_1,s_1)\}, \ \emptyset, \emptyset, \emptyset, \emptyset)$, (4) $X = (\emptyset, \emptyset, \emptyset, \emptyset, \{(s_1, m)\})$.

The algorithm Refine-game controls the possible refinements from a failure witness of Fwitness. Each change X is used to the modification and recoloring of the game graph by Recolor-game (which is supposed to call the 3-valued model cheker). A change is done relative to the model, i.e., if an edge (m,n) corresponds to the transition (s_i, s_j) in the model, all edges (r,s) which correspond to (s_i, s_j) should be removed of the game graph and if the subgraphs from nodes s are no more accessible from the root node they must be desconsidered by other search for failure witnesses. If the model checker results $\perp$, all the other failure witnesses in Nwitness (determined by Recolor-game) are considered (one at a time) to complement X by call Refine-game recursively. When the result of model checking is T the model $M(X)$ is returned, the game is restored to a previous state in order to other failures witnesses from Nwitness be considered and achieve all possible complementations for the change X.

The algorithm Refine-play generates the change X according to Failure $= (m, n)$, i.e., the change generated depends on the cause of the failure which is relative to the node m or n. Consider node m of type $(s_i \vdash \psi)$ and n of type $(s_j \vdash \chi)$. Node m can be: a AX node $(s_i \vdash AX\psi)$, a EX node $(s_i \vdash EX\psi)$, a disjunctive node of type $s_i \vdash \psi \vee l$, or a conjunctive node of type $s_i \vdash \psi \wedge l$. The conditions specified in the algorithm cover the cases described below that represent the possible changes required.

A node EX is true if it has a must child colored with true, it is false if all its may children are false and otherwise it is $\perp$. If node m is a EX node and n is colored T and (m, n) is a may transition, it should be transformed into a must transition. A may edge to a node of type $s_k \vdash V$ that represents loop in the graph and V is a greatest fixpoint variable (ν) (formulas of type EG) is also changed to must. A node AX is true if all its may (including must) children are colored true, it is false if it has a must child colored false, otherwise it is $\perp$. If node n is colored F or $\perp$ (not of type $s_j \vdash l$) the may transition (m, n) should be cut, if it is $\perp$ and of type $s_j \vdash l$ two alternatives exits: the label of s_j is changed to contain l or the transition is cut. To consider both alternatives when a failure witness of this type is found then this failure witness (m, n) is duplicated in the sequence of witnesses (Fwitness or Nwitness) and in the second one the node is represented as a negative number $(-n)$. A node $s_i \vdash \psi \wedge l$ is colored $\perp$ if it does not have a child colored F and has one or both children colored $\perp$. So, if node n of type $s_j \vdash l$ is colored $\perp$ the label of s_j should be changed. A node $s_i \vdash \psi \vee \chi$ is colored $\perp$ if it does not have a child colored T and has a child colored $\perp$. So, if node n of type $s_i \vdash l$ is colored $\perp$ its label should be changed.

Algorithm 1. Revision-game()

Input: KMTS M to revise, property φ /* X is declared as a global variable */
Output: KMTSs resultant of the changes with $s_0 \vdash \varphi$ colored T

1 Read(M, φ) ;
2 Check-model(M, φ, Fwitness); /* returns a 3-valued model checking game graph and the possible failure witnesses in case $s_0 \vdash \varphi$ colored $\perp$ */
3 **if** $s_0 \vdash \varphi$ *colored* $\perp$ **then**
4 | **repeat**
5 | | X := () ;
6 | | Refine-game(Fwitness, X) ;
7 | | Restore-game(head(Fwitness)) ;
8 | | Fwitness := tail(Fwitness) ;
9 | **until** *Fwitness* = *nil*;
10 **end**

Algorithm 2. Refine-game(Fwitness, X)

Input: Fwitness - sequence of pairs (m, n) determining the failure witness edges
Output: KMTSs resultant of the changes with $s_0 \vdash \varphi$ colored T

1 Failure := head(Fwitness);
2 Refine-play(Failure, X); /* X contains the changes to be done */
3 Recolor-game(φ, Nwitness, X); /* other failure witnesses are put in Nwitness if
    they exists ($s_0 \vdash \varphi$ is colored $\perp$) */
4 **if** $s_0 \vdash \varphi$ *is colored* T **then**
5 | Return $M(X)$;
6 | Restore-game(Failure) /* the game is restored by removing the change
    | corresponding to Failure ;
7 **else if** $s_0 \vdash \varphi$ *is colored* $\perp$ **then**
8 | **while** *Nwtiness* $\neq$ *nil* **do**
9 | | Refine-game(Nwitness, X) ;
10 | | Nwitness := tail(Nwitness) ;
11 | **end**
12 **end**

Algorithm 3. Refine-play(Change, X)

Input: Failure = (m, n) such that node m is colored $\perp$ and is of type $s_i \vdash \psi$
and node n is of type $s_j \vdash \chi$
Output: Changes X

1 **if** *node* m *is of type* $s_i \vdash EX\psi$ *and* n *is colored* T *or* $(\psi = V$ *and* V *is a*
    variable of type ν *and* n *is colored* $\perp$ *and* (m, n) *represents a loop in the game*
    graph **then**
2 | $X.P_3 := X.P_3 \cup \{(s_i, s_j)\};$
3 **else if** *node* m *is of type* $s_i \vdash AX\psi$ **then**
4 | **if** *node* n *is colored* F *or* n *is not of type* $s_j \vdash l$ *and is colored* $\perp$ **then**
5 | | $X.P_1 := X.P_1 \cup \{(s_i, s_j)\}$;
6 | **else if** *node* n *is of type* $s_j \vdash l$ *and is colored* $\perp$ **then**
7 | | **if** $n > 0$ **then** $X.P_5 := X.P_5 \cup \{(s_j, l)\};$
8 | | **else** $X.P_1 := X.P_1 \cup \{(s_i, s_j)\}$;
9 | **end**
10 **if** *node* n *is of type* $s_j \vdash l$ *and* m *is not of type* $s_i \vdash AX\psi$ **then**
11 | $X.P_5 := X.P_5 \cup \{(s_j, l)\};$
12 **end**

For the implementation of the repair of the KMTS when a property is inconsistent with the model, a similar algorithm used for the refinement can be developed. Winning strategies of player $\forall$ instead of non-losing strategies should now be considered to identify some failure witnesses, combined with other failures witnesses such as deadends nodes colored with F. The algorithm can proceed also from bottom up changing labels or eliminating transitions that are causes of the failure in the game.

6   Final Remarks

As addressed before, general sets of Kripke structures cannot be represented by a single KMTS (Proposition 2). A solution is to generalize KMTS revision to deal with a set of KMTS instead of a single model. This solution increases the revision complexity, but it is upperbounded by the complexity of CTL revision (in the worst case, each KMTS will be a Kripke structure). The set of KMTS still have on average a more compact representation, which allows the development of more efficient revision methods.

Revision over KMTS structures is significantly more efficient than Kripke revision. For example, the revision of the models of Figure 3 produces 32 repair candidates, which have to be compared to the 8 initial models in order to select the minimal ones, which involve approximately 256 comparisons. This computation can be even more complicated if it involves a fixpoint formula as EF or AG, in the sense that it increases the number of repair candidates greatly, as the number of redundant or useless change to achieve them. On the other hand, the KMTS revision is almost straightforward from M to the solution set of 4 KMTS, with almost no redundant or useless modifications. The algorithms used for the repair were specified over 3-valued model checking game which can be implemented as two $\mu - calculus$ 2-valued model checking game [12]. It is noteworthy that $\mu - calculus$ 2-valued model checking game for CTL is linear in time.

6.1   Related Work

Zhang and Ding [8] proposed the first approach on this line, improving model checking with belief update theory [11]. As shown in [4], the choice of a belief revision approach, rather then belief update, may avoid some unnecessary loss of information in static contexts. Zhang and Ding [8] do not deal with partial system information. Belief revision principles were adopted in [4], but with no focus on partial system information. Although their framework may deal with partial information by handling sets of models, its lack of a compact representation like KMTS that can make it difficult to be used in real applications. Grumberg [6] addresses KMTS representation, but the context is abstract model checking, where a KMTS model represents an abstraction of a concrete Kripke structure. Grumberg also proposes an algorithm based on 3-valued model checking to refine a KMTS with a different proposal which consists in expanding an abstract state of the KMTS (with some undefined literal) into concrete states (states of the concrete Kripke structure that was abstracted in the KMTS). Finally, in [7], the authors deal with KMTS and develop an algorithm, not using 3-valued model checking, to repair KMTS models. Two main differences distinguish their approach from ours: the focus is on abstract model checking and not on partial system specification; and their proposal does not refer to a known change theory.

7   Conclusion

In this paper we presented a new approach to the revision of a set of CTL models through the revision of a KMTS model. We considered the revision of

KMTS both when the satisfiability of a property is undefined or is inconsistent with the model. We defined a minimality criterion relative to KMTS repair and proved that it preserves the minimality criterion relative to the repair of its set of expanded CTL models as in [4]. We presented an algorithm to implement the revision in case the property is undefined. The design of an algorithm for the repair of the KMTS in case the property is false is our next goal.

The work presented here is a first step towards a framework for the automatic repair of partial specifications. In this version of this work we considered only changes of labels of states and the removal of transitions. We aim to propose a generalization of this solution from an extension of the approach presented here.

Acknowledgments. The first author was supported by the grant #2010/15392-3, São Paulo Research Foundation (FAPESP). The second author was supported by the grant #2012/16308-1, São Paulo Research Foundation (FAPESP). The third author was supported by Brazilian Research Council (CNPq) grant #304043/2010-9.

References

1. Clarke, E.M., Grumberg, O., Peled, D.A.: Model checking. Springer (1999)
2. Huth, M.: Model checking modal transition systems using kripke structures. In: Cortesi, A. (ed.) VMCAI 2002. LNCS, vol. 2294, pp. 302–316. Springer, Heidelberg (2002)
3. Alchourron, C., Gärdenfors, P., Makinson, D.: On the logic of theory change. J. Symb. Logic 50(2), 510–530 (1985)
4. Guerra, P.T., Wassermann, R.: Revision of CTL models. In: Kuri-Morales, A., Simari, G.R. (eds.) IBERAMIA 2010. LNCS, vol. 6433, pp. 153–162. Springer, Heidelberg (2010)
5. Guerra, P.T.: Revisão de modelos CTL. Master's thesis, Univ. São Paulo (2010)
6. Grumberg, O.: 2-valued and 3-valued abstraction-refinement in model checking. Information and Communication Security 25, 105–128 (2011)
7. Chatzieleftheriou, G., Bonakdarpour, B., Smolka, S.A., Katsaros, P.: Abstract model repair. In: Goodloe, A.E., Person, S. (eds.) NFM 2012. LNCS, vol. 7226, pp. 341–355. Springer, Heidelberg (2012)
8. Zhang, Y., Ding, Y.: CTL model update for system modifications. Journal of Artificial Intelligence Research 31(1), 113–155 (2008)
9. Clarke, E.M., Emerson, E.A.: Design and synthesis of synchronization skeletons using branching-time temporal logic. In: Kozen, D. (ed.) Logic of Programs, vol. 131, pp. 52–71. Springer, Heidelberg (1982)
10. Clarke, E.M., Emerson, E.A., Sistla, A.P.: Automatic verification of finite-state concurrent systems using temporal logic specifications. ACM Transactions on Programming Languages and Systems (TOPLAS) 8(2), 244–263 (1986)
11. Katsuno, H., Mendelzon, A.O.: On the difference between updating a knowledge base and revising it. In: Proc. of KR, pp. 387–395. Morgan Kaufmann (1991)
12. Grumberg, O., Lange, M., Leucker, M., Shoham, S.: When not losing is better than winning: Abstraction and refinement for the full μ-calculus. Inf. Comput. 205(8), 1130–1148 (2007)

Formal Analysis of Information Flow Using Min-Entropy and Belief Min-Entropy

Ghassen Helali, Osman Hasan, and Sofiène Tahar

Dept. of Electrical & Computer Engineering, Concordia University
1455 de Maisonneuve W., Montreal, Quebec, H3G 1M8, Canada
{helali,o_hasan,tahar}@ece.concordia.ca

Abstract. Information flow analysis plays a vital role in obtaining quantitative bounds on information leakage due to external attacks. Traditionally, information flow analysis is done using paper-and-pencil based proofs or computer simulations based on the Shannon entropy and mutual information. However, these metrics sometimes provide misleading information while dealing with some specific threat models, like when the secret is correctly guessed in one try. Min-Entropy and Belief Min-entropy metrics have been recently proposed to address these problems. But the information flow analysis using these metrics is done by simulation and paper-and-pencil approaches and thus cannot ascertain accurate results due to their inherent limitations. In order to overcome these shortcomings, we formalize Min-Entropy and Belief-Min-Entropy in higher-order logic and use them to perform information flow analysis within the sound core of the HOL theorem prover. For illustration purposes, we use our formalization to evaluate the information leakage of a cascade of channels in HOL.

Keywords: Information Flow, Min-Entropy, Belief-Min-Entropy, Information Theory, Vulnerability, Theorem Proving, Higher-order Logic, HOL4.

1   Introduction

Protecting the confidentiality of sensitive information and ensuring perfect anonymity are increasingly becoming a dire need in many fields like tele-communication, electronic payments, auctioning and voting. The information flow analysis [21] allows us to obtain quantitative estimates about information leakage, by observing the outputs and the low security inputs in a given system, and thus plays a vital role in developing secure and anonymous systems.

Various approaches for assessing the information flow have been proposed in the literature. The main idea behind the *possibilistic* approaches [1] is to use non-deterministic behaviors to model the given system. For example, the information flow analysis based on epistemic logic [8], which is a logic of knowledge and belief, and on process algebra [20], which allows us to model concurrent systems, fall under this category. The main limitation of *possibilistic* approaches

J. Iyoda and L. de Moura (Eds.): SBMF 2013, LNCS 8195, pp. 131–146, 2013.
© Springer-Verlag Berlin Heidelberg 2013

is its failure to distinguish between systems of varying degrees of protection [6]. *Probabilistic* approaches, based on information theory and statistics, overcome this limitation and are thus considered more reliable for assessing information flow. The most commonly used probabilistic measures of information flow are Shannon's entropy [2], mutual information [3] between the sensitive input and the observable output and relative entropy [5]. It has been recently shown that using such measures sometimes leads to counter-intuitive results [22]. For example, in the case of a specific threat model where the secret is correctly guessed in one try, a random variable with high vulnerability to be guessed can have larger Shannon entropy.

In the one-try model, the adversary is given only one chance to get the value of the secret. The objective here is to maximize the probability of guessing the right value of the high input in just one try and the best strategy for her is auctionning on the element having the maximum distribution. Renyi's entropy metrics [19], i.e., Min-Entropy and Belief Min-Entropy, can deal with the above mentioned threat model more effectively and are commonly used to model and analyze the information leakage in deterministic and probabilistic systems.

Traditionally, paper-and-pencil based analysis or computer simulations have been used for quantitative analysis of information flow. Paper-and-pencil analysis does not scale well to complex systems and is prone to human error. Computer simulation, on the other hand, makes use of numerical approximations for rounding computer arithmetics, which leads to analysis inaccuracies. In order to enhance the accuracy of analysis results, formal methods have been recently proposed to be used in the safety-critical analysis domain of information flow analysis. The probabilistic model checker PRISM has been used to assist in computing the transition probabilities and capacity of the Dining cryptographers protocol [13]. However, the state-space explosion problem of model checking limits the scope of its usage in information flow analysis. For example, only the case for three cryptographers has been analyzed in [13]. These limitations can be overcome by using higher-order-logic theorem proving for the analysis of information flow. The conditional mutual information has been used to formally analyse the anonymity properties of the Dining Cryptographers protocol in the higher-order-logic theorem prover HOL4 [3]. Similarly, the information and the conditional information leakage degrees have been formalized in [17] to assess the security and anonymity protocols within the sound core of HOL4. However, to the best of our knowledge, no formalization of Min-Entropy and Belief-Min-Entropy exists in higher-order logic so far. Thus, despite their enormous applications in security-critical applications, the formal analysis of the scenarios when the secret is correctly guessed in one try is not available.

This paper presents the formalization of Min-Entropy and Belief-Min-Entropy in higher-order logic. Our formalization can be used to formally reason about the threat model where the system's vulnerability is guessed in one try by an attacker within the sound core of the HOL4 theorem prover. In this paper, we build upon the information theory foundations in HOL4 [17] mainly due to their completeness and generic nature compared to the other formalizations of probability and information theories [4,11].

In order to illustrate the effectiveness and utilization of the proposed formalization, we utilize it to conduct the information flow analysis of channels in cascade [7]. A cascade channels topology in information theory is a commonly used linear connectivity strategy where the output of each communication node (e.g., server, router, switcher) acts as input of the next one. This structure is basically used in banking systems to ensure restorability, usability and conformity of such systems. Due to the safety-critical applications of communication systems, modeled as a cascade of channels, their accurate analysis for the worst case analysis is very important. The proposed Min-Entropy formalizations enables us to achieve this goal.

The rest of the paper is organized as follows: Section 2 provides some necessary details about the HOL theorem prover based probabilistic analysis infrastructure as well as notions of information theory that we build upon to analyze the information flow. Next, we describe the higher-order-logic definitions related to the Min-Entropy and Belief Min-Entropy theories in Section 3. We utilize these definitions in Section 4 to formally analyze the information flow. Then, we apply our new model in Section 5 to verify the Min-Entropy leakage of channels in cascade. Finally, Section 6 concludes the paper.

2   Preliminaries

This section describes the HOL4 environment as well as the formalization of probability and information theories, which we would be building upon to formalize the Min-Entropy and Belief-Min-Entropy metrics later.

2.1   HOL Theorem Prover

The HOL system is an environment for interactive theorem proving in higher order logic. Higher-order logic is a system of deduction with a precise semantics and is expressive enough to be used for the specification of almost all classical mathematics theories. In order to ensure secure theorem proving, the logic in the HOL system is represented in the strongly-typed functional programming language ML. An ML abstract data type is used to represent higher-order-logic theorems and the only way to interact with the theorem prover is by executing ML procedures that operate on values of these data types. The HOL core consists of only 5 basic axioms and 8 primitive inference rules, which are implemented as ML functions. Soundness is assured as every new theorem must be verified by applying these basic axioms and primitive inference rules or any other previously verified theorems/inference rules. The HOL system has has been used to formalize pure mathematics and verify industrial software and hardware systems.

One of the advantages of HOL is that it is not limited by the size of the state space. Large systems that cannot be verified using model checking can still be verified by the theorem prover. Various mathematical concepts have been formalized and saved as HOL theories. Out of this useful library of HOL theories, we utilized the theories of sets, positive integers, real numbers, measure, probability and information in this paper. In fact, one of the primary motivations of selecting the HOL theorem prover for our work was to benefit from these built-in mathematical theories.

2.2 Probability Theory

Probability provides mathematical models for random phenomena and experiments. The purpose is to describe and predict relative frequencies (averages) of these experiments in terms of probabilities of events. The HOL4 utilizes the measure theory to formalize probability theory [16] and some of the foundational notions of this formalization are given below:

- **(Probability Space):** *a measure space such that the measure of the state space is* 1
- **(Independent Events):** *Two events A and B are independent iff* $p(A \cap B) = p(A)p(B)$.
- **(Random Variable):** $X : \Omega \to \mathcal{R}$ *is a random variable iff X is* $(F, \mathcal{B}(\mathcal{R}))$ *measurable where F denotes the set of events and* $\mathcal{B}$ *is the Borel sigma algebra.*
- **(Joint Probability):** *A probabilistic measure where the likelihood of two events occurring together and at the same point in time is calculated. Joint probability is the probability of event B occurring at the same time event A occurs. Its notation is* $p(A \cap B)$ *or* $p(A, B)$.
- **(Conditional Probability):** *A probabilistic measure where an event A will occur, given that one or more other events B have occurred. Its notation is* $p(A|B)$ *or* $\frac{p(A \cap B)}{p(B)}$.
- **(Expected Value):** $E[X]$ of a random variable X is its Lebesgue integral with respect to the probability measure. The following properties of the expected value have been verified in HOL4 [16]
  1. $E[X + Y] = E[X] + E[Y]$
  2. $E[aX] = aE[X]$
  3. $E[a] = a$
  4. $X \le Y$ then $E[X] \le E[Y]$
  5. X and Y are independent then $E[XY] = E[X]E[Y]$
- **(Variance and Covariance):** Variance and covariance have been formalized in HOL4 using the formalization of expectation. The following properties have been verified:
  1. $Var(X) = E[X^2] - E[X]^2$
  2. $Cov(X, Y) = E[XY] - E[X]E[Y]$
  3. $Var(X) \ge 0$
  4. $\forall a \in R, Var(aX) = a^2 Var(X)$
  5. $Var(X + Y) = Var(X) + Var(Y) + 2Cov(X, Y)$

The above mentioned definitions and properties have been utilized to formalize the foundations of information theory in HOL4 [16].

2.3   Information Theory

Information theory [14,5] is used in many fields of engineering and computer science, such as signal processing, data compression, storing and communicating data to quantify information. Recently, it found an enormous application in the domains of cryptography and information flow analysis [23]. Various information theoretic notions, such as the *entropy, the mutual information, the relative entropy, the conditional entropy* and *the Renyi's entropy*, are used to reason about the uncertainty of a random variable.

Let X and Y denote discrete random variables, with x and y and $\mathcal{X}$ and $\mathcal{Y}$ denoting their specific values and set of all possible values, respectively. Similarly, the probability of X and Y being equal to x and y is denoted by $p(x)$ and $p(y)$, respectively, their joint probability is denoted by $p(x, y)$. Now, the widely used information theoretic measures can be defined as:

- **(The Shannon Entropy):** It measures the uncertainty of a random variable

$$H(X) = -\sum_{x \in \mathcal{X}} p(x) log\, p(x)$$

- **(The Conditional Entropy):** It measures the amount of uncertainty of X when Y is known

$$H(X|Y) = -\sum_{y \in \mathcal{Y}} p(y) \sum_{x \in \mathcal{X}} p(x|y) log\, p(x|y)$$

- **(The Mutual Information):** It represents the amount of information that has been leaked

$$I(X; Y) = I(Y; X) = H(X) - H(X|Y)$$

- **(The Relative Entropy or Kullback Leiber Distance):** It measures the inaccuracy or information divergence of assuming that the distribution is q when the true distribution is p

$$D(p\|q) = \sum_{x \in \mathcal{X}} p(x) log\, \frac{p(x)}{q(x)}$$

- **(The Guessing Entropy):** It measures the expected number of tries required to guess the value of X optimally

$$G(X) = \sum_{1 \le i \le n} ip(x_i)$$

- **(The Rnyi Entropy):** It is related to the difficulty of guessing the value of X

$$H_\alpha(X) = \tfrac{1}{1-\alpha} log\left(\sum_{x \in \mathcal{X}} P[X = x]^\alpha\right)$$

The above measures are used to analyze the information flow from different aspects. Entropy, Mutual Information and Relative Entropy, operate over the quantity of information and the degree of uncertainty while the Guessing Entropy determines the number of attempts to decrypt a secret. Mhamdi [15] and Coble [3] formalized the notions of Entropy, Conditional Entropy, Relative Entropy and Mutual Information in HOL4, while Hölzl [11] formalized the same concepts in Isabelle/HOL.

3   Formalization of Min-Entropy and Belief Min-Entropy

Information theoretic measures of Min-Entropy and Belief Min-Entropy overcome the limitations of Shannon's entropy in evaluating the security of guessing the secret in *one try* [23]. We explain these measures along with their corresponding higher order-logic formalizations in this section. In the following subsections, X, Y and B denote the random variables that model the high input (the secret), the output (the observable) and the attacker's belief about the system behavior (the extra knowledge), respectively, and p and q denote probability spaces.

3.1   Formalization of Min-Entropy

The Min Entropy H_∞ of a random variable X is a special case from the Rényi Entropy when $\alpha = \infty$.

Definition 1 *(The Min-Entropy).*
The Min-Entropy of a random variable X is given by

$$H_\infty(X) = -log \max_{x \in \mathcal{X}} p(x)$$

This can be formalized in HOL4 as follows:

```
⊢ ∀ X p.
   min_entropy X p =
   - log (extreal_max_set (IMAGE
   (λx. distribution p X {x}) (IMAGE X (p_space p))))
```

In this definition, the function `extreal_max_set` returns the maximum of a given set, `IMAGE f s` returns the image of a given set s by a function f and `p_space p` is the state space of the Ω of the probability space p.

It can be observed from the above definition that the Min-Entropy measure is primarily the negative logarithm of the vulnerability, or in other words, the worst-case probability that an adversary A can guess the secret correctly in one try:

$$H_\infty(X) = -log(V(X)) = -log(\max_{x \in \mathcal{X}} P[X = x]).$$

The Min-Entropy measures the initial uncertainty only and the remaining uncertainty can be quantified by the conditional Min-Entropy.

Definition 2 *(The Conditional Min-Entropy).*
Observing the output Y, the probability of guessing the secret X is

$$H_\infty(X|Y) = -log(\sum_{y \in \mathcal{Y}} \max_{x \in \mathcal{X}} P[Y = y]P[X = x|Y = y])$$

This can be formalized in HOL4 as follows:

```
⊢ ∀ X Y p.
    conditional_min_entropy p X Y =
    - log ∑   (λy. extreal_max_set
          Y(Ω)
        (IMAGE (λx. distribution p Y{y}*
          conditional_distribution p X Y ({x},{y})) (X(Ω))))
```

In the above definition, we utilized the `conditional_distribution p X Y` that refers to $P(X|Y)$. This quantity relates two behaviors, i.e., the input X and the output Y, and this makes the Conditional Min-Entropy a good measure to map the remaining uncertainty, which is nothing but the probability of guessing the secret input having the observable.

3.2   Formalization of Belief Min-Entropy

The Belief Min-Entropy allows us to deal with the attacker's extra knowledge or beliefs about the system behavior. This measure is actually a refinement of the Min-Entropy since it takes into account another parameter, i.e., *belief*, that is expected to increase the reliability of the analysis.

Let p_ρ and p_β denote the distributions related to the system behavior and the adversary's belief, respectively. Given an additional information $B = b$, the adversary chooses a value having the maximal conditional probability according to her belief, that is a value $x' \in \Gamma_b$, such that $\Gamma_b = argmax_{x \in \mathcal{X}} p_\beta(x|b)$, and $argmax_{x \in \mathcal{X}} p_\beta(a|b)$ returns the elements from $\mathcal{A}$ having the maximal conditional-distribution. In case of more than one value of A with the maximal conditional probability, the attacker uniformly and randomly picks a single element from Γ_b.

Definition 3 *(The Belief Min-Entropy).*
Let X be the input random variable and B the adversarys extra knowledge about X. Then the Belief Min-Entropy of X, denoted $H_\infty(X : B)$, is defined as

$$H_\infty(X : B) = -log(\sum_{b \in \mathcal{B}} \frac{1}{|\Gamma_b|} p(b) \sum_{x \in \mathcal{X}} p(x|b))$$

In order to formalize the Belief Min-Entropy in HOL4, we first define the belief vulnerability, which can be extended to obtain the Belief Min-Entropy by applying the converse logarithm.

```
⊢ ∀ p1 p2 X B.
  belief_vulnerability p1 p2 X B =
  SIGMA (λb. ────────────────── *
             |belief_set p1 p2 X B b|
      (distribution p1 B {b}) *
          (SIGMA (λx. conditional_distribution p1 X B ({x},{b}))
          (belief_set p1 p2 X B b)))
      (B(Ω1))
```

where the function `belief_set p1 p2 X B b` models Γ_b in HOL4 and $\Omega1$ refers to p_space p1. Now, in order to model the Belief Min-Entropy, we need to define the relationship between the attacker's belief and the observable output. The belief b is compatible with the observation y, if there exists an input $x \in \Gamma_b$ verifying $p_\rho(y|x) > 0$ and in this case, the attacker is able to choose the appropriate values for guessing the secret. $\Gamma_{b,y}$ denotes the set of the possibilities that the adversary can choose and is defined as follows:

$$\Gamma_{b,y} = \begin{cases} arg\max_{x \in \mathcal{X}} p_\beta(x|b,y) & \text{if } b \text{ and } y \text{ are compatible} \\ arg\max_{x \in \mathcal{X}} p_\beta(x|y) & \text{otherwise} \end{cases} \tag{1}$$

The above definition is formalized as the HOL4 function `belief_conditionned_set`, which we will use later to model the remaining uncertainty that will be a function of the conditional belief vulnerability.

Definition 4 *(The Conditional Belief Vulnerability).*

$$V(X|Y:B) = \sum_{y \in \mathcal{Y}} \sum_{b \in \mathcal{B}} p_\rho(y,b) \frac{1}{|\Gamma_{b,y}|} \sum_{x \in \Gamma_b \ p(x|y,b)}$$

The above definition can be formalized in HOL4 as follows:

```
⊢ ∀ p1 p2 X B Y. conditional_belief_vulnerability p1 p2 X B Y =
  ∑ ∑ joint_distribution p1 B Y ({b},{y}) * ──── *
  y b                                          |Γ_{b,y}|
  ∑    belief_conditional_distribution p1 X Y B ({x},{y},{b})
x∈Γ_{b,y}
```

Now, we can apply the converse logarithm to get the conditional Belief Min-Entropy.

$$H_\infty(X|Y:B) = -log(V(X|Y:B))$$

Based on the previous measures, we define the information leakage that determines how much information has been leaked from the input to the output.

information leakage = initial uncertainty - remaining uncertainty

Next, we will use the definitions, presented in this section, to formally reason about their classical properties, which in turn allow us to conduct formal information flow analysis with the HOL4 theorem prover.

4   Formal Analysis of Information Flow

The main focus of this paper is on the analysis of the threat model of guessing the critical information in one try, which is usually considered as the worst case scenario and cannot be handled by the Shannon entropy as we mentioned earlier. In this section, we formally verify that the definitions, presented in the previous section, can handle this particular model.

In regards to information flow analysis, Min-Entropy allows us to measure uncertainties. The following theorem provides a lower bound to the initial uncertainty.

Theorem 1 *(Lower Bound of the Min-Entropy).*

$\vdash \forall$ X p b. FINITE $(\Omega) \land \Omega \neq \emptyset \land$ random_variable X p Borel $\land$
  $(\forall$x. x $\in$ X$(\Omega) \Rightarrow$ (distribution p X $\{$x$\}) \leq \frac{1}{2^b})) \land$
  $(\forall$x. x $\in \Omega \Rightarrow \{x\} \in$ events p$) \land$
  $X(\Omega) \in$ subsets Borel$) \Rightarrow$
  b $\leq$ (min_entropy X p)

where Ω = p_space p. If this initial uncertainty is uniformly distributed over the input set $\mathcal{X}$, then the initial uncertainty is equal to $|\mathcal{X}|$:

Theorem 2 *(Initial Uncertainty for Uniform Distribution).*

$\vdash \forall$p X. FINITE $(\Omega) \land$
  random_variable X p Borel $\land$
  $\forall$x. x $\in$ X$(\Omega) \Rightarrow$ distribution p X $\{$x$\}$ = 1 / $|$X$(\Omega)|$
  $\Rightarrow$ min_entropy X p = log $|$X$(\Omega)|$

The first assumption, in the above theorems, is required because the maximum of a set is well-defined for finite sets only.

Another useful aspect related to information leakage is the remaining uncertainty that represents the model of the aposteriori behavior. If a program is deterministic and the initial distribution is uniformly distributed, then its information leakage depends on the output set only. This result can be formally verified as the following theorem:

Theorem 3 *(Information Leakage of Deterministic Program).*

$\vdash \forall$ X Y p c. $(\forall$x. x $\in$ X$(\Omega) \Rightarrow$ distribution p X $\{$x$\}$ = $\frac{1}{|X(\Omega)|}) \land$
  deterministic_cond Y c $\Rightarrow$
  information_leakage p X Y = log $(|$Y$(\Omega)|)$

where the assumptions model the determinism condition and the uniform distribution. Next, we analyze the information flow considering the attacker's belief. For this purpose, we include another random variable B that models the adversary's extra knowledge about the high input. Under the condition of a total inaccurate belief, the following theorem holds:

Theorem 4 *(Initial Uncertainty of Total Inaccurate Belief).*

⊢ ∀A B sp ev p1 p2. FINITE (p_space (sp,ev,p2)) ∧
   FINITE (p_space (sp,ev,p1)) ∧
   ∀a b. (a,b) ∈ totally_inaccurate_belief_set sp ev p1 p2 A B ⇒
   belief_min_entropy sp ev p1 p2 A B = +∞

According to the above theorem, when the attacker has no information about the secret input, the initial vulnerability of the system tends to zero. The proof of this result is based on the Bayes' rule and our definition of the Belief Min-Entropy.

The following theorem verifies that the conditional Min-Entropy is always less then or equal to the Belief Min-Entropy:

Theorem 5 *(Min-Entropy and Belief Min-Entropy).*

⊢ ∀X B sp ev p1 p2.
   ∀x b. (b ∈ B(Ω1)) ∧
     (belief_set (sp,ev,p1) (sp,ev,p2) X B b ≠ ∅) ∧
     (x ∈ (belief_set (sp,ev,p1) (sp,ev,p2) X B b)) ∧
   conditional_distribution (sp,ev,p1) B X ({b},{x}) ≤ $\frac{1}{|B(\Omega 1)|}$ ⇒
   min_entropy A (sp,ev,p1) ≤ belief_min_entropy sp ev p1 p2 X B

The interpretation of the previous result is that the vulnerability of a system is greater in the presence of the extra knowledge. Similarly, the following theorem provides the belief initial uncertainty in the deterministic case.

Theorem 6 *(Deterministic Belief Initial Uncertainty).*

⊢ ∀X B sp ev p1 p2 c.
   ∀x b. x ∈ belief_set (sp,ev,p1) (sp,ev,p2) X B b ∧
     b ∈ B(Ω1) ∧
   ∀x. (x ∈ belief_set (sp,ev,p1) (sp,ev,p2) X B b) ⇒
     distribution (sp,ev,p1) X {x} = $\frac{1}{|X(\Omega 1)|}$ ∧
   events (sp,ev,p1) = POW (Ω1) ∧
   deterministic_cond B c ⇒
   log $\frac{|X(\Omega 1)|}{|B(\Omega 1)|}$ ≤ belief_min_entropy sp ev p1 p2 A B

Next, just like in the case of Min-Entropy, we verify that the remaining belief uncertainty is lower bounded by conditional Min-Entropy joint to the adversary's belief, i.e. $H_\infty(A|O, B) \leq H_\infty(A|O : B)$, which can be expressed as the following HOL4 theorem:

Theorem 7 *(Lower Bound for Belief Remaining Uncertainty).*

⊢ ∀X B Y p1 p2. FINITE (Ω) ∧ random_variable X p1 Borel ∧
   random_variable B p1 Borel ∧ random_variable Y p1 Borel ∧
   ∀x. x ∈ (Ω) ⇒ {x} ∈ events p1
   ⇒ conditional_joint_min_entropy p1 X B Y ≤
     conditional_belief_min_entropy p1 p2 X B Y

Thus, the belief remaining uncertainty under the deterministic conditions is bounded by $log(\frac{|\mathcal{A}|}{|\mathcal{O}|.|\mathcal{B}|})$. Now we can formally verify the following result in HOL4.

Theorem 8 *(Deterministic Remaining Belief Uncertainty).*

```
⊢ ∀X Y B p q c c'. FINITE Ω ∧ Ω ≠ ∅ ∧
    ∀x b y. x ∈ belief_conditionned_set p q X B Y b y ∧
    ∀b. b ∈ B(Ω) ∧ ∀y. y ∈ Y(Ω) ∧
    ∀x. x ∈ Ω ⇒ {x} ∈ events p ∧
    ∀x. x ∈ x(Ω) ⇒ distribution p X {x} = 1/|X(Ω)| ∧
    deterministic_cond Y c ∧ deterministic_cond B c' ⇒
 log (|X(Ω)|/(|Y(Ω)|.|B(Ω)|)) ≤ conditional_belief_min_entropy p q X B Y
```

where `belief_conditionned_set p q X B Y b y` = $\Gamma_{b,y}$ denotes the set of possible adversarys choices according to her belief and low observation.

The proof of the above theorem is primarily based on the Min-Entropy properties under deterministic conditions. Finally, Theorems 6 and 8 can be used to reason about the belief information leakage for deterministic programs.

$$log|\mathcal{Y}| \leq IL_\infty(X;(Y:B))$$

From the above result, we conclude that the belief behavior helps the adversary in choosing more reliable initial knowledge based on the observations. The above mentioned properties have been verified before [9] but the main novelty of our work was to re-verify these results using an interactive theorem prover. Based on the soundness of theorem proving, the formally verified theorems are guaranteed to be accurate and contain all the required assumptions. Moreover, these formally verified results can be built upon to reason about information flow analysis of various applications within the sound core of a theorem prover. For illustration purposes, the information leakage of cascade of channels is formally analyzed in the next section. These added advantages have been attained at the cost of human effort in formalizing and interactively verifying the above mentioned results. The proof script [10] is composed of 3400 lines of code and took about 1000 man-hours of development time.

5   Application: Channels in Cascade

A channel [7] is a triplet $(\mathcal{A}, \mathcal{B}, \mathcal{C}_{\mathcal{AB}})$, where $\mathcal{A}$ is a finite set of the critical inputs, $\mathcal{B}$ is the observable output and $\mathcal{C}_{\mathcal{AB}}$ is the channel matrix representing the transitional probabilities from the input to the output of the channel. The channels are frequently connected in a cascade manner such that the outputs of the previous stage act as the input to the next one. In cascaded channels, the final output is produced in n steps, where n represents the number of cascaded channels.

The major goal of this section is to formally reason about the information flow of channels in cascade and analyze the information leakage in such systems.

We will first formalize the notions of channels and cascade of channels in higher-order logic. These definitions, along with our formally verified results of the previous section, will then be used to formally reason about the measure of quantity of information and the information leakage of a two cascaded channel model.

5.1   Formalization of Channels and Cascade of Channels

A channel can be formalized in HOL4 using the following function:

Definition 5 *(Channel).*

```
⊢ ∀X Y p f. channel p X Y f =
    random_variable X p Borel ∧
    random_variable Y p Borel ∧
    ∀x y. x ∈ X(Ω) ∧
    y ∈ Y(Ω) ∧
    f(x,y) = conditional_distribution p Y X ({y},{x})
```

The predicate channel accepts a probability space p, the random variables X and Y representing the finite sets of the critical inputs and the observable outputs, respectively, and a function f that models the channel matrix $\mathcal{C}_{AB}$ in terms of the conditional probabilities of obtaining the output b such that the input is a.

Now the behavior of a cascade of two channels, i.e., $(\mathcal{X}, \mathcal{Z}, \mathcal{C}_{\mathcal{X}\mathcal{Z}})$ and $(\mathcal{Z}, \mathcal{Y}, \mathcal{C}_{\mathcal{Z}\mathcal{Y}})$, is equivalent to the channel $(\mathcal{X}, \mathcal{Y}, \mathcal{C}_{\mathcal{X}\mathcal{Z}} * \mathcal{C}_{\mathcal{Z}\mathcal{Y}})$ [7]. This definition of a cascade of two channels can be formalized in HOL4 as follows:

Definition 6 *(Cascade Channel).*

```
⊢ ∀X Z Y p f g. cascade_channel p X Z Y f g =
    channel p X Z f ∧
    channel p Z Y g ∧
    ∀x y. joint_distribution p X Y ({x},{y}) =
    ∑_z joint_distribution p X Z ({x}, {z}) *
    conditional_distribution p Y Z ({y}, {z})
```

5.2   Information Flow Analysis of Channels in Cascade

In order to analyze the information flow for the worst case scenario, i.e., when $\mathcal{A}$ recovers the critical information in one guess, we model the apriori distribution as a function of the maximum input distribution and the aposteriori behavior is expressed as a function of the maximum over $\mathcal{X}$ of the distribution of guessing a while observing b.

$$leakage = Min\text{-}Entropy(X) \text{ - } conditional\ Min\text{-}Entropy(X|Y)$$
$$IL_\infty(X,Y) = H_\infty(X) - H_\infty(X|Y)$$

Now, the leakage in a cascade of channels can be evaluated using Min-Entropy and the corresponding proof goal can be expressed in HOL4 as follows:

Theorem 9 *(Information Leakage of Channels in Cascade).*

Let $(\mathcal{X}, \mathcal{Y}, C_{\mathcal{XY}})$ be the cascade of $(\mathcal{X}, \mathcal{Z}, C_{\mathcal{XZ}})$ and $(\mathcal{Z}, \mathcal{Y}, C_{\mathcal{ZY}})$. Then we have $\mathcal{IL}_\infty(\mathcal{X}, \mathcal{Y}) \leq \mathcal{IL}_\infty(\mathcal{X}, \mathcal{Z})$ This theorem can be expressed in HOL4 as

```
⊢ ∀ p X Z Y f g.
  · cascade_channel p X Z Y f g ∧
    FINITE (Ω) ∧
    Ω ≠ ∅ ∧
    events p = POW (Ω) ∧
    ∀x. 0 < distribution p Y {x} ∧
    ∀x. 0 < distribution p Z {x} ∧
    (∀x. x ∈ Ω ⇒ {x} ∈ events p) ⇒
    information_leakage p X Y ≤ information_leakage p X Z
```

Using some arithmetic simplification, the proof goal can be simplified to the level of vulnerabilities:

$$V_\infty(X|Y) \leq V_\infty(X|Z)$$

Now, using the property of cascade (*third conjunct in Definition 6*), we obtain

$$p(A = a|B = b) = \sum_c p(A = a, C = c) * p(B = b|C = c)$$
$$\leq \sum_c max_a \ \ p(A = a, C = c) * p(B = b|C = c)$$

Next, we simplify the above subgoal by using the properties of summation along with the fact that the sum of the conditional distributions over the first state space of any random variable is equal to 1.

$$V(A \mid B) \leq \sum_c \max_a \ p(A{=}a \ , \ C{=}c)$$

The above subgoal can now be verified based on arithmetic simplification. This concludes the proof of Theorem 9, which consists of about 850 lines of HOL code.

5.3   Discussion

Due to the formal nature of the model and the soundness of the mechanical theorem prover, the analysis is guaranteed to be free of approximation and precision errors and thus the results obtained are mathematically precise and confirmed the results of paper-and-pencil based analysis approaches. This precision of analysis is a novelty that, to the best of our knowledge, has not been achieved by any other existing computer-based probabilistic analysis approaches. In the Definition 6 of the cascade channel behavior, the transition functions, f and g, are general functions that provide generic results. In model checking approach parameters and functions should be specified. Furthermore the result verified in Theorem 9 can be extended to the Min-Entropy analysis of information leakage of n channels in cascade using induction techniques. We can prove that the Min-Entropy leakage of n channels in cascade will not exceed the leakage of the first channel. The main key to verify this property is the definition of the cascade condition. Mathematically, we can express the connection of n channels as follows

Let X_0 be the random variable modeling the input of the system and X_n the one modeling the output, thus

$$\forall\, i.\ (0 \leq i \leq n) \Rightarrow P(X_0, X_i) = \sum_{\mathcal{X}_{i-1}} P(X_0, X_{i-1}) * P(X_i | X_{i-1})$$

Based on what we defined previously and what already existed, this condition can be formalized in HOL4 as

```
⊢ ∀X p f n. n_cascade_channel p X n f =
    ∀i. (1≤i≤n) ⇒ channel p (X (i-1)) (X i) (f i) ∧
    ∀x y i. joint_distribution p (X 0) (X i) (x,y) =
        ∑ joint_distribution p (X 0) (X (i-1)) (x,z) *
        z
    conditional_distribution p (X (i-1)) (X i) (z,y)
```

The ability to express and verify generic properties, quantified for all values of the variables, is the main strength of theorem proving as can be seen from the above definition and the property related to the information leakage of n channels in cascade. This property is an ongoing task, once verified, can hold for any number of cascade of channels and can be specialized to obtain expression and values for particular scenarios. Probabilistic model checking, which is the other main stream formal method, cannot provide such generic results due to the inherent state-space explosion problem.

6   Conclusion

This paper presents a formalization of vulnerability, belief-vulnerability, Min-Entropy and Belief Min-Entropy in higher-order logic. These metrics provide more reliable information flow analysis compared to the traditional definitions of quantitative information flow based on Shanon entropy for some corner cases. One such threat model being the case when an adversary can guess the secret input value in one try, given the observable output. The proposed formalization can be built upon to conduct the information flow analysis within the sound core of a theorem prover and thus the analysis is guaranteed to be free of approximation and precision errors. For illustration purposes, we performed the information flow analysis of a cascade of two channels using the HOL4 theorem prover and the analysis results were found to be generic and accurate.

The proposed higher-order-logic formalization can be used in analyzing many other applications. We are particularly aiming to apply it for the formal information flow analysis of the Crowds protocol [18] and Freenets [12]. Moreover, our work can be extended to analyze information flow in a reverse way, i.e. starting from a specific leakage bound we evaluate the input set with respect to the output set. This formalization can be used to formally ensure a specific level of security of critical information.

References

1. Andrea, S.: Possibilistic information theory: A coding theoretic approach. Fuzzy Sets Systems 132(1), 11–32 (2002)
2. Backes, M., Kopf, B., Rybalchenko, A.: Automatic discovery and quantification of information leaks. In: Proceedings IEEE Symposium on Security and Privacy, pp. 141–153. IEEE Computer Society (2009)
3. Coble, A.R.: Anonymity, information, and machine-assisted proof. Technical report, University of Cambridge, Computer Laboratory, Cambridge UK (July 2010)
4. Coble, A.R.: Anonymity, information, and machine-assisted proof. PhD thesis, King's College, University of Cambridge, Cambridge UK (2010)
5. Cover, T.M., Thomas, J.A.: Elements of Information Theory. Wiley-Interscience (1991)
6. Nguyen, H.T., Dubois, D., Prade, H.: Fundamentals of fuzzy sets, possibility theory, probability and fuzzy sets: Misunderstandings, bridges and gaps. In: Fundamentals of Fuzzy Sets. The handbooks of Fuzzy Sets Series, pp. 343–438. Kluwer (2000)
7. Espinoza, B., Smith, G.: Min-entropy leakage of channels in cascade. In: Barthe, G., Datta, A., Etalle, S. (eds.) FAST 2011. LNCS, vol. 7140, pp. 70–84. Springer, Heidelberg (2012)
8. Halpern, J.Y., O'Neill, K.R.: Anonymity and information hiding in multiagent systems. Journal of Computer Security 13(3), 483–514 (2005)
9. Hamadou, S., Sassone, V., Palamidessi, C.: Reconciling belief and vulnerability in information flow. In: Proceedings IEEE Symposium on Security and Privacy, pp. 79–92. IEEE Computer Society (2010)
10. Helali, G.: Formal analysis of information flow using min-entropy and belief min-entropy, http://hvg.ece.concordia.ca/projects/prob-it/min_beliefInfo.php
11. Hölzl, J.: Construction and Stochastic Applications of Measure Spaces in Higher-Order Logic. PhD thesis, Institut für Informatik, Technische Universität München, Germany (October 2012)
12. Clarke, I., Sandberg, O., Wiley, B., Hong, T.W.: Freenet: A distributed anonymous information storage and retrieval system. In: Federrath, H. (ed.) Designing Privacy Enhancing Technologies. LNCS, vol. 2009, pp. 46–66. Springer, Heidelberg (2001)
13. Palamidessi, C., Chatzikokolakis, K., Panangaden, P.: Anonymity Protocols as Noisy Channels. Information and Computation 206(2-4), 378–401 (2008)
14. Massey, J.L.: Guessing and entropy. In: Proceedings IEEE International Symposium on Information Theory, p. 204 (1994)
15. Mhamdi, T.: Information-Theoretic Analysis using Theorem Proving. PhD thesis, Department of Electrical and Computer Engineering, Concordia University (December 2012)

16. Mhamdi, T., Hasan, O., Tahar, S.: Formalization of entropy measures in HOL. In: van Eekelen, M., Geuvers, H., Schmaltz, J., Wiedijk, F. (eds.) ITP 2011. LNCS, vol. 6898, pp. 233–248. Springer, Heidelberg (2011)
17. Mhamdi, T., Hasan, O., Tahar, S.: Quantitative analysis of information flow using theorem proving. In: Aoki, T., Taguchi, K. (eds.) ICFEM 2012. LNCS, vol. 7635, pp. 119–134. Springer, Heidelberg (2012)
18. Reiter, M.K., Rubin, A.D.: Crowds: anonymity for web transactions. ACM Transactions on Information Systems Security 1(1), 66–92 (1998)
19. Renyi, A.: On measures of entropy and information. In: Proceedings Berkeley Symposium on Mathematics, Statistics and Probability, pp. 547–561 (1961)
20. Schneider, S., Sidiropoulos, A.: CSP and anonymity. In: Martella, G., Kurth, H., Montolivo, E., Bertino, E. (eds.) ESORICS 1996. LNCS, vol. 1146, pp. 198–218. Springer, Heidelberg (1996)
21. Smith, G.: Principles of secure information flow analysis. In: Malware Detection. Advances in Information Security, pp. 291–307. Springer (2007)
22. Smith, G.: On the foundations of quantitative information flow. In: de Alfaro, L. (ed.) FOSSACS 2009. LNCS, vol. 5504, pp. 288–302. Springer, Heidelberg (2009)
23. Smith, G.: Quantifying information flow using min-entropy. In: Quantitative Evaluation of SysTems, pp. 159–167 (2011)

Theorem Proving Graph Grammars: Strategies for Discharging Proof Obligations*

Luiz Carlos Lemos Junior, Simone André da Costa Cavalheiro, and Luciana Foss

Universidade Federal de Pelotas, Centro de Desenvolvimento Tecnológico
Rua Gomes Carneiro, 1, 96010-610, Pelotas - RS, Brazil
{lclemos,simone.costa,lfoss}@inf.ufpel.edu.br

Abstract. One way of developing reliable systems is through the use of Formal Methods. A Graph Grammar specification is visual and based in a simple mechanism of rewriting rules. On the other hand, verification through theorem proving allows the proof of properties for systems with huge (and infinite) state space. There is a previously proposed approach that has allowed the application of theorem proving technique to graph grammars. One of the disadvantages of such an approach (and theorem proving in general) is the specific mathematical knowledge required from the user for concluding the proofs. This paper proposes proof strategies in order to help the developer in the verification process through theorem proving, when adopting graph grammar as specification language.

1 Introduction

In the present scenario we find a wide variety of software and hardware systems that are increasingly complex. In this situation, it is important to adopt strategies for increasing reliability. A way of achieve such a goal is using formal specification and verification. A formal specification is carried by a mathematical model, with well-defined syntax and semantics and formal verification can guarantee system properties.

There are several specification languages, among them, graph grammars (GG) [1] stand out, which are visual, based on rewriting rules and capable of describing complex behaviours. In graph grammars, states are modelled as graphs and state changes are described by graph rules. Likewise, there are a number of verification techniques, and one of them is Theorem Proving [2]. In this technique both, the system and the desired properties are described using mathematical descriptions and logic. The verification strategy consists of finding a proof from axioms and intermediary lemmas of the system. This technique is particularly interesting [3] for systems with big or infinite state space, since it does not require the construction of (any fragment of) the state space.

Previous work [4,5,6] has allowed the verification of systems specified in graph grammars through theorem proving. This technique proposed a relational and logical approach to GG, providing the coding of graphs and rules with relations. The relations that define a grammar determine axioms that can be used to develop proofs. The

---

* The authors gratefully acknowledge financial support received from CNPq and FAPERGS, specially under Grants, ARD 11/0764-9, PRONEM 11/2016-2 and PRONEX 10/0043-0.

J. Iyoda and L. de Moura (Eds.): SBMF 2013, LNCS 8195, pp. 147–162, 2013.

rule application is described by an event such as an inference rule (when a set of variables satisfies guard conditions, the rule is applied). This approach was translated into Event-B structures [7], allowing the use of theorem provers compatible with this language (available in the Rodin platform [8]) for demonstrations of properties. The proof process is semi-automatic, requiring user interaction.

When modelling a system in Event-B, Rodin makes a syntactic (static check) and a dynamic verification. In these verifications the tool generates proof obligations to ensure invariants are preserved, guard conditions and actions are well defined, formulas are meaningful, among others. These obligations are stated in order to ensure system consistency. Some are completed automatically, others need user intervention. The knowledge of both the system and the tool required for completing the proofs hinders the use of this proposal.

This work presents the proof obligations generated by a GG specification in Rodin, as well as establishes the provers that discharge them. Also it proposes proof strategies to assist the developers when discharging semi-automatic proof obligations generated by the specification of atomic properties in the model. Next sections are organised as follows. Section 2 introduces the graph grammar formalism. Section 3 presents the mapping of graph grammars into Event-B structures. Section 4 presents the proof obligations generated by a GG in Event-B, indicating the respective provers to discharge them. Section 5 describes strategies for discharging proof obligations generated by the specification of atomic properties. Section 6 concludes and discusses future works.

2   Graph Grammars

Graph Grammar is a specification language suitable for representing complex situations, because it is simple and visual. A graph is defined by two sets and two functions. A graph morphism is defined by two partial functions. The identifiers used in next definitions (prefixed with `inv_`, `grd_`, `axm_` and `act_`) are those used in the Event-B model (meaning respectively, invariant, guard condition, axiom and action) in Section 3.

Definition 1 (Graph and graph morphism). *A **graph** G is a tuple $(vertG, edgeG, sourceG, targetG)$, where $vertG$ is a set of vertices, $edgeG$ is a set of edges, and $sourceG, targetG: edgeG \rightarrow vertG$ are total functions, defining source and target of each edge, respectively. Given two graphs $G = (vertG, edgeG, sourceG, targetG)$ and $H = (vertH, edgeH, sourceH, targetH)$, a **(partial) graph morphism** $f: G \nrightarrow H$ is a tuple $(f\_V: vertG \nrightarrow vertH, f\_E: edgeG \nrightarrow edgeH)$ such that f commutes with source and target functions:*

$$\text{grd\_srctgt:} \quad \forall e \in dom(f\_E) \cdot f\_V(sourceG(e)) = sourceH(f\_E(e)) \text{ and}$$
$$\forall e \in dom(f\_E) \cdot f\_V(targetG(e)) = targetH(f\_E(e))$$

A graph morphism is said to be total or injective if both of its components are total or injective functions, respectively.

A typed graph is defined by two graphs connected by a total graph morphism (typing morphism). A typed graph morphism is a graph morphism that satisfies a compatibility condition, which establishes that the mapping of components must preserve types.

Definition 2 (Typed Graph, Typed Graph Morphism). *A **typed graph** is given by a tuple* $G^T = (G, tG, T)$ *where* G *and* T *are graphs and* $tG = (tG\_V, tG\_E)$ *is a typing morphism from* G *over* T, *i.e.,* $tG \colon G \to T$ *is a* total graph morphism *(*inv_tG_V *and* inv_tG_E*). A **(typed) graph morphism from*** G^T **to** H^T *is defined by a morphism* $g = (g\_V, g\_E)$ *from* G *to* H, *s.t. the typed morphism compatibility condition is satisfied:*

$$\texttt{grd\_vertices:}\ \forall v \in dom(g\_V) \cdot tG\_V(v) = tH\_V(g\_V(v))\ \text{and}$$
$$\texttt{grd\_edges:}\qquad \forall e \in dom(g\_E) \cdot tG\_E(e) = tH\_E(g\_E(e))$$

A rule is composed of two typed graphs and a morphism between them, which describes a possible behaviour of the system.

Definition 3 (Rule). *A **rule** typed over* T *is a typed graph morphism* $\alpha = (\alpha\_V, \alpha\_E) \colon$ $L^T \rightarrowtail R^T$, *where:* L^T *and* R^T *are graphs typed over* T; α *is injective (*axm_alphaV *and* axm_alphaE*);* $\alpha\_V \colon vertL \rightarrowtail vertR$ *is a total function (*axm_alphaV*).*

Definition 4 (Graph Grammar). *A **(typed) graph grammar** is a tuple* $GG = (T, G0, R)$, *where* T *is a graph, called type graph;* $G0$ *is a graph typed over* T, *called initial graph; and,* R *is a set of rules typed over* T.

The occurrence of the left-hand side (LHS) of a rule in a state graph is called match.

Definition 5 (Match). *Let* $r = (\alpha \colon L^T \rightarrowtail R^T)$ *be a rule, with* L^T *and* R^T *typed graphs over* T. *Let* $G^T = (G, tG, T)$ *be a typed graph with* $tG = (tG\_V, tG\_E)$. *A **match** m of rule* r *in* G^T *is defined by a total typed graph morphism* $m = (m\_V, m\_E) \colon L^T \to G^T$, *such that* $m\_E \colon edgeL \rightarrowtail edgeG$ *is injective.*

The behaviour of a GG is given by rule applications. A rule is applied only if there is a match of the rule in the state graph. When a rule is applied a new state is generated.

Definition 6 (Rule Application). *Let* $r = (\alpha \colon L^T \rightarrowtail R^T)$ *be a rule and* $m = (m\_V, m\_E)$ *be a match of* r *in a typed graph* G^T. *A **rule application** $G^T \overset{r,m}{\Rightarrow} H^T$, or the application of* r *to* G^T *at* m, *generates a typed graph* $H^T = (H, tH, T)$, *with* $H = (vertH, edgeH, sourceH, targetH)$, *as follows:*

- $vertH = vertG \uplus (vertR - rng(\alpha\_V))$ (act_vert);
- $edgeH = (edgeG - rng(m\_E)) \uplus edgeR$ (act_edge);
- *for all* $e \in edgeH$ (act_src *and* act_tgt)

$$sourceH(e) = \begin{cases} sourceG(e) & \text{if } e \in edgeG \\ \overline{m}(sourceR(e)) & \text{otherwise} \end{cases}$$

$$targetH(e) = \begin{cases} targetG(e) & \text{if } e \in edgeG \\ \overline{m}(targetR(e)) & \text{otherwise} \end{cases}$$

where $\overline{m} \colon vertR \to vertH$ *is defined by:*
$$\overline{m}(v) = \begin{cases} m\_V(v') & \text{if } v \in rng(\alpha\_V) \text{ and } v = \alpha\_V(v') \\ v & \text{otherwise} \end{cases}$$

— *for all* $v \in vertH$ *and all* $e \in edgeH$, $tH = (tH\_V, tH\_E)$ *is defined by* (`act_tV` *and* `act_tE`)

$$tH\_V(v) = \begin{cases} tG\_V(v) \text{ if } v \in vertG \\ tR\_V(v) \text{ otherwise} \end{cases}$$

$$tH\_E(e) = \begin{cases} tG\_E(v) \text{ if } e \in edgeG \\ tR\_E(v) \text{ otherwise} \end{cases}$$

Next we use the GG language to specify the Token Ring protocol [9]. In this protocol, a special signal, called a token, is passed from station to station in only one direction. A message can be transmitted only by stations that hold the token (active stations). The transmission circulates for all the ring and finishes when the message returns to the original station. Then the station that started the transmission becomes standby and the signal token is passed for the next station, restarting the cycle. In our example there is only one token, so a single station can transmit at a given time. We also allows the addition of new stations into the network at any time.

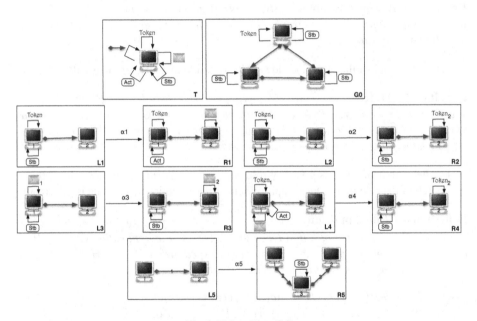

Fig. 1. Token Ring GG

Figure1 illustrates the graph grammar for the example. The type graph T defines a single type of node ▪ (Node), and five types of edges ▪ (Message), Token (Token), ↔ (Next), (Act) (Active Station) and (Stb) (Standby Station). ▪ represents a network station and ▪ defines a portion of data. The Token is a special signal which enables stations to transmit. ↔ connects each station. One station with edge (Act) transmits some information through the network. One station with edge (Stb) is standby, and can receive a message. The initial graph $G0$ was set with three nodes, and none of the stations are transmitting (there is no edge of type $\boxed{Act}$).

The behaviour of this protocol is given by the rules. In this representation, the morphism is not explicitly represented, but we consider that the items with the same name and type are mapped. In the rule $\alpha 1$ a standby station that holds the token becomes active and sends a message to the next station. It is also possible that a standby station holding the token directly passes it to the next station (rule $\alpha 2$). When a message arrives at a standby node, it goes directly to the next station (rule $\alpha 3$). In rule $\alpha 4$ the message is received by the transmitting station, which returns to the standby mode and pass the token to the next station. In this specification, at each instant of time new nodes can be added into the ring, by rule $\alpha 5$. This model generates an infinite state-space.

3   Graph Grammars in Event-B

An Event-B model [10] consists of a context (static part) and a machine (dynamic part). In the context are defined sets, constants and axioms. In the machine are defined variables, invariants and events. A model is called correct if all set of proof obligations generated from the model is discharged. An extensive tool support through the Rodin Platform [8] makes Event-B especially attractive.

The Event-B model and its behaviour is similar to a graph grammar. There is a concept of state (set of variables in Event-B and a graph in GG) and a transition is considered an atomic operation in the current state (an event that updates the variables in Event-B and a rule application in a graph grammar). Each stage should preserve the properties of the state. In Event-B these properties are treated as invariants, and in graph grammars, they are related to the graph structure. A graph grammar with n rules, α_1 to α_n and $i \in \{1, ..., n\}$, can be modelled in Event-B as follows:

1. Context
   (a) The *sets* of the model are $vertT$, $edgeT$, $vertLi$, $edgeLi$, $vertRi$ and $edgeRi$ (the sets of vertices and edges of all graphs);
   (b) The *constants* represent the vertices and edges of the type graph and rules and also the names of typing functions tLi_V, tLi_E, tRi_V and tRi_E, source and target functions, $sourceT$, $targetT$, $sourceLi$, $targetLi$, $sourceRi$ and $targetRi$, and rules $alphaiV$ and $alphaiE$;
   (c) The *axioms* define explicitly all sets and functions of the model.
2. Machine
   (a) The *model variables* are specified by $vertG$, $edgeG$, $sourceG$, $targetG$, tG_V and tG_E (current state of the system);
   (b) The *invariants* define the types of variables;
   (c) The *initialisation action* sets the initial values for the variables $vertG$, $edgeG$, $sourceG$, $targetG$, tG_V and tG_E (specifying the initial graph $G0$);
   (d) The *set of events* defines the rule applications. Guard conditions guarantee the occurrence of a match (conditions for the rule to be applied).

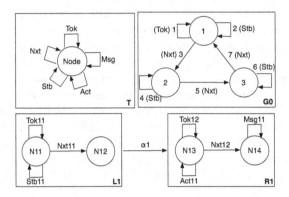

Fig. 2. Alternative Representations for Type Graph T, Initial Graph $G0$ and Rule $\alpha 1$

Static Part: The static part of graph grammars is specified in the context. Figure 2 presents an alternative representation for graph T and rule $\alpha 1$ of Figure 1.

The event-B specification is show in Figure 3. For specifying the type graph T, we define as sets, $vertT$ and $edgeT$; as constants, the names of the vertices ($Node$) and the edges (Nxt, Tok, Msg, Stb, Act), as well the names of the source and target functions ($sourceT, targetT$); in the axioms, we define these sets explicitly (e.g., axm_vertT is defined by $partition(vertT, \{Node\})$ meaning that $vertT = \{Node\}$).

```
CONTEXT   ctx_T
SETS
    vertT, edgeT  // Type graph T
    vertL1, edgeL1  // Graph L1
    vertR1, edgeR1  // Graph R1
CONSTANTS
    Node Nxt Tok Msg Stb Act sourceT targetT  // Constants of type graph T
    N11 N12 Tok11 Stb11 Nxt11 sourceL1 targetL1 tL1_V, tL1_E  // Constants of graph L1
    N13 N14 Tok12 Act11 Nxt12 Msg11 sourceR1 targetR1 tR1_V tR1_E  // Constants of graph R1
    alpha1V, alpha1E  // Morphism components
AXIOMS
    axm_vertT :  partition(vertT, {Node})  // Type graph T
    axm_edgeT :  partition(edgeT, {Nxt}, {Tok}, {Msg}, {Stb}, {Act})  // Type graph T
    axn_srcTtype :  sourceT ∈ edgeT → vertT  // Type graph T
    axn_srcTdef :  partition(sourceT, {Nxt ↦ Node}, {Tok ↦ Node},
        {Msg ↦ Node}, {Stb ↦ Node}, {Act ↦ Node})  // Type graph T
    axm_tgtTtype :  targetT ∈ edgeT → vertT  // Type graph T
    axn_tgtTdef :  partition(targetT, {Nxt ↦ Node}, {Tok ↦ Node},
        {Msg ↦ Node}, {Stb ↦ Node}, {Act ↦ Node})  // Type graph T
    :  ...
    axm_tR1_V :  tR1_V ∈ vertR1 → vertT  // Typing morphism graph R1
    axm_tR1_V_def :  partition(tR1_V, {N13 ↦ Node}, {N14 ↦ Node})  // Typing morphism graph R1
    axm_tR1_E :  tR1_E ∈ edgeR1 → edgeT  // Typing morphism graph R1
    axm_tR1_E_def :  partition(tR1_E, {Tok12 ↦ Tok}, {Act11 ↦ Act},
        {Msg11 ↦ Nxt}, {Msg11 ↦ Msg})  // Typing morphism graph R1
    axm_alpha1V :  alpha1V ∈ vertL1 ↠ vertR1  // Vertex Morphism Component from graph L1 to R1
    axm_alpha1V_def :  partition(alpha1V, {N11 ↦ N13}, {N12 ↦ N14})
    axm_alpha1E :  alpha1E ∈ edgeL1 ↠ edgeR1  // Edge Morphism Component from graph L1 to R1
    axm_alpha1E_def :  partition(alpha1E, {Tok11 ↦ Tok12}, {Nxt11 ↦ Nxt12})
```

Fig. 3. (Part of) GG Specification in Event-B

To define a rule in Event-B, it is necessary to specify the two typed graphs and the morphism. Graphs $L1$ and $R1$ are specified analogously T. The typing morphism names $tR1\_V$ and $tR1\_E$ are declared as constants while their definitions are explicitly defined in the axioms (axm_tR1_V, $axm\_tR1\_V\_def$, axm_tR1_E, $axm\_tR1\_E\_def$). The morphism components are also declared as constants ($alpha1V$, $alpha1E$) and explicitly specified in the axioms ($axm\_alpha1V$, $axm\_alpha1V\_def$, $axm\_alpha1E$, $axm\_alpha1V\_def$).

Dynamic Part: The dynamic part of a graph grammar is specified in the machine. A set of variables define the state graph and a set of invariants determine its types. Both are illustrated in Figure 4.

```
MACHINE  mch_trAll
SEES  ctx_GG
VARIABLES
    vertG, edgeG, sourceG, targetG, tG_V, tG_E
INVARIANTS
    inv_vertG :  vertG ∈ ℙ(ℕ)
    inv_edgeG :  edgeG ∈ ℙ(ℕ)
    inv_sourceG :  sourceG ∈ edgeG → vertG
    inv_targetG :  targetG ∈ edgeG → vertG
    inv_tG_V :  tG_V ∈ vertG → vertT
    inv_tG_E :  tG_E ∈ edgeG → edgeT
EVENTS
Initialisation
    act_vertG :  vertG := {1, 2, 3}
    act_edgeG :  edgeG := {1, 2, 3, 4, 5, 6, 7}
    act_srcG :  sourceG := {1 ↦ 1, 2 ↦ 1, 3 ↦ 1, 4 ↦ 2, 5 ↦ 2, 6 ↦ 3, 7 ↦ 3}
    act_tgtG :  targetG := {1 ↦ 1, 2 ↦ 1, 3 ↦ 2, 4 ↦ 2, 5 ↦ 3, 6 ↦ 3, 7 ↦ 1}
    act_tG_V :  tG_V := {1 ↦ Node, 2 ↦ Node, 3 ↦ Node}
    act_tG_E :  tG_E := {1 ↦ Tok, 2 ↦ Stb, 3 ↦ Nxt, 4 ↦ Stb, 5 ↦ Nxt, 6 ↦ Stb, 7 ↦ Nxt}
Event  alpha1 ≙
    any
        mV  mE  newEmsg  newEact
    where
        grd_mV :  mV ∈ vertL1 → vertG
        grd_mE :  mE ∈ edgeL1 ↣ edgeG
        grd_newEmsg :  newEmsg ∈ ℕ \ edgeG
        grd_newEact :  newEact ∈ ℕ \ edgeG
        grd_E1E2 :  newEmsg ≠ newEact
        grd_vertices :  ∀v·v ∈ vertL1 ⇒ tL1_V(v) = tG_V(mV(v))
        grd_edges :  ∀e·e ∈ edgeL1 ⇒ tL1_E(e) = tG_E(mE(e))
        grd_srctgt :  ∀e·e ∈ edgeL1 ⇒ mV(sourceL1(e)) = sourceG(mE(e)) ∧
            mV(targetL1(e)) = targetG(mE(e))
    then
        act_E :  edgeG := (edgeG \ {mE(Stb11)}) ∪ {newEmsg, newEact}
        act_src :  sourceG := ({mE(Stb11)} ⩤ sourceG) ∪ {newEact ↦ mV(N11),
            newEmsg ↦ mV(N12)}
        act_tgt :  targetG := ({mE(Stb11)} ⩤ targetG) ∪ {newEact ↦ mV(N11),
            newEmsg ↦ mV(N12)}
        act_tE :  tG_E := ({mE(Stb11)} ⩤ tG_E) ∪ {newEact ↦ Act, newEmsg ↦ Msg}
```

Fig. 4. State Graph and Events in Event-B

The initial graph and rule applications are specified by events in Event-B. Figure 2 also shows an alternative representation for the initial graph $G0$ of the token ring example. Vertices and edges are named with natural numbers with its types described into the brackets. The initialisation event, depicted in Figure 4, defines $G0$. It is responsible for initialising the value of each state variable.

Other events determine the behaviour of the system, specifying the rule applications. Figure 4 shows the specification for rule $\alpha 1$. Guard conditions guarantee the occurrence of a match, and the actions specify the value of the modified variables. If there are values for the variables mV, mE, $newEmsg$, $newEact$ satisfying the guard conditions, then the rule is applied. Guard conditions grd_mV, grd_mE, $grd\_vertices$, grd_edges and grd_srctgt guarantee that the pair (mV, mE) defines a match of the rule in the state graph. The conditions $grd\_newEmsg$, $grd\_newEact$ and grd_E1E2 ensure that $newEmsg$ and $newEact$ are new free edges names. The actions act_E, act_src, act_tgt and act_tE modify the state graph. In this case, an Stb edge is deleted and two new edges are created, one of type Act and other one of type Msg.

4   Proof Obligations Generated from a GG Specification in Rodin

When specifying a system in Event-B, the Rodin platform executes a static (syntactic) and a dynamic verification. In these verifications proof obligations are generated, which must be demonstrated in order to ensure (part of) the correctness of the model. These properties can be discharged using provers that comes with the tool or external ones, which can be installed in the form of plugins. Some of the proof obligations are proved automatically, while other ones depend on the user interaction.

Proof obligations generated by a GG specification in Rodin are basically of two kinds, to ensure well-definedness conditions (labelled with WD) or to preserve invariants (labelled with INV). In the Event-B specification, the set of variables define the state graph and the invariants specify their types. Proof obligations are generated to guarantee the preservation of their types by the initialisation event and by the events that specify the rules. The corresponding proof obligation are generated whenever a variable is modified by an event, in order to guarantee its type preservation. Other proof obligations aim to ensure that guards conditions (conditions for applying a rule) and actions (responsible for updating the values of some variables) are well-defined.

The main provers available for Rodin are NewPP, PP (predicate prover) and ML (mono-lemma). The NewPP prover has three forces. In the configuration "restricted" (nPP R), all selected hypotheses and the goal are passed to New PP. In the configuration "after lasso" (nPP with a lasso), a lasso operation is applied to the selected hypotheses and the goal and the result is passed to New PP. The lasso operation selects any unselected hypothesis that have a common symbol with the goal or a hypothesis that is currently selected. In the configuration "unrestricted" (nPP), all the available hypotheses are passed to New PP. This prover is embedded in the tool and its input language is first-order logic with the predicate $\in$. First, all function and predicate symbols that are different from $\in$ and not related to arithmetic are translated away. Then New PP translates the proof obligation to conjunctive normal form and applies a combination of unit resolution and the Davis Putnam algorithm. The PP prover, available in the Atelier-B as an external prover, also has three forces (P0, P1, PP). In the configuration "P0", all selected hypotheses and the goal are passed to PP. In the configuration "P1", one lasso operation is applied to the selected hypotheses and the goal and the result is passed to PP. In the configuration "PP", all the available hypotheses are passed to PP. The input sequent is translated to classical B and fed to the PP prover of Atelier B. PP works in a manner similar to newPP but with support for equational and arithmetic reasoning. The ML prover is also available in the Atelier-B, but different from others (PP and NewPP). ML applies a mix of forward, backward and rewriting rules in order to discharge the goal (or detect a contradiction among hypotheses). For more details see [10,7].

Table 1 presents the main proof obligations generated when specifying a GG in Event-B. They can be easily discharged by running the available provers. Besides the identification of each proof obligation, follows a brief description of it, along with the prover that must be used to discharge it.

Proof obligations identified with INITIALISATION guarantee that variables that define the state-graph, when initialised, preserve their types. The initial value of the variables describes the initial graph of the graph grammar. For instance, in the token ring example, the obligation INITIALISATION /inv/_vertG/INV is used to ensure that $\{1, 2, 3\} \in \mathbb{P}(\mathbb{N})$ (see Figure 4). Similarly, proof obligations are generated in order to ensure the type preservation by the initialisation of the other variables ($edgeG$, $sourceG$, $targetG$, tG_V and tG_E). All of them can be discharged by running P0.

Proof obligations labelled with rule/grd ensure that the guard conditions for the respective event (or rule) are well-defined. For example, in the token ring, the obligation rule1/grd_vertices/WD ensures that guard condition grd_vertices (see Figure 4) is well-defined, that is, $v \in dom(tL1\_V)$, $v \in dom(mV)$ and $mV(v) \in dom(tG\_V)$, with $tL1\_V$, tG_V and mV preserving its types.

The result of a rule application can create edges, delete edges or create vertices in the state-graph, changing the values of the corresponding variables. Proof obligations are generated in order to guarantee that the variables with their values updated preserve its types. These obligations are prefixed with rule/inv. In the token ring, rule 1 delete one Stb edge and create one Act and one Msg edges (see Figure 4). In such case, variables $edgeG$, $sourceG$, $targetG$ and tG_E are modified, and then proof obligations are generated to assure that these variables, after updating, preserve their types. E.g., it must be guaranteed that $(edgeG \setminus \{mE(Stb11)\}) \cup \{newEmsg, newEact\} \in \mathbb{P}(\mathbb{N})$.

Obligations are also generated to ensure that actions (which define the result of a rule application) are well-defined. These obligations are prefixed with rule/act. When a rule deletes an e edge, then variables $edgeG$, $sourceG$, $targetG$ and tG_E are modified. In such case, the deleted edge of the state-graph is the image of e by the mE component of the match, i.e., $mE(e)$ is deleted from $edgeG$. In the same way, are excluded the elements (pairs) of the functions $sourceG$, $targetG$ and tG_E that have $mE(e)$ as first component. In order to the respective actions be well-defined, the edge e must belongs to the domain of mE and mE must preserve its type (these are the proof obligations rule/act_E/WD, rule/act_src/WD, rule/act_tgt/WD, rule/act_tE/WD). Besides that, when a rule adds an edge with source (or target) in a v vertex, that is preserved by the rule, the source (respect. target) of the added edge must be image of v by the mV component of the match. In this case, in order to variables $sourceG$ and $targetG$ be well-defined, v must belong to the domain of mV, with mV preserving its type (these are the proof obligations rule/act_src/WD and rule/act_tgt/WD). Proof obligations of this type are demonstrated automatically.

The proof obligations described above are those generated when specifying a GG in Event-B. Following this approach [5], any other property to be verified must be stated as

Table 1. GG Proof Obligations in Event-B

Identification	Description	Provers
INITIALISATION/inv_vertG/INV	Ensure that $vertG$ preserves its type in $G0$ (at initialisation).	ML or P0
INITIALISATION/inv_edgeG/INV	Ensure that $edgeG$ preserves its type in $G0$.	ML or P0
INITIALISATION/inv_srcGtype/INV	Ensure that $sourceG$ preserves its type (a total function from $edgeG$ to $vertG$) in $G0$.	P0
INITIALISATION/inv_tgtGtype/INV	Ensure that $targetG$ preserves its type (a total function from $edgeG$ to $vertG$) in $G0$.	P0
INITIALISATION/inv_tG_V/INV	Ensure that tG_V preserves its type (a total function from $vertG$ to $vertT$) in $G0$.	ML, P0 or NewPP
INITIALISATION/inv_tG_E/INV	Ensure that tG_E preserves its type (a total function from $edgeG$ to $edgeT$) in $G0$.	P0
rule/grd_vertices/WD	Ensure that the `grd_vertices` condition (see Fig. 4) is well-defined, i.e. $v \in dom(tL\_V)$, $v \in dom(mV)$ and $mV(v) \in dom(tG\_V)$, with tL_V, tG_V and mV preserving its types.	ML or P1
rule/grd_edges/WD	Ensure that the `grd_edges` condition (see Fig. 4) is well-defined, i.e. $e \in dom(tL\_E)$, $e \in dom(mE)$ and $mE(e) \in dom(tG\_E)$, with tL_E, tG_E and mE preserving its types.	ML, P1 or NewPP
rule/grd_srctgt/WD	Ensure that the `grd_srctgt` condition (see Fig. 4) is well-defined, i.e. $e \in dom(sourceL)$, $sourceL(e) \in dom(mV)$, $e \in dom(mE)$, $mE(e) \in dom(sourceG)$, $e \in dom(targetL)$, $targetL(e) \in dom(mV)$ and $mE(e) \in dom(targetG)$, with $sourceL$, mV, mE, $sourceG$, $targetL$ and $targetG$ preserving its types.	ML or P1
rule/inv_vertG/INV	Ensure that $vertG$, when modified by a rule application, preserves its type.	ML or P0
rule/inv_edgeG/INV	Ensure that $edgeG$, when modified by a rule application, preserves its type.	ML or P0
rule/inv_srcGtype/INV	Ensure that $sourceG$, when modified by a rule application, preserves its type (a total function from $edgeG$ to $vertG$).	P0
rule/inv_tgtGtype/INV	Ensure that $targetG$, when modified by a rule application, preserves its type (a total function from $edgeG$ to $vertG$).	P0
rule/inv_tG_V/INV	Ensure that tG_V, when modified by a rule application, preserves its type (a total function from $vertG$ to $vertT$).	ML, P1 or NewPP
rule/inv_tG_E/INV	Ensure that tG_E, when modified by a rule application, preserves its type (a total function from $edgeG$ to $edgeT$).	P0
rule/act_E/WD	Ensure that the modification of variable $edgeG$ is well-defined. When an e edge is deleted, ensure that e belongs to the domain of the mE component of the match (i.e $e \in dom(mE)$) and that mE preserves its type ($mE: edgeL \rightarrow edgeG$).	Automatic
rule/act_src/WD	Ensure that the modification of variable $sourceG$ is well-defined. When an e edge is deleted, ensure that e belongs to the domain of the mE component of the match (i.e $e \in dom(mE)$) and that mE preserves its type ($mE: edgeL \rightarrow edgeG$). When an e edge is created with source (or target) in a vertex v, preserved by the rule, ensure that v belongs to the domain of the mV component of the match (i.e $v \in dom(mV)$) and that mV preserves its type ($mV: vertL \rightarrow vertG$).	Automatic
rule/act_tgt/WD	Ensure that the modification of variable $targetG$ is well-defined. When an e edge is deleted, ensure that e belongs to the domain of the mE component of the match (i.e $e \in dom(mE)$) and that mE preserves its type ($mE: edgeL \rightarrow edgeG$). When an e edge is created with source (or target) in a vertex v, preserved by the rule, ensure that v belongs to the domain of the mV component of the match (i.e $v \in dom(mV)$) and that mV preserves its type ($mV: vertL \rightarrow vertG$).	Automatic
rule/act_tE/WD	Ensure that the modification of variable tG_E is well-defined. When an e edge is deleted, ensure that e belongs to the domain of the mE component of the match (i.e $e \in dom(mE)$) and that mE preserves its type ($mE: edgeL \rightarrow edgeG$).	Automatic

an invariant, indicating that it must be true for all reachable states of the system. Proofs for such properties are developed by induction: in the base case, a proof obligation is generated to guarantee the preservation of the property for the initial graph and, at the inductive step, a proof obligation is generated for the graph resulting from the application of each rule of the grammar. In general, the discharging of such proof obligations requires intervention from the user, that must have knowledge of both, the tool and the specification. The proposal of proof strategies to help the user in the development of the demonstrations for some of these properties is addressed in the next section.

5 Proof Strategies for Atomic Properties

The translation of GG in Event-B structures has enabled the use of first-order logic to express properties of reachable states of a graph grammar. However, during the development of the case studies, we noticed that, although the specification of the behaviour of the system could be rather intuitively described with graph grammars, the verification of properties was not trivial. Properties over states are properties over graphs, typically composed of different kinds of edges and vertices. In previous work [11] we have proposed patterns for the presentation, codification and reuse of property specifications. Here, we presents proof strategies for the demonstration of specific atomic properties belonging to such patterns. Particularly, we describe proof strategies for discharging the properties presented in Figure 5. Properties must be stated as invariants in the machine.

INVARIANTS

> propFin : $finite(tG\_E \rhd \{t\})$ // The set of edges of type t of a reachable graph is finite.
> propCard : $card(tG\_E \rhd \{t\}) = 1$ // Any reachable graph has exactly one edge of type t.
> propExEdge : $\exists x \cdot x \in tG\_E \rhd \{t\}$ // Any reachable graph has an edge of type t.
> propExVert : $\exists x \cdot x \in tG\_V \rhd \{t\}$ // Any reachable graph has a vertex of type t.

Fig. 5. Properties as Invariants in Event-B

For each property, we first present the steps for discharging the proof obligation for the initial graph and after for the rules. Property propFin is required for the discharging of propCard. The steps for discharging the INITIALISATION/propFin/INV generated by propFin $finite(tG\_E \rhd \{t\})$ for the initial graph are the following:

1. Add the hypothesis $tG\_E \rhd \{t\} = \{x\}$, replacing tG_E by its value and considering x the result of tG_E restricted to the type t for the initial graph.
2. Execute the prover PP in force P1.
3. Run prover ML.

Figure 6 presents the proof tree[1] generated for the demonstration of the proof obligation INITIALISATION/propFin/INV. Each node represents a sequent and each number (from 1 to 5) represents the rule or the prover used to discharge the corresponding sequent. A set of proof tactics and rewriting rules are available within the Rodin platform [7]. Space limitations prohibit their detailing here. After adding the hypothesis three

---

[1] The set of hypotheses H in proof trees are omitted. In order to provide readability we denote H different sets of hypotheses.

sequents must be proved: (i) $\vdash \top$, that is discharged automatically with the $\top$ goal rule; (ii) $\vdash tG\_E \rhd \{t\} = \{x\}$ which is automatically simplified (through sl/ds, that corresponds to a selection/deselection of hypotheses) to the sequent $H \vdash tG\_E \rhd \{t\} = \{x\}$, discharged with P1; (iii) $tG\_E \rhd \{t\} = \{x\} \vdash finite(tG\_E \rhd \{t\})$ which is discharged with ML.

$$\frac{\dfrac{\text{True}}{\vdash \top} \; 2 \quad \dfrac{\dfrac{\text{PP RULES}}{H \vdash tG\_E \rhd \{t\} = \{x\}} \; 1}{\vdash tG\_E \rhd \{t\} = \{x\}} \; 3 \quad \dfrac{\dfrac{\text{ML RULES}}{tG\_E \rhd \{t\} = \{x\} \vdash finite(tG\_E \rhd \{t\})} \; 4}{\vdash finite(tG\_E \rhd \{t\})}}{} \; 5$$

1 PP; 2 $\top$ goal; 3 sl/ds; 4 ML; 5 ah $(tG\_E \rhd \{t\} = \{x\})$

Fig. 6. Proof Tree for Discharging INITIALISATION/propFin/INV

In order to conclude the proof of `propFin`, proof obligations must be discharged for each rule of the graph grammar that modifies tG_E. These will be those that replace tG_E by its new value, determined by the action of the respective rule. In general, a rule can both delete and create new edges, then the obligation to be discharged will be of the form $finite((((\{mE(e_1), \ldots, mE(e_j))\} \lhd tG\_E) \cup A) \rhd \{t\})$, considering that j edges are deleted and a set of A pairs are included in tG_E. In this case, the steps for discharging rule_i/propFin/INV for each rule i are the following:

1. Apply the tactic Range Distribution Left Rewrites, which after the application of some automatic tactics will generate two sequents to be proved: (i) $finite((\{mE(e_1), \ldots, mE(e_j))\} \lhd tG\_E) \rhd \{t\})$ and (ii) $finite(A \rhd \{t\})$.
2. In order to prove (i), add $(\{mE(e_1), \ldots, mE(e_j))\} \lhd tG\_E) \rhd \{t\} \subseteq tG\_E \rhd \{t\}$ as hypothesis, and conclude the subgoals running ML.
3. In order to prove (ii), add $A \rhd \{t\} \subseteq A$ as hypothesis, and conclude the subgoals running ML.

Figure 7 presents the proof tree generated for the demonstration of each proof obligation rule_i/propFin/INV. After applying the tactic range distribution left rewrites in goal, a sequence of automatic tactics are applied (rules 12 to 14 in the proof tree). They correspond to the applications of simplification rewriting rules and typing rewriter tactic (details are found in Rodin Proof Tactics [7]). Then, the tactic $\land$ goal splits the sequent into two subgoals: (i) $finite((\{mE(e_1), \ldots, mE(e_j))\} \lhd tG\_E) \rhd \{t\})$ and (ii) $finite(A \rhd \{t\})$. The subgoal (i) is discharged adding the hypothesis $(\{mE(e_1), \ldots, mE(e_j))\} \lhd tG\_E) \rhd \{t\} \subseteq tG\_E \rhd \{t\}$, remaining three sequents to be proved: $H \vdash e_1 \in dom(mE) \land \ldots \land e_j \in dom(mE) \land mE \in edgeLi \nrightarrow \mathbb{Z}$, that is discharged automatically, $H \vdash (\{mE(e_1), \ldots, mE(e_j))\} \lhd tG\_E) \rhd \{t\} \subseteq tG\_E \rhd \{t\}$ and $H \vdash finite((\{mE(e_1), \ldots, mE(e_j))\} \lhd tG\_E) \rhd \{t\})$, which are both discharged running ML. The subgoal (ii) is discharged adding the hypothesis $A \rhd \{t\} \subseteq A$, remaining three sequents to be proved: $H \vdash \top$, discharged with the $\top$ goal tactic, $H \vdash A \rhd \{t\} \subseteq A$ and $H \vdash finite(A \rhd \{t\})$, both discharged with ML.

The steps for discharging the obligation INITIALISATION/propCard/INV generated by `propCard` $(card(tG\_E \rhd \{t\}) = 1)$ for the initial graph are the following:

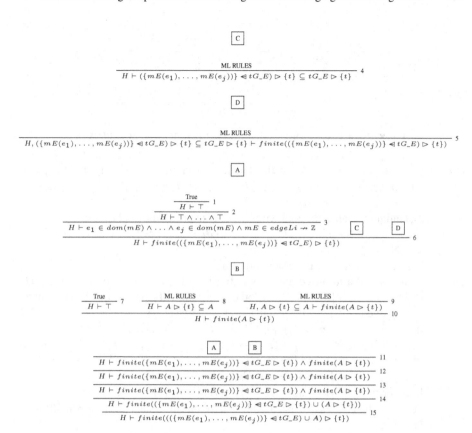

Fig. 7. Proof Tree for Discharging rule_i/propFin/INV

1. Add the hypothesis $tG\_E \triangleright \{t\} = \{e \mapsto t\}$, replacing tG_E by its initial value and considering $e \mapsto t$ the pair resultant of tG_E restricted to the type t for the initial graph.
2. Run prover PP in force P1 (lasso operation is applied to the common hypotheses).
3. Run prover PP in force P1.

Figure 8 presents the proof tree. After adding the hypothesis, three sequents must be proved: (i) $\vdash \top$, that is discharged automatically with the $\top$ goal rule; (ii) $tG\_E \triangleright \{t\} = \{e \mapsto t\}$ and (iii) $\exists x, x0.\ tG\_E \triangleright \{t\} = \{x \mapsto x0\}$, both discharged with P1.

The obligations generated by propCard for each rule will be those that replace tG_E by its new value. Since a rule can both delete and create new edges, then the general obligation to be discharged will be $card(((\{mE(e_1), \ldots, mE(e_j))\} \triangleleft tG\_E) \cup \{ed_1 \mapsto t_1, \ldots, ed_k \mapsto t_k\} \triangleright \{t\}) = 1$, considering that j edges are deleted and k edges are created. In fact, if this property is valid, the t edge or is preserved or is deleted and created by a rule application. Then, we divide our tactic into two subcases:

$$
\begin{array}{c}
\textbf{PP RULES} \\
\hline
H \vdash tG\_E \rhd \{t\} = \{e \mapsto t\} \quad 1
\end{array}
\qquad
\begin{array}{c}
\textbf{PP RULES} \\
\hline
H \vdash \exists x,\, x0 \cdot tG\_E \rhd \{t\} = \{x \mapsto x0\} \quad 2
\end{array}
$$

$$
\cfrac{\text{True}}{\vdash \top}\ 5 \quad
\cfrac{\vdash tG\_E \rhd \{t\} = \{e \mapsto t\}}{\vdash tG\_E \rhd \{t\} = \{e \mapsto t\}}\ 3 \quad 6
\qquad
\cfrac{H \vdash \exists x,\, x0 \cdot tG\_E \rhd \{t\} = \{x \mapsto x0\}}{H \vdash card(tG\_E \rhd \{t\}) = 1}\ 4 \ 7
$$

$$
\vdash card(tG\_E \rhd \{t\}) = 1 \quad 8
$$

1 PP; 2 PP; 3 sl/ds; 4 sl/ds; 5 $\top$ goal; 6 simplification rewrites; 7 simplification rewrites;
8 ah($tG\_E \rhd \{t\} = \{e \mapsto t\}$)

Fig. 8. Proof Tree for Discharging INITIALISATION/propCard/INV

The t edge is preserved: 1. Apply the default post-tactics, which simplifies the property to $\exists x,\, x0.((\{mE(e_1), \ldots, mE(e_j)\} \lhd tG\_E) \cup \{ed_1 \mapsto t_1, \ldots, ed_k \mapsto t_k\} \rhd \{t\}) = \{x \mapsto x0\}$.
2. Instantiate variables in goal with x, $x0$, converting the goal to $(\{mE(e_1), \ldots, mE(e_j))\} \lhd tG\_E) \cup \{ed_1 \mapsto t_1, \ldots, ed_k \mapsto t_k\}) \rhd \{t\} = \{x \mapsto x0\}$.
3. Run NewPP with lasso.

Figure 9 presents the generated proof tree.

The t edge is deleted and a t edge is created: 1. Add $card(\{mE(e_1), \ldots, mE(e_j))\} \lhd tG\_E \rhd \{t\}) = 0$ as hypothesis, which will generate three sub-goals to be proved: (i) $finite(\{mE(e_1), \ldots, mE(e_j)\} \lhd tG\_E \rhd \{t\})$; (ii) $\{mE(e_1), \ldots, mE(e_j))\} \lhd tG\_E \rhd \{t\} = \varnothing$; and (iii) $\exists x,\, x0.((\{mE(e_1), \ldots, mE(e_j))\} \lhd tG\_E) \cup \{ed_1 \mapsto t_1, \ldots, ed_k \mapsto t_k\}) \rhd \{t\}) = \{x \mapsto x0\}$.
2. In order to proof (i), add $\{mE(e_1), \ldots, mE(e_j))\} \lhd tG\_E \rhd \{t\} \subseteq tG\_E \rhd \{t\}$ as hypothesis, and conclude the sub-goals running ML.
3. In order to proof (ii), add $\{mE(e_i)\} \lhd tG\_E \rhd \{t\} = \varnothing$ as hypothesis, such that e_i is the t deleted edge, and discharge the sub-goals running NewPP with lasso.
4. In order to proof (iii), instantiate the variable of the existential quantifier with ed_i and t, such that ed_i is the added t edge, and discharge the sub-goal with NewPP with lasso.

Figure 10 presents the generated proof tree.

$$
\begin{array}{c}
\textbf{NewPP RULES} \\
\hline
H \vdash (((\{mE(e_1), \ldots, mE(e_j)\} \lhd tG\_E) \cup \{ed_1 \mapsto t_1, \ldots, ed_k \mapsto t_k\}) \rhd \{t\} = \{x \mapsto x0\} \quad 1
\end{array}
$$

$$
\cfrac{\text{True}}{H \vdash \top}\ 2 \quad
H \vdash (((\{mE(e_1), \ldots, mE(e_j)\} \lhd tG\_E) \cup \{ed_1 \mapsto t_1, \ldots, ed_k \mapsto t_k\}) \rhd \{t\} = \{x \mapsto x0\} \ 3
$$

$$
H \vdash \exists x,\, x0 \cdot (((\{mE(e_1), \ldots, mE(e_j)\} \lhd tG\_E) \cup \{ed_1 \mapsto t_1, \ldots, ed_k \mapsto t_k\}) \rhd \{t\} = \{x \mapsto x0\} \quad 4
$$

$$
H \vdash \exists x,\, x0 \cdot (((\{mE(e_1), \ldots, mE(e_j)\} \lhd tG\_E) \cup \{ed_1 \mapsto t_1, \ldots, ed_k \mapsto t_k\}) \rhd \{t\} = \{x \mapsto x0\} \quad 5
$$

$$
H \vdash \exists x,\, x0 \cdot (((\{mE(e_1), \ldots, mE(e_j)\} \lhd tG\_E) \cup \{ed_1 \mapsto t_1, \ldots, ed_k \mapsto t_k\}) \rhd \{t\} = \{x \mapsto x0\} \quad 6
$$

$$
H \vdash \exists x,\, x0 \cdot (((\{mE(e_1), \ldots, mE(e_j)\} \lhd tG\_E) \cup \{ed_1 \mapsto t_1, \ldots, ed_k \mapsto t_k\}) \rhd \{t\} = \{x \mapsto x0\} \quad 7
$$

$$
H \vdash card((((\{mE(e_1), \ldots, mE(e_j)\} \lhd tG\_E) \cup \{ed_1 \mapsto t_1, \ldots, ed_k \mapsto t_k\}) \rhd \{t\}) = 1 \quad 8
$$

1 $NewPP$; 2 $\top$ goal; 3 sl/ds; 4 $\exists$ goal (inst x, $x0$); 5 $\exists$ hyp ($\exists x,\, x0 \cdot tG\_E \rhd \{t\} = \{x \mapsto x0\}$));
6 simplification rewrites; 7 type rewrites; 8 simplification rewrites

Fig. 9. Proof Tree for Discharging rule_i/propCard/INV

$\mathcal{A} = \{mE(e_1), \ldots, mE(e_j)\} \lhd tG\_E$
$\mathcal{B} = \{ed_1 \mapsto t_1, \ldots, ed_k \mapsto t_k\}$
$\mathcal{C} = e_j \in dom(mE) \wedge \ldots \wedge e_j \in dom(mE) \wedge mE \in edgeLi \twoheadrightarrow \mathbb{Z}$
$\mathcal{D} = e_1 \in dom(mE) \wedge mE \in edgeLi \twoheadrightarrow \mathbb{Z}$
$\mathcal{E} = \{me(e_j)\} \lhd tG\_E$

$$\boxed{E} \quad \cfrac{\cfrac{\cfrac{\text{True}}{H \vdash \top}\ 25 \qquad \cfrac{\text{NewPP RULES}}{H \vdash ((\mathcal{A}) \cup \mathcal{B}) \rhd \{t\} = \{ed_i \mapsto t\}}\ 26}{H \vdash \exists x, x0 \cdot ((\mathcal{A}) \cup \mathcal{B}) \rhd \{t\} = \{x \mapsto x0\}}\ 24}{H \vdash card(((\mathcal{A}) \cup \mathcal{B}) \rhd \{t\}) = 1}\ 23$$

$$\boxed{F} \quad \cfrac{\cfrac{\cfrac{\cfrac{\cfrac{\cfrac{\cfrac{\text{True}}{H \vdash \top}\ 20}{H \vdash \top \wedge \top}\ 19}{H \vdash \mathcal{D}}\ 18 \qquad \cfrac{\cfrac{\text{NewPP RULES}}{H \vdash \mathcal{E} \rhd \{t\} = \varnothing}\ 21 \qquad \cfrac{\text{NewPP RULES}}{H \vdash \mathcal{A} \rhd \{t\} = \varnothing}\ 22}{H \vdash \mathcal{A} \rhd \{t\} = \varnothing}\ 17}{H \vdash \mathcal{A} \rhd \{t\} = \varnothing}\ 16}{H \vdash \mathcal{A} \rhd \{t\} = \varnothing}\ 15}{H \vdash \mathcal{A} \rhd \{t\} = \varnothing}\ 14}{H \vdash card(\mathcal{A} \rhd \{t\}) = 0}\ 13$$

$$\cfrac{\cfrac{\cfrac{\cfrac{\cfrac{\cfrac{\cfrac{\cfrac{\cfrac{\cfrac{\text{True}}{H \vdash \top}\ 10}{H \vdash \top \wedge, \ldots, \wedge \top}\ 9}{H \vdash \mathcal{C}}\ 8 \quad \cfrac{\cfrac{\text{ML RULES}}{H \vdash \mathcal{A} \rhd \{t\} \subseteq tG\_E \rhd \{t\}}\ 11 \quad \cfrac{\text{ML RULES}}{H \vdash finite(\mathcal{A} \rhd \{t\})}\ 12}{H \vdash finite(\mathcal{A} \rhd \{t\})}\ 7}{H \vdash finite(\mathcal{A} \rhd \{t\})}\ 6}{H \vdash finite(\mathcal{A} \rhd \{t\})}\ 5}{H \vdash finite(\mathcal{A} \rhd \{t\})}\ 4}{H \vdash \top \wedge, \ldots, \wedge \top \wedge finite(\mathcal{A} \rhd \{t\})}\ 3}{H \vdash \mathcal{C} \wedge finite(\mathcal{A} \rhd \{t\})}\ 2 \qquad \boxed{F} \quad \boxed{E}}{H \vdash card(((\mathcal{A}) \cup \mathcal{B}) \rhd \{t\})) = 1}\ 1$$

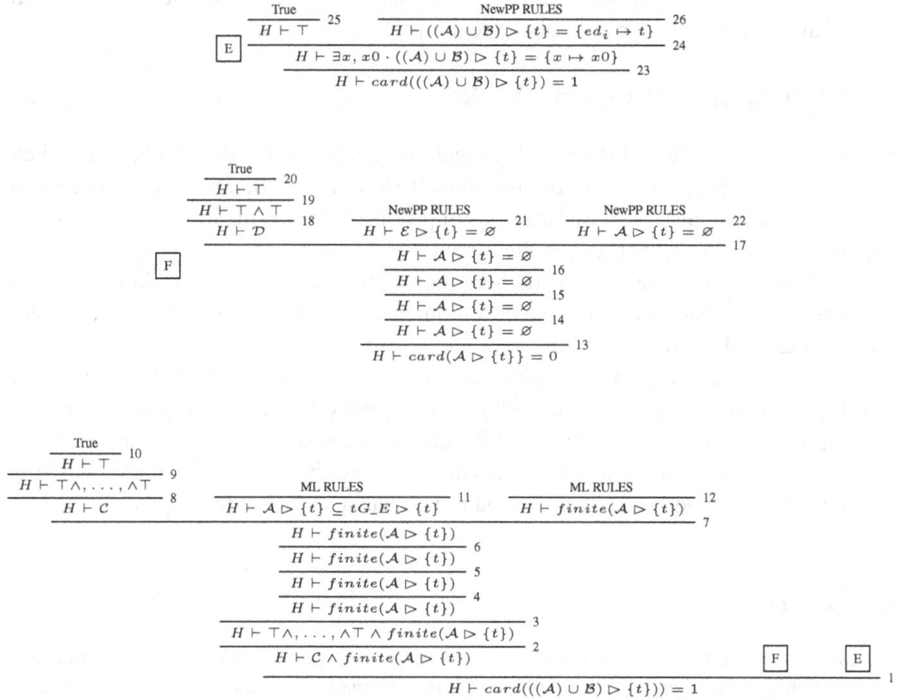

1 ah $(card(\{mE(e_1), \ldots, mE(e_j)\} \lhd tG\_E \rhd \{t\}) = 0)$; 2 generalised MP; 3 simplification rewrites; 4 type rewrites; 5 simplification rewrites; 6 $\exists$ hyp $(\exists x, x0 \cdot tG\_E \rhd \{t\} = \{x \mapsto x0\})$; 7 ah$(\mathcal{A} \rhd \{t\} \subseteq tG\_E \rhd \{t\})$; 8 generalised MP; 9 simplification rewrites; 10 $\top$ goal; 11 ML; 12 ML; 13 simplification rewrites; 14 type rewrites; 15 simplification rewrites; 16 $\exists$ hyp $(\exists x, x0 \cdot tG\_E \rhd \{t\} = \{x \mapsto x0\})$; 17 ah $(\mathcal{E} \rhd \{t\} = \varnothing)$; 18 generalised MP; 19 simplification rewrites; 20 $\top$ goal; 21 NewPP; 22 NewPP; 23 simplification rewrites; 24 $\exists$ goal (inst ed_i, t); 25 $\top$ goal; 26 NewPP

Fig. 10. Proof Tree for Discharging rule_i/propCard/INV

In order to discharge the proof obligation INITIALISATION/propExEdge/INV generated by property `propExEdge` ($\exists x \cdot x \in tG\_E \rhd \{t\}$) for the initial graph just run NewPP. Again, since a rule can preserve, delete and create edges, then we divide our proof strategies for obligations rule_i/propExEdge/INV in three cases.

All t edges are preserved: Run NewPP with lasso.
An t edges is created: (a) Instantiate existential variable in goal with $ed_i \mapsto t$, such that ed_i is the t edge that is created. (b) Run ML.
An t edge is deleted, but an t edge is preserved (a) Instantiate existential variable in goal with $mE(ed_i) \mapsto t$, such that ed_i is the t edge that is preserved. (b) Run NewPP with lasso.

In order to discharge the proof obligation INITIALISATION/propExVert/INV generated by property `propExVert` ($\exists x \cdot x \in tG\_V \rhd \{t\}$) for the initial graph just run

NewPP. For such property no proof obligations are generated for rules. This is because the component that map vertices in rules are total and injective, and then vertices can not be deleted. Proving that we have a vertex of type t in the initial graph, no other rule can delete it. Previous work has addressed that this restriction in the model is not a severe limitation for many practical applications [6].

6   Conclusions and Future Work

In this paper we presented the proof obligations generated by Rodin platform when specifying a graph grammar system in Event-B structures, indicating the strategies to discharge them. We also propose strategies of proofs for the verification of some atomic properties, declared as invariants in the model.

One of the disadvantages of using theorem proving as verification technique is that it requires user interaction during the development of the proofs, but on the other hand, it allows the verification of systems with huge or infinite state spaces. This work constitutes the first step towards the reduction of expertise required from the user when adopting such an approach. Strategies for discharging other kind of properties are being proposed. Particularly, tactics for all patterns proposed in [11] are under development. We are also investigating to which extent the theory of refinement, which is well-developed in Event-B, could be used to validate a stepwise development based on graph grammars.

References

1. Ehrig, H., Heckel, R., Korff, M., Löwe, M., Ribeiro, L., Wagner, A., Corradini, A.: Handbook of graph grammars and computing by graph transformation, pp. 247–312. World Scientific Publishing Co., Inc., River Edge (1997)
2. Robinson, J.A., Voronkov, A. (eds.): Handbook of Automated Reasoning (in 2 volumes). Elsevier and MIT Press (2001)
3. de Mello, A.M., Junior, L.C.L., Foss, L., da Costa Cavalheiro, S.A.: Graph grammars: A comparison between verification methods. In: WEIT, pp. 88–94 (2011)
4. da Costa, S.A., Ribeiro, L.: Verification of graph grammars using a logical approach. Sci. Comput. Program. 77(4), 480–504 (2012)
5. Ribeiro, L., Dotti, F.L., da Costa, S.A., Dillenburg, F.C.: Towards theorem proving graph grammars using Event-B. ECEASST 30 (2010)
6. da Costa, S.A.: Relational approach of graph grammars. PhD thesis, UFRGS, Brazil (2010)
7. DEPLOY: Event-B and the rodin platform (Mai 2013), http://www.event-b.org/ (last accessed Mai 2013)
8. Abrial, J.R., Butler, M., Hallerstede, S., Hoang, T.S., Mehta, F., Voisin, L.: Rodin: An open toolset for modelling and reasoning in Event-B. International Journal on Software Tools for Technology Transfer (STTT) 12(6), 447–466 (2010)
9. Tanenbaum, A.: Computer Networks, 4th edn. Prentice Hall Professional Technical Reference (2002)
10. Abrial, J.R.: Modeling in Event-B: System and Software Engineering, 1st edn. Cambridge University Press, New York (2010)
11. da Costa Cavalheiro, S.A., Foss, L., Ribeiro, L.: Specification patterns for properties over reachable states of graph grammars. In: Gheyi, R., Naumann, D. (eds.) SBMF 2012. LNCS, vol. 7498, pp. 83–98. Springer, Heidelberg (2012)

A Refinement Framework
for Autonomous Agents

Qin Li and Graeme Smith

School of Information Technology and Electrical Engineering
The University of Queensland, Australia
q.li2@uq.edu.au, smith@itee.uq.edu.au

Abstract. An autonomous agent is one that is not only directed by its
environment, but is also driven by internal motivation to achieve certain
goals. The popular Belief-Desire-Intention (BDI) design paradigm allows
such agents to adapt to environmental changes by calculating a new execution path to their current goal, or when necessary turning to another
goal. In this paper we present an approach to modelling autonomous
agents using an extension to Object-Z. This extension supports both
data and action refinement, and includes the use of LTL formulas to describe an agent's desire as a sequence of prioritised goals. It turns out,
however, that the introduction of desire-driven behaviour is not monotonic with respect to refinement. We therefore introduce an additional
refinement proof obligation to enable the use of simulation rules when
checking refinement.

Keywords: Autonomous agents, BDI agents, Refinement, Object-Z,
Temporal logic.

1 Introduction

The design of autonomous agents is one of the central issues of the artificial
intelligence community [1]. Such an agent has the capability to manage its own
resources and sense its environment. Its further behaviour is often determined
dynamically based on its current perception of itself and the environment as well
as a goal to achieve. This is the main difference between autonomous agents and
conventional components.

An autonomous agent is usually described in terms of not only its "physical"
features such as variables and actions but also its "mental" features such as
beliefs, *desires* and *intentions* (BDI) [2,3]. An autonomous agent in the BDI
paradigm formulates a plan (its intention) based on its current beliefs about
itself and its environment in order to achieve its desire. Its behaviour, therefore,
is derived not only from what it is able to do, but also from what it wants to
do [1].

In this paper, we use an extension to Object-Z [4] to specify autonomous
agents. The interactions between an agent and its environment are recorded with
the inputs and outputs within action definitions. If the information obtained from

J. Iyoda and L. de Moura (Eds.): SBMF 2013, LNCS 8195, pp. 163–178, 2013.
© Springer-Verlag Berlin Heidelberg 2013

the environment violates the belief of the agent (which is implicitly included in the precondition of the actions), we consider this to be divergence which can be refined in the development process. This perspective allows us to refine an agent to adapt to a hostile environment by introducing reaction mechanisms for unexpected inputs.

The desire-driven behaviour of autonomous agents is captured by restricting an agent's behaviour to paths leading to its desire. A desire is specified as a sequence of goals each specified in terms of linear temporal logic (LTL) [5]. Typical goals include getting a task done in the future which can be specified with the eventually temporal operator $\Diamond$, or maximising a reward at each step which can be specified with the always temporal operator $\Box$.

In this paper, we limit goals to refer to the state variables of an agent only, *i.e.*, a goal cannot refer to inputs and outputs from the environment. If this is necessary, the values of such variables can be recorded as part of the agent's state.

The goals are ordered with priority within the desire and we assume that the agent will have only one goal at any moment. Initially, the goal of the agent will be set to the goal of the desire with the highest priority. The agent follows an execution path which leads to the current goal taking into account interaction with the environment. If there is no path to achieve the goal, the agent sets another goal of the desire to its current goal. If none of the goals of the desire is achievable, the agent arbitrarily performs any enabled action, which we call *unmotivated* behaviour.

An alternative to unmotivated behaviour would be to remove behaviours corresponding to the agent's goals being unachievable. This would lead to specifications which are unimplementable (since we cannot guarantee that the environment will allow an agent to achieve its goals), whereas we want to be able to develop our specifications using refinement. The unmotivated behaviour in our specifications can be refined by introducing further goals when the current ones are unachievable.

The refinement theory we provide is able to justify the correctness of design and development paradigms for adapting to environments: (a) introducing local mechanisms to increase the feasibility of the desire under different environmental conditions, and (b) introducing further goals to the desire to reduce the possibility of not being able to achieve a goal belonging to the desire. To provide flexible support for (a) we allow the introduction of both variables and actions in the concrete specification. Therefore, the refinement theory and its simulation rules are based on event refinement in Event-B [6]. As mentioned above, our notion of unmotivated behaviour supports (b).

However, as we show, restricting unmotivated behaviour during the development of an agent is not monotonic with respect to refinement. In order to refine autonomous agents, therefore, we provide an additional refinement obligation. A refinement of an autonomous agent can be verified by checking both the standard simulation rules and the new proposed obligation.

The remainder of the paper is organised as follows. The specification notation and its semantics are presented in Section 2; the refinement relation and simulation rules are introduced in Section 2.1. Section 3 proposes the specification of an autonomous agent with an explicit desire presented as a sequence of LTL formulas representing goals. In Section 4 the non-monotonicity of the behaviour restriction is revealed, and the refinement obligation to aid the checking of refinement is proposed. Section 5 mentions related work and Section 6 concludes the paper and refers to future research directions.

2   Agents

At low levels of abstraction an agent can be modelled as a state machine, or state-transition system. But an autonomous agent is conveniently specified more abstractly by stating explicitly its desire. This distinguishes an autonomous agent from a general reactive component; such an agent adjusts its choice of actions to meet its desire [1]. This will be considered in Section 3. For now we represent an agent syntactically by a construct, based on the class construct of Object-Z [4], which we will call a *module*.

A module includes a state schema declaring the local variables and an invariant constraining their values, an initial state schema and a set of actions modelling state transitions. As in Object-Z, primed variables, *e.g.*, x', denote the value of state variables in the post-state of an action, and actions include a Δ-list of variables whose values they may change.

Unlike standard Object-Z, an action has both a guard and a precondition. The guard condition is stated explicitly in an action separated from the effect predicate describing the action's behaviour. The explicit guard is an extension to Object-Z aimed at allowing a more flexible notion of refinement similar to that of Event-B. Specifically, an action can be enabled in a state which is not included as a pre-state of the effect predicate; but the result is divergence.

An action is of the following form where y denotes those state variables not in the Δ-list.

```
__ Action _____
 Δ(x)                        variables which action may change
 u? : Type_of_u              input variables
 v! : Type_of_v              output variables
 a : Type_of_a               auxiliary variables
 _____
 guard(u?, a, x, y)
 _____
 effect(u?, a, x, y, x', v!)
```

In the standard semantics of Object-Z, the state variables are hidden (*i.e.*, executions are represented by sequences of actions) and the interaction variables (inputs and outputs) appear as part of the actions which occur. While such a semantics is suited to standard data refinement [7], to allow the introduction of actions we require a semantics in which the actions are hidden (*i.e.*, executions are represented by sequences of states), and hence embed the interaction variables in the states.

The interaction variables are implicitly added to the Δ-list of every action. Any reference in an action to an input variable is a reference to its pre-state value. Hence, actions cannot refer to or constrain their post-state values which represent the values of the inputs used by the next action. Any reference to an output variable is a reference to its post-state value. In the case that an action does not generate a value for a given output variable $v!$ then $v!$ is implicity assigned the special null (undefined) value ϵ.

Semantically, a module is a tuple $M = (\Sigma, I, \mathcal{A})$ where

- Σ is the set of states of the module. Each state is a function mapping the local variables and interaction variables to values which satisfy the variables' types.

$$\Sigma \; \widehat{=} \; \{\sigma \mid \sigma \in ((Var \cup In) \to Val) \cup (Out \to (Val \cup \{\epsilon\}))\}$$

  where *Var* is the set of local variables declared in the module, *In* is the set of input variables appearing in any action of the module, and *Out* is the set of output variables appearing in any action of the module. *Val* is the set of all values and ϵ is the null value for output variables.
- $I \subseteq \Sigma$ is the set of states which satisfy the module's initial condition. The initial value of each output variable is ϵ.

$$I \; \widehat{=} \; \{\sigma \mid \sigma \in \Sigma \wedge \sigma \models (init(Var) \wedge inv(Var)) \wedge \forall\, v! \in Out \bullet \sigma(v!) = \epsilon\}$$

  where *init(Var)* is the initialisation condition and *inv(Var)* is the invariant over the state variables. The input variables are not constrained initially. The values chosen represent the values of the inputs used by the first action to occur.
- $\mathcal{A} \subseteq \Sigma \times \Sigma^{\perp}$ is the transition relation specified by the actions where $\Sigma^{\perp} = \Sigma \cup \{\perp\}$ and $\perp$ denotes a divergent state in which the values of the state variables are undefined. Divergence occurs when the current state enables an action but the effect of executing the action is undefined. Divergent behaviour is modelled as maximally nondeterministic behaviour allowing it to be refined by any other behaviour. Hence, divergence can be used to abstract the details of behaviour of interest only at some lower level of abstraction. When an action results in divergent behaviour, the divergent state $\perp$, as well as any other state in Σ, may result. In this way, divergent behaviour can be distinguished semantically from maximally nondeterministic terminating behaviour.

Formally, an individual action named A is represented semantically as

$$sem\ A \; \widehat{=} \; \{(\sigma, \sigma') \mid \sigma \in \Sigma \wedge \sigma' \in \Sigma^{\perp} \wedge \sigma \models A.guard \wedge$$
$$((\sigma, \sigma') \models E(A) \vee \nexists \sigma'' \bullet (\sigma, \sigma'') \models E(A))\}$$

where $A.guard$ is the guard condition of action A and

$$E(A) \,\hat{=}\, A.\textit{effect} \wedge \textit{inv}(\textit{Var}) \wedge \textit{inv}(\textit{Var}') \wedge \forall v! \in (\textit{Out} \backslash A.\textit{out}) \bullet \sigma'(v!) = \epsilon$$

where $A.\textit{effect}$ is the effect predicate of action A, and $A.\textit{out}$ is its set of output variables.

Given that the set of all action names is $\textit{Actions}$, we have

$$\mathcal{A} = \bigcup\nolimits_{A \in \textit{Actions}} \textit{sem } A$$

For simplicity, we omit the notation $\textit{sem}$ in the rest of the paper when it causes no confusion.

The behaviour of a module is the set of all possible traces of the agent, *i.e.*, infinite sequences of states $\langle \sigma_1, \sigma_2, \ldots \rangle$ where every state is a member of $\Sigma^\perp$, $\sigma_1 \in I$, and for all $i \in \mathbb{N}_1$, (σ_i, σ_{i+1}) corresponds to the execution of an action A, or to agent inactivity. By allowing unlimited agent inactivity, we model the fact that an unmotivated autonomous agent can always choose to do nothing. This is not the case when the agent is motivated by a desire.

Formally, the set of traces of a module is defined below where for any $i \in \mathbb{N}_1$, $s[i]$ denotes the ith state in trace s.

Definition 1. *(Module Traces) For a trace s and a set $m \subseteq \mathbb{N}_1$, let $non\_div(s, m)$ be true iff s does not diverge at indices in m, i.e.,*

$$non\_div(s, m) \,\hat{=}\, \forall i \in m \bullet (s[i], s[i+1]) \in \mathcal{A} \cup \textit{Skip} \wedge (s[i], \perp) \notin \mathcal{A}$$

where $\textit{Skip} \,\hat{=}\, \{(\sigma, \sigma') \mid \forall x \in \textit{Var} \bullet \sigma'(x) = \sigma(x) \wedge \forall v! \in \textit{Out} \bullet \sigma'(v!) = \epsilon\}$

The behaviour of any module M is modelled as a set of traces, divided into the following subsets distinguished by divergence.

$nml(M)$ denotes the set of all normal, i.e., non-divergent, traces of M.

$$nml(M) \,\hat{=}\, \{s \mid s[1] \in I \wedge non\_div(s, \mathbb{N}_1)\}$$

For $n \in \mathbb{N}_1$, $div(M, n)$ denotes the set of traces of M that diverge after the nth state.

$$div(M, n) \,\hat{=}\, \{s \mid s[1] \in I \wedge non\_div(s, \{1 \,.. \, n-1\}) \wedge (s[n], \perp) \in \mathcal{A}\}\}$$

Note that it is not possible to recover from divergence; the behaviour following the nth state is undefined and hence maximally nondeterministic (all behaviours including those with the divergent state $\perp$ are included).

$tr(M)$ denotes the set of all possible execution traces of M.

$$tr(M) \,\hat{=}\, nml(M) \cup \left(\bigcup\nolimits_{n \geq 1} div(M, n)\right)$$

Example 1. Consider an agent driving a car. The agent receives information about the local traffic via an on-board navigation device. This information includes the time required to reach the destination on the current route, taking into account traffic congestion, and the time on any alternative routes which are faster than the current route. The agent can change the route it takes based on this information.

Let *Route* be a given type denoting the set of all routes and let the agent's state have two variables *current* : *Route* denoting the current route and *time* : *Route* $\nrightarrow$ $\mathbb{N}$ denoting the travel times of the current route and all alternative routes. Initially, the current route is the only route for which a time is displayed. The action *Update* models the agent receiving route information from the navigator, and the agent choosing a route based on this information.

__*Agent*_____

$current$: $Route$
$time$: $Route \nrightarrow \mathbb{N}$

_$I\!NIT$_____
$\text{dom } time = \{current\}$

_$Update$_____
$\Delta(current, time)$
$time?$: $Route \nrightarrow \mathbb{N}$

$true$

$current \in \text{dom } time?$
$\forall\, r : \text{dom } time? \setminus \{current\} \bullet time?(r) < time?(current)$
$time' = time?$
$current' \in \text{dom } time'$

Let $R1, R2, R3 \in Route$. A normal trace of the agent is:

$\langle(current = R1, time = \{R1 \mapsto 50\}, time? = \{R1 \mapsto 40, R2 \mapsto 35\}),$
$(current = R1, time = \{R1 \mapsto 40, R2 \mapsto 35\}, time? = \{R1 \mapsto 35, R3 \mapsto 20\}),$
$(current = R3, time = \{R1 \mapsto 35, R3 \mapsto 20\}, time? = \{R3 \mapsto 20\}), \ldots\rangle$

A divergent trace of the agent is:

$\langle(current = R1, time = \{R1 \mapsto 50\}, time? = \{R1 \mapsto 40, R2 \mapsto 35\}),$
$(current = R1, time = \{R1 \mapsto 40, R2 \mapsto 35\}, time? = \{R1 \mapsto 35, R2 \mapsto 40\}),$
$\perp, \ldots\rangle$

In this case, the divergence is caused by the navigator providing an input violating the precondition $\forall\, r : \text{dom } time? \setminus \{current\} \bullet time?(r) < time?(current)$.

2.1 Refinement and Simulation Rules

A refinement of an agent specification guarantees that the changes of the state variables in the concrete specification are consistent with those in the abstract specification with respect to a *retrieve relation* R. Given two modules M_1 and M_2, a retrieve relation $R : \mathbb{P}(\Sigma_1^\perp \times \Sigma_2^\perp)$ defines a correspondence between their states. Note that R maps the divergent state $\perp$ only to itself, *i.e.*, $R(\perp) = \{\perp\}$ and $R^{-1}(\perp) = \{\perp\}$. As well as allowing R to be applied as a function on sets of states (note that a single state argument is interpreted as the singleton set containing that state), we allow it to be applied as a function on traces, sets of traces and formulas. The results of the application of R to these constructs are based on its application to states. For instance, the application of R to a trace can be defined as:

$$R(s) = \{ t \mid \forall\, i \in \mathbb{N}_1 \bullet t[i] \in R(s[i]) \}$$

The application of R to a set of traces S can be defined based on its application to traces:

$$R(S) \mathrel{\widehat{=}} \bigcup_{s \in S} R(s)$$

The application of R to a formula P is also defined in terms of its application to traces:

$$R(P) = \{ Q \mid \forall\, s, t \bullet t \in R(s) \Rightarrow (s \models P \Leftrightarrow t \models Q) \}$$

Definition 2. *(Refinement) Let M_1 and M_2 be two modules. We say M_1 is refined by M_2 with respect to retrieve relation R, denoted $M_2 \sqsupseteq_R M_1$, iff $tr(M_2) \subseteq R(tr(M_1))$.*

The subscript R in $\sqsupseteq_R$ may be omitted if R is the identity relation.

Internal changes in the concrete specification may be hidden by the retrieve relation, making some of the concrete actions appear like inactivity at the abstract level. Such concrete actions are called 'stuttering actions'. Formally, action A defined in a concrete module is called a *stuttering action* if it behaves as inactivity in the abstract view, *i.e.*, $R\,;\,A \subseteq Skip\,;\,R$. Any concrete action not having that property is called a *change action*.

To prove refinement via Definition 2 is generally intractable, requiring analysis of all traces of the modules, and so as usual we consider simulations. The following simulation rules are inspired by those of Event-B [6] which allow a single abstract state transition to be refined by a sequence of concrete transitions.

Theorem 1. *(Forward Simulation) Let M_1 and M_2 be modules and R be a retrieve relation between their states. Then $M_2 \sqsupseteq_R M_1$ if*

(1) $I_2 \subseteq R(I_1)$

(2) for any change action A_2 of M_2, there exists an action A_1 of M_1 where $R\,;\,A_2 \subseteq A_1\,;\,R$.

The proof is straightforward noting that any concrete trace which has stuttering states is related to an abstract trace with inactivity, *i.e.*, *Skip*, in the corresponding positions in the trace.

Condition (2) allows the guards of a concrete change action to be stronger than that of the corresponding abstract action. This can result in the introduction of deadlock, *i.e.*, where no actions are enabled. While an agent can choose to be inactive, we would not usually want to refine an agent to one which can only be inactive in certain circumstances. Hence, as in Event-B, we propose an additional condition to prevent the introduction of deadlock.

(3) The overall guard of M_2 is weaker than that of M_1, *i.e.*,

$$R(\{\sigma \mid \sigma \models g(M_1)\}) \subseteq \{\gamma \mid \gamma \models g(M_2)\}$$

where the overall guard $g(M)$ is the disjunction of all action guards declared in module M.

3   Autonomous Agents

A module can specify the behaviour of an agent by referring to the variables it controls and the actions it can perform. In order to specify the autonomous behaviour of an agent, we need to also specify the motivation for its execution: to fulfil its desire. Hence we add a component to the standard module to represent the agent's desire.

An autonomous agent comprising a module M and desire Q will be denoted by $M?Q$. The desire Q is a finite sequence of goals, *i.e.*, $Q = \langle \Phi_1, \Phi_2, ..., \Phi_n \rangle$. Each goal is represented by a linear temporal logic (LTL) [5] formula.

Initially, the agent sets its goal to the first element of the desire sequence. To achieve this goal, the agent calculates execution paths based on its current beliefs about itself and the environment and chooses to follow a path leading to the goal. If there is no path for the agent to achieve its current goal, the agent changes its goal to the next element of the desire sequence. If no goal in the desire sequence is feasible, the agent's behaviour becomes unmotivated (choosing any enabled action). At a lower level of abstraction, the unmotivated behaviour might be refined by, for example, introducing a new goal to the desire sequence.

We define the desire-driven behaviour of an autonomous agent $M?Q$ in an inductive manner. As the base case, an agent with an empty desire sequence behaves as the definition of its module, *i.e.*, $M?\langle\rangle \mathrel{\widehat{=}} M$.

Consider an agent with only one goal in its desire sequence, *i.e.*, $M?\langle\Phi\rangle$. The traces of $M?\langle\Phi\rangle$ include:

- Any non-divergent trace of M which satisfies Φ.
- Any divergent trace of M which has satisfied Φ before divergence. After the desire has been satisfied, the agent may act in any manner available to it.

– Any trace of M in which, from a certain point, the agent has no opportunity to make a decision which will lead to its desire being satisfied while before that point the agent made acceptable choices all along the trace. Such a trace corresponds to unmotivated behaviour.

Note that a decision made by the agent is acceptable when there exists a path afterward which can satisfy the desire given a cooperative environment. That is, we do not insist the decisions of the agent guarantee that every path afterward can satisfy the desire. This reflects the fact that such decisions would be based on the agent's beliefs about the future behaviour of the environment which may, or may not, turn out to be true.

To formalise our notion of desire-driven behaviour, we first introduce some notation.

1. We use the notation Δ to denote the set of all sequences of states which do not include $\perp$. For a trace $s \in \Delta$ and LTL formula Φ, we say $s \vDash \Phi$ if and only if the temporal property Φ is satisfied by s.
2. For traces s and t, let $s =_n t$ be true iff s and t share the same prefix of length n, i.e.,

$$s =_n t \mathrel{\widehat{=}} \forall\, i \in 1..n \bullet s[i] = t[i]$$

3. For a set S of traces satisfying a desire, we let $\Gamma(s, S, i)$ denote a predicate that is true when trace s is not in the set S due to either (a) the value of inputs at point i, or (b) when i is 1, the trace's initial state (due to either the values of the state variables or the inputs to the first action). These situations are ones in which the agent has no opportunity to make a decision which will lead to the desire being satisfied.

    For case (a), (1) there does not exist a trace in S which shares the prefix of trace s up to point i, and (2) there exists a trace $u \in S$ which shares the prefix of s up to point $i - 1$ and differs from s at point i by the input values only. This case indicates that the desire is unable to be satisfied due to inputs from the environment.

    For case (b), there does not exist a trace in S which shares the same initial state as s. This case indicates that the desire is unable to be satisfied due to the initialisation of the agent or the initial inputs from the environment. Let $V \triangleleft \sigma$ denotes the state σ with variables in set V removed.

$$\Gamma(s, S, i) \mathrel{\widehat{=}} \begin{aligned} &i = 1 \Rightarrow \nexists r \in S \bullet r[1] = s[1] \,\wedge \\ &i > 1 \Rightarrow \nexists r \in S \bullet r =_i s \,\wedge \\ &\quad \exists\, u \in S \bullet u =_{i-1} s \wedge In \triangleleft u[i] = In \triangleleft s[i] \end{aligned}$$

Such a trace s contains unmotivated behaviour after point i. It would be kept in the autonomous behaviour for further refinement.

Definition 3. *(Autonomous behaviour) The behaviour of an autonomous agent $M?\langle \Phi \rangle$ is modeled as a set of traces, divided into the following subsets distinguished by divergence.*

The normal traces of $M?\langle\Phi\rangle$ are those normal traces of M which either satisfy Φ (represented by nmlsucc), or fail to satisfy Φ due to input values or their initial state (represented by nmlfail).

$$nml(M?\langle\Phi\rangle) \ \hat{=}\ nmlsucc(M?\langle\Phi\rangle) \cup nmlfail(M?\langle\Phi\rangle) \ where$$

$$nmlsucc(M?\langle\Phi\rangle) \ \hat{=}\ \{s \mid s \in nml(M) \wedge s \models \Phi\}$$

$$nmlfail(M?\langle\Phi\rangle) \ \hat{=}\ \{s \mid s \in nml(M) \wedge \exists i \in \mathbb{N}_1 \bullet \Gamma(s, nmlsucc(M?\langle\Phi\rangle), i)\}$$

The divergent traces of $M?\langle\Phi\rangle$ are those divergent traces which satisfy Φ (i.e., all non-diverging traces that do not differ before the point of divergence satisfy Φ) or fail to satisfy Φ due to input values (represented by divfail).

$$div(M?\langle\Phi\rangle, n) \ \hat{=}\ divsucc(M?\langle\Phi\rangle, n) \cup divfail(M?\langle\Phi\rangle, n) \ where$$

$$divsucc(M?\langle\Phi\rangle, n) \ \hat{=}\ \{s \mid s \in div(M, n) \wedge \forall t \in \Delta \bullet s =_n t \Rightarrow t \models \Phi\}$$

$$divfail(M?\langle\Phi\rangle, n) \ \hat{=}\ \{s \mid s \in div(M, n) \wedge \exists i \in 1..n \bullet \Gamma(s, nmlsucc(M?\langle\Phi\rangle), i)\}$$

The set of all possible traces of $M?\langle\Phi\rangle$ is

$$tr(M?\langle\Phi\rangle) \ \hat{=}\ nml(M?\langle\Phi\rangle) \cup \left(\bigcup\nolimits_{n \geq 1} div(M?\langle\Phi\rangle, n)\right).$$

Example 2. Reconsider the example agent of Section 2. Let the desire of the agent be that the time cost of the current route is always no greater than the previous current route. This can be specified in LTL as follows.

$$\Box(\exists t : \mathbb{N} \bullet t = time(current) \wedge \bigcirc(time(current) \leq t))$$

In this case, the following normal trace (where the agent does not change to a faster route) would no longer be allowed.

$\langle(current = R1, time = \{R1 \mapsto 50\}, time? = \{R1 \mapsto 45, R2 \mapsto 35\}),$
$(current = R1, time = \{R1 \mapsto 45, R2 \mapsto 35\}, time? = \{R1 \mapsto 35, R3 \mapsto 40\}),$
$\ldots\rangle$

If there is no route provided by the navigator that takes less time than the current route, the agent would have no choice but to violate its current goal. The behaviour after this point is considered to be unmotivated behaviour. Such a case is shown below where the input *time?* in the first state gives the agent no choice to satisfy its goal. The rest of the trace is unmotivated.

$\langle(current = R1, time = \{R1 \mapsto 40\}, time? = \{R1 \mapsto 50, R2 \mapsto 45\}),$
$(current = R2, time = \{R1 \mapsto 50, R2 \mapsto 45\}, time? = \{R2 \mapsto 45, R3 \mapsto 40\}),$
$\ldots\rangle$ $\qquad\qquad\qquad\qquad\qquad\qquad\qquad\qquad\qquad\qquad\qquad\qquad\qquad\square$

For an agent with more than one goal in its desire sequence, the definition is as follows.

Definition 4. *(Introducing goals) Let $M?Q$ be an autonomous agent with $Q \neq \langle\rangle$ and Φ be an LTL property. The introduction of goal Φ will take effect when the agent cannot fulfil its original desire Q. In other words, it will further restrict the unmotivated behaviour of the agent $M?Q$. The behaviour of the autonomous agent $M?(Q \frown \langle\Phi\rangle)$ can be defined as follows.*

- *The nmlsucc behaviour is extended by the traces which share the same prefix as a trace satisfying the original desire Q before point i and satisfying Φ instead from the point $i + 1$ where Q cannot be fulfilled.*

$$nmlsucc(M?(Q \frown \langle \Phi \rangle)) \mathrel{\widehat{=}} nmlsucc(M?Q) \cup \{s \mid s \in nmlfail(M?Q) \wedge \\ \exists i : \mathbb{N}_1 \bullet \Gamma(s, nmlsucc(M?Q), i) \wedge s_{i+1} \models \Phi\}$$

where s_i denotes the postfix of s beginning with the ith state.
- *The nmlfail behaviour contains the traces which cannot satisfy the new desire $Q \frown \langle \Phi \rangle$ due to the inputs or their initial state.*

$$nmlfail(M?(Q \frown \langle \Phi \rangle)) \mathrel{\widehat{=}} \{s \mid s \in nml(M?Q) \wedge \\ \exists i \in \mathbb{N}_1 \bullet \Gamma(s, nmlsucc(M?(Q \frown \langle \Phi \rangle)), i)\}$$

- *A similar definition is made for the divergent behaviours.*

$$divsucc(M?(Q \frown \langle \Phi \rangle), n) \mathrel{\widehat{=}} divsucc(M?Q, n) \cup \\ \{s \mid s \in divfail(M?Q, n) \wedge \forall t \in \Delta \bullet s =_n t \wedge \\ \exists i \in 1..n \bullet \Gamma(t, nmlsucc(M?Q), i) \wedge t_{i+1} \models \Phi\}$$

$$divfail(M?(Q \frown \langle \Phi \rangle), n) \mathrel{\widehat{=}} \{s \mid s \in div(M?Q, n) \wedge \\ \exists i \in 1..n \bullet \Gamma(s, nmlsucc(M?Q \frown \langle \Phi \rangle), i)\}$$

According to the above definition, the newly introduced goal only takes effect when the original goals are infeasible. This further restricts the behaviour of the autonomous agent by reducing its unmotivated behaviours. It is intuitive to obtain the conclusion that introducing a goal to the agent's desire sequence refines its behaviour.

Theorem 2. *Let M be a module and Q_1 and Q_2 be desires such that Q_1 is a proper subsequence of Q_2. Then we have $M?Q_2 \sqsupseteq M?Q_1$.*

Proof

1. *If $Q_1 = \langle \rangle$ and $Q_2 = \langle \Phi \rangle$, then from Definition 3, all traces of $M?\langle \Phi \rangle$ are traces of M, i.e., $tr(M?\langle \Phi \rangle) \subseteq tr(M)$. Hence, since $M?\langle \rangle \mathrel{\widehat{=}} M$, we have $tr(M?Q_2) \subseteq tr(M?Q_1)$ and therefore $M?Q_2 \sqsupseteq M?Q_1$.*
2. *If $Q_1 \neq \langle \rangle$ and $Q_2 = Q_1 \frown \langle \Phi_1, ..., \Phi_n \rangle$, then $tr(M?Q_2)$ can be obtained recursively from Definition 4 one goal at a time. It is straightforword to show that in each recursive step, any trace which does not satisfy the original goals nor the newly introduced goal but at some point has the opportunity to achieve the new goal is removed from the behaviour of the previous step. Hence we have $tr(M?Q_2) \subseteq tr(M?Q_1)$ and therefore $M?Q_2 \sqsupseteq M?Q_1$.*

4   Refinement Obligation

The desire-driven behaviour of an autonomous agent only removes a trace where it can choose another one with a shared prefix to achieve the desire. Otherwise,

the behaviour is like a standard module without desires. This allows us to refine
an agent by introducing additional goals to reduce the unmotivated behaviour
of the abstract specification. However, such a restriction is non-monotonic with
respect to the refinement order. An intuitive example is shown below.

Consider the situation shown in Figure 1 which shows a subset of the behaviours of two agents M_1 and M_2. s is the only trace which shares a prefix with
t of length k and satisfies a goal Φ.

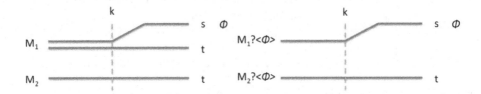

Fig. 1. Counter example for monotonicity

Consider the case where the traces s and t of agent M_1 differ at point $k + 1$
due to a local choice made by the agent. At point k, therefore, the agent has a
chance to make a local choice and follow trace s to fulfil the goal Φ. So trace t
will be removed from the behaviour of $M_1?\langle\Phi\rangle$.

Agent M_2 has all traces of M_1 apart from s. It is obvious that $M_2 \sqsupseteq M_1$
according to Definition 2. However, with the same desire $\langle\Phi\rangle$, trace t will not
be removed from the behaviour of $M_2?\langle\Phi\rangle$ since, in this case, the agent has no
opportunity to fulfil the desire. Hence the desire-driven behaviour $M_1?\langle\Phi\rangle$ is not
refined by $M_2?\langle\Phi\rangle$.

This situation arises whenever we disable a choice which can lead to an agent's
desire and hence make it impossible for the refined agent to satisfy the desire.
To avoid such refinements, we need an additional proof obligation that ensures
that the concrete agent does not introduce more unmotivated behaviour. That
is, if a concrete trace is a trace with unmotivated behaviour from a given point,
then its corresponding abstract trace is also a trace with unmotivated behaviour
from the same point.

This conclusion can be formalised by the following theorem. For simplicity,
we first explore the case of introducing a goal to the empty desire sequence.

Theorem 3. *(Refinement Obligation)*

*Let M_1 and M_2 be modules linked by a retrieve relation R and $\Phi_2 \in R(\Phi_1)$. We
have $M_2?\langle\Phi_2\rangle \sqsupseteq_R M_1?\langle\Phi_1\rangle$ if both of the following conditions hold.*

1. *$M_2 \sqsupseteq_R M_1$*
2. *For any trace of M_2 if it is impossible for the agent to make a local choice
   leading to the satisfaction of Φ_2 at a point in the trace, then from the same
   point in the corresponding trace of M_1 it is also impossible to satisfy Φ_1.
   That is, for all $s \in tr(M_1)$ and $t \in tr(M_2)$ where $t \in R(s)$, we have*

$$\forall i \in \mathbb{N}_1 \bullet (\Gamma(t, nmlsucc(M_2?\langle\Phi_2\rangle)), i) \Rightarrow \Gamma(s, nmlsucc(M_1?\langle\Phi_1\rangle)), i))$$

Proof:

Following Definition 2, we need to show that for any trace $t \in tr(M_2?\langle\Phi_2\rangle)$, each of its corresponding traces s, i.e., those traces where $t \in R(s)$, satisfy $s \in tr(M_1?\langle\Phi_1\rangle)$. According to condition 1 and Theorem 2, we get $s \in tr(M_1)$ (since $M_2?\langle\Phi_2\rangle \sqsupseteq M_2 \sqsupseteq_R M_1$).

The proof proceeds by a case analysis of traces s and t based on whether or not they are in Δ (the set of traces without $\bot$) and, if so, on their satisfaction of the respective desires. Since $s \in R(t)$ and $R(\bot) = \{\bot\} \wedge R^{-1}(\bot) = \{\bot\}$, it follows that $t \in \Delta \Leftrightarrow s \in \Delta$.

Assume $s, t \in \Delta$. In this situation, there are two cases to consider:

1. *If $t \models \Phi_2$ then its corresponding trace s satisfies Φ_1 since $\Phi_2 \in R(\Phi_1)$ (see the definition of R applied to formulas). Hence, s appears in $tr(M_1?\langle\Phi_1\rangle)$.*
2. *If $t \not\models \Phi_2$ then, according to Definition 3, its appearance in $tr(M_2?\langle\Phi_2\rangle)$ implies that there exists a point in t where the agent has no opportunity to make a choice leading to the goal Φ_2.*

$$\exists\, i \in \mathbb{N}_1 \bullet \Gamma(t, nmlsucc(M_2?\langle\Phi_2\rangle), i)$$

Hence in the corresponding trace s, Γ holds at the same point i due to condition 2. This then leads to

$$\exists\, i \in \mathbb{N}_1 \bullet \Gamma(s, nmlsucc(M_1?\langle\Phi_1\rangle), i)$$

Hence, according to Definition 3, s also appears in $tr(M_1?\langle\Phi_1\rangle)$.

The remaining case to consider is when $s, t \notin \Delta$. According to Definition 1, we can find $n > 1$ so that t diverges at the nth place, i.e., $t \in div(M_2?\langle\Phi_2\rangle, n)$.

1. *If $t \in divsucc(M_2?\langle\Phi_2\rangle, n)$, which means $\forall u \in \Delta \bullet t =_n u \Rightarrow u \models \Phi_2$, then since $\Phi_2 \in R(\Phi_1)$ and $t \in R(s)$, we have $\forall r \in \Delta \bullet s =_n r \Rightarrow r \models \Phi_1$. Hence $s \in div(M_1?\langle\Phi_1\rangle, n)$.*
2. *If $t \in divfail(M_2?\langle\Phi_2\rangle, n)$, which means $\exists\, i \in 1..n \bullet \Gamma(t, nmlsucc(M_2?\langle\Phi_2\rangle), i)$, then according to condition 2 we can conclude that $\exists\, i \in 1..n \bullet \Gamma(s, nmlsucc(M_1?\langle\Phi_1\rangle), i)$. Hence we have $s \in div(M_1?\langle\Phi_1\rangle, n)$.*

In summary, we have $t \in tr(M_2?\langle\Phi_2\rangle) \Rightarrow s \in tr(M_1?\langle\Phi_1\rangle)$ which means $M_2?\langle\Phi_2\rangle \sqsupseteq_R M_1?\langle\Phi_1\rangle$.

The refinement obligation implies that the refined agent has no more unmotivated behaviour than the abstract agent. Reconsider the counter example of Figure 1. The trace s is a trace with unmotivated behaviour in $M_2?\langle\Phi\rangle$ but not in $M_1?\langle\Phi\rangle$.

A general version of the refinement obligation for all possible desire sequences is as follows.

Theorem 4. *(General Obligation) Let $M_1?Q_1$ and $M_2?Q_2$ be two autonomous agents linked by a retrieve relation R, and Φ_1 and Φ_2 be LTL formulas with $\Phi_2 \in R(\Phi_1)$. We have $M_2?(Q_2 \frown \langle \Phi_2 \rangle) \sqsupseteq_R M_1?(Q_1 \frown \langle \Phi_1 \rangle)$ if both of the following conditions hold.*

1. *$M_2?Q_2 \sqsupseteq_R M_1?Q_1$*
2. *For all $s \in tr(M_1?Q_1)$ and $t \in tr(M_2?Q_2)$ where $t \in R(s)$ we have*

$$\forall i \in \mathbb{N}_1 \bullet \Gamma(t, nmlsucc(M_2?Q_2 \frown \langle \Phi_2 \rangle), i)$$
$$\Rightarrow \Gamma(s, nmlsucc(M_1?Q_1 \frown \langle \Phi_1 \rangle), i)$$

Proof: The proof can be done inductively based on Theorem 3.

With the refinement obligation we obtain from Theorems 3 and 4, refinement checking between two autonomous agents can be done monotonically and recursively. First we can check the refinement between their modules without desires. Then we check the obligation for each goal along their desire sequences.

The refinement obligation requires the refined agent preserve the possibility of achieving the desire under any environmental inputs. A development strategy which sufficiently satisfies the obligation is to introduce local mechanisms to adapt to environmental "hostility". The strategy includes the following three rules.

1. Weakening the precondition of actions to accept a larger range of inputs. This makes the agent handle more situations of the environment and hence reduces divergence.
2. Optimizing the decision making algorithms to improve the local decision so that the agent has a more deterministic way to achieve the desire under certain inputs than the specification does.
   For example, for the desire to take a faster route, the operation *Update* of Section 2 could be refined to always choose the fastest route, *i.e.*, by adding the predicate $time(current') = min(\text{ran } time)$.
3. Introducing additional goals to regulate the unmotivated behaviours.
   For example, for the unmotivated behaviour where the navigator provides no faster route than the current one, we introduce an alternative goal to allow the agent to choose the fastest of the provided routes.

$$\square(\nexists r : \text{dom } time \bullet time(r) < time(current))$$

With this alternative goal, the following trace from Section 3 is no longer unmotivated behaviour.

$\langle (current = R1, time = \{R1 \mapsto 40\}, time? = \{R1 \mapsto 50, R2 \mapsto 45\}),$
$(current = R2, time = \{R1 \mapsto 50, R2 \mapsto 45\}, time? = \{R2 \mapsto 45, R3 \mapsto 40\}),$
$\ldots \rangle$

Rule 1 is a conventional refinement rule. Rule 2 requires the designer to ensure the agent has a way to achieve its desire in the development. Rule 3 allows the designer to design a sequence of alternative goals when the agent fails to satisfy its current goal.

Following the above strategy, the refined agent has more reliable local mechanisms to achieve the desire than it does in the abstract specification.

5   Related Work

There is some formal work developed to specify interactions between an agent and its environment. Alternating transition systems (ATS) proposed by Alur *et al.* [8] treats an agent and its environment as the opponents of a game. Agents choose their own transitions to update the current state and the final result is the intersection of their choices. The action-based alternating transition system studied by Atkinson *et al.* [9] provides reasoning techniques for which action should be chosen by an agent in particular situations. Zhu [10] proposes a formal notation for specifying agent behaviour. The autonomous behaviour of the agent is formalised by a set of rules designed for various environmental scenarios. While the above approaches are able to specify agent-environment interactions, they do not specify the behaviour of agents as being driven by its 'mental' states (*e.g.*, desire).

Rao *et al.* [2] use a possible world model to interpret the semantics of BDI logic for autonomous agents. This is suitable for representing the belief, desire and intention of agents by assigning each of them a set of accessible worlds. However, unlike our approach, it lacks a theory to justify the correctness of the development of autonomous agents by introducing mechanisms to adapt to the environment. Aştefănoaei and de Boer [11] define a notion of refinement for BDI agents. Unlike our approach abstract and concrete specifications are not in the same notation. Therefore, their approach allows only a single refinement step from an abstract to a concrete representation of an agent, not the incremental development of an agent. More importantly, in their approach the goal of an agent is fixed. While they allow environmental hostility to be dealt with by changing plans, they don't allow the goal of an agent to be changed, nor the possibility of an agent not fulfilling its goal.

6   Conclusion

In this paper we provided a formal refinement framework to justify the correctness of the development of autonomous agents. Agents are specified in an extension of Object-Z including a desire specified by a sequence of LTL properties. The autonomous behaviour of an agent is realised by restricting its ordinary behaviour with the goals in its desire. Although this behaviour restriction is not monotonic with respect to refinement, we proposed an additional refinement obligation to allow checking refinement using ordinary simulation rules. The refinement framework can support the development of an autonomous agent by either introducing local mechanisms to adapt to environmental updates or introducing alternative goals to reduce unmotivated behaviour.

As a first step, we only considered the desire part of an agent's mental state and organised the goals within a sequence. A more general goal selection semantics will be supported in our future work as well as the explicit introduction of beliefs and intentions.

Acknowledgement. This work was supported by Australian Research Council (ARC) Discovery Grant DP110101211.

References

1. Wooldridge, M.: An Introduction to MultiAgent Systems, 2nd edn. Wiley (2009)
2. Rao, A.S., Georgeff, M.P.: BDI agents: From theory to practice. In: 1st International Conference of Multi-agent Systems (ICMAS 1995), pp. 312–319. MIT Press (1995)
3. Wooldridge, M., Jennings, N.R.: Intelligent agents: Theory and practice. Knowledge Engineering Review 10, 115–152 (1995)
4. Smith, G.: The Object-Z Specification Language. Kluwer Academic Publishers (2000)
5. Emerson, E.: Temporal and modal logic. In: van Leeuwen, J. (ed.) Handbook of Theoretical Computer Science, vol. B, pp. 996–1072. Elsevier (1990)
6. Abrial, J.R.: Modelling in Event-B. Cambridge University Press (2010)
7. Derrick, J., Boiten, E.: Refinement in Z and Object-Z, Foundations and Advanced Applications. Springer (2001)
8. Alur, R., Henzinger, T.A., Kupferman, O., Vardi, M.Y.: Alternating refinement relations. In: Sangiorgi, D., de Simone, R. (eds.) CONCUR 1998. LNCS, vol. 1466, pp. 163–178. Springer, Heidelberg (1998)
9. Atkinson, K., Bench-Capon, T.: Practical reasoning as presumptive argumentation using action based alternating transition systems. Artif. Intell. 171, 855–874 (2007)
10. Zhu, H.: Formal specification of agent behaviour through environment scenarios. In: Rash, J.L., Rouff, C.A., Truszkowski, W., Gordon, D.F., Hinchey, M.G. (eds.) FAABS 2000. LNCS (LNAI), vol. 1871, pp. 263–277. Springer, Heidelberg (2001)
11. Aştefănoaei, L., de Boer, F.: The refinement of multi-agent systems. In: Dastani, M., Hindriks, K., Meyer, J.J. (eds.) Specification and Verification of Multi-agent Systems, pp. 35–65. Springer (2010)

A Formal Semantics
for SysML Activity Diagrams

Lucas Lima, André Didier, and Márcio Cornélio

Centro de Informática, Universidade Federal de Pernambuco,
Recife, Brazil
{lal2,alrd,mlc2}@cin.ufpe.br
http://www.cin.ufpe.br/

Abstract. In this work, we propose a semantics for Activity Diagrams based on the COMPASS Modelling Language (CML): a formal specification language to model systems which is based on the CSP and VDM specification languages. A distinguishing feature of our semantics is that it is defined as part of a larger effort to define the semantics of several diagrams of SysML, a UML profile for systems engineering. We have defined a fairly comprehensive semantics for Activity Diagrams, which comprises action, object and control nodes constructors, control and object flow, interruptible regions among other features. We illustrate our semantics with diagrams of an emergency response system. We also discuss an analysis strategy which involves an integrated view of diagrams like block definition and state machines.

Keywords: Activity Diagrams, SysML, semantics, CML.

1 Introduction

The increasing size and complexity of systems have lead to a great difficulty to their description and specification. Features like concurrency and parallelism demand notations and techniques for reasoning about system properties. In a broader context, Systems Engineering is related to the design of whole systems through an iterative process that leads to the development and operation of a system. Overall, it is an interdisciplinary approach to the development of systems [2]. In this case, systems are not only software-intensive but can also involve physical components. When systems interoperate achieving results that non-interconnected systems cannot obtain, they are referred as a System of Systems (SoS) [6].

The Systems Modeling Language (SysML) [11] was proposed by the OMG with the purpose of customising the Unified Modeling Language (UML) for systems engineering applications. It allows the representation of behaviour, structure, properties, constraints, and requirements of a system. SysML has its foundations in UML 2, but it adds two diagrams (requirements and parametric diagrams) and extends some other diagrams to the system point of view, e.g. class diagram becomes block definition diagram.

J. Iyoda and L. de Moura (Eds.): SBMF 2013, LNCS 8195, pp. 179–194, 2013.
© Springer-Verlag Berlin Heidelberg 2013

SysML semantics is not formally described, its specification is given in natural language. This impacts tool construction and reasoning about system specification. In this paper, we focus on a formal semantics of SysML Activity Diagrams that follows the UML 2 token flow semantics. Our semantics is amenable to automatic verification and has the purpose of being compatible with the semantics of other SysML behavioural and structural diagrams. We describe the semantics of activity diagrams by using the Compass Modelling Language (CML) [17], a formal specification language that enables a variety of refinement-based analysis. Different existing formalisms have served as semantics for UML 2 and SysML activity diagrams. Several approaches [1,19,18,15,4] use an algebraic process language such as CSP [13]. Other formalisms used as semantic domain are Abstract State Machines [12], Petri nets [14,3], and *Activity Calculus* [8]. CML allows a better representation for object nodes and flows through the definition, assignment and manipulation of typed variables.

The semantics we propose covers a rich set of elements of SysML activity diagrams: control nodes, object nodes (action pins, and activity parameters), control and object flows. We give semantics for different kinds of actions: call behaviour action, send signal, accept event, call operation, opaque, and value specification. We also deal with interruptible regions. From the meta-model that corresponds to these elements, we define a translation function into CML model (or part of a model). In this paper, we do not present the functions itself, but we apply them to two different activity diagrams to exemplify the CML models we obtain. For the complete set of semantic mappings, see [9]. Currently, the functions of the different types of diagrams are being implemented in Artisan Studio [1], thus, CML models can be automatically generated from SysML models.

This paper is organized as follows. We describe the Compass Modeling Language (CML) in Section 2. In Section 3, we informally describe the semantics of SysML activity diagrams. We present the application of our formal semantics of SysML activity diagrams in Section 4; we use two diagrams to exemplify the use of the translation functions. We discuss related work in Section 5. Final remarks and future work appear in Section 6.

2   CML

The COMPASS modelling language (CML) [17] is a formal specification language that integrates a state based notation similar to VDM++ [5], a process algebraic notation like CSP [13] and Dijkstra's language of guarded commands. It supports the specification and analysis of state-rich distributed specifications. Additionally, CML supports step-wise development by means of algebraic refinement laws. The soundness of the laws is established with respect to the formal semantics of CML, defined in the Unifying Theories of Programming [7]. CML tools include an Eclipse-based development environment (parser and type-checker) with plug-ins that support simulation, theorem proving and model checking (still on development).

---

[1] http://www.atego.com/products/artisan-studio/

A CML specification comprises two main constructs: *Processes* and *Classes*. Global definitions can be placed at the top of the specification, where global *types* and *functions* are defined. There are some sections to define *channels* and *chansets*, which are used when defining the behaviour of a system. A *Class* contains the definition of a state, functions and operations. A *Process* defines the behaviour of a system. It may be defined either by the composition of other processes through the use of specific operators (basically, CSP operators like parallel or choice) or by defining an internal dynamic behaviour using a CML *Action*.

An *Action* is the basic behavioural unit in CML. It specifies a flow of events using communicating processes combined via CSP-like operators. Examples of actions are `Skip`, `Stop` (canonical deadlock) and assignment; an *Action* prefixing (`a -> P`) denotes a channel event `a` that is followed by an *Action* `P`. When specifying a *Process* in terms of previously defined *Actions*, we must define a main *Action* that starts the behaviour of the *Process* (similar to the function *main* of several programming languages, like Java or C).

CML is suitable to describe activity diagram semantics due to its compositional nature. The usage of parallelism operators allows to define semantic mappings for each constructor separately. Moreover, the representation of data can be simplified due to the definition of state in CML processes. An example of a subset of CML is presented in Section 4 when we show the CML models resulting from the application of the translation functions. For a complete description of the CML language, please see Woodcock *et al.* [16].

3   SysML Activity Diagrams

SysML [11] is built as a UML profile, that is, it reuses part of the UML metamodel [10] and extends it with some specific features from system engineering. It consists of 9 diagrams, two of them are new (requirement and parametric), some preserve the same semantics from UML (e.g., sequence diagrams) and the others have the base semantics from UML with some extensions, which is the case of activity diagrams, block definition and internal block diagrams. The latter two are extensions of class diagram and composite structure diagram, respectively.

Activity diagrams are a visual representation of UML/SysML activities. Activities represent a description of a coordinated behaviour with emphasis on the sequence of actions and conditions. The representation of this organised ordering of execution is described in terms of control and object flows. The former imposes an ordering of events and the latter describes the flow of data through an activity. Nodes are used together with flows to describe the execution of some behaviour. There are three types of nodes: control, object and actions. Control nodes affect the ordering of execution in the behaviour; object nodes describe the data that flows through the activity, and actions are basic units of behaviour. An action takes a set of inputs and converts them into a set of outputs, though either or both sets may be empty. There are a large number of action types, each one with a specific meaning, for example, sending a signal, performing an operation call, or even invoking another activity diagram. Figures 1 and 2 show two examples of activity diagrams where most of the previous elements are used. They both represent the behaviour of how an emergency central unit must act when receiving a critical call; they are used in Section 4 to demonstrate the usage of our semantic mappings. Our semantics provides meaning for other elements not depicted in theses figures, e.g. interruptible regions, for more details see [9].

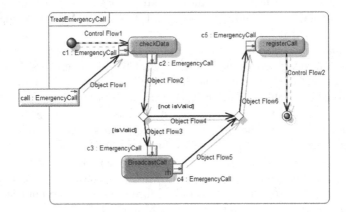

Fig. 1. Activity diagram for handling an emergency call

Figure 1 details the beginning of the process for treating an emergency call. One extension of SysML is the distinction between the two types of flows. Control flows are represented by dashed edges, whilst object flows are depicted as solid edges. Four control nodes are used, an initial node, represented by a solid circle, fires the beginning of the diagram, whilst a final node, depicted as a solid circle with a hollow circle around, ends the execution of the whole diagram. The white diamonds represent decision and merge node. A decision node has one input and may have multiple outputs. The output to be executed depends on the boolean guards of each edge. The ones that are evaluated to true may be executed, however only one may be chosen for each input arrival. Merge nodes act as relays where they just retransmit to the output edge the input arrived.

Regarding actions, *checkData* and *registerCall* represent operation calls of the owner of this activity and *BroadcastCall* is a call behaviour action, which invokes another activity diagram, in this case it is the diagram depicted in Figure 2. Finally, input and output pins together with the input parameter of the activity are examples of object nodes used. They have a name and the type of the item that flows through them (e.g., *call*, $c1$, ..., $c5$ are object nodes of the type *EmergencyCall*). Pins provide values to actions (input pin) or return some result values (output pin) from them. Parameters have similar semantics, however instead of working with actions, they are used in the context of an activity. Nevertheless, sometimes a pin may correspond to a parameter when used with a call behaviour action, which is the case of the *BroadcastCall* action in Figure 1, whose pins correspond to the parameters of the activity of the same name depicted in Figure 2.

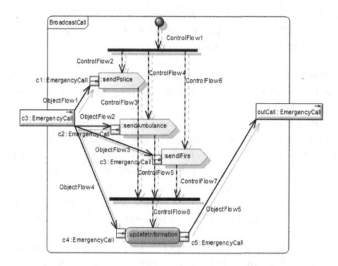

Fig. 2. Activity diagram for broadcasting an emergency call

Figure 2 illustrates the behaviour of an activity that broadcasts a call received as parameter. As the call must be sent in parallel to the police, ambulance and fire department, a fork node splits one control flow into three. The three pentagons represent a send signal action and they are responsible for emitting the signals according to their names. After the signal emissions, the three control flows are synchronised by a join node.

Activities in SysML can be linked to blocks to specify their behaviours. Activity diagrams can be used for different purposes. For example, in our semantics an activity can be used to describe the behaviour of an operation from a SysML block, thus, each time a block receives an operation call it must trigger the corresponding activity in order to respond to such request. In the next section, we provide a translation of the activities presented so far to demonstrate the usage of our semantics.

4   CML Semantics for Activity Diagram

Our approach to formalise activity diagrams involves three main elements: the syntax of the source language (SysML/UML metamodel elements), a rich and expressive semantic domain based on a well-defined mathematical theory (CML), and mappings from the elements of the syntax to the semantic domain. The way we link SysML/UML to CML is through the definition of translation functions, which receive as input the metamodel elements of activity diagrams and provide the corresponding CML model as output. However, in order to yield a consistent CML model that allows the application of analysis techniques integrating different types of diagrams, we must assume that the SysML model is sufficiently complete (not too abstract) to allow such derivation. This completeness is described in terms of guidelines that gives insights to the modeller on which information must be explicitly declared when a formal analysis is desired. The guidelines do not affect the expressiveness of the language. Some examples of these guidelines are expressed below:

Entity Definition. The block that owns or participate in an activity must be defined in a block definition diagram together with its operations and properties.

Explicit Information. Some elements must have enough information to allow a consistent generated model. For example, guards of output edges from a decision node must have concrete and well-defined guards according to the properties of a block or object data that flows through the diagram.

Simplification Assumptions. This is a group of guidelines that provides alternatives to the use of certain elements, where they have an equivalent counterpart, or define how they can be used. For more details see [9].

The adequacy to the guidelines allows the generation of analysable CML code. Nevertheless, even if the model is too abstract, in some cases we can still provide the respective CML model, however, no analysis is guaranteed to be feasible. The complete set of translation functions and their description can be seen in [9]. Next we illustrate our semantics by showing the result of the application of our translation functions to the examples described in Section 3.

4.1 Structure of the CML Specification

Figure 3 gives an outline of the formal model resulting from our examples. We use ellipsis in the CML extracts to hide possible CML code not relevant to be explained at the moment and commentary lines (starting by //) to introduce which elements are the translation target. Here we use BC and TEC as acronyms for the names of the activities, *BroadcastCall* and *TreatEmergencyCall*, respectively. Our translation strategy is compositional and is based on the parallelism operator. Each diagram is represented by a pair of processes, one representing the internal organization of the diagram (`ad_internal_BC` and `ad_internal_TEC`) and the other composes this internal representation with other activities that may be used inside itself as call behaviour actions (`ad_BC` and `ad_TEC`). Such composition is detailed in Section 4.6. Inside the internal representation, each node of a diagram becomes a CML action and the transitions between nodes are represented by channels. All nodes are composed in parallel and the synchronisation alphabet of each node is the set of all edges that arrives or leaves the node. Such approach allows a compositional translation where each node can be translated individually.

The *channels* section declares the events used to communicate information in the activities. They are used to represent flows and specific events. Control flows are mapped to the `control` channel, which is indexed by a natural number associated to the edge (we assume a diagram is preprocessed, inserting these index numbers). Object flows use one channel per edge where each channel is typed according to the data that flows through itself. They are named according to the activity diagram and the index of the edge, then obj_BC_1: EmergencyCall; is the object edge from the *BroadcastCall* diagram (edge number 1) along with data of type *EmergencyCall*. Some other channels are used for internal control of the activity and they are explained further according to their usage.

```
channels
   ...
process ad_internal_BC = ...
process ad_BC = ...
process ad_internal_TEC = ...
process ad_TEC = ...
```

Fig. 3. Outline of the formal model of the example in Figures 1 and 2

4.2   Internal Activity Process

This process details the internal structure of an activity diagram. Every node and possible flows between them are described through the use of CML actions and channels. Moreover, there are CML actions for controlling the beginning and ending of an activity. It also specifies a main action, which composes all of these elements in parallel to simulate the connections between nodes.

Figure 4 illustrates the corresponding CML internal process corresponding to the diagram of Figure 1. It consists of the process signature which receives as parameter the identification of the block instance (CentralUnit_id, where *CentralUnit* is the name of the block) that owns the activity. The set of channels Hidden is used to hide communications that should only be visible internally. The CML actions consist of the nodes definition and other control events followed by a main action (after the @ character) that uses the previous actions.

The *actions* section defines CML actions for nodes and interruptible regions (when they exist). In this example we have three control nodes (CNode1, CNode2 and CNode3) related to the initial, decision and merge nodes, whilst the final node is handled by END_ACTIVITY. Also, we have three CML actions, one for each action node, followed by the six object nodes: five of them are pins and one is a parameter of the action. The number appended to the actions uniquely identifies them inside this process. All these nodes are composed in an alphabetised parallelism by the CML action Nodes (omitted here due to space limitation.). Besides them, there are two control actions responsible for the beginning (START_ACTIVITY) and the end of the activity (END_ACTIVITY).

The CML action START_ACTIVITY provides the event that fires the beginning of the diagram execution (the event startActivity_TEC is externally visible). This event is indexed by the ID of the block instance (CentralUnit_id) and receives parameters of the activity (x_call). The next step is to assign the value of the parameters to the corresponding variables declared in the main action. The termination of an activity diagram may happen due to different factors.

```
process ad_internal_TEC = CentralUnit_id: ID @ begin
chansets
    Hidden = {|control, endDiagram, endFlow, obj_BC_1, ...|}
actions
    START_ACTIVITY = startActivity_TEC.CentralUnit_id?x_call ->
            atomic (call := x_call)
    END_ACTIVITY = control.2 -> endDiagram.TEC -> Skip
    //Control Nodes
    CNode1 = ...
    CNode2 = ...
    CNode3 = ...
    //Actions
    CheckData_1 = ...
    BroadcastCall_2 = ...
    RegisterCall_3 = ...
    //Object Nodes
    ObjNode_1 = ...
    ...
    ObjNode_6 = ...
    Nodes = ...
    //Main Action
    @
    mu X @ (( dcl call: EmergenceCall := null @
            START_ACTIVITY;(Nodes [|{|control.2|}|] END_ACTIVITY);
            endActivity_TEC.CentralUnit_id);X )\ Hidden
end
```

Fig. 4. Internal process of the SysML activity diagram from Figure 1

Reaching a final node should end the diagram execution because it halts any other flow in the diagram. On the other hand, flow final nodes only finish a flow of execution and not the whole diagram. Therefore, when final nodes exist, the diagram must end when any of them is reached. In their absence, the diagram ends when all ends of flows happen. Figure 4 shows an example in which there is a final node. It synchronises with the event that leads to this element (`control.2`), then it fires the `endDiagram.TEC`, which halts all activity nodes because they can be interrupted by such event stopping all activity flows. This interruption mechanism is shown further in the translation of nodes. We use the interruption operator of CML (/\).

At the bottom of the process, we have the main action, which is recursive. Initially, it declares a variable for the parameter of the activity that is updated and referenced by further CML actions. Then, it runs the `START_ACTIVITY` action according to a synchronization with an external process. After that, the process behaves as the nodes composed in parallel with the `END_ACTIVITY` action, responsible for terminating the activity. After termination, the process offers the (visible) event `endActivity` parametrised by the ID of the caller. As there is no output parameter, no additional data is returned through this channel.

4.3 Control Nodes

Control nodes change the flow of execution inside an activity diagram. In Figure 1, there are some examples of control nodes like initial and final nodes, and decision and merge nodes. The last ones are represented by the same graphical syntax (white diamond), but with distinct semantics. Figure 5 displays a CML extract of the control nodes of the TEC and BC diagrams. All nodes can be interrupted by the same CML action (END_DIAGRAM). This action is defined in terms of the channel event (endDiagram) used by END_ACTIVITY. This is valid for actions and object nodes as well. Such interruption mechanism, mentioned in Section 4.2, is used to halt the active flows when the activity reaches its end.

```
//TreatEmergencyCall Activity
//InitialNode
CNode1 = (control.1 -> Skip) /\ END_DIAGRAM
//DecisionNode
CNode2 = (obj_TEC_2?x_2 -> ( dcl isValid: bool := false @
         CentralUnit.get_isValid.CentralUnit_id?x_isValid ->
         isValid := x_isValid ->
         if isValid -> obj_TEC_3!x_2 -> CNode2
           | not isValid -> obj_TEC_4!x_2 -> CNode2
         end)) /\ END_DIAGRAM
//MergeNode
CNode3 = (obj_TEC_4?x -> obj_TEC_6!x -> CNode3 []
         obj_TEC_5?x -> obj_TEC_6!x -> CNode3) /\ END_DIAGRAM
...
//BroadcastCall Activity
//ForkNode
CNode2 = (control.1 -> (||| i:{2,4,6} @ control!i -> Skip );
         CNode_2) /\ END_DIAGRAM
//JoinNode
CNode3 = ( ((control.3 -> Skip ) ||| (control.5 -> Skip ) |||
            (control.7 -> Skip )); control!8 -> CNode_3) /\ END_DIAGRAM
```

Fig. 5. Control nodes of the TEC and BC activities

The only output of initial nodes are their corresponding outgoing control edges. This happens to CNode1 as the event control.1 relates to the control edge number 1 that flows from the initial node. A decision node (CNode2) requires that for each attribute of a block used in the guards of the edges, we should declare local variables and assign the current attribute values to them. Blocks have specific channels to get and set attribute values. The event CentralUnit...?x_isValid acquires the value from attribute isValid of block instance CentralUnit_id of block CentralUnit. The *if* expression uses these variables to check the guards. According to the chosen guard a different edge is traversed. As this decision node deals with object nodes, the same data received at the incoming edge (x_2) is forwarded to the outgoing edges. The merge node CNode3 only relays the data to the outgoing edge obj_TEC_6. As final nodes do not have body, we do not need to create CML actions for them; their behaviour is already represented by the END_ACTIVITY action, as shown in Section 4.2.

The join and fork nodes appear in the BC example (Figure 2). The fork node CNode2 receives an incoming flow from control edge 1 and combines the outgoing control edges 2, 4 and 6 in interleaving. The join node is complementary as it receives multiple control edges and provides only one outgoing edge. Most of the nodes are recursive because they may receive another token during the same execution (e.g. in a loop situation).

4.4   Actions

Actions provide basic descriptions of behaviour and they can be combined inside activities. The TEC example demonstrates the usage of two types of actions, call operation and call behaviour, whilst the BC example, besides a call operation, employs three send signal actions.

Call Operation Action. This action refers to an operation of a block, which can be the owner of the current activity or another block linked to it. If the target block is not specified in the action, we assume that it is related to an internal operation, which is the case of our examples for the *CentralUnit* block. How the operation is designed is not relevant in these examples as we just make use of the channels related to the calls. Synchronous operation calls use two channels, one for starting the operation and another for its return. Asynchronous calls are treated as signals with a single channel event.

We present in Figure 6 the CML code corresponding to the call operation action *CheckData* of the TEC example. One of the issues to be treated is the interruption of calls, because if the diagram ends it could halt the processing of an action, leaving the entity that is actually dealing with the call in an inconsistent state, as the activity diagram will never receive its return. This is not a desirable feature, and to avoid that we define a boolean guard (end_guard), which forbids the interruption of an action once its processing has been started. Notice that the interruption mechanism at the end of the action can only happen if such guard is true. During the period between starting the call and receiving its return, the guard is assigned to false. We also declare variables for each one of the pins according to their names. Next, we interleave all incoming edges (control or object flow) and compose it sequentially with the treatment of the action, in this case an operation call. Such behaviour provides a manner for only starting the action behaviour once all incoming edges are enabled. The channel event in_TEC_checkData_1 receives the value of the input pin and assigns it to local variable c_1. Then, we have the description of the action behaviour by an operation call defined in two channels — as described earlier — and using the c_1 variable as a parameter of the operation call. After the second event, the return is assigned to the variable c_2, which is used in the output pin event (out_TEC_checkData_2!c2).

Call Behaviour Action. The Call Behaviour Action (CBA) is a special kind of action that starts the execution flow of another diagram. If the called diagram has input or output parameters, the action will have input or output

```
CheckData_1 = ( dcl end_guard: bool = true @ mu X @
  ( dcl c1, c2: EmergenceCall: ID @
    ((control.1 -> Skip) ||| (in_TEC_checkData_1?inc1 -> c1 := inc1));
    (checkData_I.op.CentralUnit_id!CentralUnit_id!c1) ->
       end_guard := false;
     checkData_O.op.CentralUnit_id!CentralUnit_id?out: checkData_O ->
     (c2 := out.call -> Skip ); end_guard := true ;
    (out_TEC_checkData_2!c2 -> Skip); X)
    /\ end_guard & END_DIAGRAM)
```

Fig. 6. The CheckData call operation action

pins. They are connected through the special channels startActivity_CBA and
endActivity_CBA as shown in Figure 7. The actual behaviour of the action —
which is the behaviour of the called diagram — is achieved by putting both
called diagram process and internal process in parallel, but only considering
those special channels for CBAs. We show this parallelism later in Section 4.6.
It follows the same action structure shown in Figure 6. The only difference is the
use of the special channel that starts and ends the called activity. The number 1
after the block name CentralUnid_id avoids name clashing if there is more than
one CBA instance for the same diagram.

```
BroadcastCall_2 = ( dcl end_guard: bool = true @ mu X @
  ( dcl c3, c4: EmergenceCall: ID @
    ((control.3 -> Skip) ||| (in_TEC_broadcastCall_1?inc1 -> c3 := inc1));
    (startActivity_CBA_TEC.CentralUnit_id.1!c3 -> end_guard := false ;
     endActivity_CBA_TEC.CentralUnit_id.1?out -> c4 := out.call -> Skip);
     end_guard := true;
    (out_TEC_broadcastCall_3!c4 -> Skip); X)
    /\ end_guard & END_DIAGRAM)
```

Fig. 7. The BroadcastCall call behaviour action

Send Signal Action. The send signal action communicates a signal whose
name is the action's name. The BC activity (Figure 2) depicts three actions
of this type where an emergency call is sent to the police, ambulance and fire
department through send signal actions. One of the parameters of these signals
is the call that should be sent. However, another parameter is needed to identify
the target object that receives the event. We omitted in this diagram due to
space limitation, but each one of these actions has another input pin that relates
to each one of the emergency units. The CentralUnit block is associated to each
one of these units, then it has the values that are passed to send signal actions.

The translation of send signal actions is similar to that of the call operation
action. They have the same guarded-end mechanism. First, the incoming edges
are interleaved, then the signal event is fired. As signals are asynchronous, only
one event is needed. Afterwards, the events of the outgoing edges happen.

4.5   Object Nodes

We use two types of object nodes in the examples, activity parameters and pins. Both can be used for input or output data. Figure 8 shows the first three object nodes of the TEC activity. The first is the activity input parameter and the other two are the input pin and output pin of the *checkData* call operation action. The activity parameter only communicates a *call* to the object edge 1 of the TEC activity (see Section 4.2 for the declaration of *call* and its usage). Pins have two channel events: one for the object edge and another for communication with the related action. Input pins (see `ObjNode_2`) receive data from the object edge and communicate it through the input event of the action ($in\_\{Activity\}\_$ $\{ActionName\}\_\{EdgeIndex\}$). Output pins (see `ObjNode_3`) receive data by the output event of the action ($out\_\{Activity\}\_\{ActionName\}\_\{EdgeIndex\}$) and send it through the object edge.

```
//Input Parameter
ObjNode_1 = (obj_TEC_1!call -> Skip )
//Input Pin
ObjNode_2 = mu X @ ((obj_TEC_1?x_2 -> in_TEC_checkData_1!x_2 -> X)
                ) /\ END_DIAGRAM
//Output Pin
ObjNode_3 = mu X @ ((out_TEC_checkData_1?x_3 -> obj_TEC_2!x_3 ->  X)
                ) /\ END_DIAGRAM
```

Fig. 8. Object Nodes of the TEC activity

Output activity parameters (e.g. in the BC activity) have a different meaning from other object nodes because they may be updated several times and they are considered ends of flow. Thus, after receiving data from an object edge and updating the output variable, two possibilities are given by an external choice operator: either it finishes the flow and waits the synchronisation with other ends of flow or it may receive more data by recursion of the CML action.

Other object nodes not illustrated in these examples (e.g. simple object nodes) have their semantics defined in [9]. The following section describe how the main process of activities is defined in terms of its internal representation together with other diagrams it may reference.

4.6   Main Activity Process

The main activity process contains the constructions for the whole behaviour of the activity diagram, as well as its internal attributes. It includes the internal behaviour and also the calls to other diagrams. For CBAs, as we mentioned in Section 4.4, the internal process is put in parallel with the main activity process of the called diagrams. We achieve that by using renaming and synchronizing on the start and end events. CBA's inner start and end events (`startActivity_BC` and `endActivity_BC`) are renamed to `startActivity_CBA_TEC`

```
process ad_TEC = CentralUnit_id: ID; @
  ad_internal_TEC(CentralUnit_id)
  [|{|startActivity_CBA_TEC.CentralUnit_id.1,
      endActivity_CBA_TEC.CentralUnit_id.1|}|]
  ad_BC [[startActivity_BC.CentralUnit_id <-
            startActivity_CBA_TEC.CentralUnit_id.1,
          endActivity_BC.CentralUnit_id <-
            endActivity_CBA_TEC.CentralUnit_id.1]]
```

Fig. 9. Call Behaviour Action process in parallel with the internal process

and `endActivity_CBA_TEC`, respectively. Then the main inner process (`TEC`) is put in parallel with the `BC` process on the renamed channels (see Figure 9).

The parallel operator "`[| |]`" only synchronizes on those specified events, even if there are other events with the same name on both diagrams. Thus, it is safe to use any number of CBAs that points to the same called diagram. The called diagram behaviour (`ad_BC`) is defined elsewhere using the same rule that generates the TEC process (`ad_TEC`), however, as it does not have CBAs, it is composed only by its internal representation.

4.7   Integration with Other Diagrams

One of our goals is to perform analysis of consistency among several diagrams. In addition to the activity diagram, we have defined semantics for block definition diagram, internal block diagram, state machine diagram and sequence diagram. These diagrams communicate with each other through the events they perform, operation calls and signals. Each one has specific purposes in the definition of the system architecture.

Thus, the designer may use block, state machine and activity diagrams to model the overall behaviour of the system. We call this set of models the *system design*. Sequence diagrams are used to model correct flows of events in the system, and we can call them *valid traces*. Once we have the CML processes from both the system design (SYS) and valid traces (TRC), we could verify using the forthcoming CML tool set that both are deadlock free and deterministic. Once these properties are verified, we combine SYS and TRC in a generalised parallelism whose synchronisation alphabet is the visible channel events of the Sequence Diagram (SYS $[|\alpha(TRC)|]$ TRC). We can now use a model checker to run a deadlock-freedom verification in order to check the correctness of the *system design* with respect to its traces. If a deadlock happens, it means that a trace of the sequence diagram cannot be reproduced by the system design. Moreover, the counter-example returned by the model checker, which is a trace, can be presented as a sequence diagram. This series of verification can uncover many design problems earlier in the development life cycle.

5   Related Work

In this section we describe previous works about the formalisation of activity diagrams. We focus on works using CSP [13] as semantic domain because it is the closest formalism to CML used so far to define semantics of activity diagrams.

Xu et al. [18,19] formalise UML activity diagrams and define a set of mapping rules from the formal model for activity diagrams into CSP. They introduce a formal meta-model for activity diagrams. This meta-model is given by a tuple composed of elements that represent the different nodes of an activity diagram, a set of directed edges, and the flow relationship between them. Translation functions are defined for each diagram, so their translation is not compositional, the diagram nodes are not translated independently. They deal strictly with control flow. There are no mapping rules for pins. They do not treat different kinds of actions. There is a limitation of their work concerning fork and join nodes as they require the number of incoming edges of a join to be the same as number of outgoing edges of a fork.

Abdelhalim et al. [1] propose the use of a subset of fUML (Foundational Subset for Executable UML) that is mapped into CSP [13]. Their focus is on analysis of dynamic behaviours. As control flow has been addressed by Xu et al. [18,19], they concentrate on mapping *SendSignalAction* and *AcceptEventAction* and signals [1]. They deal with decision node as an internal choice. Also, they map expansion region into CSP processes. They treat signals by means of an asynchronous buffer, whereas in our translation we use a one-place synchronised buffer that could receive data from an asynchronous buffer. Their communication model allows storing of signals.

Varró et al. [15] define translation rules that relate edges in an activity diagram to a process in CSP [13]. They do not deal with object nodes or object flows, just with the translation of control flow. They translate a join node separately from the fork node. However, a synchronisation event appears only in the process that reaches the join node, but not in the parallel operator that is introduced in the fork node. Also, the translation of the join node results in processes that are not similar: only one will behave as the process after the join, all the others will terminate in `Skip`. In our case, we translate fork and join nodes independently.

6   Conclusion

In this paper we proposed a semantics for SysML activity diagrams [11] by using the CML language [17] as semantic domain. Activity diagram elements are given semantics by means of translation functions. The translation is compositional, each element in a diagram can be translated independently by the use of a specific function. Our approach requires the adherence to a set of guidelines, however, they do not restrict the expressiveness of the language. For instance, it is not required that fork and join nodes appear in pairs and with equal number of output and input edges to obtain a translation. We defined a comprehensive set of translation rules for elements of activity diagrams: control nodes, object and control flows, actions, input and output pins, input and output activity parameters.

Our work is in the context of a broader effort for giving a semantics to other SysML diagrams (block definition, internal block, state machine, and sequence diagrams). The communication between them is accomplished by means of events, operation calls and signals. This allows verification of properties like deadlock in earlier stages of a system development.

There are some limitations in our work that we consider as future direction of work. The relation between actions of different blocks is established only by the invocation of other actions in a different diagram. We aim to extend such communication using activity partitions that describe the blocks responsible for each action in an single activity diagram. We have not defined functions for dealing with time constraints. This is also a future work direction.

Acknowledgments. The authors thank the anonymous referees of SBMF 2013 for comments in drafts of this work and the EU Framework 7 Integrated Project "Comprehensive Modelling for Advanced Systems of Systems" (COMPASS [2], Grant Agreement 187829). This work was partially supported by the National Institute of Science and Technology for Software Engineering (INES [3]), funded by CNPq and FACEPE (grants 573964/2008-4 and APQ-1037-1.03/08), and CNPq grant 483329/2012-6.

References

1. Abdelhalim, I., Sharp, J., Schneider, S., Treharne, H.: Formal Verification of Tokeneer Behaviours Modelled in fUML Using CSP. In: Dong, J.S., Zhu, H. (eds.) ICFEM 2010. LNCS, vol. 6447, pp. 371–387. Springer, Heidelberg (2010)
2. INCOSE Technical Board. Systems engineering handbook. INCOSE-TP-2003-002-03 (2006)
3. Boufenara, S., Belala, F., Barkaoui, K.: Mapping uml 2.0 activities to zero-safe nets. Software Engineering & Applications (2010)
4. Davies, J., Crichton, C.: Concurrency and refinement in the unified modeling language. Formal Aspects of Computing 15(2-3), 118–145 (2003)
5. Fitzgerald, J., Larsen, P.G.: Modelling Systems: Practical Tools and Techniques in Software Development. Cambridge University Press (2009)
6. Friedenthal, S., Moore, A., Steiner, R.: A Practical Guide to SysML: The Systems Modeling Language, 2nd edn. Morgan Kaufmann Publishers Inc., San Francisco (2011)
7. Hoare, T., He, J.: Unifying Theories of Programming. Prentice Hall (1998)
8. Jarraya, Y., Debbabi, M., Bentahar, J.: On the meaning of sysml activity diagrams. In: Proceedings of the 2009 16th Annual IEEE International Conference and Workshop on the Engineering of Computer Based Systems, ECBS 2009, pp. 95–105. IEEE Computer Society, Washington, DC (2009)

---

[2] http://www.compass-research.eu
[3] http://www.ines.org.br

9. Miyazawa, A., Lima, L., Cornelio, M., Iyoda, J., Cavalcanti, A.: Final Report on Combining SysML and CML. Technical Report D22.4, COMPASS Deliverable (March 2013)
10. Object Management Group. OMG Unified Modeling Language (OMG UML), superstructure, version 2.4.1. Technical report, OMG (2011)
11. Object Management Group. OMG Systems Modeling Language (OMG SysML^{TM}). Technical report, Object Management Group, OMG Document Number: formal/12-06-02 (2012)
12. Raschke, A.: Translation of uml 2 activity diagrams into finite state machines for model checking. In: Proceedings of the 2009 35th Euromicro Conference on Software Engineering and Advanced Applications, SEAA 2009, pp. 149–154. IEEE Computer Society, Washington, DC (2009)
13. Roscoe, A.W.: The Theory and Practice of Concurrency. Prentice Hall PTR, Upper Saddle River (1997)
14. Staines, T.S.: Intuitive mapping of uml 2 activity diagrams into fundamental modeling concept petri net diagrams and colored petri nets. In: Proceedings of the 15th Annual IEEE International Conference and Workshop on the Engineering of Computer Based Systems, ECBS 2008, pp. 191–200. IEEE Computer Society, Washington, DC (2008)
15. Varró, D., et al.: Transformation of UML Models to CSP: A Case Study for Graph Transformation Tools. In: Schürr, A., Nagl, M., Zündorf, A., et al. (eds.) AGTIVE 2007. LNCS, vol. 5088, pp. 540–565. Springer, Heidelberg (2008)
16. Woodcock, J., Cavalcanti, A., Coleman, J., Didier, A., Larsen, P.G., Miyazawa, A., Oliveira, M.: CML Definition 0. Technical Report D23.1, COMPASS Deliverable (June 2012)
17. Woodcock, J., Cavalcanti, A., Fitzgerald, J., Larsen, P., Miyazawa, A., Perry, S.: Features of CML: a Formal Modelling Language for Systems of Systems. In: Proceedings of the 7th International Conference on System of System Engineering. IEEE Systems Journal, vol. 6 (2012)
18. Xu, D.: et al. Towards Formalizing UML Activity Diagrams in CSP. In: Proceedings of the 2008 International Symposium on Computer Science and Computational Technology, ISCSCT 2008, vol. 2, pp. 450–453. IEEE Computer Society, Washington, DC (2008)
19. Xu, D., Miao, H., Philbert, N.: Model Checking UML Activity Diagrams in FDR. In: ACIS International Conference on Computer and Information Science, pp. 1035–1040 (2009)

Formal Analysis of Memory Contention in a Multiprocessor System

Liya Liu, Osman Hasan, and Sofiène Tahar

Dept. of Electrical & Computer Engineering, Concordia University
1455 de Maisonneuve W., Montreal, Quebec, H3G 1M8, Canada
{liy_liu,o_hasan,tahar}@ece.concordia.ca

Abstract. Multi-core processors along with multi-module memories are extensively being used in high performance computers these days. One of the main performance evaluation metrics in such configurations is the memory contention problem and its effect on the overall memory access time. Usually, this problem is analyzed using simulation or numerical methods. However, these methods either cannot guarantee accurate analysis or are not scalable due to the unacceptable computation times. As an alternative approach, this paper uses theorem proving to analyze the memory contention problem of a multiprocessor system. For this purpose, the paper presents the higher-order-logic formalization of the expectation of a discrete random variable and Discrete-time Reward Models. These foundations are then utilized to analyze the memory contention problem of a multi-processor system configuration with two processors and two memory modules using the HOL theorem prover.

1 Introduction

The extensive computation requirements in complex engineering systems and the trend to move towards smart consumer electronic devices has brought a paradigm shift towards using multi-core processors in all sorts of embedded systems. These processors usually share information with one another by accessing shared variables in a common memory space. In order to avoid concurrent updates to these shared variables, which may lead to erroneous results, only one processor at a time is allowed to access the memory. However, this configuration leads to the well-known memory contention problem, which results in an overall performance degradation as the processors may have to wait for accessing the memory. This problem is usually alleviated by using a multi-module memory, as depicted in Figure 1. The main idea is to divide the cache memory into sub-modules so that the processors can simultaneously access different sub-modules in parallel. This configuration tends to minimize the memory contention problem but cannot rectify it completely since two or more processors may want to access the same memory sub-module as well. Thus, rigorous performance analysis is conducted to determine the optimized size of sub-modules of memory for a given memory access rate.

Due to the random nature of time dependent memory access requests, the above mentioned configurations are modeled as classified Discrete-time Markov

J. Iyoda and L. de Moura (Eds.): SBMF 2013, LNCS 8195, pp. 195–210, 2013.
© Springer-Verlag Berlin Heidelberg 2013

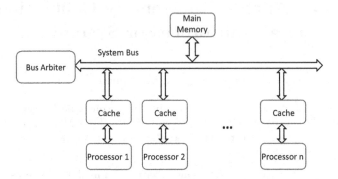

Fig. 1. A Multiprocessor System with Multimodule Memory

Chains (DTMCs) [2]. Then performance characteristics, such as the average number of memory accesses and the steady state probabilities of processors waiting, can be deduced based on the properties of classified Markov chains and Discrete-time Markov Reward Models (DMRMs) [18]. These properties are expressed in terms of the transition probabilities of the given Markov chain and thus provide useful insights for system optimization.

Traditionally, the above mentioned performance analysis is conducted analytically, using paper-and-pencil proof methods [19], computer simulations [5] or numerical methods [17]. The paper-and-pencil proof methods do not scale well to the complex multi-processor systems. Moreover, they are prone to human errors. Computer based simulations or numerical methods are scalable but due to the usage of computer arithmetic and pseudo random numbers and their inherent incompleteness cannot guarantee accurate results.

The accuracy of the above mentioned performance analysis is becoming quite important these days due to the increasing usage of multi-processor systems in safety-critical domains like medicine and transportation. Recently, probabilistic model checking has been used to analyze DMRMs (e.g., [4] and [8]). The typical model checking tools are *PRISM* [16] and *MRMC* [13], which provide precise system analysis by modeling the stochastic behaviors using probabilistic state machines and exhaustively verifying their probabilistic properties. These tools can be used for performance analysis of multi-processor systems as well. However, some algorithms implemented in these model checking tools are also based on numerical methods. For example, the Power method [15], which is a well-known iterative method, is applied to compute the steady-state probabilities (or limiting probabilities) of Markov chains in PRISM. Thus, most of the stationary properties analyzed in model checkers are time bounded. Moreover, probabilistic model checking often utilizes unverified algorithms and optimization techniques. Finally, model checking cannot be used to verify generic mathematical expressions for statistical properties, like expectation.

In order to provide an accurate and complete approach for analyzing the memory contention problem of multi-processor systems, we propose to use higher-order-logic theorem proving. The high expressiveness of higher-order logic allows us to formally express the systems that can be modeled using classified Markov chains and DMRMs. Whereas, the soundness of theorem proving guarantees the correctness and completeness of the analysis. In this paper, we develop the formalization of Discrete-time Markov Reward Models based on the formalization of expectation and conditional expectation functions for discrete random variables along with the available formalization of Discrete-Time Markov Chains (DTMCs) [10]. Compared to the work in [10], which is based on the formalized probability theory of Hurd [7], the formalization of DTMCs in the current paper is developed by building upon a more general probability theory developed by Mhamdi [12]. This update provides us with the flexibility to model time-inhomogeneous DTMCs/DMRMs or several random processes (involving DTMCs) containing distinct types of state spaces. This paper also presents the formal verification of some classical properties of expectation and DMRMs. The above mentioned formalizations allow us to analyze the memory contention problem of any multi-processor system. For illustration purposes, we formally analyze a typical multi-processor system [19] using the formalization of DMRMs and the irreducible and aperiodic Markov Chains [11].

2   Preliminaries

In this section, we present the foundations that we build upon to formalize expectation for discrete random variables and DMRM later.

2.1   Probability Theory

A *probability space* is a measure space $(\Omega, \Sigma, \mathcal{P}r)$ such that $\mathcal{P}r(\Omega) = 1$ [2]. Σ is a collection of subsets of Ω called *measurable sets*. In [12], a higher-order logic theory is developed where given a probability space p, the functions space and subsets return the corresponding Ω and Σ, respectively. Mathematically, a *random variable* is a measurable function between a probability space and a measurable space. This is formalized in HOL by a predicate random_variable X p s that returns true if X is a random variable on a probability space p and an outcome space s.

The *expectation* [20] of a random variable plays an important role in describing the characteristics of probability distributions. A *conditional expectation* represents the expected value of a *real* random variable considering a conditional probability distribution. Mhamdi [12] formalized general definitions of expectation and conditional expectation using the Lebesgue integral. These definitions can be used to find the expectations involving both discrete and continuous random variables. However, it is not a straightforward task to use these definitions to reason about the expectation of discrete random variables as the proofs of even the basic theorems require the Radon Nikodym derivative [6] and a series of intermediate theorems. In this paper, we formalize the expectation and conditional expectation for the discrete case to avoid these complex reasoning problems. These definitions are then used to formalize DMRM in HOL.

2.2 Discrete-Time Markov Chains

Given a probability space, a stochastic process $\{X_t : \Omega \to S\}$ represents a sequence of random variables X, where t represents the time that can be discrete (represented by non-negative integers) or continuous (represented by real numbers) [2]. The set of values taken by each X_t, commonly called *states*, is referred to as the *state space*. The *sample space* Ω of the process consists of all the possible state sequences based on a given state space S. Now, based on these definitions, a *Markov chain* is a Markov process [3], with finite or countably infinite state space Ω, that satisfies the following :

$$Pr\{X_{t_{n+1}} = f_{n+1}|X_{t_n} = f_n, \ldots, X_{t_0} = f_0\} = Pr\{X_{t_{n+1}} = f_{n+1}|X_{t_n} = f_n\}$$

for $0 \le t_0 \le \cdots \le t_n$ and $f_0, \cdots, f_{n+1}$ in the state space. This means that the future state is only dependent on the current state and is independent of all the other past states. The Markov property can be formalized as follows:

Definition 1 (Markov Property).

```
⊢ ∀ X p s. mc_property X p s =
  (∀ t. random_variable (X t) p s) ∧
  ∀ f t n.
    increasing_seq t ∧ ℙ(⋂ₖ∈ [0,n−1]{x | X tₖ x = f k}) ≠ 0 ⇒
    (ℙ({x | X tₙ₊₁ x = f (n + 1)}|
      {x | X tₙ x = f n} ∩ ⋂ₖ∈ [0,n−1]{x | X tₖ x = f k}) =
    ℙ({x | X tₙ₊₁ x = f (n + 1)}|{x | X tₙ x = f n}))
```

where `increasing_seq t` is defined as `∀ i j. i < j ⇒ t i < t j`. The first conjunct indicates that the Markov property is based on a random process $\{X_t : \Omega \to S\}$. The quantified variable X represents a function of the random variables associated with time t which has the type **num**. This ensures the process is a *discrete time* random process. The random variables in this process are the functions built on the probability space p and a measurable space s. The conjunct $\mathbb{P}(\bigcap_{k \in [0,n-1]}\{x \mid X\ t_k\ x = f\ k\}) \neq 0$ ensures that the corresponding conditional probabilities are well-defined, where `f k` returns the kth element of the state sequence.

A DTMC is usually expressed by specifying: an initial distribution p_0 which gives the probability of initial occurrence $Pr(X_0 = s) = p_0(s)$ for every state s; and transition probabilities $p_{ij}(t)$ which give the probability of going from i to j for every pair of states (i, j) in the state space [14]. For states i, j and a time t, the *transition probability* $p_{ij}(t)$ is defined as $Pr\{X_{t+1} = j|X_t = i\}$, which can be easily generalized to *n-step transition probability* as shown in Equation (1), and it can be formalized in Definition 2.

$$p_{ij}^{(n)}(t) = \begin{cases} \begin{cases} 0 & \text{if } i \neq j \\ 1 & \text{if } i = j \end{cases} & n = 0 \\ Pr\{X_{t+n} = j|X_t = i\} & n > 0 \end{cases} \tag{1}$$

Definition 2 (Transition Probability).

⊢ ∀ X p s t n i j. Trans X p s t n i j =
  if i ∈ space s ∧ j ∈ space s then
    if n = 0 then
      if (i = j) then 1 else 0
    else $\mathbb{P}$({x | X (t + n) x = j}|{x | X t x = i})
  else 0

Now, the Discrete Time Markov Chain (DTMC) can be formalized as follows:

Definition 3 (DTMC).

⊢ ∀ X p s p_0 p_{ij} dtmc X p s p_0 p_{ij} =
  mc_property X p s ∧ (∀ i. i ∈ space s ⇒ {i} ∈ subsets s) ∧
  ∀ i. i ∈ space s ⇒ (p_0 i = $\mathbb{P}${x | X t x = i}) ∧
  ∀ t i j. $\mathbb{P}${x | X t x = i} ≠ 0 ⇒
      (p_{ij} t i j = Trans X p s t 1 i j)

Most of the applications actually make use of *time-homogenous DTMCs*, i.e., DTMCs with finite state-space and time-independent transition probabilities [1]. The time-homogenous property refers to the time invariant feature of a random process: $\forall\ t\ t'.\ p_{ij}(t) = p_{ij}(t')$ (in the sequel, $p_{ij}(t)$ is simply written as p_{ij}).

Definition 4 (Time homogeneous DTMC).

⊢ ∀ X p s p_0 p_{ij}. th_dtmc X p s p_0 p_{ij} =
  dtmc X p s p_0 p_{ij} ∧ FINITE (space s) ∧
  ∀ t i j.
    $\mathbb{P}${x | X t x = i} ≠ 0 ∧ $\mathbb{P}${x | X (t + 1) x = i} ≠ 0 ⇒
    (Trans X p s (t + 1) 1 i j = Trans X p s t 1 i j)

Using these fundamental definitions, we formally verified most of the classical properties of DTMCs with finite state-space in HOL [11]. Some of the relevant ones to the context of this paper are presented here.

The *joint probability distribution* of a DTMC is the probability of a chain of states to occur:

$$\mathcal{P}r(X_t = S_0, \cdots, X_{t+n} = S_n) =$$
$$\prod_{k=0}^{n-1} \mathcal{P}r(X_{t+k+1} = S_{k+1}|X_{t+k} = S_k)\mathcal{P}r(X_t = S_0)$$

Theorem 1 (Joint Probability Distribution).

⊢ ∀ X p s t n S p_0 p_{ij} n.
  dtmc X p s p_0 p_{ij} ⇒
  $\mathbb{P}(\bigcap_{k=0}^{n}${x | X (t + k) x = EL k S}) =
  $\prod_{k=0}^{n-1}\mathbb{P}$({x | X (t + k + 1) x = EL (k + 1) S}|
      {x | X (t + k) x = EL k S})$\mathbb{P}${x | X t x = EL 0 S}

The Chapman-Kolmogorov Equation [2] $p_{ij}^{(m+n)} = \sum_{k \in \Omega} p_{ik}^{(m)} p_{kj}^{(n)}$ is a widely used property of time homogeneous DTMCs. It basically gives the probability of going from state i to j in $m+n$ steps. Assuming the first m steps take the system from state i to some intermediate state k and the remaining n steps then take the system from state k to j, we can obtain the desired probability by adding the probabilities associated with all the intermediate steps.

Theorem 2 (Chapman-Kolmogorov Equation).

```
⊢ ∀ X p s i j t m n p₀ pᵢⱼ.
    th_dtmc X p s p₀ pᵢⱼ ⇒
    Trans X p s t (m + n) i j =
    ∑       (Trans X p s (t + m) n i k * Trans X p s t m k j)
  k∈space s
```

The unconditional probabilities associated with a Markov chain are called *absolute probabilities*, which can be computed by applying the initial distributions and n-step transition probabilities, as $p_j^{(n)} = \mathcal{P}r(X_n = j) = \sum_{k \in \Omega} \mathcal{P}r(X_0 = k) \mathcal{P}r(X_n = j | X_0 = k)$. Using $p_i^{(n)}$ for the probability $\mathcal{P}r(X_n = j)$, we verified the following result:

Theorem 3 (Absolute Probability).

```
⊢ ∀ X p s j n p₀ pᵢⱼ.
    th_dtmc X p s p₀ pᵢⱼ ⇒
    ℙ{x | X n x = j} =
    ∑       ℙ{x | X 0 x = k}ℙ({x | X n x = j}|{x | X 0 s = k})
  k∈space s
```

2.3   Aperiodic and Irreducible Markov Chain

Aperiodic and irreducible DTMCs are considered to be the most widely used classified Markov chains in analyzing Markovian systems due to their attractive stationary properties, i.e., their limit probability distributions are independent of the initial distributions.

The foremost concept of classified DTMCs is the *first passage time* τ_j, or the *first hitting time*, which is defined as the minimum time required to reach a state j from the initial state i, $\tau_j = min\{t > 0 : X_t = j\}$.

Definition 5 (First Passage Time).

```
⊢ ∀ X x j. FPT X x j = MINSET {t | 0 < t ∧ (X t x = j)}
```

where X is a random process and x is a sample in the probability space associated with the random variable X_t.

The conditional distribution of τ_j, defined as the probability of the events starting from state i and visiting state j at time n, is expressed as $f_{ij}^{(n)} = \mathcal{P}r\{\tau_j = n | X_0 = i\}$.

Definition 6 (Probability of First Passage Events).

⊢ ∀ X p i j n.
  f X p i j n = $\mathbb{P}$({x | FPT X x j = n}|{x | X 0 x = i})

Another important notion is the probability of the events starting from state i and visiting state j at all times n, which is expressed as $f_{ij} = \sum_{n=1}^{\infty} f_{ij}^{(n)}$. It can be expressed in HOL as (λ n. f X p i j n) sums f_{ij}. Now f_{jj} provides the probability of events starting from state j and eventually returning back to j. A state j in a DTMC is called *persistent* if $f_{jj} = 1$.

The greatest common divisor (*gcd*) of a set is a frequently used mathematical concept in defining classified states. For a state j, a *period* of j is any n such that $p_{jj}^{(n)}$ is greater than 0. We write $d_j = gcd \{n : p_{jj}^{(n)} > 0\}$ as the gcd of the set of all periods.

A state i is said to be *accessible* from a state j (written $j \rightarrow i$), if the n-step transition probability of the events from state i to j is nonzero. Two states i, j are called *communicating states* (written $i \leftrightarrow j$) if they are mutually accessible. The formalization of these foundational notions is given in Table 1.

Table 1. Formalization of Classified States

Definition	Condition	HOL Formalization
Persistent State	$f_{jj} = 1$	⊢ Persistent_state X p j = ∀ x. {t | 0 < t ∧ (X t x = j)} ≠ ∅) ∧ (λ n. f X p j j n) sums 1
Periods of a State	$0 < n$ $0 < p_{jj}^n$	⊢ Period_set X p s j = {n | Persistent_state X p j ∧ 0 < n ∧ ∀ t. 0 < Trans X p s t n j j}
gcd of a Set	gcd A	⊢ GCD_SET A = MAXSET {r | ∀ x. x ∈ A ⇒ divides r x}
gcd of a Period Set	d_j	⊢ Period X p s j = GCD_SET (Period_set X p s j)
Periodic State	$d_j > 1$	⊢ Periodic_state X p s j = 1 < Period X p s j ∧ Period_set X p s j ≠ ∅
Aperiodic State	$d_j = 1$	⊢ Aperiodic_state X p s j = (Period X p s j = 1) ∧ Period_set X p s j ≠ ∅
Accessibility	$i \rightarrow j$	⊢ Accessibility X p s i j = ∀ t. ∃ n. 0 < n ∧ 0 < Trans X p s t n i j
Communicating State	$i \leftrightarrow j$	⊢ Communicating_states X p s i j = Accessibility X p s i j ∧ Accessibility X p s j i

Now, a DTMC is considered as *aperiodic* if every state in its state space is an aperiodic state; and a DTMC is said to be *irreducible* if every state in its state space can be reached from any other state including itself in finite steps.

Definition 7 (Aperiodic DTMC).

⊢ ∀ X p s p_0 p_{ij}. Aperiodic_mc X p s p_0 p_{ij} =
  th_dtmc X p s p_0 p_{ij} ∧
  ∀ i. i ∈ space s ⇒ Aperiodic_state X p s i

Definition 8 (Irreducible DTMC).

⊢ ∀ X p s p_0 p_{ij}. Irreducible_mc X p s p_0 p_{ij} =
  th_dtmc X p s p_0 p_{ij} ∧
  (∀ i j. i ∈ space s ∧ j ∈ space s ⇒
        Communicating_states X p s i j)

The above mentioned definitions are mainly used to formally specify and analyze the dynamic features of Markovian systems within the sound environment of a theorem prover. In this paper, we will be using them to formalize a behavior of the multi-processor system in Section 4.

2.4 Long-Term Properties

The long-run probability distributions (limit probability distributions) are often considered in the convergence analysis of random variables in stochastic systems. It is not very easy to verify that the stationary behaviors of a certain state exists in a generic non-trivial DTMC, because the computations required in such an analysis are often tremendous. However, in aperiodic and irreducible DTMCs, we can prove that any state in the state space possesses a convergent probability distribution, by the following theorems.

For any state i in the finite state space S of an aperiodic DTMC, there exists an $N < \infty$ such that $0 < p_{ii}^{(n)}$, for all $n \geq N$.

Theorem 4 (Positive Return Probability).

⊢ ∀ X p s p_0 p_{ij} i t.
  Aperiodic_DTMC X p s p_0 p_{ii} ∧ i ∈ space s ⇒
  ∃ N. ∀ n. N ≤ n ⇒ 0 < Trans X p s t n i i

Applying Theorem 4, we can prove that, for any aperiodic and irreducible DTMC with finite state space S, there exists an N, for all $n \geq N$, such that the n-step transition probability $p_{ij}^{(n)}$ is non-zero, for all states i and $j \in S$.

Theorem 5 (Existence of Positive Transition Probabilities).

⊢ ∀ X p s p_0 p_{ij} i j t.
  Aperiodic_DTMC X p s p_0 p_{ij} ∧ Irreducible_DTMC X p s p_0 p_{ij} ∧
  i ∈ space s ∧ j ∈ space s ⇒
  ∃ N. ∀ n. N ≤ n ⇒ 0 < Trans X p s t n i j

Utilizing Theorems 4 and 5, the convergence of the probability distributions in an aperiodic and irreducible DTMC can be verified as the following theorem:

Theorem 6 (Convergent Probability Distributions).

⊢ ∀ X p s p_0 p_{ij} i j.
  Aperiodic_DTMC X p s p_0 p_{ij} ∧ Irreducible_DTMC X p s p_0 p_{ij} ⇒
  convergent (λ t. $\mathbb{P}${x | X t x = i})

As multiprocessor systems are usually modeled as aperiodic and irreducible DTMCs, the theorems presented above are very useful in analyzing their long-term behaviors. However, to the best of our knowledge, the second requirement for analyzing multiprocessor systems, i.e., the reward or cost factors for DTMCs have not been formalized so far. Therefore, we build upon the foundations, presented in this section, to formalize the Discrete-time Markov Reward Models in order to facilitate the performance analysis of multi-processor systems in HOL.

3   Formalization of Discrete-time Markov Reward Models

In this section, we formally define expectation and conditional expectation of a discrete random variable and then use these results along with the formal DTMC definition to formalize a Discrete-time Markov Reward Model (DMRM).

3.1   Expectation

The *expectation* (also called *expected value*) of a discrete random variable X is $E[X] = \sum_{i \in space \; s_x} i Pr\{X = i\}$. Whereas, the *conditional expectation* of a discrete random variable X given a condition Y is $E[Y|X] = \sum_{i \in space \; s_x} i Pr\{Y|X = i\}$. These definitions can be formalized as:

Definition 9 (Expectation).

$\vdash \forall$ X p s_x. expec X p s_x = $\sum_{i \in space \; s_x} i \mathbb{P}\{x \mid X \; x = i\}$

Definition 10 (Conditional Expectation).

$\vdash \forall$ X Y y p s_x.
    cond_expec Y X y p s_x = $\sum_{i \in space \; s_x} i \mathbb{P}(\{x \mid Y \; x = y\} | \{x \mid X \; x = i\})$

where X is a discrete random variable, which has type 'a $\rightarrow$ real, s_x is a finite state space, and $\{x \mid Y \; x = y\}$ is a discrete event given in the conditional probability to calculate the expectation.

Utilizing these two formal definitions, we can verify some interesting properties of expectation that play a vital role in the performance analysis of multiprocessor systems. We can prove that the total expectation of a random variable X is $E[Y] = \sum_{j \in space \; s_x} E[Y|X_j] Pr\{X_j\}$. Here, X_j represents a discrete event involved in the event space (subsets s_x) and j is any state in the state space (space s_x) of random variable X.

Theorem 7 (Total Expectation).

$\vdash \forall$ X Y p s_x s_y.
    random_variable X p s_x $\wedge$ random_variable Y p s_y $\wedge$
    ($\forall$ x. x $\in$ space s_x $\Rightarrow$ $\{x\}$ $\in$ subsets s_x) $\wedge$
    ($\forall$ x. x $\in$ space s_y $\Rightarrow$ $\{x\}$ $\in$ subsets s_y) $\wedge$
    FINITE (space s_x) $\wedge$ FINITE (space s_y) $\Rightarrow$
    (expec Y p s_x =
    $\sum_{j \in space \; s_x}$ (λj. cond_expec Y X j p s_x * $\mathbb{P}\{x \mid X \; x = j\}$)))

For a random process $\{X_t\}_{t\geq0}$, with sample space $\mathbf{s_x}$, and discrete event $\{Y_t = y\}_{t\geq0}$, in the event space (subsets $\mathbf{s_y}$) (for all y in the finite state space $\mathbf{s_y}$), the total expectation of the steady-state of the random variable Y is: $\lim_{t\to\infty}\mathrm{E}[Y_t]$ $= \sum_{j\in\text{space } \mathbf{s_x}} \lim_{t\to\infty}\mathrm{E}[Y_t|X_t = j]\lim_{t\to\infty}Pr\{X_t = j\}$

Theorem 8 (Total Expectation of Steady-state Probabilities).

⊢ ∀ X Y p sₓ s_y.
   (∀ t. random_variable (X t) p sₓ) ∧
   (∀ t. random_variable (Y t) p s_y) ∧
   (∀ x. x ∈ space sₓ ⇒ {x} ∈ subsets sₓ) ∧
   (∀ x. x ∈ space s_y ⇒ {x} ∈ subsets s_y) ∧
   (∀ j. convergent (λt. ℙ{x | X t x = j}) ∧
   (∀ i. convergent (λt. cond_expec (Y t) (X t) i p sₓ)) ∧
   FINITE (space sₓ) ∧ FINITE (space s_y) ⇒
   (lim (λ t. expec (Y t) p s_y) =
   $\sum_{j\in\text{space sx}}$ (lim (λ t. cond_expec (Y t) (X t) j p sₓ) *
              lim (λ t. ℙ{x | X t x = j})))

3.2 Discrete-time Markov Reward Models

Discrete-time Markov Reward Models (DMRMs) are extended DTMCs that consider the costs, or dually bonuses (rewards). In the performance analysis of some real-world systems, DMRMs allow numerous quantitative measures of the system, such as the elapsed time, power consumption, size of message queue, net profit, etc.

Mathematically, a DMRM is defined on a DTMC $\{X_t\}_{t\geq0}$ with a real valued reward function r_{xy}, which associates a real reward (or cost) to a state x in the state space of X for all t, $t \geq 0$ by the conditional expectation of the reward (or cost) given the state x.

Definition 11 (Discrete-time Markov Reward Model).

⊢ ∀ X Y p sₓ s_y p₀ p_ij r_xy. dmrm X Y p sₓ s_y p₀ p_ij =
   dtmc X p sₓ p₀ p_ij ∧ (∀ t. random_variable (Y t) p s_y) ∧
   (∀ y. y ∈ space s_y ⇒ {y} ∈ subsets s_y) ∧
   (∀ x t. ℙ{x | Y t x = y} ≠ 0 ⇒
       (r_xy t x = cond_expec (Y t) (X t) x p s_y))

where the quantified variable X refers to the random variables involved in the underlying DTMC, Y indicates the random reward, p is the probability space, $\mathbf{s_x}$ refers to the state space of the DTMC, $\mathbf{s_y}$ represents the measurable state space of random variable Y, $\mathbf{p_0}$ and $\mathbf{p_{ij}}$ are the initial distribution and transition probability of the DTMC, and $\mathbf{r_{xy}}$ denotes the reward function. The first conjunct in this definition ensures that the underlying stochastic process is a DTMC, the second and third conjuncts constrain the expected values are discrete random variables (Y t) and the last condition gives the conditional expectation distributions by the reward function.

It is important to note that this definition provides a general DMRM, in which the state space can be finite or infinite, the underlying DTMC can be time-homogeneous or time-inhomogeneous, and the reward is a function of time (this feature facilitates the modeling of the impulse reward in some systems [4]).

Very often, the underlying DTMC in a DMRM is considered as a time-homogeneous DTMC with a finite state space and the rewards or costs are considered as constants for the corresponding states. We formalize this frequently used DMRM as follows:

Definition 12 (DMRM with Time-homogeneous Property).

⊢ ∀ X Y p s_x s_y p_0 p_{ij} r_{xy}. th_dmrm X Y p s_x s_y p_0 p_{ij} r_{xy} =
    dmrm X Y p s_x s_y p_0 p_{ij} r_{xy} ∧ FINITE (space s_y) ∧
    (∀ x t t'. r_{xy} t x = r_{xy} t' x) ∧
    (∀ t i j.
        $\mathbb{P}$\{x | X t x = i\} ≠ 0 ∧ $\mathbb{P}$\{x | X (t + 1) x = i\} ≠ 0 ⇒
        p_{ij} X p s (t + 1) 1 i j = p_{ij} X p s t 1 i j)

where the first conjunct states that this model is a DMRM, the second condition constrains that the reward space is a finite space, the third one ensures the rewards are constant for every state x in the state space of the random variable (X t) and the last conjunct refers to the time-homogeneity of the transition probabilities of the underlying DTMC.

If the underlying DTMC of a DMRM is an aperiodic DTMC, then the conditional expectations are convergent. This property can be verified as follows:

Theorem 9 (Convergent Property).

⊢ ∀ X Y p s_x s_y p_0 p_{ij} r_{xy} i.
    th_dmrm X Y p s_x s_y p_0 p_{ij} r_{xy} ∧ APERIODIC_MC X p s_x p_0 p_{ij} ⇒
    convergent (λt. cond_expec (Y t) (X t) i p s_y)

The expected cumulated reward over a long period is always of interest as the cumulative property verified in the following theorem, which can be used to obtain the expected steady-state reward.

Theorem 10 (Cumulative Property).

⊢ ∀ X Y p s_x s_y p_0 p_{ij} r_{xy} i.
    th_dmrm X Y p s_x s_y p_0 p_{ij} r_{xy} ∧ APERIODIC_MC X p s_x p_0 p_{ij} ∧
    i ∈ space s_x ⇒
    (lim (λt. cond_expec (Y t) (X t) i p s_y) = lim (λt. r_{xy} t i))

The expected steady-state reward can be achieved by applying the following theorem:

Theorem 11 (Expected Steady-state Reward).

⊢ ∀ X Y p s_x s_y p_0 p_{ij} r_{xy} i.
    th_dmrm X Y p s_x s_y p_0 p_{ij} r_{xy} ∧ APERIODIC_MC X p s_x p_0 p_{ij} ∧
    i ∈ space s_x ⇒
    (lim (λ t. expec (X t) p s_x) =
    $\sum_{y \in \text{space } s_y}$ lim (λ t. r_{xy} t i) lim (λ t. $\mathbb{P}$\{x | (Y t) x = y\}))

The HOL script of these formalizations is available in [9] and the verified theorems are used in the next section to analyze the memory contention problem of a particular multi-processor system.

4 Application

In this section, we present a formal performance analysis of a multiprocessor system by reasoning about the expectation of memory access requests.

4.1 Memory Contention Problem

Consider a multi-processor system with two memory modules and two processors. This system can be modeled as a Discrete-time Markov Reward Model (DMRM) [19], depicted in Figure 2, by assuming that access time of any memory module is a constant and all the memory modules are synchronized. The states of the system are denoted by the pair (i, j), where i represents the number of the processors waiting for the memory module 1 and j refers to the amount of the processors waiting for the memory module 2. Due to the fact that memory access time is always longer than any other data transaction of the processor, it is reasonable to assume that $0 \le i$, $0 \le j$, and $i + j = 2$ in every memory cycle. Thus, the states set $\{(1, 1), (0, 2), (2, 0)\}$ provides all the possible states of the given system. Also, q_k $(k = 1, 2)$ represents the probabilities that a processor requests a direct memory access. If both processors are accessing two different memory modules (in this case, the system stays in state $(1, 1)$) and will complete the task by the end of this memory cycle, then the expectation of the number of memory requests completed in this memory cycle is 2. If there are two requests to access memory module 1 in a memory cycle, then only one request can be completed in this memory cycle. We can obtain the same expectation when memory module 2 is requested to be accessed. We denote the random variable Y as the number of requests completed in every memory cycle in the steady state and the request state space is the set $\{0, 1, 2\}$. The conditional expectations of Y can be mathematically described as:

$$E[Y|\text{system in state } (1,1)] = 2;$$
$$E[Y|\text{system in state } (2,0)] = 1; \qquad (2)$$
$$E[Y|\text{system in state } (0,2)] = 1.$$

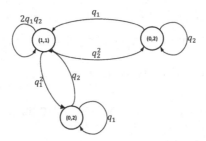

Fig. 2. The State Diagram for the Memory Interference Problem

In order to analyze the performance of such a system, we are interested in learning the steady probabilities of the states, in which the memory modules are efficiently used, and the expected number of memory requests satisfied in each memory cycle in the steady state.

4.2 Formalization of Memory Contention Problem

To formally analyze the properties of this system, we first describe this multiprocessor system in HOL. As shown in Figure 2, this kind of system can be described as a DMRM with an aperiodic and irreducible DTMC [19]. First of all, we define the state space for the requests as a general function in HOL:

Definition 13 (Request State Space).

⊢ ∀ n. request n = {(r:real) | r ∈ [0, n]}
⊢ ∀ n. request_space n = (request n, POW (request n))

where variable n refers to the number of memory modules in the system and POW (request n) is the sigma algebra of the request set. In the case of the two-processor system, at most two requests can be created in a memory cycle, thus, $n = 2$.

Now, the system state space and the transition probabilities can be formally expressed as the functions presented in Definition 14 and the conditional expected value is described as a function in Definition 15 using higher-order logic.

Definition 14 (State Space & Transition Probabilities).

⊢ sys_state = {(0, 2); (2, 0); (1, 1)}
⊢ sys_space = (sys_state, POW sys_state)
⊢ ∀ q_1 q_2 t i j. Lt q_1 q_2 t i j = case (i, j) of
$$
\begin{array}{llll}
((1,1),(1,1)) & \to & 2q_1q_2 & | \quad ((0,2),(1,1)) \to q_1 \quad | \\
((2,0),(1,1)) & \to & q_2 & | \quad ((1,1),(0,2)) \to q_2^2 \quad | \\
((0,2),(0,2)) & \to & q_2 & | \quad ((2,0),(2,0)) \to q_1 \quad | \\
((1,1),(2,0)) & \to & q_1^2 & | \quad (\_,\_) \to 0
\end{array}
$$

where sys_space is a pair, in which the first element is a set sys_state and the second element is the sigma algebra of sys_state, the function Lt returns the transition probabilities.

Definition 15 (Conditional Expected Requests).

⊢ ∀ t i j. rewards t (i, j) =
    if (i, j) = (1, 1) then 2 else
    if (i, j) = (2, 0) then 1 else
    if (i, j) = (0, 2) then 1 else 0

where the function rewards corresponds to Equation (2).

These functions can now be used to model the multiprocessor system of Figure 2 as follows:

Definition 16 (Multiprocessor Model).

⊢ ∀ X Y p q_1 q_2 p_0. opera_sys_model X Y p q_1 q_2 p_0 =
   th_dmrm X Y p sys_space (request_space 2) p_0 (Lt q_1 q_2) rewards ∧
   Aperiodic_DTMC X p sys_space p_0 (Lt q_1 q_2) ∧
   Irreducible_DTMC X p sys_space p_0 (Lt q_1 q_2) ∧
   0 < q_1 ∧ 0 < q_2 ∧ q_1 < 1 ∧ q_2 < 1 ∧ (q_1 + q_2 = 1)

where variable X indicates the system state (the pair containing the number of requests for each memory module) at discrete time points, variable Y refers to the requests, which is a random variable, p denotes the probability space, q_1 and q_2 are the parameters in the transition probabilities described previously, and function p_0 represents a general initial distribution, the request state space is request_space and the system state space is sys_space, which are defined in Definition 13 and 14, respectively.

Note that, the definitions presented above provide the flexibility on modifying the argument, i.e., n in Definition 13, or the functions in Definitions 14 and 15 in case of describing more complex systems.

4.3   Performance Analysis of Memory Contention

As the underlying DTMC in the model described in Definition 16 is an aperiodic and irreducible DTMC, we can directly apply Theorem 6 to prove that for all states in the system state space, the probability distributions are convergent in the long-term as the following theorem.

Theorem 12 (Convergence of the State Distribution).

⊢ ∀ X Y p q_1 q_2 p_0 i.
   opera_sys_model X Y p q_1 q_2 p_0 ∧ i ∈ space sys_space ⇒
   convergent (λ t. $\mathbb{P}\{x \mid X\ t\ x = i\}$)

Applying Theorems 2, 3, 5 and 6, we obtain the steady-state probabilities (the limit of the probability mass functions for all states in the state space):

Theorem 13 (Steady Probabilities).

⊢ ∀ X Y p q_1 q_2 p_0.
   opera_sys_model X Y p q_1 q_2 p_0 ⇒
   $\lim_{t \to \infty} \mathbb{P}\{x \mid X\ t\ x = (2,\ 0)\} = \frac{q_1^3}{1 - 2q_1 q_2}$ ∧
   $\lim_{t \to \infty} \mathbb{P}\{x \mid X\ t\ x = (0,\ 2)\} = \frac{q_2^3}{1 - 2q_1 q_2}$ ∧
   $\lim_{t \to \infty} \mathbb{P}\{x \mid X\ t\ x = (1,\ 1)\} = \frac{q_1 q_2}{1 - 2q_1 q_2}$

Utilizing the formalizations of expectation presented in Section 3.1, we can prove the expectation of the number of memory requests completed per memory cycle in the steady state in the following theorem:

Theorem 14 (Expected Steady-state Rewards).

$\vdash \forall$ X Y p q_1 q_2 p_0. opera_sys_model X Y p q_1 q_2 p_0 $\Rightarrow$
$\lim_{t\to\infty}$ (λ t. expec (Y t) p request_space) = $\frac{1-q_1q_2}{1-2q_1q_2}$

Theorems 13 and 14 can be used for optimizing the system design. For example, we can obtain the maximum value of the expectation of completed requests from Theorem 14 and find out the conditions to achieve the best efficiency ($q_1 = q_2 = 1 / 2$). Similarly, when $q_1 = 0.97$ and $q_2 = 0.03$, we can obtain the steady-state probability $\lim_{t\to\infty} \mathbb{P}\{x \mid X\ t\ x = (0, 2)\} = 2.8669e^{-5}$ by applying Theorem 13, however, classical simulators, such as Matlab, compute $\lim_{t\to\infty} \mathbb{P}\{x \mid X\ t\ x = (0, 2)\} = 0$ due to the underlying algorithms for accelerating the convergent speed and the round-off error in the intermediate steps. Moreover, the algorithms can never provide a positive transition probability matrix, which exists according to Theorem 5, because of the round-off errors or the slow convergent speed. Our approach can overcome all these problems and provide accurate results.

Our general definition of DMRMs offers the flexibility of describing the states as arbitrary types, such as the pairs in this application, instead of the abstract non-negative integers. On the other hand, this application illustrates an approach to formally analyze the distributed systems using theorem proving. It is important to note that the system can be more complex (i.e., the number of the processors and memory modules can be very large), and we can analyze it by defining new functions, such as sys_space, request_space, Lt and rewards.

The proof script for modeling and verifying the properties of the memory contention in a multiprocessor (two processors and two memory modules) is about 700 lines long and is available in [9]. The ability to formally verify theorems involving DMRMs and the short script clearly indicates the usefulness of the formalization, presented in the previous sections in this paper, as without them the reasoning could not have been done in such a straightforward way.

5   Conclusion

This paper presents a method to formally analyze the performance of multiprocessor systems based on the formalization of Discrete-time Markov Reward Models (DMRMs) using higher-order logic. Due to the inherent soundness of theorem proving, our work guarantees to provide accurate results, which is a very useful feature while analyzing stationary behaviors and long-term expectation on certain key measures for a system associated with safety or mission-critical systems. In order to illustrate the usefulness of the proposed approach, we formally analyzed the memory contention problem in a system with two processors and two memory modules, which is modeled as a DMRM with the underlying aperiodic and irreducible DTMC, using the formalizations of DTMCs. Our results exactly matched the results obtained using paper-and-pencil analysis in [19], which ascertains the precise nature of the proposed approach.

As DMRMs have been widely applied in performance and reliability analysis, especially in predicting the reliability for fault-tolerant systems and software, the presented work opens the door to a new and promising research direction on formally analyzing the Discrete-time Markov Reward Models. We plan to apply the formalization presented in this paper to formally analyze some real-world systems modeled as DMRMs. Also, we plan to extend our work to the Continuous-time Markov Reward Models (CMRMs) and Markov Decision Process (MDP), which will enable us to formally analyze software reliability and hardware performance of a wider range of systems.

References

1. Baier, C., Katoen, J.: Principles of Model Checking. MIT Press (2008)
2. Bhattacharya, R.N., Waymire, E.C.: Stochastic Processes with Applications. John Wiley & Sons (1990)
3. Chung, K.L.: Markov Chains. Springer (1960)
4. Cloth, L., Katoen, J., Khattri, M., Pulungan, R.: Model checking Markov Reward Models with Impulse Rewards. In: International Conference on Dependable Systems and Networks, pp. 722–731. IEEE Computer Society Press (2005)
5. Gamerman, D., Lopes, H.F.: Fundamentals of Applied Probability Theory. Chapman & Hall/CRC (2006)
6. Goldberg, R.R.: Methods of Real Analysis. Wiley (1976)
7. Hurd, J.: Formal Verification of Probabilistic Algorithms. PhD Thesis, University of Cambridge, UK (2002)
8. Kwon, Y., Agha, G.: A Markov Reward Model for Software Reliability. In: International Parallel and Distributed Processing Symposium, pp. 1–6. IEEE (2007)
9. Liu, L.: HOL Script: Formal Analysis of Memory Contention in a Multiprocessor System (2013), http://hvg.ece.concordia.ca/projects/prob-it/dmrm.html
10. Liu, L., Hasan, O., Tahar, S.: Formal Reasoning About Finite-State Discrete-Time Markov Chains in HOL. Journal of Computer Science and Technology 28(2), 217–231 (2013)
11. Liu, L., Hasan, O., Aravantinos, V., Tahar, S.: Formal Reasoning about Classified Markov Chains in HOL. In: Blazy, S., Paulin-Mohring, C., Pichardie, D. (eds.) ITP 2013. LNCS, vol. 7998, pp. 295–310. Springer, Heidelberg (2013)
12. Mhamdi, T., Hasan, O., Tahar, S.: Formalization of entropy measures in HOL. In: van Eekelen, M., Geuvers, H., Schmaltz, J., Wiedijk, F. (eds.) ITP 2011. LNCS, vol. 6898, pp. 233–248. Springer, Heidelberg (2011)
13. MRMC (2013), http://www.mrmc-tool.org/trac/
14. Norris, J.R.: Markov Chains. Cambridge University Press (1999)
15. Parker, D.A.: Implementation of Symbolic Model Checking for Probabilitics Systems. PhD Thesis, University of Birmingham, Birmingham, UK (2002)
16. PRISM (2013), www.prismmodelchecker.org
17. Sczittnick, M.: MACOM - A Tool for Evaluating Communication Systems. In: International Conference on Modelling Techniques and Tools for Computer Performance Evaluation, pp. 7–10 (1994)
18. Tijms, H.C.: A First Course in Stochastic Models. Wiley, New York (2003)
19. Trivedi, K.S.: Probability and Statistics with Reliability, Queuing, and Computer Science Applications. John Wiley & Sons (2002)
20. Yates, R.D., Goodman, D.J.: Probability and Stochastic Processes: A Friendly Introduction for Electrical and Computer Engineers. Wiley (2005)

Algebraic Graph Transformations
with Inheritance

Michael Löwe, Harald König, Christoph Schulz, and Marius Schultchen

FHDW Hannover University of Applied Sciences,
Freundallee 15, 30173 Hannover, Germany
{Michael.Loewe,Harald.Koenig,Christoph.Schulz}@fhdw.de,
Marius.Schultchen@web.de

Abstract. In this paper, we propose a new approach to inheritance in
the context of algebraic graph transformation by providing a suitable
categorial framework which reflects the semantics of class-based inheritance in software engineering. Inheritance is modelled by a type graph
T that comes equipped with a partial order. Typed graphs are arrows
with codomain T which preserve graph structures up to inheritance. Morphisms between typed graphs are "down typing" graph morphisms: An
object of class t can be mapped to an object of a subclass of t. We prove
that this structure is an adhesive HLR category, i.e. pushouts along
extremal monomorphisms are "well-behaved". This infers validity of classical results such as the Local Church-Rosser Theorem, the Parallelism
Theorem, and the Concurrency Theorem.

Keywords: Graph transformation, Inheritance, Adhesive HLR category.

1 Introduction

Developing appropriate models to mimic reality has always been an important
part of software engineering. However, the relation between coding and modelling
has changed over time. Today, model-driven engineering focuses on generating
code from appropriately detailed and formalised models, hoping that developing
the model and using a mature and well-tested code generator is less error-prone
than letting programmers write most of the code themselves. This reasoning,
however, is only valid if model development is relatively easy. Typically, different graphical notations help people to structure the problem in various ways.
Consequently, *graphs* or graph structures play an important role in software
engineering today, compare e.g. the UML [13], a modelling language which is
currently the de facto standard for modelling object-oriented systems.

If one looks more closely at object-oriented systems, one realises that it is
impossible to analyse or build object-oriented software in an efficient way without
making use of specialization or *inheritance*.[1] Therefore, it is sensible to require
that the graphical notation supports aspects of inheritance well.

---

[1] In this paper, we do not differentiate between type specialization (subtyping) and
class inheritance, because the differences are mostly relevant in the context of type
theory, which we do not discuss, and because most mainstream OOP languages do
not differentiate between these concepts.

J. Iyoda and L. de Moura (Eds.): SBMF 2013, LNCS 8195, pp. 211–226, 2013.
© Springer-Verlag Berlin Heidelberg 2013

On the one side, graphs are well suited for modelling static aspects of software, e.g. the class and inheritance structure. On the other side, behavioural aspects of the system, e.g. state changes, can be modelled using *graph transformations* which formally describe when and how a graph (here: state of an object-oriented system) can change into another graph (here: another system state). Graph transformations, especially algebraic graph transformations based on adhesive HLR categories[2], have been studied for a long time and are a well-known tool in the context of software engineering.

However, if we want to combine a graphical notation supporting inheritance with graph transformations, which therefore have to operate on graphs with inheritance, there are relatively few approaches, which differ in flexibility and "readability". In this papier, we propose a new approach which binds the inheritance hierarchy to the type graph (only); objects are typed by providing a typing morphism into the type graph which preserves the graph structure up to inheritance. Morphisms between graphs are allowed to relate objects of different types as long as the target object is at least as specialised as the source object.[3] Upon this notion of inheritance, we build a suitable category and show that this category is an adhesive HLR category, such that many interesting results from the field of algebraic graph transformations can be applied immediately.

The paper is structured as follows: Section 2 develops some basic notions and defines the category $\mathcal{G}^T$ which is used in the subsequent sections. Sections 3, 4, and 5 analyse the properties of monomorphisms, pushouts, and pullbacks in $\mathcal{G}^T$. In section 6, we prove the main result of this paper, namely that $\mathcal{G}^T$ is an adhesive HLR category. Section 7 demonstrates the usefulness of our approach by means of a practical example. We discuss related approaches in section 8. Finally, section 9 summarises the results and discusses future work.

Due to space limitations, some of the proofs have been omitted. They can be found in [12].

2   Basic Definitions

$\mathcal{G}$ denotes the usual category of multi-graphs whose objects $G = (V_G, E_G, s_G : E \to V, t_G : E \to V)$ have vertices, edges, and the usual source and target mappings $s_G, t_G : E \to V$, resp.[4] Morphisms $f : G_1 \to G_2$ are pairs of mappings compatible with the graph structure, i.e. they obey the rules $f \circ s_{G_1} = s_{G_2} \circ f$

---

[2] Adhesive high-level replacement (HLR) categories introduced in [2, 5] combine high-level replacement systems[4] with the notion of adhesive categories[10] in order to be able to generalize the double pushout transformation approach from graphs to other high-level structures as e. g. Petri nets using a categorial framework. Generally, adhesiveness abstracts from exactness properties like compatibility of union and intersection of sets.

[3] We call this property "down-typing".

[4] These notations will remain fixed in that for any $X \in \mathcal{G}$ we will always write V_X, E_X, s_X, t_X for the constituents of X without defining them explicitly.

and $f \circ t_{G_1} = t_{G_2} \circ f.$[5] If a graph is used as a class diagram, its vertices represent the available classes and its edges model directed associations. We formalise class-inheritance by an additional partial order on the vertices of a type graph:

Definition 1 (Type Graph). *A type graph is a pair* $(T, \leq)$ *where* T *is a graph and* $\leq \; \subseteq V \times V$ *is a partial order with a largest element* $O \in V_T$[6].

This definition reflects the basic nature of class models. It still lacks additional annotations like multiplicities, abstractness properties or other constraints. The forthcoming definition of object structures, however, shows that it is reasonable to interpret edges as associations with multiplicity "0..*" on both ends.

Definition 2 (Typed Graph). *Let* $I \in \mathcal{G}$ *and* $(T, \leq)$ *be a type graph. A mapping pair* $(i_V : V_I \to V_T, i_E : E_I \to E_T)$, *written* $i : I \to T$, *is called* T-*typed graph if the conditions (1) and (2) hold:*[7]

$$i \circ s_I \leq s_T \circ i \tag{1}$$
$$i \circ t_I \leq t_T \circ i \tag{2}$$

Condition (1) means that subtypes inherit all attributes of all their super-types. Condition (2) formalises the fact that referenced objects at run-time may appear polymorphically: They may possess any subtype of the corresponding association target, cf. Fig. 1. This concept coincides with the definition of "clan morphism" if the underlying relation I in [9] is a partial order.

In the sequel, the type graph $T := (T, \leq)$ will be fixed, i.e. we speak of "typed graphs" instead of "T-typed graphs".

Definition 3 (Type-Compatible Morphism). *Given two typed graphs* $i : I \to T, j : J \to T$, *a graph morphism* $m : I \to J$ *is type-compatible, written* $m : i \to j$, *if*

$$j \circ m \leq i \tag{3}$$

on V_I *and*

$$j \circ m = i \tag{4}$$

on E_I. *If in (3) "$\leq$" can be replaced by "=", m is called* strong. *A strong morphism* f *from* i *to* j *will be denoted* $i \xrightarrow{\;f\;} j$.

It follows that type-compatible morphism can map an "object" of type c to an "object" the type of which is a subtype of c. This is especially useful when

---

[5] Sometimes in the literature the two components f_V and f_E of f are explicitly differentiated. We will not do that, because it will always become clear from the context which component is used.

[6] The letter "O" shall remind of the class "Object" in Java, which is a super class of all other classes, hence the inheritance order's largest object.

[7] If $f, g : X \to Y$ are two mappings into a partially ordered set $Y = (Y, \leq)$, we write $f \leq g$ if $f(x) \leq g(x)$ for all $x \in X$.

matching a graph transformation rule, since one can match many specialised objects by using an object of a general type.

Strong morphisms are closed under composition:

Proposition 4. *Let $i : I \to T$, $j : J \to T$, and $k : K \to T$ be some typed graphs, and let $m : i \to j$ and $n : j \to k$ be two strong morphisms. Then $n \circ m$ is also strong.*

Proof. $k \circ (n \circ m) = (k \circ n) \circ m = j \circ m = i.$ $\qquad\qquad\qquad\qquad\qquad$ □

Definition 5 (Category $\mathcal{G}^T$). *Let T be a type graph. We define $\mathcal{G}^T$ to be the category which has typed graphs as objects and type-compatible morphisms between them as arrows.*

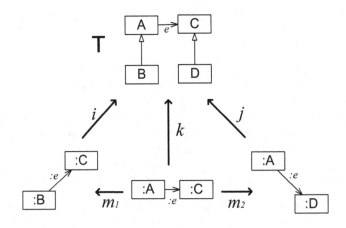

Fig. 1. Typed graphs and type-compatible morphisms

The main effects are shown in UML-styled Fig. 1: T is the top graph in which nodes are rectangles and the partial order is depicted by arrows with end-triangles (reflexive elements and the largest element O are not shown). There are three typed graphs i, j, k, their typing being highlighted by names $:X$ whenever they map to X. Since B inherits association e, i is a well-typed object structure. Since A-objects may polymorphically be linked to C- or D-objects j is an admissible typing. Moreover, m_1 and m_2 are two type-compatible morphisms (e.g.: $m_1(:A) = :B$ yielding $i(m_1(:A)) = B < A = k(:A)$[8]).

In the sequel, we let

$$\tau : \begin{cases} \mathcal{G}^T \to \mathcal{G} \\ (g : G \to T) \xrightarrow{\ f\ } (h : H \to T) \mapsto G \xrightarrow{\ f\ } H \end{cases}$$

be the functor which forgets the typing structure.

---

[8] $<$ being short for: $\leq$ and $\neq$.

3 Monomorphisms and Epimorphisms

In order to investigate categorial properties of $\mathcal{G}^T$, we analyse the nature of monomorphisms and epimorphisms: First, a straightforward argument shows that any injective $m : i \to j$ is a monomorphism. The reverse statement is also true, but we need the existence of the largest element O of $\leq$: If $m : g \to h$ is a monomorphisms then $m(v_1) = m(v_2)$ can be detected by mappings $k_1, k_2 : \{:O\} \to G$ with $k_i(:O) = v_i$ $(i \in \{1, 2\})$.[9] If we do not require the existence of a largest element, assume T contains the three types A, B, and C such that $C < A$ and $C < B$, then the non-injective $m \colon \{:A, :B\} \to \{:C\}$ with $m(:A) = m(:B) = :C$ is a monomorphism, as there do not exist any morphisms $p, q : X \to \{:A, :B\}$ which map some element $x \in X$ to $:A$ and $:B$, resp., due to the missing common supertype of A and B.

Surjective morphisms coincide with the class of epimorphisms. In contrast to monomorphisms, however, the proof of this fact does not make use of the largest element and is proven in the same way as the corresponding fact in $\mathcal{G}$.

Proposition 6. *Epimorphisms of $\mathcal{G}^T$ are exactly the surjective morphisms. Monomorphisms of $\mathcal{G}^T$ are exactly the injective morphisms.*

Conventionally, in category theory, *extremal* monomorphisms are often the right choice if (ordinary) monomorphisms do not represent embeddings: A monomorphism m is said to be *extremal*, if any decomposition $m = m' \circ f$ with an epimorphism f already forces f to be an isomorphism. In $\mathcal{G}^T$ a morphism $m : \{:B\} \to \{:A\}$ with $A < B$ is monic and epic (cf. Proposition 6) but no isomorphism, because a hypothetical inverse n would have to "upcast" $(n(:A) =:B)$, which is not possible. Thus m is not extremal, because $m = id \circ m$.[10]

Proposition 7 (Strong Monos and Extremal Monos coincide). *A monomorphism in $\mathcal{G}^T$ is extremal if and only if it is strong.*

Because of this result, it is reasonable to denote an extremal mono m from i to j by $i \overset{m}{\rightarrowtail} j$.

4 Pushouts

In order to define and apply double-pushout graph transformation rules in the category $\mathcal{G}^T$, we need to analyse how pushouts can be constructed. The first observation is that pushouts do not always exist: Let T be the discrete graph[11] with $V_T = \{O, B, C\}$ and $\leq = \{(B, O), (C, O)\}$ together with reflexive pairs. Then

$$\{:C\} \longleftarrow \{:O\} \longrightarrow \{:B\}$$

---

[9] The notation $\{x\}$ is short for the graph $(\{x\}, \emptyset, \emptyset, \emptyset)$.

[10] In topoi, an epic monomorphisms necessarily becomes an isomorphism. Hence this example shows that $\mathcal{G}^T$ is not a topos. In the next sections there will be many other aspects detecting this property (e.g. the fact that some limits and some more co-limits do not exist).

[11] A graph with empty edge set.

obviously possesses no pushout. Even if one restricts down-typing to at most one of the given morphisms, pushouts along monomorphisms need not exist, because

$$\{1{:}B, 2{:}C\} \longleftarrow\!\!\!< \{1{:}O, 2{:}O\} \longrightarrow \{12{:}O\} \ ,$$

where the left leg maps according to the numbers (and hence is monic) and where the right leg identifies the objects $1{:}O$ and $2{:}O$ by mapping them to $12{:}O$, does not admit a pushout. This behaviour has its roots in the fact that B and C are incomparable and do not possess a common subtype.

Our goal is to find a feasible criterion for a span

$$j \xleftarrow{\ \beta\ } g \xrightarrow{\ \alpha\ } h \tag{5}$$

to admit a pushout. For this we denote with $\bigwedge A$ the *greatest lower bound* of a subset $A \subseteq V_T$ if it exists[12]. Let furthermore $G := \tau(g)$, $H := \tau(h)$, and $J := \tau(j)$ with the above introduced forgetful functor. We denote with $[h, j] : H + J \to T$ the disjoint union of h and j and we need the usual relation

$$\sim := \{(\alpha(x), \beta(x)) \mid x \in G\} \tag{6}$$

on $H + J$, for which $\equiv$ denotes the smallest (sortwise) equivalence on $H + J$ which contains $\sim$. An equivalence class of $\equiv$ will be written $[v]_\equiv$ or $[v]$. Let $H +_G J := (H + J)/_\equiv$ together with the canonical graph morphisms $\overline{\alpha} : J \to H +_G J$ and $\overline{\beta} : H \to H +_G J$ (which map v to $[v]_\equiv$) that make up the $\mathcal{G}$-pushout of α and β.

Theorem 8 (Characterisation of Pushouts). *The span* (5) *admits a pushout in* $\mathcal{G}^T$ *if and only if*

$$\forall v \in V_{H+J} : \bigwedge \{[h, j](x) \mid x \in [v]_\equiv\}$$

exists. If this condition is met, the square

$$\begin{array}{ccc} g & \xrightarrow{\ \alpha\ } & h \\ {\scriptstyle \beta}\big\downarrow & & \big\downarrow{\scriptstyle \overline{\beta}} \\ j & \xrightarrow[\ \overline{\alpha}\ ]{} & p \end{array} \tag{7}$$

is a pushout in $\mathcal{G}^T$, *where* $p : H +_G J \to T$ *is defined by*

$$p([v]) = \bigwedge \{[h, j](x) \mid x \in [v]\}$$

on vertices and $p([e]) = [h, j](e)$ *on edges.*

Corollary 9. $\mathcal{G}^T$ *has all pushouts along extremal monomorphisms. In such a pushout the extremal mono is preserved under the pushout.*

---

[12] The notation $\bigwedge$ shall remind of "intersection" (of sets): For any set X, any indexed set $(Y_i)_{i \in I}$ with $Y_i \in (\wp(X), \subseteq)$ always has a greatest lower bound, namely $\bigcap_{i \in I} Y_i$.

Proof. If α is an extremal mono, it is a strong monomorphism by Proposition 7. This means, that for any $v \in V_{H+J}$ the set $[v]$ is a singleton (if $v \in V_H$ is not in the image of α), or it is of the form $\{\alpha(y) \mid y \in \beta^{-1}(\beta(x))\} \cup \{\beta(x)\}$ for some $x \in V_G$. In the first case, the greatest lower bound is $h(v)$, in the latter case, by strongness, it is $j(\beta(x))$. Thus, by Theorem 8, the pushout can be constructed with the usual construction in $\mathcal{G}$ such that $\overline{\alpha}$ becomes an embedding, hence a strong (thus extremal) mono. □

Theorem 8 can be alternatively formulated as

Corollary 10. *A commutative diagram* $\mathcal{D} =$

$$
\begin{array}{ccc}
g & \xrightarrow{\ \alpha\ } & h \\
\beta \downarrow & & \downarrow \delta \\
j & \xrightarrow[\ \gamma\ ]{} & q
\end{array}
$$

s.t. $\tau(\mathcal{D})$ *is a pushout in* $\mathcal{G}$, *is a pushout in* $\mathcal{G}^T$ $\iff$ $\forall v \in V_{\tau(q)} : q(v) = \bigwedge \{[h,j](x) \mid [\gamma,\delta](x) = v\}$.

Proof. Let $i : \tau(q) \to \tau(p)$ be the canonical $\mathcal{G}$-isomorphism between the given pushout $\tau(\mathcal{D})$ and the canonical pushout in $\mathcal{G}$ (τ applied to (7)). Then for all $x \in H + J$, $v \in V_{\tau(q)}$ we obtain $[\gamma,\delta](x) = v \Leftrightarrow i([\gamma,\delta](x)) = i(v) \Leftrightarrow [\overline{\alpha},\overline{\beta}](x) = i(v)$, thus

$$[\gamma,\delta](x) = v \Leftrightarrow x \in i(v) \tag{8}$$

"$\Rightarrow$": By Theorem 8, $\bigwedge S_v$ exists and (7) is pushout. Thus, i is a $\mathcal{G}^T$-isomorphism. Then $q = p \circ i$ and (8) yield $q(v) = p(i(v)) = \bigwedge \{[h,j](x) \mid x \in i(v)\} = \bigwedge \{[h,j](x) \mid [\gamma,\delta](x) = v\}$.

"$\Leftarrow$": The definition of q and (8) yield the characterising condition of Theorem 8. Hence (7) is a $\mathcal{G}^T$-pushout. Moreover, by (8) and the definition of p we have $p(i(v)) = \bigwedge \{[h,j](x) \mid x \in i(v)\} = \bigwedge \{[h,j](x) \mid [\gamma,\delta](x) = v\} = q(v)$, such that i is a $\mathcal{G}^T$-isomorphism and the given square is a $\mathcal{G}^T$-pushout. □

Note that the results of this section remain true even if we do not claim the existence of a largest element O.

5   Pullbacks

In this section we characterise those co-spans of $\mathcal{G}^T$ which admit pullbacks. The situation is *not* dual to the situation in Section 4 because of the existence of the largest element: If T consists of nodes $\{A, B, C, O\}$ with no edges where $\leq$ is generated from $\{(A,B), (A,C), (B,O), (C,O)\}$, the co-span

$$\{:C\} \longrightarrow \{:A\} \longleftarrow \{:B\}$$

possesses the pullback

$$\{:C\} \longleftarrow \{:O\} \longrightarrow \{:B\} \ .$$

But pullback construction fails in more complex situations: Let a type graph be given by the class diagram in Fig. 2, in which the partial order is generated by the depicted arrows.

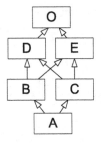

Fig. 2. A type graph

Then the co-span

$$\{:C\} \longrightarrow \{:A\} \longleftarrow \{:B\}$$

admits no pullback, because there are two incompatible candidates, namely the spans

$$\{:C\} \longleftarrow \{:D\} \longrightarrow \{:B\} \quad \text{and} \quad \{:C\} \longleftarrow \{:E\} \longrightarrow \{:B\} \ ,$$

and a minimal candidate

$$\{:C\} \longleftarrow \{:D, :E\} \longrightarrow \{:B\} \ , \tag{9}$$

for which, however, two different mediators exist from

$$\{:C\} \longleftarrow \{:O\} \longrightarrow \{:B\} \ .$$

This example shows that it seems to be difficult to find a feasible criterion for a pullback to exist without claiming the existence of a largest element: If we omitted O in Figure 2, there would indeed be a pullback, namely the span (9) (which seems to be weird because the middle graph possesses two vertices – note that monos are still preserved by pullbacks because both morphisms in (9) are now monos, see the example in the first paragraph of Section 3).

In order to avoid these degenerate limits we return to the original situation in which O exists. We want to find a necessary and sufficient criterion for a co-span

$$j \xrightarrow{\ \beta\ } g \xleftarrow{\ \alpha\ } h \tag{10}$$

to admit a pullback which is feasible enough to be used in practical contexts. It turns out that the existence of pullbacks heavily depends on the existence of *least upper bounds* of two nodes of T. We use the notation $B \lor C$ to denote the least upper bound if it exists.[13]

We abbreviate $J := \tau(j)$, $G := \tau(g)$, and $H := \tau(h)$. $H \times_G J$ is the pullback object of α and β in $\mathcal{G}$ together with projections $\pi_1 : H \times_G J \to H$ and $\pi_2 : H \times_G J \to J$. It turns out that the two above examples fully characterise the limitations for the existence of pullbacks:

Theorem 11 (Characterisation of Pullbacks). *The co-span* (10) *admits a pullback if and only if*

$$\forall(v_1, v_2) \in V_{H \times_G J} : h(v_1) \lor j(v_2) \text{ exists.}$$

If this condition is met, the square

$$
\begin{array}{ccc}
g & \xleftarrow{\ \alpha\ } & h \\
{\scriptstyle\beta}\big\uparrow & & \big\uparrow{\scriptstyle\pi_1} \\
j & \xleftarrow[\pi_2]{} & p
\end{array}
\tag{11}
$$

is a pullback in $\mathcal{G}^T$, *where* $p : H \times_G J \to T$ *is defined by*

$$p(v_1, v_2) = h(v_1) \lor j(v_2)$$

on vertices and

$$p(e_1, e_2) = h(e_1)(= j(e_2))$$

on edges.

We obtain the following consequences:

Corollary 12.

(1) If in (10) *at least one morphism is strong, the pullback exists.*

(2) If in $(T, \leq)$ *all pairs have a least upper bound, all pullbacks exist.*

(3) If T *is finite and* $\leq$ *represents a hierarchy, i.e. if each node in* $V_T - \{O\}$ *has exactly one direct super node[14], all pullbacks exist.*

(4) Extremal monomorphisms as well as strong morphisms are preserved under pullbacks.

Proof. 12(1), 12(2), and 12(4) are immediate consequences of Theorem 11 and the fact that pullbacks preserve monos in $\mathcal{G}$. 12(3) can be easily proved by induction over path lengths from $h(v_1)$ to O and $j(v_2)$ to O, respectively.   □

Theorem 11 can be alternatively formulated:

---

[13] The notation $\lor$ shall remind of "union" (of sets): For any set X, any two elements $Y_1, Y_2 \in (\wp(X), \subseteq)$ have always a least upper bound, namely $Y_1 \cup Y_2$.

[14] As is the case in each programming language that prohibits multiple inheritance.

Corollary 13. *A commutative diagram* $\mathcal{D} =$

$$
\begin{array}{ccc}
g & \xleftarrow{\ \alpha\ } & h \\
{\scriptstyle\beta}\big\uparrow & & \big\uparrow{\scriptstyle\delta} \\
j & \xleftarrow[\ \gamma\ ]{} & q
\end{array}
$$

s.t. $\tau(\mathcal{D})$ *is a pullback in* $\mathcal{G}$*, is a pullback in* $\mathcal{G}^T$ *if and only if* $\forall z \in V_{\tau(q)} : q(z) = h(\delta(z)) \vee j(\gamma(z))$.

Proof. "⇒": $\mathcal{D}$ and (11) yield a canonical $\mathcal{G}^T$-isomorphism $i \colon q \to p$, such that for $z \in V_{\tau(q)}$, $q(z) = p(i(z)) = p(\pi_1(i(z)), \pi_2(i(z))) = p(\delta(z), \gamma(z)) = h(\delta(z)) \vee j(\gamma(z))$.

"⇐": Let $i \colon \tau(q) \to \tau(p)$ be the canonical $\mathcal{G}$-isomorphism between $\tau(\mathcal{D})$ and τ applied to (11). Then $q(z) = h(\pi_1(i(z))) \vee j(\pi_2(i(z))) = p(\pi_1(i(z)), \pi_2(i(z))) = p(i(z))$, thus i is $\mathcal{G}^T$-isomorphism, hence $\mathcal{D}$ is $\mathcal{G}^T$-pullback. □

6   Adhesiveness

In this section, we intend to show that $\mathcal{G}^T$ is an adhesive HLR category for the class $\mathcal{M}$ of all extremal monomorphisms.

Theorem 14. $\mathcal{G}^T$ *is an adhesive HLR category for the class* $\mathcal{M}$ *of all extremal monomorphisms.*

Proof. Due to Prop. 4 and [1, Prop. 7.62(2)], $\mathcal{M}$ is closed under composition (also with isomorphisms) and decomposition[15], resp. Moreover, $\mathcal{G}^T$ has all pushouts and pullbacks along $\mathcal{M}$, and $\mathcal{M}$-morphisms are preserved under pushouts and pullbacks (cf. Corollaries 9 and 12). It remains to show that pushouts along $\mathcal{M}$-morphisms are VK squares, cf. [2, Def. 4.9]. Let therefore a commutative cube be given with a pushout along the extremal mono α at the bottom and two rear pullbacks (Fig. 3). From Corollaries 9 and 12(4) we can deduce that $\overline{\alpha}$ and α' are extremal monos, too (which is already indicated in Fig. 3).

We now show that the top face in Fig. 3 is a pushout ⟺ the two front faces are pullbacks.

"⇒": By Corollary 9 and Proposition 7 $\overline{\alpha}'$ is strong. Applying τ to the cube shows that front and right faces are pullbacks in $\mathcal{G}$ (by adhesiveness of $\mathcal{G}$). By Corollary 13 it suffices to show that $c = d \circ \overline{\alpha}' \vee h \circ i_1$ and $b = d \circ \overline{\beta}' \vee i \circ i_2$ on vertices. The first statement follows immediately, because $\overline{\alpha}'$ is strong and thus for any $x \in V_{\tau(c)}$

$$
c(x) = d(\overline{\alpha}'(x)) \text{ and } h(i_1(x)) \le c(x)
$$

s.t. $c(x) = d(\overline{\alpha}'(x)) \vee h(i_1(x))$.

---

[15] "Decomposition" means: $g \circ m$ an extremal mono ⇒ m an extremal mono.

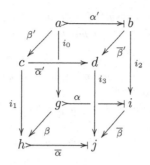

Fig. 3. Commutative cube

In order to show the second statement, we let $z \in V_{\tau(b)}$ be arbitrary. If z is in the image of α', i.e. $z = \alpha'(z')$ for some $z' \in V_{\tau(a)}$, we obtain

$$
\begin{aligned}
b(z) &= a(z') & \text{Strongness of } \alpha' \\
&= c(\beta'(z')) \vee g(i_0(z')) & \text{Cor. 13 applied to left rear pullback} \\
&= d(\overline{\alpha}'(\beta'(z'))) \vee i(\alpha(i_0(z'))) & \text{Strongness of } \overline{\alpha}' \text{ and } \alpha \\
&= d(\overline{\beta}'(z)) \vee i(i_2(z)) & \text{Top and right rear faces commute.}
\end{aligned}
$$

If z is not in the image of α', the pushout construction of Theorem 8 shows that $\overline{\beta}'(z)$ is not in the image of $\overline{\alpha}'$, such that by Corollary 10

$$b(z) = d(\overline{\beta}'(z))$$

which yields $b(z) = d(\overline{\beta}'(z)) \vee i(i_2(z))$, because $i(i_2(z)) \leq b(z)$.

"$\Leftarrow$": Assume all four side faces are pullbacks. By adhesiveness of $\mathcal{G}$ the top face is a pushout in $\mathcal{G}$ such that by Corollary 10 it suffices to show that $d \circ \overline{\alpha}' = c$ and $d \circ \overline{\beta}' = b$ on $\tau(b) - \alpha'(\tau(a))$. The first statement is immediate because $\overline{\alpha}'$ is strong by Corollary 12(4).

Let $z \in \tau(b) - \alpha'(\tau(a))$. Because the rear face is a pullback, $i_2(z) \in \tau(i) - \alpha(\tau(g))$. By the pushout property of the bottom face, Corollary 10 yields $j(\overline{\beta}(i_2(z))) = i(i_2(z))$. Thus by Corollary 13

$$b(z) = d(\overline{\beta}'(z)) \vee i(i_2(z)) = d(\overline{\beta}'(z)) \vee j(\overline{\beta}(i_2(z))) = d(\overline{\beta}'(z)) \vee j(i_3(\overline{\beta}'(z)))$$

But $j \circ i_3 \leq d$, such that

$$b(z) = d(\overline{\beta}'(z))$$

as desired. $\square$

Proposition 15. *In $\mathcal{G}^T$, binary coproducts are compatible with $\mathcal{M}$.*

We conclude this section with the main result of this paper: If all graph transformation rules in $\mathcal{G}^T$ are spans $L \leftarrowtail K \rightarrowtail R$ of two extremal monomorphisms, we obtain the well-known concurrency theorems for the DPO-approach:

Corollary 16. *The following results for graph transformation based on $\mathcal{G}^T$ and the class $\mathcal{M}$ of all extremal monomorphisms are valid due to Theorem 14 and Proposition 15:*

- *Local Church Rosser Theorem for pairwise analysis of sequential and parallel independence [2, Thm. 5.12]*
- *Parallelism Theorem for applying independent rules and transformations in parallel [2, Thm. 5.18]*
- *Concurrency Theorem for applying edge-related dependent rules simultaneously [2, Thm. 5.23]*

7 Example

Consider a simple model of a file system (Fig. 4). On the one hand, we have the file system itself and directories, which both can contain other file system objects and, thus, are called *containers*. On the other hand, we have directories and files, which are part of a (unique) container and, thus, are called *containees*.[16] Directories can be created by the rule in Fig. 5a (file creation is done by a similar rule). Fig. 5b allows to delete a file system object by unlinking it from its container.[17]

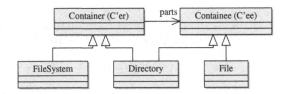

Fig. 4. File system model

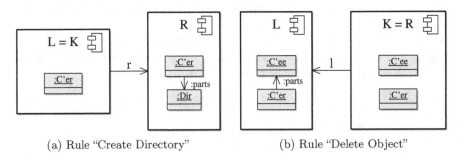

(a) Rule "Create Directory"   (b) Rule "Delete Object"

Fig. 5. Example rules

---

[16] We do not cover container uniqueness in this example.

[17] Some sort of a garbage collector is needed to physically delete all objects that are not part of any container. These rules are not shown in this example but can be modelled by using NACs (negative application conditions) [2].

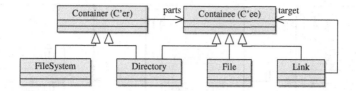

Fig. 6. File system model with links

Now we extend the file system model by links (see Fig. 6).[18] Creating a link is handled by the rule in Fig. 7. The rule in Fig. 8 allows to retarget a link; the figure also demonstrates how the rule can be applied to a concrete instance G.

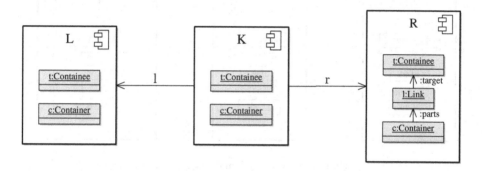

Fig. 7. Rule "Create Link"

In this example, the advantage of being able to define a graph transformation rule on an abstract level should have become clear. For each containee, we only need *one* rule to create the containee, instead of one rule for each concrete container. It is not necessary to change or extend the rule to delete a file system object. Retargeting a link can be specified by *one* single rule (independent of whether the old and new targets of the link are directories, files, or links), whereas without any abstraction, nine rules would be necessary.

8   Related Work

There are relatively few approaches that integrate inheritance or inheritance-like features into graph transformation. Most of these research lines are based on algebraic graph transformation, either on the double pushout approach [2] or on the single-pushout approach [11].

---

[18] A (symbolic) *link* is a reference to another file system object, which can be a link itself. Typically, operating systems confine the link depth in order to sort out circular references.

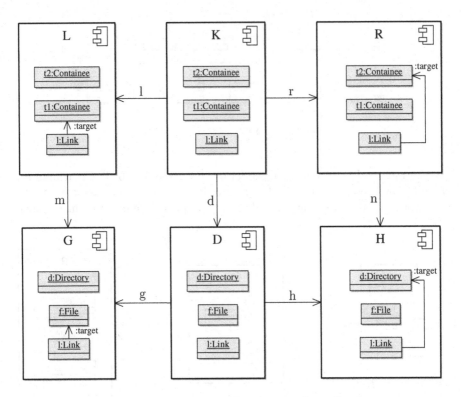

Fig. 8. Rule "Retarget Link" and a sample application

H. Ehrig et al. [2] introduce inheritance as an additional set of inheritance edges between vertices in the type graph. This structure is not required to be hierarchical. Cycle-freeness is not necessary, since they do not work with the original type graph. Instead they use a canonically flattened type structure, in which inheritance edges are removed and some of the other edges are copied to the "more special" vertices. By this reduction, they get rid of inheritance and are able to reestablish their theoretical results. E. Guerra and J. de Lara [8] extend this approach to inheritance between vertices *and* edges.

F. Hermann et al. [9] avoid the flattening and define a weak adhesive category based on the original type graph *with* inheritance structure. The morphisms in the rules are restricted to those which reflect the subtype structure: if an image of a morphism possesses subtypes, all these subtypes have pre-images under the morphism. This feature considerably restricts applicability to examples as in section 7.

U. Golas et al. [7] also avoid the flattening process. They, however, require that the paths along inheritance edges are cycle-free (hierarchy) and that every vertex has at most one abstraction (single inheritance). For this set-up, they devise an adhesive categorial framework comparable to our approach which is, however, restricted to single inheritance.

A. P. L. Ferreira and L. Ribeiro [6] introduced a graph transformation framework for object-oriented programming based on single-pushout rewriting. They allow vertex and edge specialisations in the type graph and show that suitably restricted situations admit pushouts of partial morphisms. Their framework is shown adequate as a model for object-oriented systems. They do not address further categorial properties like adhesiveness.

9   Conclusion

Since our introduced formal foundation is enriched with *inheritance*, it is better capable of modelling static structures of object-oriented systems. Although there have been similar approaches (see Section 8), the innovation of our work is the proof that our framework is well-behaved w.r.t. the interplay of pushouts and pullbacks (adhesiveness). Consequently, important theorems on concurrent applications of graph transformation rules are valid. This enables controlled manipulation and evolution of object graphs with inheritance based on the general theory of algebraic graph transformations.

The presented inheritance concept increases the value of graph transformation techniques for applications. But beside the specification of associations (i.e. admissible object linkings) and inheritance (property transfer between classes), (UML-)class diagrams also specify attributes, object containment relations (composition), instantiation restrictions (abstract classes), arbitrary mulitiplicities, and other limiting constraints. Hence, there is one important direction for future research: Is adhesiveness invariant under enlargements of $\mathcal{G}^T$ such as introduction of attributes [3], addition of abstractness predicate, or sketched OCL[19] constraints [14]?

It is also a goal of forthcoming research to define *single pushout rewriting* [11] with inheritance: For this, transformation rules $r : L \to R$ with r a *partial* type-compatible morphism have to be introduced, conflict freeness and more generally "deletion injectivity" have to be made precise. In addition to static inheritance features introduced above, we conjecture that simple inclusion relations of rules lead to a better formal understanding of *overwriting* (a rule by a larger rule). Consequently, the effect of replacing an application of a rule r by a super rule r' could also be interpreted as a negative application condition [2], if r' is the identity.

Finally, the overall research goal must be to integrate all important object-orientation concepts to graph transformations, which will result in a comprehensive visual formal framework to be applied to object-oriented modelling and meta-modelling.

References

[1] Adámek, J., Herrlich, H., Strecker, G.E.: Abstract and Concrete Categories: The Joy of Cats. Free Software Foundation (2004)

---

[19] Object Constraint Language.

226   M. Löwe et al.

[2] Ehrig, H., Ehrig, K., Prange, U., Taentzer, G.: Fundamentals of Algebraic Graph Transformation. Springer (2006)
[3] Ehrig, H., Prange, U., Taentzer, G.: Fundamental theory for typed attributed graph transformation. In: Ehrig, H., Engels, G., Parisi-Presicce, F., Rozenberg, G. (eds.) ICGT 2004. LNCS, vol. 3256, pp. 161–177. Springer, Heidelberg (2004)
[4] Ehrig, H., Habel, A., Kreowski, H.J., Parisi-Presicce, F.: Parallelism and concurrency in high-level replacement systems. Mathematical Structures in Computer Science 1, 361–404 (1991)
[5] Ehrig, H., Padberg, J., Prange, U., Habel, A.: Adhesive high-level replacement systems: A new categorical framework for graph transformation. Fundam. Inf. 74(1), 1–29 (2006)
[6] Lüdtke Ferreira, A.P., Ribeiro, L.: Derivations in object-oriented graph grammars. In: Ehrig, H., Engels, G., Parisi-Presicce, F., Rozenberg, G. (eds.) ICGT 2004. LNCS, vol. 3256, pp. 416–430. Springer, Heidelberg (2004)
[7] Golas, U., Lambers, L., Ehrig, H., Orejas, F.: Attributed graph transformation with inheritance: Efficient conflict detection and local confluence analysis using abstract critical pairs. Theoretical Computer Science 424, 46–68 (2012)
[8] Guerra, E., de Lara, J.: Attributed typed triple graph transformation with inheritance in the Double Pushout approach. Tech. Rep. UC3M-TR-CS-06- 01, Universidad Carlos III de Madrid (2006)
[9] Hermann, F., Ehrig, H., Ermel, C.: Transformation of type graphs with inheritance for ensuring security in e-government networks. In: Chechik, M., Wirsing, M. (eds.) FASE 2009. LNCS, vol. 5503, pp. 325–339. Springer, Heidelberg (2009)
[10] Lack, S., Sobociński, P.: Adhesive categories. In: Walukiewicz, I. (ed.) FOSSACS 2004. LNCS, vol. 2987, pp. 273–288. Springer, Heidelberg (2004)
[11] Löwe, M.: Algebraic approach to single-pushout graph transformation. Theoret. Comput. Sci. 109, 181–224 (1993)
[12] Löwe, M., König, H., Schulz, C., Schultchen, M.: Algebraic graph transformations with inheritance. Tech. Rep. 02013/03, University of Applied Sciences, FHDW Hannover (2013)
[13] Pilone, D.: UML 2.0 in a Nutshell. O'Reilly (2006)
[14] Rutle, A., Wolter, U., Lamo, Y.: A diagrammatic approach to model transformations. In: Proceedings of the 2008 Euro American Conference on Telematics and Information Systems (EATIS 2008), pp. 1–8. ACM (2008)

Generating Protocol Software from CPN Models Annotated with Pragmatics

Kent Inge Fagerland Simonsen[1,2], Lars M. Kristensen[1], and Ekkart Kindler[2]

[1] Department of Computer Engineering, Bergen University College, Norway
{lmkr,kifs}@hib.no
[2] DTU Compute, Technical University of Denmark, Denmark
{kisi,ekki}@dtu.dk

Abstract. Model-driven software engineering (MDSE) provides a foundation for automatically generating software based on models that focus on the problem domain while abstracting from the details of underlying implementation platforms. Coloured Petri Nets (CPNs) have been widely used to formally model and verify protocol software, but limited work exists on using CPN models of protocols as a basis for automated code generation. The contribution of this paper is a method for generating protocol software from a class of CPN models annotated with code generation pragmatics. Our code generation method consists of three main steps: automatically adding so-called derived pragmatics to the CPN model, computing an abstract template tree, which associates pragmatics with code templates, and applying the templates to generate code which can then be compiled. We illustrate our method using a unidirectional data framing protocol.

1 Introduction

Model-driven software engineering (MDSE) [4] provides a foundation for highly automated generation of software based on models. The use of models allows software designers to focus on the problem domain and abstract from the details of underlying implementation platforms. If the MDSE process uses modelling languages with a formal semantics, we gain the additional advantage that the models can be verified, e. g. by model checking [2]. The combination of formally verified models from which code is generated automatically increases the confidence in the resulting implementation being correct with respect to the formally specified properties.

Coloured Petri Nets (CPNs) [9,10] have been widely used for formal modelling and verification of protocol designs [14,3], but limited work has been done on developing methods that support the use of CPN models as a basis for automated code generation of protocol software [13,16]. CPNs extend ordinary Petri nets with a programming language for defining data types and using inscriptions for modelling data and data manipulation. In addition, CPNs provide a module concept that allows large CPN models to be structured as a hierarchically related set of modules. CPN uses Standard ML (SML) as programming language.

J. Iyoda and L. de Moura (Eds.): SBMF 2013, LNCS 8195, pp. 227–242, 2013.

The contribution of this paper is a method for automated code generation from CPN models based on a modelling methodology for constructing *descriptive models* of protocols and on adding *code generation pragmatics* to the CPN models. The notion of descriptive models is firstly intended as a means for creating models that are helpful in understanding and conveying the operation of the considered protocol. Secondly, a descriptive model is close to a verifiable version of the same model and sufficiently detailed to serve as a basis for automated code generation when annotated with code generation pragmatics. The relationship between descriptive models and verification models was discussed in [12]. In this paper, we concentrate on the pragmatics, the modelling methodology for constructing descriptive models, and on the steps of the code generation.

The pragmatics that we integrate into the CPN language are syntactical annotations that are associated with CPN model elements. The primary purpose of the pragmatics is to add enough details for generating code without cluttering the model and making it verbose which would ultimately render it unreadable and too complex for verification purposes. It should be noted that pragmatics are purely syntactical annotations for code generation purposes, and hence our method does not affect the formal semantics of CPNs. The pragmatics fall into three types: structural, control flow, and operation pragmatics. Our method defines a set of core pragmatics that are applicable to all protocols. In addition, our method is extensible in that it allows the modeller to easily add new pragmatics if required by a specific protocol or a specific protocol domain under consideration.

The code generation consists of three main steps, starting from a CPN model that the modeller has annotated with a set of pragmatics that makes the protocol structure and the control flow explicit. The first step is to automatically compute for the CPN model, a set of *derived pragmatics* that identify common control flow structures and operations, such as sending and receiving packets, or manipulating states. In the second step, an *abstract template tree* (ATT) is constructed providing an association between pragmatics and code generation templates. Essentially, every node of the ATT will be associated with a code template. In the third step, the ATT is traversed and code is emitted by invoking the code templates associated with each node of the ATT rather than translating SML. A key feature of our method is that the generated code resembles what a human programmer would have developed. This is advantageous with respect to code inspection, maintainability, and performance.

This paper is organised as follows. Section 2 presents our modelling methodology and the explicit pragmatics. In Sect. 3, we introduce automatically derived control flow and operation pragmatics. In Sect. 4, we cover ATTs and their use in code generation. In Sect. 5, we discuss related work, and, in Sect. 6, we sum up conclusions and outline directions for future work. Due to space limitations, we cannot present our method in full detail here. These can be found in the technical report [22]. A very early and preliminary version of these ideas was presented as an extended abstract [21]. A prototype of a tool supporting the approach presented in this paper is available: PetriCode. For more information on the tool, we refer to the tool's home page [18]. We assume that the reader is familiar with the basic concepts of Petri nets (places, transitions, tokens, enabling, and firing rule), and we introduce CPN specific concepts only briefly as we proceed. A comprehensive introduction to CPNs is given in a textbook [10].

2 Modelling Methodology and Explicit Pragmatics

To present our modelling methodology we use, as a running example, a unidirectional framing protocol. The overall service provided by this protocol is to send *messages* of arbitrary length from a sender to a receiver by splitting up the message into smaller *packets* sent across a unidirectional channel. The channel is assumed to be reliable and to preserve the order of the transmitted packets. The protocol uses a *final bit* in each transmitted packet indicating whether the payload of the packet is the final (last) part of the larger message. As we proceed with presenting the CPN model, we introduce the basic set of explicit pragmatics that are central to our method and which the modeller uses as part of the construction of the CPN model. Pragmatics are by convention written in ⟨⟨ ⟩⟩ to distinguish them from, e.g., place and transition names and SML inscriptions.

2.1 Protocol System Level

Figure 1 shows the top-level module of the CPN model which constitutes the *protocol system level*. The purpose of the protocol system level is to specify the *protocol principals* and the *channels* connecting them. This module has three CPN *substitution transitions* (transitions with double lined borders) named Sender, Channel, and Receiver. Substitution transitions constitute the basic structuring mechanism of CPNs and each substitution transition has an associated submodule modelling the details of the compound behaviour represented by the substitution transition. The two substitution transitions Sender and Receiver represent the two principals of the protocol, and the substitution transition Channel represents a channel between them. We use the ⟨⟨principal⟩⟩ pragmatic to specify which substitution transitions represent protocol principals, and the ⟨⟨channel⟩⟩ pragmatic to specify substitution transitions representing channels. The channel pragmatic has three associated *properties* specifying that the channel is unidirectional, reliable (i. e., the channel does not loose packets), and that it preserves the order of packets. Our modelling methodology includes a set of channel modules for common channel types and the specific module to be used in the model is selected based on the properties specified for the channel pragmatic. The two *socket places* (places connected to a substitution transition) SenderChannel and ReceiverChannel connecting the principal substitution transition to the Channel are implicitly considered *channel places* which means that messages (tokens) added and removed from these places are considered to be sent and received, respectively. In CPNs, a socket place can be associated with a *port place* in the submodule of the substitution transition. This has the effect that the two places, conceptually, become the same place; this way, sockets provide the means by which modules in CPNs exchange tokens.

Fig. 1. The protocol system level

We require in our modelling methodology that the protocol system module consists of one or more substitution transitions representing principals. A socket place at the protocol system level can be connected to at most one principal substitution transition and at most one channel substitution transition. This requirement is needed since we use the socket places connecting principals and channels to identify which channel or principal a message is intended for.

The concept of a channel represents a means for communication between *endpoints* as determined by the colour set (data type) Endpoint which consists of a name identifying the endpoint and an input and an output buffer for packets transmitted on the channel. In CPNs, the data type of a place is by convention written below the place and determines the kind of tokens that may reside on the place. The protocol system level and the modelling of channels are parameterised by colour sets (data types) used to identify channels and the specific packets transmitted. This means that we assume only the existence of these two types and do not make any assumptions on how they are realised. The concrete implementation of the Packet colour set in a protocol model depends on the protocol data units exchanged among the principals in the protocol under consideration. For code generation purposes, the implementation of the EndpointId colour set depends on the concrete channel used to realise the communication between the principals. If for instance, the channel is realised using the transport layer of the TCP/IP protocol stack, then the Endpoint colour set will consist of a host (IP address) and a port (a process). Hence, in a TCP/IP context, an endpoint can be implemented as a TCP/IP socket. The colour sets also have an associated class of functions that play a central role in being able to recognize common structural patterns in the CPN models, which are captured by the operation pragmatics to be presented in Sect. 3.

2.2 Principal Level

The submodules of principal substitution transitions in the protocol system module constitute the *principal level modules*. Each principal level module specifies the *services* that are provided by the corresponding principal and the life-cycle of the principal. In addition to specifying constraints on the order of service uses, the principal level modules may also model the state to be maintained across invocation of the services. The explicit modelling of the methods that constitute the service is required in our method in order to generate code that can be integrated into different code contexts.

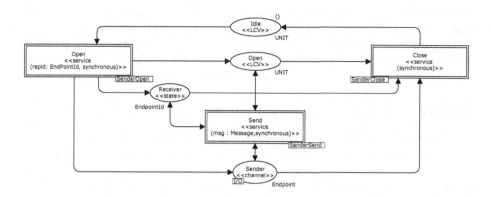

Fig. 2. The Sender module

Here, we concentrate on the sender principal as a representative example. Figure 2 shows the principal level CPN module for the sender. This module is the submodule of the Sender substitution transition in Fig. 1. The module has three substitution transitions annotated with the ⟨⟨service⟩⟩ pragmatic to indicate that they represent services that are to be exposed by the implementation, i.e., be externally visible. In this case, the sender has three services: Open (for opening the communication with the receiver), Send (for sending a message), and Close (for closing the communication with the receiver). The parameters of the ⟨⟨service⟩⟩ pragmatic specify the parameter and return types, and properties of the services. In this case, all three services provided by the sender principal are synchronous services as specified by the synchronous property of the ⟨⟨service⟩⟩ pragmatics. Our method also supports asynchronous services which, however, are not discussed here (see [22] for details).

The principal can be in two different states as modelled by the places Idle and Open with the colour set UNIT containing just a single value ( ) (called unit and representing a black token). When there is a unit token on Idle, this means that no communication is initialised, and when there is a unit token on Open this means that messages can be transmitted to the receiver. A third implicit state is also possible when neither the Idle nor Open places have a token. This state is reached when the client is busy opening, sending or closing. A place modelling a principal life-cycle state is annotated with the ⟨⟨LCV⟩⟩ pragmatic (Life Cycle Variable). The open service can be invoked only when the principal is in Idle and, once Open, messages can be sent, and the communication can be closed. In the latter case, the sender returns to the Idle state. The sender maintains another state variable Receiver, which represents the endpoint created by Open, and is used by Send in order to send messages. State variables are indicated using the ⟨⟨state⟩⟩ pragmatic. The *port place* Sender (bottom) is associated with the SenderChannel socket place in Fig. 1 and hence any token added (removed) to Sender will be added (removed) to SenderChannel and vice versa. In the sender module, the place Sender has been annotated with the ⟨⟨channel⟩⟩ pragmatic which is derived from the fact that the associated socket place at the protocol system level is connected to a channel substitution transition (see Fig. 1).

The principal level modules do not specify how a wrong use of the services should be handled, e. g. when the send service is invoked in a state where the sender is not Open. The associated error handling is platform dependent.

2.3 Service Level

The submodules of the substitution transitions annotated with ⟨⟨service⟩⟩ on the principal level specify the detailed behaviour of the principals for each of the principal's services. The detailed behaviour is modelled in a control flow oriented manner using ⟨⟨ID⟩⟩ pragmatics on places to make the control flow explicit. Modelling the services in a control flow oriented manner serves two main purposes. The first purpose is to provide for comprehensible models in that the explicit control flow provides a reading path to the model of the service. This is in contrast to a pure event-oriented approach to modelling (as discussed in [3] for example) from which no control flow is explicit and which consists of modelling a protocol principal using a single place to represent its state and a set of transitions connected to this place which changes the state of the principal depending on packets sent and received. The second purpose of modelling in a control flow oriented manner is to automatically generate code with a structure that resembles what a human programmer would implement. This makes it easier to inspect and maintain automatically generated code, and provides code with better performance since it reflects the intended use of the constructs provided by the target programming language.

As a representative example of a service level module, we consider the send service of the sender principal which is shown in Fig. 3 (left). At this level, the ⟨⟨service⟩⟩ pragmatic is used on ordinary (non-substitution) transitions to indicate the single entry point for the corresponding service primitive. Hence, it is possible to have only one transition annotated with ⟨⟨service⟩⟩. The message to be sent is represented by the parameter msg of the ⟨⟨service⟩⟩ pragmatic. Transitions representing the termination/completion of the service are annotated with the ⟨⟨return⟩⟩ pragmatic. We assume that there is exactly one transition in a service level module that is annotated with ⟨⟨return⟩⟩. In general, the ⟨⟨return⟩⟩ pragmatic may take parameters representing return values. The parameters for the open service specifies the endpoint of the receiver principal. These parameters are stored in the Receiver state variable and also an endpoint is created on the Sender channel place which the sender will use for sending packets.

Places modelling the control flow in the send primitive are annotated with an ⟨⟨ID⟩⟩ pragmatic. From a control flow perspective, the send operation has an overall sequence (starting at transition Send and ending at transition Completed), and a repeat-until loop (starting at place Start and ending in place PacketSent). The operation of the send primitive is to first partition the message to be sent into a sequence of smaller sub-messages which is placed on Outgoing. In CPNs, the expression associated with arcs specifies the tokens to be removed and added when transitions occur. The expressions may contain free variables which

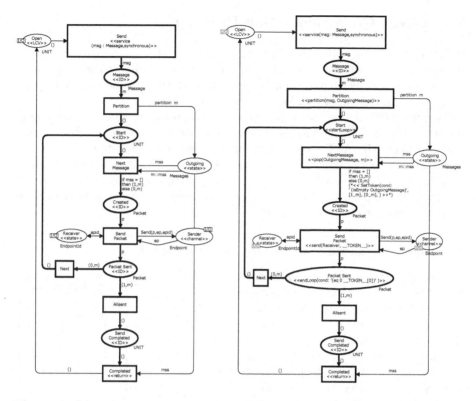

Fig. 3. The SenderSend module with explicit pragmatics (left) and derived pragmatics added (right). The derived pragmatics are discussed in Sect. 3

determines possible modes in which a transition may occur. As an example, the Partition transition in Fig. 3 (top) has a variable m of type Message which in an occurrence of Partition will be bound to the value of a token present on place Message. When the transition occurs, it will remove the corresponding token from Message, and add tokens to the outgoing places Start and Outgoing obtained by evaluating the expressions on the corresponding arcs. The partition function takes a message as argument, and constructs a list of submessages that is added as a token on place Outgoing. Also, a unit token will be added to place Start. The sender then executes a loop in which a packet is sent for each sub-message.

The modelling of the sender includes some intermediate states (e. g., Send-Completed) which makes the model more verbose, but is used in our method for recognising control flow constructs. It is worth noting that, in the model of the send service, the token is removed from Open while the send operation is in progress; this prevents any further sending or invocation of close while a send operation is executed (the protocol is not designed for concurrent sends).

3 Derived Code Generation Pragmatics

Before we discuss how the actual code generation works, we discuss some additional pragmatics which are used by the code generator. Since these pragmatics can be automatically derived from the net (model) structure and the arc inscriptions, these pragmatics are called *derived pragmatics*.

The first kind of pragmatics concerns the control flow, which indicate how the net structure of a service module is decomposed into control flow blocks that constitute the ATT (see Sect. 4 for more details). Therefore, this kind is called *control flow* pragmatics. The second kind of pragmatics, called *operation pragmatics*, helps generating the code for the actual operations that are to be executed. We explain these pragmatics by the help of the SenderSend module example, which was shown in Fig. 3.

3.1 Block Structure and Control Flow Constructs

CPNs (and Petri nets in general) do not enforce any particular structure with respect to the modelling of the control flow of the service primitives. In order to be able to generate code that uses the control flow constructs of typical programming languages, we assume that the net structure induced by places of the service level modules that are marked with $\langle\langle\mathsf{ID}\rangle\rangle$ can be decomposed into *control flow blocks*. For the Send primitive in Fig. 3(left), the part corresponding to control flow blocks has been graphically indicated in bold. Formally, the

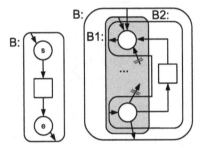

Fig. 4. Blocks: Atomic and loop

block structure decomposition is defined by having different types of blocks, which inductively define the block structure of a net. Due to space limitations, we cannot go into the details of this definition here (see [22] for the technical and formal details). There are four types of blocks: *atomic*, *choice*, *loop*, and *sequence*, and two of these patterns are sketched in Fig. 4. The pattern in Fig. 4(left) captures that an atomic block consists of a start place (top), a single transition, and an end place (bottom). The pattern in Fig. 4(right) specifies that a loop block has a single start place (top), a body (indicated by ...) and an end place (bottom) and a single transition (right) capturing the iteration by connecting the end place and the start place. For the SenderSend module in Fig. 3 the control flow can be decomposed into a block, which is a sequence, where the first element of that sequence is an atomic block, the second is a loop, which again consists of a sequence of two atomic blocks.

For code generation purposes we, systematically decompose each service level module into blocks where the containment of the blocks defines the structure of the ATT. For the actual code generation, it is sufficient to identify the start and end of loops and choices – actually the places where they start and end – with some additional pragmatics: $\langle\langle\mathsf{startLoop}\rangle\rangle$, $\langle\langle\mathsf{endLoop}\rangle\rangle$, $\langle\langle\mathsf{branch}\rangle\rangle$, and $\langle\langle\mathsf{merge}\rangle\rangle$.

For the SenderSend module, these additional pragmatics are shown on the right-hand side of Fig. 3. Note that the ⟨⟨endLoop⟩⟩ has a parameter, which represents the exit *condition* of the loop. The ⟨⟨branch⟩⟩ pragmatic for a choice has a *condition* parameter too, but we do not have a choice in this example. Our technology comes with a simple syntax for formulating these conditions, which resembles the syntax of Lisp. In our example, the expression (eq 1 __TOKEN__[0]) checks whether the first component (referred to by index 0) of the control flow token (referred to by __TOKEN__) is equal to 1, which reflects the inscription of the arc leaving the loop. We use this condition parameter and the specific syntax for conditions in order to be independent of SML. By adding the condition as a parameter of the ⟨⟨endLoop⟩⟩ pragmatic, we do not need to restrict the annotations of CPN models – at the price of, sometimes, being forced to add the condition of the ⟨⟨branch⟩⟩ and ⟨⟨endLoop⟩⟩ pragmatics manually.

3.2 Operation Pragmatics

The *operation pragmatic* is associated with transitions and describes an operation associated with the execution of the transition in a programming language independent way.

The right-hand side of Fig. 3 shows three examples of these pragmatics. The ⟨⟨send⟩⟩ pragmatic is an example of a protocol independent pragmatic. It represents sending a message to another principal, which is represented by the pattern for this transition. The parameters of the ⟨⟨send⟩⟩ pragmatic define the target of the send (here identified by the end point on place Receiver) and the actual message to be sent (here, the message is contained in the current token).

The other two operation pragmatics are more specific to this particular protocol: ⟨⟨partition⟩⟩ splits a message into the sequence of chunks that are supposed to be sent – actually a list of these chunks. The ⟨⟨pop⟩⟩ operation, obtains and removes one chunk from the list.

As mentioned above, some of the operation pragmatics are part of the general method, and for these there will be direct code generation support available defined by so-called template bindings. These bindings are discussed in Sect. 4. In addition, a protocol developer can add own protocol specific pragmatics; in that case, the developer must provide the corresponding templates and bindings at some point in order to generate the code.

4 Abstract Template Trees and Code Generation

The actual generation of code from a CPN model annotated with explicit and derived pragmatics proceeds in three phases: The first phase is the construction of an ATT which serves as an intermediate representation in the code generation. The second phase binds code generation templates to the nodes of the ATT corresponding to the target platform under consideration. The third phase is to traverse the ATT and invoke the code generation templates in order to emit code. Below, we illustrate the three code generation phases using the annotated send service module shown in Fig. 3 (right) as an example. The target platform considered in our example is the Groovy programming language. Groovy is a multi-paradigm language that runs on the Java Virtual Machine. It was chosen as a target because it is an optionally typed multi-paradigm language with features that makes it fairly easy to generate code for while still being a realistic platform for industrial applications.

An ATT is an ordered tree of nodes and resembles abstract syntax trees. The two major types of nodes in the ATT are *leaf* (operation) nodes and *container* nodes. A leaf node does not have children and contains pragmatics for one or more sequential operations such as sending on a channel or accessing a state variable. A container node has in addition to associated pragmatics, an ordered list of child nodes. The types of container nodes at the service level corresponds to the different types of blocks introduced in Sect. 3. The root node of the ATT represents the entire protocol system. The generation of the ATT is implemented by a guided walk through the CPN model. This walk starts at the protocol system module and, for each ⟨⟨principal⟩⟩ pragmatic, it generates a corresponding node in the ATT. On the next level, the generator looks for modules annotated with a ⟨⟨service⟩⟩ pragmatic and adds corresponding nodes. Each service module contains exactly one transition with the ⟨⟨service⟩⟩ pragmatic, which is the starting point for the method modelled by the sub-module. The subsequent set of nodes is constructed according to the block structure rules described in Sect. 3.

The sub-ATT corresponding to the sender send service is shown in Fig. 5. The node at the top represents the sender send service. The child nodes of the Send node correspond to the overall sequence performed by the send service: partitioning the message, executing the loop where submessages are sent, and then completing the service. The child nodes of the Start node correspond to the body of the loop.

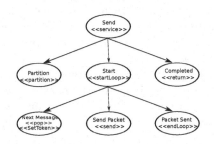

Fig. 5. Sub-ATT for sender send service

When the ATT has been generated, in order to generate code for a particular platform, the pragmatics represented by the nodes of the ATT must be bound to code generation templates. This is done by means of a *template descriptor*. A template descriptor contains a line for each pragmatic that need to be translated into code for a specific platform. The template binding for a pragmatic contained in an ATT node is determined by the line for the pragmatic contained in the template descriptor.

The template descriptor is specified in a simple domain specific language (DSL). An extract of the binding descriptor for generating Groovy code covering three of the pragmatics from Fig. 5 can be seen in Listing 1. Each line of the template descriptor consists of a name followed by a left-parenthesis followed by key value pairs where the keys can be pragmatic which contains the name of the pragmatic, template which corresponding value is the path to the template, isContainer which indicates whether this pragmatic denotes a container or a isMultiContainer. The multi-container flag is primarily an implementation detail in our tool used to indicate whether or not the container is of type loop or choice.

Listing 1. Extract of binding descriptor for the Groovy platform

```
partition(pragmatic: 'partition', template: 'groovy/partition.tmpl',
         isContainer: false, isMultiContainer: false)
send(pragmatic: 'send', template: 'groovy/send.tmpl',
         isContainer: false, isMultiContainer: false)
startLoop(pragmatic: 'startLoop', template: 'groovy/loop.tmpl',
         isContainer: true, isMultiContainer: true)
```

Generating the protocol software consists of traversing the ATT and invoking the associated templates for each node as described by the template binding. When a pragmatic is transformed to code, its template is run through the template engine together with a number of parameters given by the pragmatic definition and the CPN structure. The templates are sown together by replacing a special tag in the container templates, %%yield%%, with the text of the underlying templates in order.

As an example of a container template, the template for the loop pragmatic for the Groovy language is given in Listing 2 (left). The template creates a while-loop which continues while the __LOOP_VAR__ variable is true. The body of the loop is populated by replacing the %%yield%% directive with the code generated by the templates of the sub-nodes in the ATT. The __LOOP_VAR__ is updated at the end of the loop by the ⟨⟨endLoop⟩⟩ pragmatic which is always present as the last child element of a loop. The ⟨⟨send⟩⟩ is an example of an operation pragmatic. Listing 2 (right) shows the template for the ⟨⟨send⟩⟩ pragmatic which requires two parameters: one is the name of the socket that the message should be sent on, and the other is the variable that holds the message to be sent.

Listing 2. Examples of templates for loops (left) and send (right)

```
%%VARS:__LOOP_VAR__%%          ${params[0]}.getOutputStream()
__LOOP_VAR__ = true                .newObjectOutputStream()
while(__LOOP_VAR__){               .writeObject(${params[1]})
    %%yield%% }                %%VARS:${params[1]}%%
```

As an example of the generated code, the loop in the sender service in the Sender principal is shown in Listing 3. The loop is started by defining a variable, __LOOP_VAR__. After the __LOOP_VAR__ is defined, the loop is entered. Inside the loop, the next fragment is code from the template bound to the ⟨⟨pop⟩⟩ pragmatic. This code removes the first element from OutgoingMessage and assigns it to variable m. Then, the code for the ⟨⟨setToken⟩⟩ pragmatic on the arc between the transition NextMessage and the place Created is generated. This code sets the __TOKEN__ variable in the code according to the conditional statement in the pragmatic: if OutgoingMessage is empty then the message is prefixed by 1, otherwise it is prefixed by zero. The next pragmatic that is found on the control flow path is the ⟨⟨send⟩⟩ pragmatic on the transition Send Packet. The socket Receiver is used to send the value of the __TOKEN__ variable. Finally, the template associated with the ⟨⟨endLoop⟩⟩ pragmatics has generated the code for updating __LOOP_VAR__ according to the conditional expression given as a parameter to the ⟨⟨endLoop⟩⟩ pragmatic.

Listing 3. The generated code for the loop of the sender send service

```
__LOOP_VAR__ = true
while(__LOOP_VAR__){
def m = OutgoingMessage.remove(0)
if(OutgoingMessage.size() == 0){
__TOKEN__ = [1,m]
} else {
__TOKEN__ = [0,m]
}
Receiver.getOutputStream().newObjectOutputStream().
        writeObject(__TOKEN__)
__TOKEN__
__LOOP_VAR__ = 1 == __TOKEN__[0]
}
```

5 Related Work

The goal of our code generation method is to generate code from models close to descriptive models that are amenable to verification with little or no modification. Also, the code that is generated should be readable, portable and maintainable. Furthermore, we would like to be able to easily integrate our code into third party software and have a great deal of flexibility in the way code is produced.

There are many methods for modelling and analysing protocol software using languages such as High Level Petri Nets [7], temporal Petri Nets [23], ESTELLE [5] and LOTOS [15]. Some methods support automatic code generation such as state charts [24], SPI [20], SDL [8] and UML [1]. Due to space limitations, we focus our discussion on approaches that use general purpose languages (UML and CPNs) equipped with additional information for a specific domain. In the rest of this section, we discuss several related works and finally, at the end, contrast and sum up the key differences between each of the related work items and our approach.

In [19], possible methods for code generation from high level Petri Nets (HLPNs), such as CPNs, are discussed and a new hybrid of the discussed approaches is presented. The general methods for code generation from HLPNs are, according to [19]: structural analysis, simulation based, and reachability graph based. The method proposed in the paper is a hybrid of simulation based and structural analysis methods.

In [16], the author describes an approach for generating code from CPNs for an access control system. The generation takes advantage of the fact that CPNs use the SML programming language for all inscriptions. This means that it is fairly simple to generate SML code that simulates the CPN in SML code. And by using external libraries, the CPN can interact with other devices through a specialized protocol for access control systems. The paper also presents a case study where the techniques discussed are used to generate an access control system for an industrial actor. A somewhat similar approach is also taken in [11] where the core of a tool for scheduling courses of actions is created based on a CPN model. The model is extracted from the modelling tool and executed as an SML program.

Process-Partitioned CPNs (PP-CPNs) [13] have been used to automatically generate code for several purposes including protocols. Code is generated from PP-CPNs by first translating the PP-CPN into a control flow graph (CFG), then translating the CFG into an abstract syntax tree (ASTs), first of an intermediary language then to an AST that is dependent on the target platform. From the platform dependent AST, code is generated. In [13], PP-CPNs are used to model and obtain an implementation for the DYMO routing protocol using the Erlang programming language and platform.

In [17], a UML profile named Graphical Protocol Description Language (GPDL) is used together with a textual language called GAEL to model and generate code for protocols. The approach uses stereotypes to annotate UML diagrams with information used for code generation. The stereotypes and GAEL annotations are used though a series of transformations to generate code. In [17], the authors produce SDL code, but are able to produce code for any platform.

In the terminology of [19], our code generation method is based on structural analysis, but it is also based on user input in the form of explicit pragmatics. The pragmatics coupled with templates makes it possible to be platform independent and create readable and maintainable code which has an interface based on the services described on the principal level. The template approach also gives the modellers flexibility, by modifying the templates, to create code in their own style. The methods presented in [19,16,11] are all based on simulating the models. The simulation methods conflicts with our goals of readable code as the purpose of the code can easily be lost in the details of the operations of the simulator. Also the code generated by the simulation methods is not likely to be efficient in particular due to the complex enabling computation that needs to be performed in each step of the execution. The method presented in [13] constrains the models more than our method since we have the possibility to add more pragmatics to expand the range of functionality. Also, [13] does not model how services can be used, so it does not allow the modeller to control how third party applications could be integrated with the generated code. In contrast to our approach, the approach in [13] is also bound to the Erlang platform where our approach, through templates is platform independent. Also, our approach provides more flexibility in the operations that can be modelled by allowing users to define additional pragmatics. The approach in [17], despite being based on UML, has several similarities with our approach such as annotating the models with stereotypes which are similar to our pragmatics. However, the stereotypes are predefined in a UML profile and does not offer the same flexibility in modelling as our templates that may be user defined. Also the GPDL models use a separate language, GAEL, to provide additional information in addition to the platform information which in our case is contained in templates and template bindings.

6   Conclusions and Future Work

In this paper, we have presented a method for automatically generating code for protocol software from CPN models. The method was discussed by a simple, but complete example of a communication protocol. The code generation approach has been realized in a tool that was used to generate the code examples in this paper. The tool can be accessed from the project website [18].

The main objective of our method is that code can be generated from what we call *descriptive models*. Descriptive models are typically used for understanding and explaining how a protocol works on a high level of abstraction. Descriptive models focus on concepts and not on technical details and, in many cases, these models can be used – with some tweaking – also for analysing and verifying protocols. Today, it is typical practise to use models for analysing a protocol and its specification and for verification of the protocol. Then, the protocol software is implemented manually based on these models. Our method makes it possible to use the same descriptive model for analysis and verification as well as for code generation – in both cases, the models are moderately extended.

In our method, we chose to use Coloured Petri Nets (CPNs) [9] as modelling language for descriptive models since they have successfully been used for modelling, analysing, and verifying various kinds of systems [10] for a long time now. Over the time, specific modelling styles, principles, and disciplines have developed for using CPN for that purpose. These styles and principles are mostly used informally – sometimes not even mentioned at all. In our method, we needed to make them into more rigorous rules.

Since descriptive models are conceptual in nature and on a high level of abstraction, they often do not capture some technical aspects and implementation details. Examples of such information not contained in descriptive models are the API and the interface for calling the services or operations of a protocol. Our method caters for that by *pragmatics* that can be added to different elements of the model. This way, it is possible to attach additional information without compromising the overall structure of the original model. And our example shows, that all relevant technical information can easily be added to the model in this way. We argue that adding pragmatics will not add significantly to the modelling effort. One reason for this is that explicit pragmatics, to a large extent, represent concepts the modeller would be aware of while modelling, so adding them should add little more time than looking up and adding the pragmatics. Also, derived pragmatics are added automatically and therefore require no additional action from the modeller. Adding new pragmatics is relatively simple since all that is required is to add templates and describe the pragmatic and template bindings in simple specialized languages. Our approach also provides the modeller with a modelling framework through the required model levels. This could also add structure and thereby perhaps even reduce the modelling effort. Our method comes with some predefined pragmatics which are of general use. But, our method is open for adding more pragmatics if need should be. Moreover, pragmatics can be used for adding more technical information which could be derived automatically. This way, it is possible to gradually extend the degree of automation of our method without changing the method itself.

Another objective of our method is the generation of code for different target languages and platforms. To this end, ATTs and template bindings were introduced; by replacing the templates and template binding, code for a different platform can be generated. In a way, a set of templates along with a template binding can be considered as a characterization of a target platform. And the code generator can be customized for different platforms by modifying templates. The concepts of principals and services in our approach, lend themselves nicely to the object oriented paradigm where principals can be realized as classes, and services can be realized as methods. The control-flow block structure fits well with imperative paradigm with loops and conditional statements. Therefore, it seems likely that it would be simple to create templates for languages and platforms with roots in these paradigms such as Java, Python and C. For functional languages and platforms, which do not have control flow structure such as loops and conditionals, this could be a little more difficult. A last objective of our method is the readability of the generated code. This might be a bit subjective, although some metrics exists [6]. With control blocks, ATTs, and templates reflecting these constructs in the target language, we try to emulate code written by human programmers. A detailed evaluation, however, is future work.

We have shown that our method works for a simple example and for one target platform. An evaluation for larger examples and other target platforms is future work. Likewise, we still need to show that the same CPN models can be used for verification as well as code generation. Though verification is not the main focus, future work will, at least, demonstrate that verification from the model is possible in principle. A first step towards verification was taken in [12].

References

1. Alanen, M., Lilius, J., Porres, I., Truscan, D.: On modeling techniques for supporting model driven development of protocol processing applications. In: Model-Driven Software Development, pp. 305–328. Springer (2005)
2. Baier, C., Katoen., J. -P.: Principles of Model Checking. MIT Press (2008)
3. Billington, J., Gallasch, G.E., Han, B.: A coloured Petri net approach to protocol verification. In: Desel, J., Reisig, W., Rozenberg, G. (eds.) ACPN 2003. LNCS, vol. 3098, pp. 210–290. Springer, Heidelberg (2004)
4. Brambilla, M., Cabot, J., Wimmer, M.: Model-Driven Software Engineering in Practice. Synthesis Lectures on Software Engineering. Morgan & Claypool Publishers (2012)
5. Budkowski, S., Dembinski, P.: An introduction to Estelle: A specification language for distributed systems. Computer Networks and ISDN Systems 14(1), 3–23 (1987)
6. Buse, R.P.L., Weimer, W.R.: A metric for software readability. In: Proc. of ISSTA 2008, pp. 121–130. ACM, NY (2008)

7. Choppy, C., Dedova, A., Evangelista, S., Hong, S., Klai, K., Petrucci, L.: The NEO Protocol for Large-Scale Distributed Database Systems: Modelling and Initial Verification. In: Lilius, J., Penczek, W. (eds.) PETRI NETS 2010. LNCS, vol. 6128, pp. 145–164. Springer, Heidelberg (2010)
8. Hannikainen, M., Knuutila, J., Hamalainen, T., Saarinen, J.: Using SDL for implementing a wireless medium access control protocol. In: Proc. International Symposium on Multimedia Software Engineering, pp. 229–236 (2000)
9. Jensen, K.: Coloured Petri nets and invariant methods. Theoretical Computer Science 14, 317–336 (1981)
10. Jensen, K., Kristensen, L.M.: Coloured Petri Nets - Modelling and Validation of Concurrent Systems. Springer (2009)
11. Kristensen, L.M., Mechlenborg, P., Zhang, L., Mitchell, B., Gallasch, G.E.: Model-based development of a course of action scheduling tool. International Journal on Software Tools for Technology Transfer 10, 5–14 (2008)
12. Simonsen, K.I.F., Kristensen, L.M.: Towards a CPN-based modelling approach for reconciling verification and implementation of protocol models. In: Machado, R.J., Maciel, R.S.P., Rubin, J., Botterweck, G. (eds.) MOMPES 2012. LNCS, vol. 7706, pp. 106–125. Springer, Heidelberg (2013)
13. Kristensen, L.M., Westergaard, M.: Automatic Structure-Based Code Generation from Coloured Petri Nets: A Proof of Concept. In: Kowalewski, S., Roveri, M. (eds.) FMICS 2010. LNCS, vol. 6371, pp. 215–230. Springer, Heidelberg (2010)
14. Kristensen, L.M., Simonsen, K.I.F.: Applications of Coloured Petri Nets for Functional Validation of Protocol Designs. In: Jensen, K., van der Aalst, W.M.P., Balbo, G., Koutny, M., Wolf, K. (eds.) ToPNoC VII. LNCS, vol. 7480, pp. 56–115. Springer, Heidelberg (2013)
15. Leduc, G., Germeau, F.: Verification of security protocols using LOTOS-method and application. Computer Communications 23(12), 1089–1103 (2000)
16. Mortensen, K.H.: Automatic code generation method based on coloured Petri net models applied on an access control system. In: Nielsen, M., Simpson, D. (eds.) ICATPN 2000. LNCS, vol. 1825, pp. 367–386. Springer, Heidelberg (2000)
17. Parssinen, J., von Knorring, N., Heinonen, J., Turunen, M.: In: Proc. TOOLS 2000, pp. 82–93 (2000)
18. PetriCode, Project Web Site, http://kentis.github.io/nppn-cli/
19. Philippi, S.: Automatic code generation from high-level Petri-nets for model driven systems engineering. Journal of Systems and Software 79(10), 1444–1455 (2006)
20. Pozza, D., Sisto, R., Durante, L.: Spi2Java: automatic cryptographic protocol Java code generation from spi calculus. In: Proc. of Advanced Information Networking and Applications, vol. 1, pp. 400–405 (2004)
21. Simonsen, K.I.F., Kristensen, L.M., Kindler, E.: Code generation for protocols from CPN models annotated with pragmatics – extended abstract. In: 24th Nordic Workshop on Programming Theory (November 2012)
22. Simonsen, K.I.F., Kristensen, L.M., Kindler, E.: Code Generation for Protocol Software from CPN models Annotated with Pragmatics. Technical Report IMM-Technical Reports-2013-01, Technical University of Denmark, DTU Informatics (January 2013), http://bit.ly/WwH2hf
23. Suzuki, I.: Formal analysis of the alternating bit protocol by temporal Petri nets. IEEE Transactions on Software Engineering 16(11), 1273–1281 (1990)
24. Wagstaff, K., Peters, K., Scharenbroich, L.: From protocol specification to state-chart to implementation. Technical Report CL08-4014, Jet Propulsion Laboratory (2008)

Author Index